The
Ayn Rand Cult

The
Ayn Rand Cult

JEFF WALKER

Open Court
Chicago and La Salle, Illinois

To order books from Open Court,
call toll-free 1-800-815-2280.

Open Court Publishing Company is a division of Carus Publishing Company.

Copyright © 1999 by Carus Publishing Company

First printing 1999

Printed and bound in the United States of America.

Library of Congress Cataloging-in-Publication Data

Walker, Jeff, 1952-
     The Ayn Rand cult / Jeff Walker.
         p.   cm.
     Includes bibliographical references (p.   ) and index.
     ISBN 0-8126-9390-6 (pbk. : alk. paper)
     1. Rand, Ayn—Appreciation—United States.   2. Fiction—
Appreciation—United States—History—20th century.   3. Women and
literature—United States—History—20th century.   4. Authors and
readers—United States—History—20th century   5. United States—
Intellectual life—20th century.   6. Philosophy and literature.
7. Objectivism (Philosophy)   I. Title.
PS3535.A547Z97   1999
813'. 52—dc21   98-459555
                                                                      CIP

To my late parents,
Robert M. Walker and Ruth E. Walker,
and to Anne

Contents

Preface

Ayn Rand (1905–1982) was a remarkable phenomenon in American cultural life. She wrote two popular novels which not only became best-sellers, but continue to sell decades later. She attracted adherents to some ideas which had been unduly neglected and which would later come into their own again. She stimulated many young people to think about important issues, and unlike some modern writers who have attracted a devoted following, she did not try to impress with mystifying terminology: whatever you may think of Rand's arguments, they are always clearly and forcefully expressed. She helped to break down the barrier between pop culture and serious intellectual debate.

There are many books and articles which expound Rand's ideas, either to advocate them or to criticize them, and there will be many more. This book doesn't compete with those works: it is not primarily an examination of the doctrinal content of Objectivism. It would be missing the point of *The Ayn Rand Cult* to see it as primarily an attempt to refute Rand's theories. There are points where I agree with Rand and points where I disagree with her, but I am mainly concerned with the fact that Rand's movement became a cult, that it functioned like a typical cult, and that this caused considerable unnecessary unhappiness for many people. The identification of the organized Objectivist movement as a cult has been made repeatedly over the years by a great many individuals who consider themselves Objectivists in all essentials, and who hold a much higher estimation of Rand's attainment as a thinker than I do. The cultishness of a cult is not changed by the correctness or incorrectness of some of its teachings, or even of all of them.

The official Objectivist movement, led at first by the Nathaniel Branden Institute, and today by the Ayn Rand Institute, has played a very important role in the history of Objectivism. But it has always been true, and is now more true than ever, that the number of sympathizers with and admirers of Rand's ideas outside the official movement has greatly exceeded the number of those affiliated with it. There are many people who have been affiliated with an Objectivist group and have then left or been ejected. Most often, they then still think of themselves as Objectivists. There are many others, influenced by Rand's writings, who have never had any formal affiliation, but who are free-lance Objectivists. To keep things simple, I refer to all the people in both these categories as 'neo-Objectivists'.

Obviously, the people I call neo-Objectivists do not all agree on everything, and if I cite one of them in support of some point I am making, it does not follow that other neo-Objectivists will agree with that point. Nor does it follow that a neo-Objectivist quoted in support of some point I am making will necessarily agree with any other point I make elsewhere in the book. Nothing I say here is meant to suggest that all neo-Objectivists are cultists. Many of them certainly are not, which often helps to explain why they never joined, or why they voluntarily or involuntarily left, Objectivist organizations. Nevertheless, I do not think that Objectivism is a neutral doctrine which by bad luck happened to become the doctrine of a cult: I show that many aspects of Rand's thinking are conducive to cultishness.

It was during my research for a Canadian Broadcasting Corporation (CBC) two-hour radio program on Rand, aired in 1992, that I began to sense that the closer to Rand a given follower was, the less real perspective he or she had on Rand, even after time and distance had separated them. The Brandens seemed so brand*ed* by their prime years at her knee that no other mindset could subsequently dislodge Rand's. The same appeared true for the other former members of her entourage, if to a lesser extent.

The more I saw, the more I realized that, not only was this a classic cult phenomenon, but that Rand's post-1943 writings themselves could not be fully grasped except as documents of a cult leader forming, consolidating, and splintering her cult following. Rand's biography is mainly of interest insofar as the Russian revolution landed hard on her family and drove her to the U.S. where she became a well-known writer. Far more fascinating in the Rand saga are the underground currents that swelled up to support an enduring cult phenomenon. This is where the real lessons for individuals and societies lie.

In identifying Objectivism as a cult, I do not intend to be wholly negative. Cults can have bad effects on people's lives, but they can also perform useful services. For many, experience in a cult can serve as a valuable agency of change, providing some stepping stones toward life goals chosen independently of the cult. The cult's doctrines offer the acolyte a structured system of beliefs which makes sense of the world, and which may well afford insights not easily available to mainstream thought. One should not compound the downside of cultism by a display of anti-cult fanaticism; excesses of enmity can sometimes be as harmful within mainstream thinking, with its knee-jerk hostility to all cults, as among the cults themselves.

The material for this book was selected from a much larger mass of information. In most cases, a point substantiated by quoting one or two people could have been further corroborated by citations from many sources, but I wanted to keep this book an easily readable work for the general reader rather than a scholarly compilation cluttered with numerous footnotes. To find the source of any quotation, see the 'Sources' section at the back of the book.

I interviewed the following people in person: Michael Berliner, Allan Blumenthal, Joan Blumenthal, Barbara Branden, Nathaniel Branden, Roy Childs, Albert Ellis, Antony Flew, Mary Gaitskill, Allan Gotthelf, Hank Holzer, Erika Holzer, John Hospers, David Kelley, Paul Kurtz, Ronald Merrill, William O'Neill, Leonard Peikoff, John Ridpath, Robert Sheaffer, Kay Nolte Smith, Philip Smith, and Joan Kennedy Taylor. By phone I talked with Edith Efron, Leisha Gullison, Virginia L. L. Hamel, Robert Hessen, Ralph Raico, and Murray Rothbard.

I conducted most of these interviews in 1991–92, and they were used in preparing the two-hour CBC program *Ideas: The Legacy of Ayn Rand* (1992), which was until recently available in the U.S. in tape cassette form. I thank the Canadian Broadcasting Corporation for permitting me to draw upon those interviews in preparing the present book.

I thank Max Allen, Anne Collins, Albert Ellis, Brian Goldman, Anne Michaels, and Jim Polk, who all encouraged me to write this book.

Chronology of the Objectivist Movement

1905   February 2nd, Alissa Rosenbaum born in Petrograd (St. Petersburg).

Abortive Russian Revolution.

1907   *The Secret of the League* by Ernest Bramah published.

1914   Alissa vacationing in Western Europe when World War I breaks out.

1917   February, democratic revolution and Kerensky regime.

'October Revolution' (Bolshevik coup).

Rosenbaums' business nationalized and their apartment building expropriated.

1918   Rosenbaum family flees Petrograd for the Crimea.

1918–1921   Russian civil war: Bolsheviks versus Whites.

Alissa completes high school in Crimea.

1921   Crimea falls to Bolsheviks; Rosenbaums return to Petrograd.

1921–1924   Alissa follows three-year degree program at the University of Leningrad.

1925   Alissa works as a tour guide at Peter and Paul Fortress.

Letter from mother's Portnoy relatives in Chicago arrives.

Alissa attends first year of film-school program in Petrograd.

1926   Alissa, now Ayn, arrives in America for six-month 'visit' with Chicago relatives.

Ayn Rosenbaum, now Rand, moves to Hollywood and has a fortuitous encounter with Cecil B. DeMille.

1927   Rand becomes a scriptwriter with the DeMille studio, soon to close.

Rand re-encounters Frank O'Connor after meeting and then losing track of him.

1928   Rand plans her first novel, *The Little Street,* never to be written.

1929   Rand marries Frank O'Connor, in order to stay in the U.S.

1930   Nathan Blumenthal (later known as Nathaniel Branden) born.

1932   Rand sells her screen original, *Red Pawn,* to Universal studios.

1933   Leonard Peikoff born.

1934   First version of *The Night of January 16th* opens in Los Angeles.

Rand moves to New York City for Broadway production.

1935   *Night of January 16th* has a successful run on Broadway.

1936   *We the Living* published.

1938   *Anthem* published in Britain.

1940   Rand campaigns for Republican presidential candidate Wendell Willkie.

Rand meets and befriends Isabel Paterson.

1941   December, Rand finally finds publisher for *The Fountainhead.*

1943   *The Fountainhead* published.

The God of the Machine by Isabel Paterson published.

The Discovery of Freedom by Rose Wilder Lane published.

Rand sells the film rights to *The Fountainhead* for $50,000.

1944   *The Road To Serfdom* by Friedrich Hayek published.

Rand moves back to Hollywood, writes screenplays for Hal Wallis studio.

1947   Rand testifies as a friendly witness before HUAC.

Rand breaks with her friend and mentor Isabel Paterson.

First meeting of the Mont Pèlerin Society in
   Switzerland.
1949 *Fountainhead* movie released.
1950 Nathan Blumenthal (Nathaniel Branden) and
   Barbara Weidman meet Rand in Los Angeles.
1951 The Brandens move from Los Angeles to New York
   City, and the O'Connors soon follow.
   Leonard Peikoff is introduced to Ayn Rand by
   Nathaniel Branden.
1951–1952 Rand's inner circle, 'the Collective', takes shape.
1953 Nathaniel Branden weds Barbara Weidman.
1954 Rand begins a platonic 'romance' with Nathaniel
   Branden.
1955 The Rand-Branden romance becomes a full-fledged
   sexual affair.
1957 *Atlas Shrugged* published.
1958 What will soon become the Nathaniel Branden
   Institute (NBI) begins, as Branden initiates
   lectures on Rand's philosophy.
   Murray Rothbard and his Cercle Bastiat briefly
   intersect with Rand's inner circle.
1960–1962 John Hospers has many philosophical discussions
   with Rand.
1962 *The Objectivist Newsletter* begins publication.
1962 John Hospers is excommunicated by Rand.
   Who Is Ayn Rand? by Nathaniel and Barbara
   Branden published.
1964 April, Rand pushes Nathan to resume their affair,
   she at age 59, he at 34.
   The Virtue of Selfishness published.
   Leonard Peikoff obtains his Ph.D. in philosophy
   from NYU.
1966 *Capitalism: The Unknown Ideal* published.
1966–1971 *The Objectivist* journal published.
1967 NBI moves to offices in the Empire State Building,
   signing 15-year $500,000 lease.
1968 Edith Efron is excommunicated by Rand.

The Break: The Brandens and all who will not shun them are excommunicated by Rand.

NBI is disbanded.

Is Objectivism a Religion? by Albert Ellis published.

1969   Nathaniel Branden obtains certification as a psychologist in New Jersey.

The Psychology of Self-Esteem by Nathaniel Branden published.

1971–1976   Rand publishes The Ayn Rand Letter.

1971   *With Charity toward None* by William O'Neill published.

The Romantic Manifesto published.

The New Left: The Anti-Industrial Revolution published.

1972   Nathaniel Branden attacks Rand in a *Reason* magazine interview.

The Disowned Self by Nathaniel Branden published.

1973   Rand re-united with her younger sister Nora, to the ultimate disappointment of each.

1974   Rand has surgery for lung cancer.

1978   The Blumenthals and the Kalbermans break with Rand.

1979   Rand's husband Frank dies.

1980   Rand's last TV appearance (*Donahue*).

1981   Rand's last Ford Hall appearance.

1982   6th March, Ayn Rand dies.

The Ominous Parallels by Leonard Peikoff published.

1985   Ayn Rand Institute starts up.

The Philosophic Thought of Ayn Rand edited by Douglas Den Uyl and Douglas Rasmussen published.

The Early Ayn Rand published.

Elegy for a Soprano by Kay Nolte Smith published.

1986   *The Passion of Ayn Rand* by Barbara Branden published.

1989 *Judgment Day: My Years with Ayn Rand* by Nathaniel
        Branden published.
        David Kelley excommunicated from ARI by Leonard
        Peikoff.

1990 Institute for Objectivist Studies founded by David
        Kelley.
        Truth and Toleration by David Kelley published.

1991 *Objectivism: The Philosophy of Ayn Rand* by
        Leonard Peikoff published.
        Two Girls, Fat and Thin by Mary Gaitskill published.
        The Ideas of Ayn Rand by Ronald Merrill published.

1992 John Agliaro buys 15-year option on *Atlas* film
        rights from Peikoff for $1.1 million.

1994 George Reisman and Edith Packer excommunicated
        from ARI by Leonard Peikoff.

1995 *Letters of Ayn Rand* published.
        Ayn Rand: The Russian Radical by Chris Sciabarra
        published.

1996 *Capitalism* by George Reisman published.
        Peikoff becomes a radio talk-show host on KIEV.

1997 *Journals of Ayn Rand* published.

1998 ARI-authorized documentary *Ayn Rand: A Sense of
        Life* is nominated for an Oscar.
        Helen Mirren, Peter Fonda shoot *The Passion of Ayn
        Rand* for Showtime TV.

1999 Plans for a movie of *Atlas Shrugged,* and re-makes of
        The Fountainhead and *We the Living* are in
        various stages of development.

Introduction:
The Most Peculiar Cult
on Earth

In a furious rage, the 63-year-old woman glared at the handsome young man seated in front of her, and in a choked voice, with a heavy Russian accent, placed a curse on his penis: "If you have an ounce of morality left in you, an ounce of psychological health, you'll be impotent for the next twenty years! And if you achieve any potency, you'll know it's a sign of still worse moral degradation!" Having delivered this imprecation, she violently slapped his face—once, twice, and some witnesses say, even a third time.

These slaps rang out like pistol shots. And these shots would soon be heard round the world. For this was the first great schism in the Objectivist movement. The woman was Ayn Rand, believed by her followers to be the greatest thinker since Aristotle, though some said, not to damn her with faint praise, the greatest thinker of all time. That she was the greatest novelist of all time almost went without saying. The young man was Nathaniel Branden, second greatest living intellect, who had brought the followers into the fold and had done more than anyone to convince them of Rand's greatness, and incidentally of his own.

In the weeks that followed, the rank and file, the 'students of Objectivism' (they were not permitted to call themselves 'Objectivists') would be asked to take sides. Without knowing the cause of this violent rupture, the students of Objectivism would be asked to shun Branden and anyone who continued to associate with him. Many of them did just that, because Ayn Rand asked them to. Others refused to denounce Branden until they were shown a reason, and these were excommunicated, anathematized, boycotted, and blacklisted forever by official Objectivism. Their close friends abruptly stopped speaking to them. Some of Branden's own sisters and cousins would never speak to him again. One of the loyal Randians who shunned Branden was a young man named Alan Greenspan. The face-slaps would drastically change thousands of lives, and oddly enough, they continue to do so. And it would be years before the full story which led up to them would come out.

Prior to this dramatic incident in New York City on 23rd August, 1968, Objectivism had grown by leaps and bounds. You might think that the Break between Rand and Branden would put an end to all that, and so it seemed for a while. In fact, things turned out differently. Some of the history of the Objectivist movement can be found in this book, but let me just mention here a few of the highlights of the year 1998. A Showtime cable TV movie, *The Passion of Ayn Rand*, based on Barbara Branden's biography of the same name, finished shooting, with Helen Mirren as Ayn Rand, Eric Stoltz as Nathaniel Branden, and Peter Fonda as Frank O'Connor. The documentary movie, *Ayn Rand: A Sense of Life*, premiered and appeared in theaters across the U.S. and Canada, and was nominated for an Academy Award. The views of neo-Objectivist philosopher David Kelley dominated a popular John Stossel TV special on 'Greed'.

Since her death in 1982 several books on Rand have appeared, most notably, Barbara Branden's biography *The Passion of Ayn Rand* (1986), Nathaniel Branden's memoir *Judgment Day: My Years with Ayn Rand* (1989), and Chris Sciabarra's *Ayn Rand: The Russian Radical* (1995). Reading these three volumes will leave one with some understanding of what Ayn Rand and her movement were all about—but not much.

The Sciabarra book is precisely the kind of academic exercise that Rand would have felt justified her contempt for academic philosophy. Apparently not an Objectivist, Sciabarra is nonetheless so sympathetic a critic as to invite the label of 'neo-Objectivist'. *Ayn Rand: The Russian Radical* goes to great lengths to suggest that Rand's philosophy is to a significant extent an outgrowth of various Russian influences present during her youth and is as systematic and radical as Marx's. Yet what Rand in fact took from her strictly Russian milieu was little more than a perceived need to counter Marxist ideology with an alternative in-depth complex of ideas.

The Passion of Ayn Rand and *Judgment Day* are works by the pair who were her greatest champions between 1950 and 1968. Both Brandens strive to preserve the Randian core of what they learned in their 18 years with her. Both strive also to expose Rand's volcanic temper and moralizing judgmentalism. Though both Branden books appear critical at times, and some unattractive wrinkles are sculpted in, care is taken to avoid knocking Rand off her pedestal. It was the Brandens, after all, who placed her there.

Ron Merrill's *The Ideas of Ayn Rand* (1991) points to Rand's Nietzschean influences but argues unpersuasively against what seems obvious to non-Objectivists, namely that Rand clung to certain Nietzschean ideas throughout her life, despite an overlay of Aristotelianism that she displayed in later years. The dismissal by Rand's followers of the importance of her Jewish background indicates another blind spot. Without an appreciation of that background, an understanding of her philosophy and of the whole Rand phenomenon is incomplete, to say the least. I disclose the Nietzschean and Jewish roots of Rand's thinking, especially in Chapter 10.

To ignore the insider reports of Rand's personality problems is to neglect the origin of crucial components of her philosophy—and of her movement which came to embody some of her own psychological peculiarities and to reinforce their presence in the Objectivist philosophy.

Where did Rand acquire her obsession with 'selfishness', ability, brains, and captains of industry as heroic role models? These and much more were part of the business literature of the 1920s Business Civilization that greeted Rand during her first impressionable years in America. Such literature is cavalierly dismissed by Rand herself as well as by her spokesmen, but to read actual excerpts from it come as an eye-opener to many of Rand's admirers. Many of Rand's ideas are taken directly from 1920s business theory, which therefore pops up in several places in this book.

The reputation that Rand turned into a cult phenomenon is based on *Atlas Shrugged*. That thousand-page-plus opus is acclaimed by adherents as wildly original. Yet, as I show in Chapter 11, it is derivative of particular novels and other works. Moreover, *Atlas Shrugged* was written very much to serve as pro-business propaganda. The Francisco speech on 'money' is even a product of consultation with her favorite real-life businessman.

The more sophisticated economic thinking that grew into a revival of economic liberalism in the 1980s and 1990s was done by others, particularly Friedrich Hayek, whom Rand hated but who was its true intellectual epicenter. Just as playwright Maksim Gorki, despite substantial disagreements with the Bolsheviks, conveyed Bolshevism's ideological message via his 'socialist realism', so novelist and essayist Rand, despite substantial disagreements with the business community, conveyed its preferred *laissez-faire* ideology through her 'romantic realism'.

There have been other Ayn Rands, before and after Ayn Rand. Throughout this book, I draw attention to the striking parallels between Rand and such figures as Mary Baker Eddy, Edward Bellamy, Count Alfred Korzybski, L. Ron Hubbard, Werner Erhard, and Bhagwan Rajneesh. The phenomena she represents are common and recurring ones that say a great deal about the nature of individuals and society. Rand's was but one of several waves of cultism that rolled out of America's peculiar religious heritage during the era of that heritage's disintegration and reshaping. Re-integration was the hallmark of all these new religious movements, the very term 'integration' constituting for Rand a kind of rallying cry.

In her fiction Rand portrayed a constellation of values—reality, objectivity, reason, egoism, individual rights, heroism, and *laissez faire*—that underwent severe contortions during their attempted embodiment by a real-life movement. As many government interventions in the economy accomplish precisely the opposite of their intent, so Rand's formative influences made it likely that she would adopt a set of ideas which, if probed deeply enough or if embodied in real people, could be seen as accomplishing precisely the opposite of her intent. That opposite is the ultimate destination of her exclusive concern for the Nietzschean overachiever, who must be protected via absolutized individual rights, which are justified only by Reason.

The Objectivist movement began in the living room of Rand's New York City apartment in late 1951 through 1952. Canadians Nathan Blumenthal and wife-to-be Barbara Weidman from Toronto and Winnipeg respectively, both students at New York University, and soon various of their relatives and acquaintances such as later chief of the Federal Reserve Alan Greenspan, sat at Rand's feet, listening spellbound to her read from her work-in-progress *Atlas Shrugged* and discourse upon ideas. Ten years earlier Ayn Rand herself had sat at the feet of *her* guru, novelist and conservative firebrand Isabel Paterson, listening to 'Pat' discourse on American history and politics.

By the time Rand was writing the scenes about her Galt's Gulch utopia in *Atlas Shrugged*, she had gathered around her a parallel, if junior, Galt's Gulch, its members too lecturing to each other on their professional specialties from the perspective of Rand's philosophy. It was basically Ayn's 'Blumenthal bunch' but she dignified it as 'the Class of '43', given that their admiration for *The Fountainhead* (1943) was what had drawn them to her. Privately they referred to themselves facetiously as 'The Collective', as if they made up a communist-like cell of party faithful, disciplined to unquestioningly carry out the dictates of a central authority. But as time passed, permissible jokes became fewer, and this particular insiders' joke became more appropriate to the grim reality.

Reinforcing the emerging hierarchy which placed Nathan second as Rand's special protégé and intellectual heir, Ayn and Nathan began a sexual affair in 1955, kept secret from all but their spouses, who were persuaded to give their consent to it. By 1957, some of Rand's more youthfully optimistic disciples were convinced that the world would be almost instantly converted *to* her selfishness-based *laissez-faire* capitalism, from the collectivist corruption she had dramatized in *Atlas Shrugged*. Just as the novel ends with society in ruins and the heroes of Galt's Gulch about to descend from their Nietzschean mountain retreat to set all things right, so 'the Collective' saw itself as the personal vanguard of Ayn Rand's philosophic and literary genius, preparing to instruct a society grateful for Rand's solutions.

Critical reaction to *Atlas Shrugged* was only sporadically favorable, mostly mixed, and often downright hostile. Rand, seeing her *magnum opus*, despite its commercial success, derided by virtually all established intellectual voices, sank into despondency. Nathan, lacking the credentials to continue practising as a psychologist in the state of New York, and thinking instead about making a living by teaching Rand's philosophy explicitly, devised and delivered in early 1958 a lecture series introducing *Atlas Shrugged*'s biggest fans in the New York area to Objectivism. Within a few years hundreds were enrolling at his Nathaniel Branden Institute (NBI), not just in the intro course (usually two or three times), but in supplementary courses given by himself or by other members of the Collective, with Rand herself sometimes in attendance to answer students' questions.

The success of the venture proved to be just the tonic Rand needed to emerge from her depression, restoring her confidence that in the longer-term her ideas might have a major impact upon America. Unfortunately, by then the darker facets of her personality were prevailing, and any tiny step toward greater acceptance of her ideas would be partially negated by the autocratic manner in which they were conveyed. Objectivism had begun as Ayn Rand's way of dealing with the world; the Objectivist movement evolved into the way her admirers would have to deal with Ayn Rand.

Nonetheless, Rand's inner circle swelled with new admirers and NBI swelled the lower ranks with hundreds and soon thousands of 'students of Objectivism'. The *Objectivist* newsletter and then journal that Branden and Rand started up would by 1968 have 21,000 subscribers. Rand herself spoke to overflowing halls on the campuses of more than a dozen universities. Branden delivered radio broadcasts. Both Brandens collaborated on the biographical *Who Is Ayn Rand?* Essays by Rand and inner circle members were collected and published as books such as *The Virtue of Selfishness* and *Capitalism: The Unknown Ideal.* Soon there was a book service, there were NBI social events, and an entire institutionalized social network, like a church. It appeared that via this burgeoning community, Rand's philosophy might indeed exert a countervailing effect upon the 1960s' increasingly collectivist and non-rational ethos.

In fact the predominant ethos of the 1960s would reach deep into the 1970s, while the Objectivist movement would implode in the second half of 1968. Why this happened provides an indication of just how personal an extension of Ayn Rand was her philosophy and the movement attempting to embody and spread it. Between 1964 and 1968, unbeknownst to Rand and everyone else except Barbara from whom he had separated, Nathaniel Branden engaged in an affair with a gorgeous model, 35 years Rand's junior, who in 1969 would become his second wife. Branden was convinced that if Rand found out, *that* would be the end of the movement and his leadership of it. During that entire period, Rand was with great exasperation trying to re-ignite the sexual affair with Branden and to puzzle out his tortured explanations of why unfathomable personal problems were getting in the way.

When at long last the truth did come out, Rand *did* explode with rage at Branden's betrayal and systematic deception of her. As feared, NBI was dissolved and both Brandens were mercilessly expelled along with anyone who took their side. Students of Objectivism were as stunned by this Break as they were ignorant of its real cause. The most hard-core fanatics rallied to Rand's side, but a large percentage of students, utterly disillusioned, simply drifted away. The Brandens, separately and with new partners, fled the poisonous atmosphere of recrimination in New York, for California.

In New York, while Objectivism's formal lecture bureau was gone, some inner circle loyalists such as Barbara Branden's cousin

Leonard Peikoff continued to give lectures on her philosophy. But the juice had been squeezed out of the movement. Most former adherents found their way toward libertarian political activism or psychotherapeutic cults. By 1973 Rand was in ill-health and soon ceased all formal communication with her followers, save her yearly public address at Ford Hall in Boston. Newsletters published by acolytes with her conditional approval partly filled the vacuum. But since Rand had no stomach for spearheading a dynamic movement herself and since no one else with Branden's entrepreneurial flair came to the fore, the movement shrank to the point that few even spoke of there being a movement as such during the 1970s and early 1980s. The uncharismatic Leonard Peikoff became Rand's replacement intellectual heir largely by default—she had fallen out with everyone else.

Contrary to appearances, the Objectivist movement was merely in hibernation. The Reagan era brought a quasi-Randian free-market economics to the forefront of national politics and Nathaniel Branden's obsession, self-esteem, to the forefront of therapy and educational policy. When Rand died in 1982, the albatross of her oppressive personality was lifted from that remnant of her following which *did* want a vibrant movement. By 1985 funding was in place for an Ayn Rand Institute (ARI) in Los Angeles, with Peikoff having veto power over its decisions.

For a while it seemed if the reawakening of interest in Rand's ideas would be accompanied by an easing of the intolerant moralizing that had become a hallmark of Objectivism. That brief halcyon period soon encountered thunderheads, first Barbara Branden's *The Passion of Ayn Rand* (1986), and then Nathaniel Branden's *Judgment Day: My Years with Ayn Rand* (1989), which together subjected Rand's reputation to a critical dousing which was very mild but still completely unacceptable to Peikoff and ARI.

With Peikoff evidently looking for an excuse to purge those who had expressed any sympathy for either Branden volume, Objectivist philosopher David Kelley's accepting an invitation to address a gathering of libertarians handed Peikoff that excuse. (Libertarians are hated by Objectivists.) Kelley was summarily excommunicated for expressing tolerance of ideological sympathizers who largely accepted Rand's politics and economics but had the effrontery to designate her metaphysics, epistemology, ethics, and aesthetics as merely optional.

Kelley responded in 1990 by forming a New York-based, more tolerant alternative to ARI that he called the Institute for Objectivist Studies (IOS). He took a a significant proportion of Objectivist scholars and rank-and-file with him. This second great rift continues to reverberate throughout the revived Objectivist movement and as the century closed, ARI and IOS would be more at loggerheads than ever.

A third rift, the product of internecine squabbling at ARI, occurred in 1994 when Peikoff excommunicated economist George Reisman and his wife, psychologist Edith Packer, the two who for a decade had been operating the ARI-affiliated Thomas Jefferson School (TJS), basically a summer school for Objectivists. In response, a number of former ARI stalwarts joined Reisman in virulently denouncing ARI and Peikoff. Both 1990s rifts have narrowed ARI's base of financial support and rendered the Objectivist movement no less unedifying a spectacle today than at the time of the Rand-Branden Break in 1968.

Nonetheless, about 400,000 copies of books by Rand, or by her current or former followers, continue to sell every year, probably more than enough to keep up a constant flow of new recruits to Objectivism. The Ayn Rand cult is alive and well on planet Earth.

1

The Cult While the Guru Lived

Rand's Adolescent Recruits

When the disciple is ready, the guru arrives.
Old saying

Nearly always, new converts to Objectivism are *young*. In the 1960s, the core of the Objectivist rank-and-file consisted of college kids, many of them converted or first attracted when in high school. Even Rand's inner circle, the Collective, mostly comprised 'thirsty' young people drinking up her ideas, ideas so potently spiked with her charisma as to be absolutely convincing. "She could convince you to walk into a firing squad," declares Erika Holzer.

Ron Merrill opens his book on Rand's ideas with: "I was fifteen—a common age for converts to the ideas of Ayn Rand." Barbara Branden read *The Fountainhead* at age 15. Eric Nolte was 16. Libertarian philosopher and former Objectivist Eric Mack first read Rand as a high school junior. Roy Childs felt obliged to remark upon his "late" start, not reading Rand until his last year of high school because he wasn't normally a reader of fiction. Sympathetic critic Robert Hunt suggests that *Atlas Shrugged* "demands the fervent elitism of late adolescence in order to be read with conviction. A taste for Rand must be acquired early or not at all." A former Objectivist recalls that when he was a teen, in the spring of 1966, the assistant pastor at the Lutheran Church he attended gave him his copy of *Atlas Shrugged*, much the way that eventual neo-Objectivist leader David Kelley discovered Ayn Rand. Says Kelley, "By the time I went to college, . . . I knew these were my basic values."

Normally cults reach out and assertively recruit. The Rand cult was fortunate: there was no need for hard missionary work. At the back of every copy of *Atlas Shrugged*, one paperback page-turn after the inspiring conclusion, the young reader scarcely having had a moment to catch his or her breath, found "A MESSAGE FROM THE AUTHOR," virtually an invitation to join the Objectivist movement. It was a highly unusual pitch for the 1960s, if not for later decades. These back-of-the book invitations help to explain the growth and resilience of the Rand cult, then and now. The sales of Rand's novels are so high, year after year, that a tiny percentage of readers responding to these invitations supplies the official Objectivist organization with a steady flow of new recruits.

The youthful students of Objectivism who were recruited in such surprising numbers in the 1960s typically came equipped with a basic education but little or no prior knowledge of the subjects that Objectivism pronounced upon, subjects like philosophy, history, economics, and literature. Typically, recruits learned the Objectivist line on all these subject areas, and *then*, perhaps, began to learn a little about them. The students' first exposure to these subjects was through a Randian lens.

Pierpont describes Rand's readership as the largely abandoned class of thinking nonintellectuals. Joan Kennedy Taylor concurs: "Many thought that Rand had invented *laissez-faire* capitalism . . . . dentists, engineers, and so on loved this vision of a techno-logically advancing logical world, but this was the first they had dealt with ideas in any grand sense." Taylor, having grown up with people in the arts and having gone to a liberal arts college, was not quite as overwhelmed by Rand's ideas as most of her fellow students of Objectivism, for whom these were the only ideas in the world.

Many former cultists say that early college classes destabilized their worldview and bewildered them, preparing them for the certainty offered by the cult. Rand criticized professors for disorienting students, while in effect capitalizing upon the disorientation. Kay Nolte Smith recalls that a friend took her in 1957 to an NYU lecture by Rand who said that everyone has a philosophy of life, the only choice being whether one is going to know it consciously or not. For Smith this was "a blinding epiphany. I thought 'my God, she's right'—everybody's actions are governed by some kind of thoughts," so it's incumbent on us to know consciously what those are. "And the idea that one could be consistent in one's thoughts, I found wonderfully attractive."

Atlas Shrugged was most people's entry to the cult. The part that casual readers skip is the part Objectivists-to-be dwell upon: Galt's 35,000-word speech, which Jane Hamblin called the longest burst of sustained histrionics since Wagner's *Ring of the Nibelungs*. Rosalie Nichols recalls that reading *Atlas Shrugged* a second time snapped the last ties holding her to her pre-Objectivist friends. "I had always been lonely, and it had been getting worse with every shattered relationship. Now I felt totally isolated. But then I reasoned. I exist. Ayn Rand exists. There must be others. I have to find them." For Nichols, Rand's philosophy "made it easier to understand people and harder to get along with them, . . . easier to identify the influences in our culture and harder to live in it, . . . stimulated my desire to study and made it almost impossible to read a textbook, . . . fueled my ambitions and convinced me how difficult it would be to achieve them in this society. . . . I became more and more particular and less and less satisfied."

The Spell of Ayn Rand

Newsweek remarked about Rand in 1961 that no she-messiah since Aimee McPherson could so hypnotize an audience. Of the Rand-based figure in her novel, *Elegy For a Soprano*, Kay Nolte

Smith writes that, "people responded less to her ideas than to the strength with which they were held." There can be something peculiarly magnetic about someone who seems completely unconflicted. Those lacking self-confidence tend to look to such a person for certainty. In Mary Gaitskill's Objectivism-satirizing novel *Two Girls, Fat and Thin,* the Randian-in-the-making character, recalling her first attendance at a lecture by the great Granite (Rand), rhapsodises, "I imagined myself in a psychic swoon, lush flowers of surrender popping out about my head as I was upheld by the mighty current of Granite's intellectual embrace."

Rand was impressive on an interpersonal level, according to followers. Even John Kobler, an unsympathetic 1960s journalist, could not avoid mentioning her "huge blazing hazel eyes" that fronted a "personality as compelling as a sledgehammer." "We were young and she was not," recalled Kay Nolte Smith. "I thought she was a genius. One of the things that was dazzling to me was her superb command of the language. She could just talk magnificently on any subject without any hemming or hawing or note consulting, and then she could marshal an argument on practically any subject, that—at least at that time in my life, given my age and knowledge and experience—I was simply unable to refute, had I cared to. And if you think to yourself, I have to be able to go by rational arguments, and you're unable to refute them, then you're really in a bind, which is where we all were." Rand spent virtually all of her productive time after the publication of *Atlas Shrugged* in 1957 consolidating and communicating what she believed to be rational arguments *for* her ideas and *against* opposing ideas. She became good enough at it to dazzle already-starstruck university students.

To former student of Objectivism Ron Merrill, it seemed that Rand *radiated* intelligence. "You could almost physically feel it . . . you would ask her a question and she would look at you with those incredible eyes and you could just see—almost like a fire burning behind them—the power of her intelligence . . . she was *never* at a loss . . . ask her a question and instantly out came an answer that you could never have thought of on your own." She could improvise on the spot, with a perfect answer, even

regarding something she hadn't previously thought about, "in perfect sentences, with all the grammatical elements in the right
place." Merrill could well understand how people "would give up
anything to be so close to a person of such stellar intellect." It
doesn't come across when you see her from a distance or on tape,
Merrill insisted. "You had to get up close, talk to her, her attention
focused on you," like a magnifying glass in the sun. Merrill is correct that neither razor-sharp intelligence nor unusual articulate-
ness is evident on extant video and audio tapes of Rand.

Former associates cite Rand's unshakeable arrogance and self-
assurance, emulated by the follower, who, secretly not so self-
assured, relied heavily upon Rand. She came to embody Reason.
The highest value became earning her approval, the gravest sin—
incurring her displeasure. Kramer and Alstad suggest that a guru
can become a disciple's personal living god, igniting even greater
emotion than an ethereal one. An early 1970s open letter to Ayn
Rand proudly confessed its author a Randian cultist. "I worship
you. . . . I owe you my life. . . . I think you are the greatest thinker
and writer who ever lived. . . ." Published albeit obscure novelist
Shane Dennison recalls that, as imagined from afar in the 1960s,
Rand and Branden "were *gods*, man, they'd said it all."

Rajneesh's sannyasins came to view their Master as a powerful,
unquestioned, and unquestionable authority. Likewise Kay Nolte
Smith recalls the "commonly held and voiced view that Ayn was
never wrong . . . about anything having to do with any aspect of
thought or of dealing with human beings." Leonard Peikoff,
today's Pope-like leader of orthodox Objectivism, tells us that
Rand "discovered true ideas on a virtually unprecedented scale"
and that a moral person would greet this "with admiration, awe,
even love. . . . If you . . . accept Objectivism, you live by it," and you
revere Ayn Rand for defining it. To her most devoted followers,
Rand is very much an 'Eastern' guru, that is, perfect enlightenment in the flesh. In the West, the only perfection is heavenly. In
the East, the guru's enlightenment is all-encompassing, applying
everywhere in the past, present, and future. Peikoff echoes that
sense of finality with respect to Rand.

Against the World

Hatred is the most accessible and comprehensive of all unifying agents.

Eric Hoffer, *The True Believer*

Rand bullied her inner circle, the Collective, who in turn bullied the students of Objectivism, who in turn bullied possible converts. Merrill writes that to the extent that the Collective passively accepted the sort of intellectual bullying of which they accuse Rand, "they corrupted her—as slaves always corrupt their masters. Surrounded as she was by the distorting mirrors of her sycophantic admirers, it is not surprising that Rand lost touch with reality." When NBI students intellectually bullied outsiders, they were no more in touch with reality than Rand. According to Nathaniel Branden, "If people didn't get it, we only had two responses: It's useless to talk; go read *Atlas Shrugged* and *The Fountainhead*. And then, if the book's converted you, we'll do the fine polishing with you. If not, the hell with you."

Rand gave public talks every April (except one year owing to ill health) at Boston's Ford Hall Forum between 1961 and 1981, attended by overflow audiences of her admirers. She would field questions, but the event was so in-group-oriented that its informal moniker became 'Objectivist Easter', as Objectivist an institution as NBI, which in effect it replaced in 1969. The rapt admirers did not ask tough questions.

Many of the cult aspects of the Objectivist movement were exposed by the founder of Rational Emotive Behavior Therapy (REBT), Albert Ellis, in his 1968 book *Is Objectivism a Religion?* It grew out of his public debate with Branden in May 1967 on the respective merits and shortcomings of Ellis's and Branden's therapies. Probably because of the amount of unbecoming heckling of Ellis by Rand herself and by the largely Objectivist crowd, as well as the commotion Rand raised when Ellis attacked the appropriateness of Rand's characters as role models, Branden subsequently refused Ellis permission to distribute audiotapes of the debate. His justification was that Ellis's arguments had been "devoid of intellectual content."

The explicit message of Objectivism is optimistic, benevolent, and life-affirming, but Objectivism, beginning with Rand's writings, is actually more preoccupied with contempt and disgust for the real world. Robert Bidinotto has concluded that, for many Objectivists, morality is identified with suffering, and the roots of *Atlas Shrugged* in the Promethean tragedy link heroism to martyrdom. While paying lip service to positives, Rand dwells on the negatives, and passes on this attitude to her followers. Ultimately, Objectivists come to feel they are in society but not of it. Holding standards alien to those of mainstream society can then excuse lack of progress in one's education or career. The Objectivist martyr is even reluctant to pursue great challenges, for if not successful, he will feel like a failure, which in Objectivism amounts to moral failure. Then he feels guilty about unproductiveness. George Smith maintains that the Objectivist martyr is caught up in a vicious cycle of rules and guilt, with devastating results.

Eric Mack says that what had the most negative impact upon him emotionally and psychologically was the notion conveyed by Rand's novels that one should be "devoted to the choice and pursuit of a world-historic career, and *not at all* to personal relations" which were destined to work out somehow as adjunct to one's main world-historic mission, or not to work out, in which case they weren't worthy of it.

John Ridpath, associate professor of economics and intellectual history at York University in Toronto, and foremost Canadian exponent of orthodox Objectivism, agrees that part of the price of becoming an Objectivist is "cutting yourself off progressively from your own culture." That vile culture invites such loneliness and seeming hopelessness that one tends to withdraw. Perhaps Ridpath's perspective springs directly from a passage in *Atlas Shrugged,* in which a beleaguered Hank Rearden achieves some sense of identification with "fanatical sects . . . who believed that man was trapped in a malevolent universe ruled by evil for the sole purpose of his torture."

Rosalie Nichols quit a government job because she was being paid with money stolen from tax payers. She dropped out of university because she found the subject-matter to be distorted, biased, or false. Even its presentation was all chopped up and disconnected, in contrast to Objectivism, where one finds the answers to all issues integrated into one big pyramid. Distancing herself from statism thus became an almost total withdrawal from the social sphere. Depressed by the whole culture, she would read *Atlas Shrugged* for an hour every night in order to get to sleep in a cheerful mood.

Atlas Shrugged's secondary railroad hero Dan Conway denounces villain Jim Taggart as "lice." At another point Dagny's words to brother Jim "were not addressed to anything human." Elsewhere Galt's gang describe their enemies as "inanimate objects" or as "refuse." Letters to the editor in defense of Ayn Rand dismiss her critics not just as 'hoodlums' and 'thugs', but as 'cockroaches'. Rand herself deploys "vermin" in one letter and her orthodox heirs would dismiss Barbara Branden, until late 1968 ranked number three in the Objectivist movement, as 'lice.' Considering that lice and cockroaches are owed no moral consideration, and that in any case, as Nathaniel Branden put it, "once somebody is declared an 'enemy' of Ayn Rand, all morality is suspended," one shudders at what *some* literal-minded Objectivists might do to an enemy they saw as posing a threat to the future of the Objectivist movement and hence of civilization.

The only sector of humanity that Rand *seemed* to approve of was businessmen. Belying that impression, she wrote in the 1960s that the real "money-*maker*" is a discoverer who transforms his discovery into actual products, money-makers in Alan Greenspan's view constituting less than 15 percent of businessmen. Overwhelmingly, in Rand's view, actual businessmen are "money-*appropriators*" whose goal is to get rich not by conquering physical nature, not by thought, not by producing, but by social manipulations that result in the shifting of pre-existing wealth from its owners' pockets to theirs.

Tacitly, say David Kelley, Chris Wolf, and other former cult participants, Objectivists held that there had to be something mentally and morally wrong with those who would not quickly embrace Objectivism. Since these outsiders would not accept the truth, they must be 'evading facts' and thus be motivated by evil. Objectivism was so clear, so well laid out out, so manifestly true, that refusal to swallow it must mean basic irrationality. Kelley now points out that it's perfectly possible for a reasonable person to be quite familiar with Objectivist principles and yet, in good faith, not be convinced. It speaks volumes for the character of the movement he left that he feels he actually needs to say this.

An unrepentant Peikoff has used the term "inherently dishonest ideas," referring to ideas so blatantly false that they can be believed only through a deliberate act of evasion. He includes as examples: non-objective art such as that featured in Museum of Modern Art exhibits, non-Aristotelian logic (such as fuzzy logic, presumably, or perhaps even all modern logic), pragmatism as developed by American philosophers or illustrated by American politics since Jefferson, and egalitarianism (and here Peikoff means not just equality of outcomes but also equality of opportunity). Peikoff adherent Peter Schwartz has characterized Islam, Kantianism, and Marxism as inherently irrational and labels libertarianism an evil doctrine. Peikoff insists that all the leaders of such movements are necessarily evaders on a major scale, their ideas being anti-reason and anti-reality and thus anti-man and anti-values.

The way marriages are handled shows similarities across cults and cultishly fanatical political movements. Rothbard recalls that the top Randian leadership presumed to bring about appropriate marriages, one explicitly asserting that she knew all the rational young men and women in New York and could match them up. At one Randian wedding ceremony, "the couple pledged their joint devotion and fealty to Ayn Rand" and "read aloud a passage from the sacred text," *Atlas Shrugged.* If a match that should be working wasn't, Objectivist psychotherapy would bring the couple to see Reason. Writes Margaret Thaler Singer, "When one partner of a married pair is recruited into a cult, pressure is put on that person to get the partner to join. If the partner doesn't, most of the time the cult, in effect, breaks up the marriage." Rothbard reports of Objectivist circles in New York in the late 1950s that when hectoring failed to persuade, many marriages were actively broken up by the cult leadership, one partner being sternly informed that his or her spouse was insufficiently Randworthy. Rothbard's wife Joey, a Christian, was a problem for Branden, who grilled Murray as to whether she had listened to his anti-God tape and been converted by it. (Branden still markets a version of this tape in *Psychology Today* ads for lectures by various therapists.) Rothbard recalls one Randian so brainwashed that she agreed she deserved her expulsion for having married a non-Objectivist.

Henry Scuoteguazza, looking back from 1991, tells us that in his experience, Objectivists use only one main criterion in choosing a friend: Is he or she an Objectivist? As a result, they have few friends in the working and everyday world. Joan Kennedy Taylor recalls the romantic implications of that stance, namely that in the heyday, Objectivists were only supposed to go with Objectivists, a recipe for a rather constricted love life. Scuotteguazza laments that having tried for decades to live by Rand's ideas, he is still faced with the question of why the Objectivist ethics hasn't made a more positive impact on the lives of Objectivists. His tentative answer is that those ethics don't help the individual choose from among the innumerable values that may be rational but aren't particularly appropriate for oneself. Moreover, what little guidance Rand's virtue of selfishness actually provides boils down to: 'Be rational, and always pass moral judgment. And . . . oh, by the way, have fun.' But when obsessive rationality and the judging of others are the top priorities, whither fun?

NBI: The Objectivist Church

Nathaniel Branden's original intention was to give just one course on Objectivism, in large part to help lift Ayn Rand out of her *Atlas*-reviews depression by demonstrating the public's interest in the book's ideas. The concept took off beyond Branden's imagination. By the mid-1960s, says Joan Kennedy Taylor, "The whole Nathaniel Branden Institute network was very powerful." Even on the west coast there were people "listening to taped lectures, writing letters to people back east, having Objectivist celebrities come by and visit their group." Murray Rothbard recollected that any town's NBI representative "was generally the most robotic and faithful Randian in his particular area, and so attempts were made . . . to duplicate the atmosphere of awe and obedience pervading the mother section in New York."

A magazine writer of that time, Dora Jane Hamblin, was not impressed by what she saw at NBI. "They are practically humorless, laughing only at key expressions of disdain for religion (the word 'God', pronounced aloud in class, provokes paroxysms of laughter) . . . They leave their lectures armed with formula answers for the obvious questions from outsiders. In an argument with outsiders, if one Objectivist were strangled in mid-sentence, another could finish it precisely. . . . Mastery of such glibness requires several class sessions and assiduous readings of The Works . . ." A taped seminar in Detroit is described as "almost liturgical," featuring "an immaculate white-clothed altar with a tape-recorder tabernacle." Objectivists found such depictions insulting at the time, but in retrospect, most wince at their accuracy.

Gurdip S. Sidhu, M.D., recalled that in 1967–68 he attended a few courses at NBI, along with a few social events. "The courses were characterized by little significant discussion except questions directed at clarifications. . . . No alternative opinions were ever offered." At social events "most participants were aloof, displaying an air of enlightened detachment. Cheerful talk was confined to a few small groups only . . . an 'in' crowd. Now, belatedly, I learn they were mostly members of the Blumenthal family." It also struck Sidhu that everyone in that circle was a chain smoker—a strange way of showing their conviction that life is the highest value.

One student recalls of NBI classes and get-togethers unexpectedly high degrees of uniformity, conformity, uneasy self-consciousness, posing, overcautiousness, and coldness, "the young men in their suits and ties, sitting rigidly staring ahead, conscientiously unsmiling," the women no more real, most "concentrating on looking cold and glamorous." Another remarks upon the clannishness, even at non-live taped lectures. He found students to be inhibited, humor-deprived, and caddishly snide. Questions raised in a politely challenging way were often met with anger or contempt. Later, Barbara Branden would note the contradiction in Rand's attitude. She would abuse students for not grasping some point, while claiming to be challenging two thousand years of philosophy. If so, one might think, her philosophy was bound to be assimilated only with difficulty.

One student of Objectivism found obsequious, even selfless conformity to be all too prevalent. Ron Merrill, always ready to defend the Objectivist movement against charges of cultishness, concedes that as the 1960s wore on 'true believers' *did* come to infest the ranks of Objectivists at his school, M.I.T; the philosophy's doctrines *did* seem to harden into virtual dogma; and dissenters *were* formally excommunicated.

Followers were not permitted to call themselves 'Objectivists'. Only Ayn and Nathan could do that. The approved term was 'student of Objectivism'. "That was the relationship that Ayn wanted with everybody, teacher-student . . . that relationship went on with Peikoff until she died," says Taylor. "Greenspan may be the one person who graduated from . . . her student to . . . independent intellectual. I'm not sure anyone else was allowed to." Rand declared that the term 'Objectivism' was her own intellectual property, that only she and those she explicitly sanctioned could be designated 'Objectivists'. In an early 1960s letter she referred to her movement's role of spreading a new culture, specifying that "we are not and do not regard ourselves as teachers." But, of course, the followers were students.

Barbara Branden has tried to defend Rand by saying: "She wasn't aware of the whole cult atmosphere," the fact that for most students "real understanding wasn't necessary but only to know what the master was saying." Yet in a 1960 letter of warning to Rand, Hospers had written of NBI that "the rather dogmatic and brief presentation, the oversimplification of some points, and the sort of 'I'm right and everyone else is wrong' manner of the presentation, tends to MAKE slavish dogmatists out of the audience." In her reply to Hospers, Rand dismisses any and all students so "cowardly" as to feel intimidated in this way. Tough on them. Her lectures' aim, she says, not "to provoke intelligent comment" but rather, paraphrasing George Washington, "to raise a standard to which the wise and honest can repair." Rand states that the lectures are not given to convert antagonists—a redundant remark, for only those in agreement with the ideas of *Atlas* were invited to enrol. She says she is hurt by Hospers's "concern for any weakling's needs, ideas, and interests, as against mine; it implied that they must be considered because they have not developed their minds, but I can claim no consideration, because I have." Thus, while dismissing Hospers's fears that students would become mindless dogmatists, Rand rejects the notion of genuine dialogue with them.

Students of Objectivism, recalls Taylor, "either accepted everything, or they were corrected. If they did not accept the correction they were out." Her aging father, Deems Taylor, a composer of operas, was a friend of Rand. Once "he was talking about dying and how matter is neither created nor destroyed so why should the soul be?, and Ayn said to me, 'At his age this is meaningful to him. Just let it alone'." No student of Objectivism, even an elderly one, would have been allowed to get away with such 'mystical claptrap'. Taylor explains that Rand respected people who had developed independently of her and met her on some common playing field of achievement more than she respected people who really admired her and came to be students. Nathaniel Branden said later that Rand "never had much respect for most of her followers."

The Cult's Pecking Order

Objectivism constantly praised individual independence, thinking for oneself, having confidence in one's mental capacity to make decisions, and not being intimidated by the opinions of others. While this incessant litany of inspiring words droned on ineffectually, the actual conduct of the Objectivist organization was the exact opposite. No one dared to think for themselves, except Rand. Within the Collective, Rand's inner circle, everyone hung on Rand's every whim, assuming that if their views ever conflicted with hers, they had to be in the wrong. The rank and file of the organization, the students of Objectivism, would do and say anything to win the approval of the Collective. The Collective treated the students with undisguised condescension and haughtiness. The Collective was fond of saying to the students: "Our job is to tell people *what* Objectivism is; your job to tell them *that* it is."

Nathaniel Branden says that Rand made it "abundantly clear to us that fighting for Objectivism meant fighting for Ayn Rand. . . . Loyalty to Ayn and love of her work was really more important than who you were as a person." Philip Smith says with reference to gurus like Rand that "everybody around you become tools in your crusade. They're not people any more. They're tools." His wife, Kay Nolte Smith, reflecting upon her ouster by Rand, laments that previous devotion and a tremendous amount of time and effort had not registered at all. "I did feel used, because it all added up to zero."

Philip Smith regards Eddie Willers as the most significant character in *Atlas Shrugged*. Willers is supposed to epitomize the ideal common man. "Imagine the view she had of the common man to indicate that Eddie Willers is the ideal," observes Smith. "He's sort of a non-entity with no life of his own who does everything Dagny wants him to do. He cuts the ribbon." When 'the Mind' has left the culture, the good person like Eddie Willers is left to perish. "So all the common man does is sit there and adore, obey, take orders from the brilliant people in the world. If that is her view of the common man, imagine what she thought of herself in relation to society and what other people should be doing for her. That's what she wanted from everyone around her." In Rand's early play, *Ideal* (1934), heroine-worshipper Johnnie pronounces himself "a man who is perfectly happy!" and then blows his brains out. Why? Because he'd just taken the rap for a murder he believed screen goddess Kay Gonda, Johnnie's highest reverence, had committed. But it turns out she was only pretending to have committed the murder, to test the loyalty of her supposed fans. Kay, a stand-in for Rand, comments later that allowing Johnnie that final dramatic gesture was, "the kindest thing I have ever done." It prefigures the ideal of devotion Ayn Rand would one day expect from her inner circle, the 'Collective'.

Rand learned the history of philosophy mostly by talking to Leonard Peikoff and Barbara Branden, both graduate students in philosophy, Barbara stopping at a master's. Rothbard notes that in Barbara Branden's biography, by not focusing on the cult she avoids unpleasant facts such as that while the Brandens had to abase themselves before Rand, everyone else crawled before the Brandens, and that Barbara herself was held up as 'the most beautiful woman in the world', the greatest living female after Rand and (via her master's thesis) 'the solver of the free will problem'.

Novelist Kay Nolte Smith says of Rand that, "it is painful to write a book and have critics say things that are either nasty or ill-informed. She got rid of that. She built a group in which no one was allowed to do anything but praise her for her novels for the rest of her life." To Objectivists, this may not seem like the main function of the Collective and the Objectivist movement. Yet being more interested in power than in truth is merely to be consistent with the actual rather than professed values of most of the rest of the world. If nothing else, the guru comes to enjoy the power of being others people's emotional center.

Within hierarchies, categorical separation of good and evil can facilitate the control of personnel. Kramer and Alstad explain that such dualistic thinking reinforces hierarchy because absolutizing the distinction between persons A and B legitimates their place-ment at different rungs of the ladder. Decades later before a mostly Objectivist audience, David Kelley would grant that the Objectivist movement "always had an inner circle, an extremely well-defined hierarchy . . . in which people often knew to within several decimal places their exact distance from the center," (laughter of recognition throughout the audience) "whose mem-bers are ranked as much by loyalty as by merit. Many are con-temptuous and condescending toward those below them, fearful and fawning toward those above."

Peikoff disapproves of those who drift away from Ayn Rand's orbit, a revealing metaphor suggesting a massive gravitational center and passive inertial bodies. According to Rothbard's recollection, the central axiom of Objectivism's *un*official creed was, "Ayn Rand is the greatest person that has ever lived or ever shall live." In fact there was a "consuming concern with greatness and rank." A friendly but perfectly serious dispute broke out: Was Nathaniel Branden tied with or ahead of Aristotle for second greatest thinker of all time? Real disputes were resolved by appeal to the authority closest to Ayn Rand.

The Objectivist movement quickly took on characteristics of the Communist Party of the Soviet Union. An exiled Trotsky explained in 1927 that, "Within an order such as the Party had now become, the effect of psychological affinity with the leader is to suppress rational thinking and enhance feelings of fanatical solidarity, the herd-instinct, mindlessness." The Party "inhabits two storeys, on the upper one they decide everything, and on the lower one they only hear about what is decided."

The Collective

By September 1950 Ayn Rand was reading from her work in progress, *Atlas Shrugged*, to Nathan and Barbara and within a few years to the relatives and friends they had gathered into Rand's fold in New York City. The Rand circle's beginnings are reminiscent of Rajneesh's—informal, exciting, enthusiastic, and a bit chaotic; in Bombay, Rajneesh followers could keep their jobs and attend evening lectures or drop in at his apartment during their free hours.

The core of the Collective was largely made up of Canadian Jews, most of them closely related. Nearly all the Collective, Rand included, came upon the ideas of America's founding fathers as outsiders. Leonard Peikoff, a lowly member of the Collective, though he was one day to become Rand's heir, hailed from Manitoba, as did Joan Mitchell Blumenthal, Rand's close friend for a quarter-century, and Barbara Weidman (Barbara Branden). With Toronto natives Nathan Blumenthal (Nathaniel Branden), a Blumenthal sister and her husband, and cousin Allan Blumenthal, Rand's inner circle was nearly complete. Barbara Branden states that her brother Sidney, wife Miriam, and Nathaniel's two other sisters and their husbands, Florence and Hans Hirschfeld and Reva and Sholey Fox, might have become regular rather than irregular inner circle members had they been New York City residents. Also by the late 1950s, Nathan's nephews Jonathan and Leonard Hirschfeld moved to New York, and Barbara's nephew, Jim Weidman, spent summers with them. Elsewhere Barbara comments, without irony, on the early inner circle, "It was like a family, it really was." And Nathaniel Branden has said of those days, also without intentional irony, "I did not believe in the kinship of blood, only ideas."

Earlier, Rand had enjoyed a circle of friends in both Hollywood and New York, including the Henry Hazlitts and the Ludwig von Miseses, and 'girlfriends' Marjorie Hiss, Faith Hersey, and Isabel Paterson (known to friends as 'Pat'). But with her new inner circle, the Collective, she could talk about what she really cared about and her listeners would be as spellbound by her as Rand had been by Pat. The Blumenthal bunch, 25–35 years younger than she, were so awestruck and so proud of being a part of her life that they made it impossible for her to continue normal relationships with her own peers. They were, as Roy Childs put it, "barking at her feet all the time. Nobody wanted to deal with these hangers-on." Childs thought that "they encouraged terrible behavior on her part."

For Rand, the kernel of her cult was an attempted real-life embodiment of her Galt's Gulch fantasy in *Atlas Shrugged*, with mostly young disciples standing in for accomplished professionals. It isn't surprising, given Rand's goal of eliminating any emotion unworthy of Reason as defined by her philosophy, that "to disparage feelings was a favorite activity of virtually everyone in our circle, as if that were a means of establishing one's rationality. All we achieved was to drive our own feelings underground." But, continues Nathaniel Branden, any emotional outbursts from *Ayn* were not merely tolerated as the price of access to genius, but rather "were uncritically interpreted as manifestations of irreproachable rationality." Thus was the group cathartic for Rand, and repressive for everyone else. When Nathaniel Branden eventually informed Rand that he would no longer have sex with her, she demanded by way of compensation that he devote his life exclusively to Objectivism: in other words, 'Abandon my ego and preach the morality of egoism.' This was only the most extreme form of what Rand—*and* Branden—expected of all students of Objectivism.

The top Randians never quite communalized. However Murray Rothbard, an adjunct member of Rand's circle for several months in 1958, recalls that most of the New York movement resided in Manhattan's East 30s, several associates even living in Rand's very apartment building. According to Rothbard's friend Ralph Raico, Murray was for a time being groomed to be co-equal with Nathaniel Branden. The Collective assumed it had to be a top priority for Rothbard and his Cercle Bastiat of libertarian friends to maximize contact with the top Randians. Rothbard recalls that at the final get-together before his July 1958 ouster, Branden asked him why he was seeing the Collective only twice a week. Rothbard refrained from telling Branden the truth, that he couldn't stand any of these "posturing, pretentious, humorless, robotic, nasty, simple-minded, . . . dazzlingly ignorant people." Ralph Raico found them reminiscent of a Communist Party cell, yet constantly posing, like English majors.

By February 1958, Rothbard saw that the marriage of the two groups was destined for dissolution. In addition to "the trumpeting by these ignoramuses of their own greatness," Rothbard lost patience with the Rand-Branden personality cult that was forming, the atmosphere of unrelenting nastiness, and the brandishing of Randian cigarette holders and dollar-sign-monogrammed gold cigarette lighters. Rand had at least created some worthwhile fiction, but her acolytes had yet to create anything.

The Holzers joined the Collective several years later. Erika Holzer recalls that Rand combined her ideas and her extraordinary charisma with an oppressive moralism, in a sort of package deal. So "you got sucked in. You didn't want to give up this experience . . . though there was a great deal of pain at the time, and fear . . . it was exciting, it was like being on another planet, it was us against the world." Erika's husband Hank, who became Rand's attorney, remembers leaving after all-night sessions with Rand, exhausted but feeling they had just come from a consistently rational universe, "a window on what life might be." Like "sitting in the pristine light," enthuses Erika, "It was irresistible!" (In *Atlas Shrugged,* when John Galt permits Dagny to enter his secret laboratory, a metaphor for Rand's philosophy, "It was like crossing the border into a different universe.")

Nathaniel Branden later concluded that he and others thrived at the forefront of Rand's intellectual crusade because "we were ecstasy addicts . . . that was the key . . . that need for an ecstatic state of consciousness." Generating religious ecstasy typically entails being part of a like-minded group intent upon yielding to the higher power its members all believe in, Rand in this case. The group reinforces and amplifies the ecstasy. Kay Nolte Smith writes of the authority such charisma can exert upon impressionable minds that "it could give you power over something more important than their livelihoods . . . their souls." In any group united by a belief system its members equate with reality itself, some will have staked career and soul on that system, which they therefore feel must be maintained.

A Reign of Terror

Because Rand's associates thought the survival of civilization was at stake, those disinclined to agree with them were deemed betrayers or enemies. Mary Ann Sures spoke for all when she exclaimed, "It's wonderful to be a part of history!" Similarly, the docility and fear of excommunication among early members of Freud's psychoanalytic 'church' can be explained by a concomitant fear of forfeiting a place in history.

The Holzers insist that apart from themselves, those closest to Rand for any significant stretch of time would admit, if they're frank, that the relationship took far more out of them than they gained, Rand being so difficult, so hard to deal with, so nasty, so unkind, and so insensitive. Joan Kennedy Taylor recalls of mid-1960s Collective member Edith Efron that she was not simply hurt emotionally, but psychologically damaged by Rand. Taylor also recalls that while inner circle discussions were presumed by outsiders to be an ongoing intellectual renaissance, in actuality when they weren't strictly Blumenthal clan gossip, they were about someone's transgression.

Rajneesh's followers, initially rebels and adventurers, became frightened conformists who could no longer trust in themselves. Hospers sums up Rand's inner circle similarly: "They became shivering-scared disciples who dared not say the wrong thing lest they incur her wrath. . . . Rand said she wanted people imbued with reason around her . . . she actually got on the whole . . . a bunch of adoring sycophants." Efron suggests that you'd be "better off with Rand if you were . . . a malleable nothing . . . the kind of special adoration the youngsters gave her . . . she could not get from an adult."

Ayn Rand not only admired Frank Lloyd Wright as she did no one else and modelled aspects of Howard Roark after him, she even partly modelled herself after him. She also became like him in ways she may never have understood. Rand met Wright and visited him at Taliesin in the 1940s, and found to her dismay that his students were hero-worshipping serfs. "Anything he said was right, there was an atmosphere of worshipful, awed obedience . . . their work . . . was badly imitative of Wright." Although Wright purported to be trying to elicit intellectual independence from his students, open admiration for architecture other than Wright's was interpreted as betrayal. Rand's shocked description of Wright's idolization is a close prefiguring of her own cult 20 years later.

Murray Rothbard recalls that even in the early days of the Objectivist movement, "fear was common, fear of displeasing, using an incorrect word or nuance, smiling at an unworthy person, being found out for some ideological or personal deviation." Erika Holzer confirms that within the Collective and on its periphery, "there was a lot of fear." At an Objectivist lawyer's lecture, someone asked if the subpoena was a violation of rights. He replied that he had to think about it, but this was merely code for having to check this point with Rand. A rank-and-file student recalls being so scared of asking Rand a question in 1963 that he got a friend to ask it for him. Rothbard recollects one top 1960s

Randian who had grave doubts about a certain philosophical tenet, but feared that to ask his question about it might mean excommunication. So he waited years for someone else to ask it. It's a measure of the Objectivist movement's authoritarian past that the head of a later more tolerant institution devoted to Rand's ideas felt obliged to assure patrons that at *its* events one is "not denounced on moral grounds for asking the wrong kinds of questions."

Here's a characteristic Ayn Rand moment, as recounted by Hamblin. At an NBI lecture a question submitted anonymously in writing asked why Rand employed, as a term of moral approval, the alienating term 'selfishness'? Her enraged answer: "Do not *any of you* begin a question telling me what alienates people! A person of self-esteem would *never* address a question of that kind to another person of self-esteem!" If government giveaways are *un*selfishness, "then let me be selfish! And tell your alienated friends to make the most of it," she roared, to loud sustained applause. Recalls Philip Smith, "We'd see her cut down people right, left and center at these lecture periods . . . She'd treat them as if Attila the Hun had just got up." Kay Smith adds, "Phil's not exaggerating . . . she would just cut people's heads off." Philosopher Eric Mack has a "vivid *un*pleasant memory" of Rand's treatment of questioners. "Might not religious faith play a useful role in helping one endure tribulations?" someone once asked, to which Rand angrily retorted "What sort of inadequate and corrupt psychology would lead someone to ask that?" Hospers remembers how very quickly Rand could whip out the iron fist behind the velvet glove and just tear a person to ribbons. At the NBI lectures it became somewhat embarrassing. She'd become incendiary over some small thing and after having this spate of venom turned upon them, most people simply left and never came back. Eventually Nathaniel Branden had to bar her from the lectures. These were, after all, his paying customers.

Not that Branden always took a back seat to Rand in the intolerance department. Mack recalls that when a number of philosophy students taking a course with Peikoff in 1965 gathered at Nathaniel Branden's apartment, with Rand an imposing though silent presence, "Branden began a long harangue about how grotesque it was for people to claim to have read Rand's works and still raise the sorts of philosophical questions that Peikoff had reported to them. . . . Of course, we were all shell-shocked and there were no questions."

It was just as bad inside the Collective. Erika Holzer recalls that "if we said something that might reveal a bad premise, . . . she would nail us. It got to be you were nervous about speaking up." Kay Nolte Smith explained: "You could say, 'That was a fascinating point, Ayn; it made me think of this or that thing', and you could just sort of have a discussion about it. But could you say, 'You know, Ayn, I don't think I really agree with this'? No!"

Philosopher George Walsh is one of the very few already-mature intellectuals who ever converted to Objectivism. Useful as he thereby was to her cause, Rand would put up with minor acts of insubordination on his part that she wouldn't abide in others. Walsh recalls that when he was writing an article on radical 1960s Marxist icon Herbert Marcuse for the *Objectivist*, "she would make editorial changes sometimes which I didn't agree with." On one occasion Walsh was giving a factual exposition of some idea of Freud's, and Rand inserted the word 'obscene'—"the obscene doctrines of Freud." "So I said . . . I would withdraw the whole article if she didn't agree to drop it, and she agreed after a short argument."

Since having the right psychology should lead to one's having the right opinions, fellow Objectivists expressing wrong opinions were suspected of having been led astray by a faulty psychology. To attack someone's thought processes or motives in such cases was a favorite Rand strategy, says Nathaniel Branden, a strategy one might add that had already been perfected by Freudians. "She taught her whole circle to do it," he adds, estimating that in 1971 three quarters of the students of Objectivism had adopted it. Yet Branden had ranked a close second to Rand within that circle and he had been the chief instructor of students of Objectivism.

First the Trial, then the Beheading

Because of the powerful combination of belief, loyalty, dependency,
guilt, fear, peer pressure, lack of information, and fatigue, . . .
members do not readily leave cults.

Margaret Thaler Singer

Formal trials of offenders were a frequent event. What typically were the 'big' offences, big enough to warrant convening the group to hear charges? According to Nathaniel Branden's later recollection: being friendly with anyone critical of Rand or being caught gossiping about a fellow member of the Collective. Such a transgression would generate her instant denunciation and the transgressor's categorization as a villain within the typology of her novels—an Ellsworth Toohey or a Lillian Rearden or whoever, pronounced with the authority of a supreme arbiter in matters of the human soul. In this, Branden says he can't recall anybody openly questioning Rand's policy, not even once. At any subsequent trial, Branden himself would usually serve as prosecutor. In retrospect he says he is appalled at his own ruthless behavior in that role.

Early expulsions occurred in 1958 involving the 'Cercle Bastiat', a handful of libertarians led by Rothbard, impressed enough by *Atlas* to meet with Rand's Collective for several months. One of these joint Collective-Cercle Bastiat meeting, with neither Rothbard nor Rand in attendance, became a recitation of Holy-Roller type testimonials, each acolyte answering the question 'Who has been the most intellectually important person in my life?' Of course, each was supposed to nominate Rand. One Bruce Goldberg, not quite getting the real point of the exercise, named Ralph Raico, for having converted him to libertarianism. Goldberg was given the gate permanently and Raico left with him.

Then came Rothbard's expulsion. Already under suspicion for having a Christian wife, having religious friends like libertarian historian Leonard Liggio, being a non-smoker, and not spending enough time with the Collective, he was now accused of plagiarism. Rothbard had written a paper for a symposium headed by Helmut Schoeck (author of the standard classical liberal work,

Envy, later to be carried by the orthodox Objectivist Second Renaissance Books). Nathan phoned Rothbard saying that his paper plagiarized from *Atlas Shrugged* and from Barbara's master's thesis on free will. The Collective members did not understand that the ideas allegedly plagiarized were intellectual commonplaces which had been around for decades or centuries. You will appear at your trial on Wednesday at 4:00, Branden ordered. Rothbard failed to show; he *was* tried *in absentia* and denounced. Next came a letter from Branden threatening to present to Helmut Schoeck evidence incontestably establishing guilt. The evidence was duly presented. Schoeck responded that the claim of plagiarism was ludicrous. Rothbard cautiously added to the paper citations of sources earlier than *Atlas Shrugged* for all the supposedly plagiarized ideas.

Roy Childs recalls a typical target of and setting for excommunication, that is, an NBI student being put on trial in Rand's apartment. "Remember the young ballerina who had some irrational this or that, and they tore her apart, Nathaniel strutting back and forth in the apartment, Ayn applauding, and she was reduced to tears and gave up her career?" Several sources recollected that this kind of incident happened constantly, "day in, day out, it was happening all the time." Barbara's *Passion of Ayn Rand* gives the impression that this sort of thing happened once in a blue moon. According to Nathaniel Branden, Barbara "sometimes played the role of Lord High Executioner herself." "Nathaniel was the first son of a bitch," said Childs, but Barbara did not come across in her book as being the "hatchet woman" she was.

Whether they belonged to the Collective or to a wider circle of followers, people didn't miss their trials. There was no question of not showing up, Rothbard and Barbara Branden excepted. Even when it was expected to hurt like hell, if Rand had something to say about a given person, that person thought it terribly important to know. Purge protocol meant appearing to hear the charges (or else being tried *in absentia*) after which, usually the closest friend of the excommunicatee wrote, as Rothbard related, "a bitter, febrile, and portentous letter, damning the apostate." Barring unusual circumstances, the break had to be permanent and total.

The worst sin was to question the legitimacy of the whole procedure or to refuse to take a stand until one knew all the facts.

In most cults, expellees are "denounced and defiled. They are entered on a roster of non-people. Horrendous lies are told about them to reinforce the cult's line on why they are no longer members," writes Margaret Thaler Singer. Such denunciation is not a pleasant prospect for someone thinking of leaving. An ad taken out at the back of a booklet defending Rand posthumously against both Brandens' books salutes "the Heroic Accomplishments of Ayn Rand" and dismisses "those Wimps Who Blame Her for their own Personal Problems." Only cult members in good standing can tell the truth.

Kay Nolte Smith was excommunicated in the mid-1970s for making unauthorized changes to a few lines of dialogue for a public performance of Rand's play *Penthouse Legend (Night of January 16th)*. Smith concedes she shouldn't have done so but insists it was not a big deal. For that one mistake she was drummed out, 15 years of prior devoted association notwithstanding. "It almost got to be a badge of honor to get drummed out," said Smith. "I was invited back in after four years and I declined; I had come to my senses . . . it was a major traumatic life experience," its splendors attached to "a lot of agony. I think that's true of everybody." Hospers recalls of his leave-taking from Rand that, "along with the pain and desolation, I felt a sense of release from an increasing oppressiveness," because he was thereby avoiding "the web of intellectually-stifling allegiances and entanglements" that so many of her true disciples ensnared themselves in.

Usually Rand's fallings-out with associates took the form of: 'Get out of my life forever; you're immoral.' With the Holzers she explicitly left the door open. However, they never again knocked on that door, mainly because Hank found her so difficult to deal with that he didn't want to represent her legally again. Toward the end, there wasn't enough of an inner circle left to perform the excommunicatory function. Instead, with seeming deliberateness, she insulted and antagonized the Blumenthals in an unrelenting quest to prove to the Blumenthals' satisfaction that their aesthetic tastes were irrational. Eventually they could stand it no longer and abandoned her.

When asked to comment on the seeming intellectual dishonesty of excluding from the *Ayn Rand Lexicon* (1986) the at-one-time approved writings of those later excommunicated, Phil and Kay Nolte Smith jointly asserted, "But that's the essence of it. These are Papal Bulls that are coming out. It's like the Holy Roman Church in that sense. That's why it's a cult. Excommunication is not just a funny word here: it's literal. When you are excommunicated you are not recognized again, you do not exist, so why would they mention your name in any of their publications?"

In *Lectures on Fiction-Writing*, a course given by Rand in the late 1950s, both Brandens were in the audience, a fact confirmed by Karen Reedstrom. On tapes of these lectures now distributed by Second Renaissance Books, the Brandens' voices are drowned out by a narrator summarizing their questions or comments. It's reminiscent, comments Reedstrom, of old Stalinist purges, where photographs would be doctored to remove people who had been disgraced.

Kelley also confirmed that the writings of those people who wrote under Rand's auspices but later broke with her tend to disappear down the memory hole. Nathaniel Branden's essays appear in every reprinting of *The Virtue of Selfishness*, but post-1968 volumes such as the *Ayn Rand Lexicon* include not a word of his. Yet Rand never actually repudiated any of Branden's articles and lectures and seemingly had no substantive disagreements with them, having herself contributed to them via discussion and editing. That readers might profit intellectually from such writings must for the orthodox be weighed against the prospect that their now-verboten authors might thereby profit financially or exert influence in competition with orthodox leaders.

Some of the attitudes cultivated by a cult linger after leaving it and dissipate very slowly. Typically these include: a hypercritical attitude toward others and society, a condemnatory attitude toward normal human failings, harshness even toward one's self, emptiness at no longer being a world saver and loss of the sense

of being among an elite. The Holzers say of their departure from
the inner circle that it was hard to walk away from, and that with
a sense of relief came a sense of loss that took years to get over.

The ex-cultist needs to re-establish his *own* belief system and
moral values, and sort them out from ones adopted in the cult.
Often he or she fears joining any group. Barbara Branden argues
that the reluctance of most former Objectivists to get involved in
(further) cults counts against classifying the Objectivist movement as a cult. However, subsequent cult-*shyness* after leaving a
true cult is probably even more common than jumping into
another one, just as after a romance has gone sour, most prefer
uninvolvement for a while to rebounding straight into someone
else's arms.

What Would John Galt Do?

Christians faced with any major decision are admonished to ask
'What would Jesus do?' Students of Objectivism, were recommended to ask 'What would John Galt, or Howard Roark, or any
of the heroic characters in Rand's two major novels, do?'
Discussions among Objectivists would often refer to these characters, as if they were simultaneously familiar acquaintances, ora-
cles of profound wisdom, and perfect exemplars of all the virtues.
Novelist Mary Gaitskill found it "kooky" that anyone would parrot
the characters in a novel, and judge real people by how they mea-
sured up to those characters.

Just as Christian fundamentalists are exhorted to read the
Bible every day, students of Objectivism were expected to keep
rereading *Atlas Shrugged* for the rest of their lives. Eric Mack
recalls that after devouring Rand's works and becoming a 'boy
Objectivist', he felt obliged to reread Rand's novels regularly for
the next six years. Rothbard remembers being chided for not
rereading Rand, by someone who boasted that he had already
thrilled to *Atlas Shrugged* 35 times.

Atlas Shrugged was not just a sacred text: it was an alternative
reality into which Rand and her most dedicated followers disappeared, like Alice down the rabbit hole. Looking back in 1996,

Nathaniel Branden maintained that the 1960s Objectivists lived in the world of Rand's novels. "We sure as heck didn't exist in the real world." They experienced events in Rand's novels as if they were as real as anything happening in the real world, and they experienced day-to-day events in the real world in the context of Rand's novels. The result was a dangerous propensity for highly simplified explanations. Objectivists would say of real people: 'He's a Peter Keating, he's a James Taggart, she's a Lillian Rearden'. They shared a "simplified, fictionalized, stylized way of looking at everything." Branden goes so far as to say, "I didn't live in the United States in the 1950s. I lived in *Atlas Shrugged*. I have very little sense of the Fifties."

What was the nature of the novel Branden and many others were living in during the 1950s? Rand had written in 1946 that she wanted *Atlas Shrugged* to be extreme, simplified, stylized and impressionistic, like an undetailed sketch of a skyline. In the early 1960s she said in the context of *Atlas Shrugged* that in cultural matters she didn't like being bound by choices others had made. "I want to be in my own universe, of my own abstractions . . . where everything is made by me except the metaphysical human abstraction. It has to be things as they might be, but from then on I want things as they ought to be, as I want to make them. In *Atlas* I felt completely as if I'm building the whole universe." In the name of objectivity, Branden and company were living within someone else's fantasy.

Rand's fiction was the Objectivists' only refuge from the hostile and contemptible world. Allan Blumenthal explains that, "Because they had learned the philosophy predominantly from fiction, the students of Objectivism thought they had to be like Ayn Rand heroes: they were not to be confused, not to be unhappy, and not to lack confidence. And because they could not meet these self-expectations, they bore the added burden of moral failure." The late Roy Childs, who may have coined the term 'Randroids' to describe the Galt-imitating robots produced by the cult, relates that many Objectivists "became so alienated from the world that they only felt at home inside . . . the world she created" and "couldn't do anything except talk about John Galt and *Atlas* and

Dagny and Howard Roark and these people as though they were real figures. They read and reread these books and that was their life."

Atlas Shrugged may be Objectivism's greatest strength, but it is doubtless also a weakness. For many people, especially those already conversant with literature or philosophy, there has to be something ridiculous about a movement touting this as great literature or great philosophy. Kay Nolte Smith would prefer that Objectivists take *Atlas* the way non-Objectivist readers do. "I'd say there are a lot of good ideas in this book and it's got a wonderful story but you can't take it literally as a guide to life." For Rand and the Brandens in the 1960s, and for Peikoff and Binswanger in the 1990s, this was heresy. The book is a guide to life, *the* guide to life, the *only* guide to life.

What Would Ayn Rand Do?

Rand's fictional heroes are ideal human beings, creations of Rand's imagination. But the afterword of *Atlas Shrugged* solemnly warns readers not to "tell me that such men as I write about do not exist. That this book has been written—and published—is my proof that they do." This was the beginning of a recurring theme. Rand and her followers came to believe that there was at least one perfect hero alive—Ayn Rand, she having earned that designation by writing *Atlas Shrugged* and living its creed. Merrill recalls that at a 1967 debate between psychologist Albert Ellis and Nathaniel Branden, when Ellis asserted that Rand's fictional heroes were impossible, "Rand stood up and yelled, 'Am I impossible?' She started yelling at the moderator busy trying to calm her down." Rand came to regard herself and the Brandens as real-life counterparts of John Galt, Francisco, and Dagny. Before NBI audiences for years she pointed to the Brandens and even her husband Frank as real-life heroes and role models.

Rand's real-life inner circle, the Collective, and her fictional Galt's Gulch gang in *Atlas Shrugged* came into being as fraternal twins during the mid-1950s. The Gulch gang would never miss each other's lectures, and the same was expected of the Collective.

Their attitude was that since Randians are the most rational people around, one should want to spend all one's non-working time with them, especially the Collective. The dollar sign was the logo for Galt's gang, as it would become for Randians, despite Rand having written in a letter, "The sign of the dollar is a symbol introduced by me in fiction to symbolize the cause of the particular group of men in my story. It would be improper to introduce a symbol for philosophy in real life."

Ethological and psychological studies indicate that social animals, such as humans, do imitate their leaders' behavior. By the 1960s, legions of New York students of Objectivism were looking to Rand and the Brandens for cues as to what music they should be listening to, what fashions they should be wearing, and what careers they should pursue. At a deeper level, formerly likable or at least tolerable young people were transmogrified into grim, belligerent poseurs robotically mouthing Randian slogans in imitation of fictional heroes *and* of their supposed real-life counterparts.

Many availed themselves of the pretext for changing Jewish or other ethnic-sounding names to punchy Anglo-Saxon ones like those Rand gave her heroes. Or they named their children after Rand characters much as Comrade Sonia in *We The Living* ponders the ideologically-resonant names 'Ninel' ('Lenin' backwards), 'Octiabrina', 'Marxina', or 'Communara' for her unborn child. There were probably more posters of the Manhattan skyline on the apartment walls of young Objectivists aping Rand's city worship than clichéd opening shots of that skyline in Hollywood movies. One student recalls the austere, businesslike manner of Hank Rearden or Dagny Taggart as the favored pose of most students, some even donning Francisco D'Anconia or Ayn Rand capes and waving their cigarettes about in absurdly-long holders like Rand's. Murray Rothbard, asked by one Randian why he didn't smoke, pleaded an allergy, eliciting the response, "Oh, that's OK, then."

Neo-Objectivist Murray Franck recalls that when he met Rand at NBI, she told him that his brother should shave off his moustache, facial hair signalling something to hide. Allan Blumenthal confirms this Randian bias, which circulated and made beards and moustaches practically outlawed around NBI. Beards were also 'out' in Stalinist Russia. The same bias later turned up in Werner Erhard's *est*.

A dampening of humor is almost universal in cults. Cult personality transformation brings about inflexible thinking and constricted feeling, both inimical to a sense of humor. Rand herself was highly suspicious of humor. Among Objectivists, wit was all but prohibited, except in the rather crass and sneering *Atlas Shrugged* style. Humor might imply that one was not serious about one's values, that one was trying to undermine the metaphysically significant.

Longtime Objectivist David Kelley concedes with some embarrassment the movement's pressure toward conformity in both thought and action. Even in an ideological community he suggests, one "does not expect the degree of uniformity—down to matters of personal dress and style, aesthetic preferences, beliefs about political strategy or sexual psychology—that characterized the Objectivist movement, especially in its earlier days." Even Peikoff has openly regretted that some felt guilty for not having orange hair like Howard Roark, not living in New York City, or not liking skyscrapers.

Fred Smith, president of the Competitive Enterprise Institute, remarks that most Objectivists in time come to "regret their childish *Übermensch* pretensions" inspired by Rand's novels. Childs recalls that an enormous number of those bowled over by Rand "had grandiose ambitions that bore no relationship to what they were going to do with their lives." One perfectly normal young woman who could have done some acceptably good writing or taught English "wanted to be another Victor Hugo, changed her name to [a variation on the name of one of Rand's favorite writers] and had a pretentious nine novels planned out . . . Not having the technique or the training for it, she just dropped out of sight and became sort of a farmer in the Midwest."

Donway relates that as a youth he was doing well in writing. Then he read Ayn Rand on writing. It hadn't occurred to him previously that he'd been writing realistic, naturalistic fare. Rand "made it sound like part of the international Communist conspiracy." He started writing, badly, in the Rand-approved romantic mode. His instructor was dismayed that his subsequent stories lost all feeling and authenticity and asked him where his vision had gone. Donway was unreachable, classifying his instructor as just one of the bad guys attacking Romanticism. He then dismissed as sub-human a character in a novel by the instructor, who subsequently refrained from recommending him for further courses. Naturally, Donway interpreted this as 'Howard Roark expelled by the Dean'.

John Ridpath has never had to worry about straying from Rand's party line in such matters. He still asserts that "if looked into more deeply, I predict . . . you would actually find that it is true" as Rand said, that "Beethoven *did* have a malevolent sense of life," as did Victor Hugo. Ridpath has invariably found "after I've looked into something . . . that lo and behold, in essence she had her finger on it correctly."

Rand made aspiring writers feel that there was nothing worth writing about but heroes. Kay Nolte Smith found that saying to herself, 'I am now going to write about a hero' would simply immobilize her brain. Phil Smith recalls that Edith Efron was always working on a novel, yet neither she nor Barbara Branden, also an aspiring novelist, ever published any fiction. Other than Peikoff, none of the Collective published books until after breaking with Rand. Kay Nolte Smith remarks that it was just a tremendously inhibiting, intimidating experience to write for, with, or under Rand.

Erika Holzer, author of *Eye for an Eye* (made into a 1996 movie starring Sally Field), learned from Rand how not to treat young writers, whose egos can be fragile. Rand tore Holzer's 1970s-era screenplay apart, finding *nothing* good about it. Seemingly, everything she did was wrong and when Holzer left Rand's apartment she remembers turning to husband Hank and saying "I'll just stick to the law. I'm hopeless." She suggests that it was wrong of Rand not to smooth it out with, '*This* is bad but you can do this and this, there's no need to give up.' Holzer did give up writing fiction for years. Decades later, "I went back to that screenplay as a published, experienced professional writer, and it's *not* that bad."

The Break

For I have sworn thee fair, and thought thee bright,
Who art as black as hell, as dark as night.

William Shakespeare, Sonnet 147

In 1967 NBI had graduated 25,000 students and Objectivism's New York City headquarters had a mailing list of 60,000. A year later it would all be over.

Philosopher George Walsh, on the fringe of the inner circle, describes the atmosphere in Rand's apartment in July 1968, Branden having told Rand that their affair was over but still withholding that he had been lying to her for the past four years in denying his other extramarital affair. Walsh was told Nathan was out of town, but he showed up briefly. "There was a great tenseness in the air . . . I realized that something odd was going on that I couldn't figure out but there was no evidence as to what it was. This was an experience I was destined to repeat again and again in Objectivist circles." Still, when it did come, he was stunned by Rand's denunciation of Branden. Yet many rank-and-file students had long suspected what those closest to Rand blinded themselves to: rumors of a Rand-Branden affair circulated well before the 1968 Break.

Taylor explains that she took Branden's side, "with qualifications, . . . if I knew a pickpocket was being framed for murder I would come to his defense, and that was my view of what was going on. I was appalled by the lack of intellectual integrity exhibited by people calling up, passing off as gospel all kinds of rumors about Nathaniel Branden stealing money or not having written any of the articles he signed in the *Objectivist*. The whole thing was, 'You must decide to side with Ayn Rand without knowing the facts', and I refused to do so." Rationality and individualism drew people like Taylor into Objectivism, but the suppression of both ideals eventually drove them out.

Jack Wheeler recalls that as fire-breathing Objectivists he and his friends took Rand's side and wrote off Branden as the epitome of evil. Then they received the letter of self-defense Branden sent to Objectivist subscribers, which made obvious to discerning adults that this was largely a case of 'Hell hath no fury like a woman scorned'. Some people claimed that the Break had philosophical causes. Ron Merrill countered decades later that the 'Great Schism' constituted childish squabbling, not disagreement on matters of substance. The real cause was Rand's "sordid sexual affair" with Branden. David Kelley too dismisses the idea that substantive issues were at stake in this or any other rupture in Objectivism, the trigger always some act deemed an insult or injury to Ayn Rand personally. Many "were more upset at what they thought had been done to Ayn Rand than they would have been were it done to themselves. They seethed with borrowed anger."

Taylor recollects of the 1968 Break that what really shocked her was so many students acting in complete contradiction to a philosophy advocating that one make judgments based on the evidence and on one's own independent thinking. She received phone calls demanding to know which side she was on and threatening to cut off all business dealings with her if she was on the wrong side. And this was even prior to Rand's making *any* comments on the matter.

Rand and the Collective began blacklisting Branden supporters and all those unwilling to repudiate the Brandens solely on the basis of Rand's say-so. Many subscribers to *The Objectivist* found themselves barred from all Objectivist activities and their subscriptions cancelled. Barbara Branden at the time cited a "religious mania" and "moral frenzy" of ostracism and of every "ugly pressure that can be brought to bear." Those later caught having purchased any Nathaniel Branden book were blackballed.

The equivalent of loyalty oaths were suddenly required for registering in Objectivist courses given by inner-circle members Mary Ann Sures and Peikoff in Washington, D.C. Branden was denounced as a moral monster, with no specific reason or evidence supplied. David Kelley recalls that it wasn't uncommon during this schism (and subsequent ones) to hear the appeal to authority—'If Rand says someone is an anti-Objectivist masquerading as a real Objectivist, the author of *Atlas Shrugged* is hardly likely to be wrong about it.' One Rand supporter maintained that Branden's only moral option was to commit suicide, another that he could hypothetically be assassinated without compunction.

Keith Edwards, then NBI's business rep in Detroit, received a letter from Rand's attorney, seeking any evidence that Edwards might have regarding Branden's behavior. He wrote back that the whole thing was being carried a bit too far. Edwards was instantly blackballed. Rand's associates began acting dictatorially toward the Detroit students, telling them what books not to read, so the Detroit Objectivist society closed up shop.

Walsh relates how his effort to bring Rand and academic philosophy together foundered. Following the denunciation of Branden, the philosophers he had been assembling—Objectivists and Objectivist sympathizers—to make up a discussion group on Objectivism within the American Philosophical Association suddenly fell away. They either didn't answer or explained that obviously personal matters they didn't want to touch with a barge-pole were mixed up in it. Walsh himself refused to believe reports of a Rand-Branden affair. Once Peikoff had ascertained that Walsh was in no way associated with Branden, the two met, Peikoff imploring him: How could anyone possibly believe that the author of *Atlas Shrugged* had done anything fundamentally wrong? Walsh then met with Rand who asked him not to associate with her enemies. Tibor Machan recalls that nearly two years later, in 1970, three young Rand loyalists tried to persuade him to withdraw a philosophical paper of his from *The Personalist* because its editor John Hospers had dared publish an essay by Nathaniel Branden shortly after the Break, something no 'moral' person could have done.

That Branden had been acting irrationally, notes Sid Greenberg, many NBI students found "absolutely unintegratable in the light of Branden's all-encompassing knowledge" and happiness seemingly achieved, "through rationality and objectivity." ('Integration' is Objectivist jargon for making all the information at one's disposal fit together rationally.) For many, it was no longer unthinkable that Rand herself might not be a monument to absolute intellectual integration and moral perfection. Greenberg says the Break angered, bewildered, and disillusioned many students of Objectivism but eventually relieved them of the tension of trying to emulate Randian heroes or Objectivist rationality.

The Break left an even more fanatical rump movement in New York City. Lecture series by the Blumenthals on music, by Hank Holzer on law, by Mary Ann Sures on art, and by Peikoff on philosophy were presented here and there. The *Objectivist* journal did continue, if with several thousand fewer subscribers than at its 1968 peak circulation of 21,000. But the movement's creative energy was soon syphoned off by activist political libertarianism centered in California.

Leonard Peikoff was named heir to Rand's estate. He was also to become acknowledged as her 'intellectual heir' though apparently Rand never designated him as such, as she had earlier designated Nathaniel Branden.

Barbara Branden's personal reflections in 1986 summed up the sense of intense engagement culminating in disorienting disengagement that so many experienced with the Rand cult, especially in conjunction with the Break of 1968. "In the name of reason we were doing everything possible to give up our souls. It was a horrifying paradox. It appalls me when I look back on it." Afterwards she spent "whatever time was required to realize there is no contradiction—I can be perfectly reasonable and remain who I am—and to find and accept and cherish again the girl I had been at 19 when I met Ayn Rand, and to know that's who I always was. And that's who I am today, after a great many years of struggle. Probably hundreds, thousands of people went through their own variation of the same experience."

2

Entrails:
The Anatomy of the Cult

Is Objectivism a Cult?

I am not a cult.

Ayn Rand

Erika Holzer and Kay Nolte Smith, each former members of
Rand's Collective and subsequently successful novelists, both told
me that although they considered Rand's movement indisputably
a cult, they found it incongruous that a cult could attract the
highly intelligent, well-educated, sometimes brilliant individuals
who attached themselves to Ayn Rand. How *could* such acutely
intelligent people have been taken in by Rand's pretensions to
infallibility?

Both Holzer and Smith are mistaken in their view that cultism
and high intelligence mutually repel. Their mistake is shared by a
great many people, whose view of 'cults' is modelled after sensa-
tional media accounts of Jim Jones and Heaven's Gate. In reality,
the membership of most cults is fairly well-educated and middle-
class, and most cults never come close to anything like mass suicide. The Rajneesh movement of the 1970s and 1980s was

similarly attractive to a cross section of well-educated Westerners who rejected their Judaic, Christian, or Marxist roots. Among them were doctors, dentists, academics, lawyers, business people, movie actors, artists, and therapists. Other typically middle-class and college-educated cults include Scientology and *est*.

Typically, people who join cults are educated young adults, not emotionally disturbed prior to joining, possessed of an idealistic orientation, disenchanted with traditional religions and political authorities, and seeking new meanings and new authorities or exemplars.[1] Rajneesh's movement was primarily a cult for successful mid-career people disillusioned with professional and material achievement. Rand's was a cult for a younger crowd, predisillusioned with the world by Rand's novels but inspired to heroically rise above it by means of a meaningful career and material success.

Former Objectivist and current libertarian Joan Kennedy Taylor remembers: "A lot of people who came to Objectivism were obviously very interested in and prone to accept extremely strongly managed groups that were almost cults. A lot of former students of Objectivism in the sixties went into *est*. Some went into Scientology. There was a general move to accept some kind of transfiguring dominance, which may say something about why many people came to Rand in the first place." Holzer has observed that some like herself came to Objectivism from religious backgrounds, "frying pan to fire, so to speak" and "there was that same kind of almost thought control." Researching the Objectivist movement for her novel, *Two Girls, Fat and Thin*, Mary Gaitskill found that a high proportion of those she spoke to came from, and were rebelling against, very religious Jewish or Catholic families. It made sense that they would be drawn to something else like a religion but seemingly not one itself. Says philosopher John Hospers, "She did not espouse a religious faith, but it was certainly the emotional equivalent of one."

Observers of Objectivism have time and again referred to it as a cult, or have raised the question of whether it can be characterized as a cult. Psychiatrist Allan Blumenthal and his wife Joan, both close associates of Rand, subsequently declared, "It was a cult from top to bottom," a view echoed by writer Edith Efron and other former members of Rand's Collective such as Robert Hessen. Barbara Branden referred to Objectivism as a cult, but reversed herself when she came to write *Passion of Ayn Rand*. Perhaps this switch might have been influenced by marketing considerations: the obvious target readership for her book was the numerous former students of Objectivism, who might resent the description of their youthful folly as something as unsavory as a 'cult'. But Barbara has also remarked, "in my not calling it a cult, . . . I'm sort of skating on thin ice. . . . God knows there were cult-like aspects."

Murray Rothbard and a number of longer-term participants see the Objectivist movement as obviously a cult. More hesitant, Nathaniel Branden observes in *Judgment Day* that there was a cultish aspect to the Objectivist world even if it didn't constitute a cult as defined in the dictionary. This is as typical of Branden as it was of Rand—telling us what's in the dictionary without first bothering to look. By standard dictionary definitions, Objectivism is clearly a cult.[2] In refusing to admit that the Objectivist move-ment was an out-and-out cult, Branden avoids the further admis-sion that he himself was a cult builder and a cult leader. His successor Leonard Peikoff doesn't seem so sensitive, declaring in 1987 that "if I am . . . her apologist or glamorizer, then so be it. I am proud to be cursed as a 'cultist', if the 'cult' is unbreached ded-ication to the mind and to its most illustrious exponents." If.

While the cult that formed around Ayn Rand didn't lead to Jonestown, Solar Temple, or Heaven's Gate-style mayhem—very few cults do—suicides, murderous motives and death threats *have* been associated with it. Leonard Peikoff has received death threats from unstable onetime students of Objectivism, as have Joan and Allan Blumenthal, longtime Rand intimates who became two of her sterner critics. Psychologist Albert Ellis and libertarian Jerome Tuccille, who published books lambasting the Objectivist mentality, in 1968 and 1971 respectively, both received death threats from a man who eventually turned himself in to Ellis for therapy. When Nathaniel Branden's second wife Patrecia accidentally drowned, Rand loyalists whispered amongst themselves, 'How did he kill her?' while Branden himself wondered if she'd been murdered by some Rand loyalist. After all, it had been bandied about after his expulsion in 1968 that normal standards become inoperative when dealing with moral criminals like Branden, eliciting Patrecia's comment, "This is what their ideals mean in the real world."

A rational person may easily become involved in a cult, if only because a cult is typically a far different entity than it appears on the surface. As one's involvement increases, it is easy to slip into an authoritarian relationship without realizing it. Kramer and Alstad suggest that the very fact that so many intelligent people can be seduced unawares by a guru's charm merely indicates just how susceptible we all are to authoritarian control.

As for the not-so-rational young person, while adolescent rebellion undercuts adult authority, it does not reject authoritarianism itself. Teenagers generally look for new idols to follow; a shift of allegiance can provide the illusion of liberation. Members of a cult experience relief upon joining, the degree of their affiliation increasing with the degree of anxiety relieved and exclusivity felt. The bluster of autonomy ultimately gives way to the very need for dependency that they are fighting during this life stage, that need actually attracting them sometimes to the totalistic demands of some charismatic group. Their independent stance generates the very stress whose alleviation will legitimate conversion to both the guru and her worldview: 'I am a truthseeker; this guru makes me feel fantastic; therefore her message must be true'. It is the conversion experience *per se* rather than the specific beliefs adopted which generates the euphoria, its power centered in the psychological transformation from utter confusion to absolute certainty. Old beliefs melt; new ones fill the void; the new ones freeze. One's new beliefs and new identity must be upheld and defended so that the wonderful feelings attendant upon that certainty will continue to radiate rather than evaporate. From the ecstatic experiencing of 'truths' and the glow of rebirth often emerges a compulsive sharing of cult insights and dogma. Soon come increasing demands on the member's time and loyalty.

Cults try to impose an all-encompassing control upon their members' actions. They also tend toward ideological totalism in their zealous adherence to some extremist worldview. Cults offer simplistic, all-but-instantaneous solutions. They promise an expanded consciousness, well-being, and a righteous certainty on the moral or political plane. The 'we' feeling imparted generates a sense of belonging to a powerful and protective group within which the individual's personal potential can at last be actuated. Typically there is boundless reverence for the cult leader. Few would dare to disturb the atmosphere of euphoria, the feeling of fellowship. And the effort to prove others wrong solidifies the foundations of the member's beliefs.

Every cult has a leader, a body of beliefs, a prophecy, ways of dealing with personal problems, and acts of submission to the leader. Its group dynamics generate illusions of invulnerability and unanimity, suppress personal doubts, and provide rationalizations, ethical blinders, and stereotypes of outsiders. Psychologist David Barash suggests that the cult's system of beliefs becomes a psychological exoskeleton: "Like the carapace of a recently molted crab, the cult's ideology quickly hardens around the member, providing form and structure, and at least the illusion of security, an intensely protective and all-embracing family."

Kay Nolte Smith pointed to the grotesque absurdity of a philosophy of freedom and individualism whose adherents are not permitted to read disapproved books. "It's really bizarre. But that is the way it is in that world, and that's why it's a cult; and it is the most peculiar cult on the face of the earth, because it's based on being an individual and being rational." Kay's husband Phil interjected: "This is really a wild phenomenon—forming a cult of Reason—it's a contradiction in terms."

While most Objectivists would strenuously deny that Rand's following constitutes a cult, and some, more plausibly, would admit that it's a cult for some, but classify their own brand of enthusiasm for Rand's ideas as non-cultish, it is evident that Rand's interpretations of reason and individualism were quite conducive to cultism. To her, reason was 'Reason': an adherence—

allegedly via logical and scientific thinking only, that is, without recourse to faith or feelings—to a kind of absolute certainty in all important aspects of life that religion and mythology once provided. Individualism meant a principled upholding of the primacy of individual rights. Rand's reason and individualism were really Absolute Reason in defense of Absolute Individual Rights.

Most cults don't survive long. Ones that do must invent their own bureaucracy, a quasi-priesthood and an official scripture. Roy Childs has observed of any system of thought that a core of cultists is what kicks the system into motion beyond the lifespan of the author, for without followers, usually fanatics, to propagate it, the founder's message dies.

An Adulated Leadership

In a cultic relationship the guru fosters in followers a dependency based upon the belief that she possesses extraordinary talent, insight, or knowledge. Cults become extensions of the leader, a mirror of her ideas, her style, her every desire. Ideas became vested in Rand as a person and in her associates. A cult flaunts its exoteric creed, that is, its public agenda, but it operates according to an esoteric creed, a private agenda. To Rothbard, the guiding spirit of Rand's movement was personal power for Ayn Rand, the Brandens, and other leading disciples. Power and money figured among the goals, authority flowing downward, volunteer labor (such as assisting at NBI) or cash payments (for courses and so forth) flowing upward. Rothbard found it painful to witness cultists humiliatiating themselves in the name of their own self-interest.

A cult is an authoritarian structure whose leadership feels unconstrained by tradition or higher authority. Says Kay Nolte Smith: "If you define a cult as something in which people are obliged to honor and obey the dicta of the head, I believe that was true of Objectivism." Rand wielded a particularly strong hand as cult leader, because she was no mere authoritative interpreter of a special doctrine, but its creator.

Objectivism did put and still puts a premium on loyalty to and adoration of the leader. One of its great assets during the first decade was having a familial bond, that is, the ties of the Blumenthal clan, reinforce the loyalty bond. Devotion was enforced through psychological sanctions and the threat of excommunication. In Objectivism, ideological purity was demanded and doubters expelled. Little effort was made to hear the side of the accused, to whom were attributed the worst of motives.

One was not permitted to dislike the top Randians. Such wrong emotions implied wrong ideas. One had to 'fess up to wrong emotions and then purchase Objectivist therapy, or keep quiet. The idea was to inculcate everyone with Objectivist theory, track down the Objectivist premises underlying anyone's deviance from theory, and eliminate those premises. Like most modern gurus, Rand attached to her ideas the patina of science for added credibility.

Thought Control

It is the true believer's ability to 'shut his eyes and stop his ears'
to facts that do not deserve to be either seen or heard which is the
source of his unequalled fortitude and constancy.

Eric Hoffer, *The True Believer*

Like other cult authorities, notes Rothbard, ranking Objectivists tried to limit students' exposure to other ideas, except as dealt with brusquely, patronizingly, and in a haranguing mode in Objectivist publications. Constant 'party' activity helped prevent straying, and promoted identification with the group. In New York each evening a top Randian would lecture on his specialty to other members. Rand and Branden even cooked up 'the understanding premise', essentially a demand that members of the Collective spend the bulk of their spare time reading extensively in economic and philosophic literature supportive of Objectivism.

The payoff was to feel part of the elect. Intelligent or happy *outsiders* couldn't really be what they seemed. And Randians didn't really have to concern themselves much with individuality and reason, apart from Rand's. The subordination of will and of intellect to abstract doctrine that marked the Jesuits now marked the Randians. Part of the *unofficial* doctrine (tacitly understood but not necessarily formulated explicitly) was that basic truths can be ascertained at a glance by a focused mind committed to rationality, akin to a Nietzschean act of will.

James Gordon laments that for all the subtlety of their argumentation and intelligence, Rajneesh's sannyasins did interpret the world in black and white terms. One party was right, one wrong. How close one was to Rajneesh determined one's proximity to truth. Gordon found when speaking with Rajneesh that anyone who was not totally with him, anyone who harbored the slightest doubts, Rajneesh regarded as against him. As with so much that has been written about Rajneesh, this all holds true of Rand.

Kay Nolte Smith observes that Rand lost a lot of possible converts "by the savagery of her attack . . . she was very, *very* heavy-handed. But that's the way she saw the world and that's the way she lived; you were either with her or against her." As Rothbard recalled, nobody could get away with remaining neutral on any issue of concern to the leadership, a policy that Peikoff's ARI keeps alive to this day. Kramer and Alstad write that cults promote black-and-white thinking, an all-or-nothing point of view, based on the stark polarity of 'right-wrong', 'good-bad', and 'sinner-saint'. Hence the cult demands purity. With no in-between, members must judge themselves and others by the cult's all-or-nothing standard. Certainty about what *is* can be used both to rid oneself of inner conflict and to manipulate those less certain.

Smith sees the tragedy of the official movement, both NBI and ARI, as flowing from its insistence that everything Rand ever wrote is true. One cannot take one piece of the pie without having the whole. "You can't do it. They won't allow it. That's what led to the cult aspect and to a lot of the personal unhappiness, and guilt feelings about being kicked out. It's just had so many devastating consequences. It's the monolithic nature of her philosophy and her views, upon which she insisted, that's really been the source of all the trouble. It was all or nothing at all with her. That's the way she was, ideologically and personally. The basic issues were unchangeable and unchallengeable. She thought Objectivism was complete with the publication of *Atlas Shrugged*."

Orthodox ARI Objectivist John Ridpath has had no problem with Rand's totalism. Anything he might have taken 'on faith' from her would always be confirmed upon further investigation. He says that after he had studied Nietzsche in depth, he found that what Rand had said about Nietzsche was "exactly true." After studying Kant he agreed that "Kant, in his attack both on reason and on rational self-interest, is as Ayn Rand properly characterized him, the evilest man in human history."

In the sphere of music Rand did appear to have cut her followers some slack. Peikoff informs us that she regarded music as "the *only* art in which there was not yet an objective vocabulary. The ultimate evaluation of music she regarded as a subjective matter *until* the day comes that someone defines an objective vocabulary." Yet even with respect to her theory of music, relates Kay Nolte Smith, "she would admit she didn't know everything that was going on and then talk for the rest of the evening as if she did."

If one *could* detect within the official Objectivist movement during the four years after Rand's death a thaw, or at least a token effort to rein in moralistic judgmentalism, the publication of Barbara Branden's *Passion of Ayn Rand* in 1986 put an end to it. It seems that this book and then Nathaniel Branden's *Judgment Day* (1989) so undermined the belief in Rand as 'moral perfection itself', that these works had to be repudiated lest runaway revisionism douse the Randian torch Peikoff was intent on brandishing brightly before the world.

By the 1990s neo-Objectivist Chris Wolf would express exasperation over Objectivists who would do credit to the Spanish Inquisition. Even non-enemies who simply espouse ideas incompatible with Objectivism, he observes, often find their character, honesty, and integrity under attack, with the result that many dismiss Objectivism as simply another nutty cult. Indeed, "the infighting, warring factions, and schisms would rival those of any religious cult. . . . Friendships, marriages, and lifetime associations are torn apart by disagreements among Objectivists . . .

accompanied by tremendous bitterness and character assassination." Sadly, Wolf concludes, Rand unwittingly unleashed a reign of intellectual terror, something enticing only to power-lusting non-entities.

The ideological and personal crises that cult dogma ultimately produces make one a steel-hardened cadre or drive one out. The ocean of ex-communists was always vaster than the party membership and this is the case with Objectivism. When great adversity strikes, many depart, but those who hang in tend to believe even more strongly, such as those hanging in with orthodoxy after the Rand-Branden rift of 1968 or the Peikoff-Kelley rift of 1989. (See my next chapter.)

A favorite method whereby hardline Objectivists counter critics is to accuse them of one heretical dichotomization or another (such as theory versus practice or mind versus body). But it is Objectivism's obsessive dichotomization of the rational versus the irrational which divides Objectivists within and without. Even seemingly rational *non*-Objectivists aren't really rational, because by definition a pre-Objectivist or ex-Objectivist lacks insight into his own values, which must be rationally grounded to be rational at all.

It is the often undeniable 'irrational-self-destructive' link that Rand so emphasizes which allows her to morally condemn much of the behavior Victorians once condemned. Whereas, for example, Victorians argued that heavy drinking was bad because it erodes crucial social bonds, Rand would argue against it because it diminishes one's prospects of survival and personal happiness. Victorians were just as morally opposed to indulging irrationality, but largely because it conflicted with social and religious imperatives. For Rand, to condone irrationality is to condone both self-destructiveness and parasitic dependence on rational men.

Orthodox Objectivist Peter Schwartz writes that one must not reduce matters of justice to a cost-benefit analysis. Moral judgment, not pragmatic calculation, is what must determine with whom one associates. To indicate that Schwartz's position is actually harsher than Rand's, neo-Objectivist Robert Bidinotto cites something she once said during an obscure television interview:

"In judging people of mixed premises, as most people are, you have to balance, in effect hierarchically, the seriousness of their virtues and of their vices, and see what you get in the net result." But that is merely mainstream morality, and in direct contradiction to the criteria of judgment she recommends elsewhere.

Bidinotto does usefully point out that the Peikoffians' designation of complex abstract doctrines like Marxism as *inherently* evil gives them an easy way to instantly write off the millions of proponents of such doctrines as moral lepers. Peikoff in this case exempts only "the illiterate, the retarded and the very young" from willful evil. But this approach treats every abstraction as a perception, making any dissent from accepted Objectivist doctrine a blindness. Kelley cautions that if Objectivists assume that anyone who rejects Objectivist ideas is *ipso facto* an irrationalist, Objectivism will join Marxism and Freudianism as secular religions.

Kelley also says that perhaps an occupational hazard of espousing a fighting creed is "treating every intellectual dispute as an occasion for moral condemnation, and finding . . . depravity in every opponent." However, he hastens to add that "if we approach ideas with the question: good or evil?, we will avoid debate for fear of sanctioning evil-doers. We will substitute condemnation for argument, and adopt a non-intellectual, intolerant attitude."

What Kelley actually means by *non intellectual* is something stronger: *anti-intellectual*, and the term would have to be applied to the bulk of the Objectivist movement, affiliated with Peikoff-ARI and the Reismans' Jefferson School, if not so much to Kelley's own Institute of Objectivist Studies. The Peikoffians condemn practically any form of communication with non-Objectivists if such communication could conceivably redound to the greater benefit of the latter. An example is Peikoffian condemnation of any Objectivist addressing a libertarian gathering, an insidious kind of intimidation, for if a speaker's views can be equated with the views of those sponsoring the event in question, one's range of permissible speaking engagements shrinks to the vanishing point.

Objectivism allegedly promotes self-esteem. However, remarks Bidinotto, people of real self-esteem will not put up with a movement where just one slip-up results in having one's character impugned. Thus the movement is self-limiting. At present, hard-line Objectivists dismiss the neo-Objectivists as 'snarling wimps' fearful of making moral judgments and resentful of those not so timid. The consequent unlikelihood that Objectivism will ever be tested and found wanting on a large scale should allow it to long retain its doctrinal purity and its attractiveness as a cult.

The contract for joining the Objectivist Study Group (OSG), an internet newsgroup run by orthodox Objectivist Robert Stubblefield, also specifies what will constitute grounds for expulsion from the group. It warns subscribers not to belittle Objectivism with "humor." Taking ideas seriously does not preclude humor; but laughter is only appropriate at the metaphysically insignificant. Stubblefield illustrates what else will not be tolerated with the example of "a student of Objectivism who tells others a statement in one of Ayn Rand's articles is 'illogical'. He has ignored the difference between the effort he took to utter his accusation and the effort it takes to create a publishable article. He has ignored the difference between his mind, with its particular psycho-epistemology, and hers, which had a lifetime of never using a concept without identifying the facts of reality that gave rise to it. He has ignored what that careless accusation tells others about his attitude toward ideas." (But still, after ignoring all this, he could be *right*.)

George Walsh suggests that a problem in the movement is that so many Objectivists want Objectivism to be like Newtonian mechanics, that is, a complete deductive system, where all problems are a matter of making the proper calculations that take one from principle to application. Such people laser-focus on some key principles which function like a coach's formula for winning. Hospers traces that tendency back to Rand herself: "With her, it was as if she were developing a Euclidean geometry from a set of axioms," whereas he was a gadfly puncturing the axioms or revealing their meaning to be confused. His approach "wearied her, bored her, and ultimately repelled her."

A Destructive Cult?

Not all cults are classified as 'destructive'. Cult expert Eric Merrill Budd writes that a destructive cult "intentionally induces extreme dependency upon a person or group through excessive manipulation and control." According to Budd, the first step is to destabilize the recruit's sense of reality and identity. The cult then attempts to foist a new regime of thought-behavior-emotion upon the recruit who, after sufficient indoctrination, is outfitted with a new identity, a new perspective on reality and a new purpose.

Budd lists nine practices or tendencies characteristic of a destructive cult. Eight of them apply to the Objectivist movement.

1. Control of communication with the outside world, an attempt to cut off contact with conflicting ideas and with criticisms. (In Objectivism, it was: don't buy books contradicting or criticizing Rand, thereby helping your enemies profit from their own evil and *your* destruction.)

2. Claims of special knowledge by the leader, who is the focal point for enlightenment or salvation, and to whom members are expected to pay homage. The leader, says Galanter, "is reputed to have the potential of bringing a resolution to the problems of humanity." (Rand was the "greatest mind on the planet," according to her protégé Nathaniel Branden, a view naturally shared by other Objectivists.)

3. Demands for perfection and purity, and an inordinate number of rules to follow. Thoughts and actions must be directed completely toward the purpose of the group and its ideology. (Perfectly true of Objectivism, as I show throughout this book.)

4. Continual disclosure to group superiors of wrongful thoughts or actions. While self-criticism is encouraged, not so criticism of the cult, which is met with shunning. (Objectivism's sanctioned psychologists served as confessors and secret police for the movement at large, Nathaniel Branden for the Collective. Following August 1968, students were excommunicated simply for asking their thera-

pists what lay behind the Break. Shunning is a classic cult trait, developed in Objectivism to a high art. The shunned would be put on trial, put on probation or, more dramatically, designated as irrational enemies of Objectivism, and officially excommunicated, after which anyone communicating with them would himself be shunned.)

5. Elitism and separation from family and friends who don't understand. Members are led to believe they are spearheading a great effort to save the world. Feeling part of a vanguard fuels moral righteousness and emotionally isolates insiders from outsiders, binding them closer to one another. And in interacting with followers, the leader comes to believe the grandiose role they accord her. Kramer and Alstad remark that, "Gurus and disciples need each other, but as roles, not as human beings, which makes real human connection almost impossible." Withdrawal from old relationships can actually make the recruit feel temporarily better if those were a major source of conflict, as they often are with adolescents. (All true of Objectivism, which also devalues prior family ties, those ties being as '*un*chosen' as identification with the cult's mission is chosen. Where the prior relationships are not a source of conflict, an alternative to withdrawal from them is the aggressive recruiting of family, friends, and acquaintances—the route Nathaniel Branden took.)

6. A black-and-white view of the world, the notion that the forces of good and evil are sharply and definitively divided. Everyone disinclined to favor the cult's views is written off as evil. The world at large is depicted as evil, violent, decadent and as nearing a state of collapse. But thankfully a replacement utopia is waiting in the wings in the form of the leader's blueprint for a new order. Part of the convert's initial zeal for conveying the group's message is the presumption that the leader's ideology will be as unassailable and infectious for others as for himself. (Peikoff felt this way back in 1957; the whole country would soon be converted by *Atlas Shrugged*.) However, once it dawns on

the group that humanity is too blind or dumb to acknowledge the guru's wisdom and transcendent authority, the party is over and the apocalyptic phase ensues. (For Rand, all states with any degree of government intervention beyond her permissible bare minimum were sliding toward fascism or communism—this was not an uncommon view in the 1940s. The cure was *laissez faire,* but a *laissez faire* mandated for purification by the Randian rational self-interest epitomized by the heroes of *Atlas Shrugged.* At the personal level, an unextinguished iota of altruism would put one on the slippery slope to unforgivable evil.)

7. Unquestioning obedience and total commitment, making one's other concerns secondary, with harsh reproaches or sanctions for doubt or disobedience. Individual well-being becomes subordinated to maintaining the ideology that justifies the hierarchy. Kramer and Alstad call this feature "ideological uncaringness." (Absolutely true of NBI and later of ARI, as I show in the previous chapter and the following one.)

8. Special, loaded terminology deployed to control communication and separate members from the outside world via buzzwords and code terms. (Even ex-Objectivists can be heard mouthing such Randianisms as 'holding the full context', 'A is A', 'the facts of reality', 'there are no contradictions in reality', 'second-hander', 'blank out', 'whim-worshipper', 'man *qua* man', 'anti-life', and of course 'moocher', 'looter', and 'witchdoctor'. The most complicated of human problems and relationships are often simplistically reduced to a single phrase or word. For Objectivists, such words included 'rational', 'irrational', 'evil', and 'altruism'.)

9. Deceptive and manipulative techniques of recruiting. This is the feature of destructive cults least applicable to official Objectivism, and the reason is clear: Objectivism has never had to work hard to recruit, because of the steady flow of applicants generated by Rand's books. Reading *Atlas Shrugged* leaves many an adolescent in the state of

epiphanic enthusiasm that other cults don't have the chance to instill until a first or second live seminar. The excited young reader of any Rand book finds a card inside ready for mailing to Objectivist headquarters. Today, a thousand of these cards come in each month to the Ayn Rand Institute. (Works by Rand and her orthodox apostles sell a total of over 250,000 copies each and every year.) The keen young fan may soon find himself spending on Objectivist courses, an Objectivist newsletter, books from an Objectivist book service and so forth. Drawing youths into a cult when they're expecting a network truly committed to reason and individualism is perhaps deceptive, and Objectivist psychotherapists drawing their patients into the cult in the 1960s and 1970s *was* manipulative. But Rand's literary power over the adolescent mind has rendered unnecessary the aggressive recruitment usually required for cult growth.

By Budd's criteria, the 1960s Objectivist movement was really two types of destructive cult in one. It was political, and thus characterized by party discipline, rigid doctrine, and revolutionary fervor. It was also therapeutic-educational, in its dispensing of insight, motivation, and special knowledge for dealing with career and life problems, and in its being led by a self-styled maverick with few if any credentials, this applying to both Rand and Mr. Branden. All Objectivists are born anew in regard to their worldview and their place within it.

Religions exert control over others by positing a different realm superior to everyday life, calling it spiritual and then having authorities issue directives on how to attain that higher realm. Typically this engenders an uncomfortable dichotomy between the spiritual and the merely mundane that requires mediation by those spiritual authorities. Objectivism's version of this is its positing of a black-and-white distinction between the rational and the irrational. It even goes conventional religion one better by vaporizing the buffer zone, in this case between what is clearly rational and what is clearly irrational (that is, the non-rational zone). For

Rand, what cannot be justified as rational is immoral. There is no room for 'moral grayness'. Members must be in and stay in all the way, or they're out.

Budd tells us that destructive cults operate as authoritarian hierarchies. Kramer and Alstad suggest that one knows one is involved in an authoritarian group when: "No deviation from the party line is allowed. Anyone who has thoughts or feelings contrary to the accepted perspective is made to feel wrong or bad for having them. . . . Whatever the authority does is regarded as perfect or right. Thus behaviors that would be questioned in others are made to seem different and proper. . . . One trusts that the leader or others in the group know what's best. . . . It is difficult to communicate with anyone not in the group. . . . One finds oneself defending actions of the leader (or other members) without having firsthand knowledge of what occurred."

Doubt is not a route to the guru's inner circle. Once in, extracting oneself is an even harder road. Most participants achieve a power and sense of specialness they wouldn't have otherwise, each becoming an authority in the eyes of those ranking below them. In Rand's inner circle, Nathaniel Branden was her head hatchetman, but the rest also served as hatchetmen with lesser degrees of authority.

Budd suggests a number of ways to determine whether an organization is a destructive cult: Ask the leadership tough questions. (Try this in Objectivism and you encounter hostility.) Talk to former members and critics, and ask what they like least about the guru. Observe: do members tend to associate only with other members, act and speak the same, go through obvious personality changes? (Yes. Yes. Yes.) Kramer and Alstad add: Observe how gurus treat and refer to those who leave their fold. In Objectivism, they are excoriated and perhaps even wished an untimely demise.

Utopianism and Apocalypticism

Objectivism's utopic vision is one of a social order energized by a constitutional ban on all forms of initiatory violence and fraud—

this ban being implemented by a government monopoly on the retaliatory use of force whose sole function is to protect individual rights by ensuring internal and external security and the sanctity of contracts—the social order made up of multiple networks of individuals egoistically and heroically striving by rational means toward rational goals whose achievement, due to the very nature of Man, renders them happier than would any alternative arrangement.

In a typical cult, its utopic vision is merely implied while its apocalyptic scenario is depicted in graphic detail. Such is the case in Objectivism's founding document, *Atlas Shrugged*. The utopian forecasts certain disaster unless he has his way. Rand once speculated in such 'either-or' extremes. The Aristotelian philosopher of *Atlas* is Hugh Akston who tells Dagny: "I am writing a book . . . defining a moral philosophy . . . it could save the world . . ." A world failing to heed this book will perish.

This represents Rand's view, and hence Peikoff's view, of *Atlas Shrugged*. In echo, Peikoff said in the 1980s, "If we fail" at carrying Rand's legacy into the future "there will be no future for us or for mankind . . . I think there is still time. Despite everything we have against us, we can see to it that Ayn Rand's ideas *do* save the world." Rajneesh too said in the 1980s that if we cannot create the new man in the coming 20 years then humanity has no future. Peikoff specifies that the end result of any mixed economy is dictatorship, which the U.S. is in the process of illustrating. Even neo-Objectivist Ron Merrill foresaw a rerun of communism or fascism given America's present course, citing the movement of political correctness as the current carrier of the collectivist-authoritarian virus, which in its racialist, feminist and environmentalist guises is expanding and taking over.

There is the utopian carrot. There is the apocalyptic stick. John Ridpath reassures us that, "Ayn Rand's discoveries *will* come to be understood for what they are and applied," but "there is *no* chance that we will have a capitalist future without that." Peikoff has said that if the few real Objectivists, "who understand the issues, speak out, . . . the long range result will be a new lease on life for mankind." But to not speak out, to instead tolerate the Brandens and other dissidents would reduce us to their status—"frauds in the short-term and monsters long-range." Submit completely to the genius of Ayn Rand or Mankind's lease on life will not be renewed.

Cult leaders claim discovery of new knowledge or *reclaim* exclusive access to ancient knowledge, or more often, combine both, by way of justifying a special life mission. Absent a successful completion of that mission, we are all doomed. Those who buy into this 'continual crisis' mentality lose sight of the fact that most 'crises' are really long-term though manageable problems. Societies *do* typically muddle through.

Strong empathizers have the advantage of often being able to anticipate the next move of their opponent. Rand prescribed contempt for her intellectual opponents, a stance precluding empathy. But elitist contempt for the non-elect can lead to grossly underestimating them. Objectivists have consistently underestimated the average American and thus are at a loss to explain the resilience of capitalism in an America that may have read Rand's novels but never accepted her philosophy.

Rand declared in her final speech in 1981 that to win an Objectivist future "requires your *total* dedication and a *total break with* the world of your *past* . . . Fight with the *radiant certainty* and *absolute rectitude* of knowing that yours is *the* Morality of Life and that yours is *the* battle for *any* achievement, *any* value, *any* grandeur, *any* goodness, *any* joy that has *ever* existed on this earth" (my emphases). One has to admire the chutzpah of usurping all worthwhile values of all civilizations past, present, and future. It is absolutism in overdrive.

In response to Randian and libertarian fundamentalism, Edith Efron wrote in 1978 that however radical one's theory, gradualism is not just one political option among many. It is in fact the *only* political approach, all others constituting a "cultist hallucination, or a nihilistic desire for destruction and disaster—or both." However, gradualism does not excite or mobilize. Utopian apocalypticism does.

'Scientific' Cults as a Response to the Decline of Traditional Religion

Charismatic groups emerge, observes Marc Galanter, when mainstream societal values appear inadequate in the face of major social issues. An inadequately addressed major social issue that Rand's *Atlas Shrugged* and her later essays addressed was the gradual trading-off of economic freedom for regimented security requiring government interventions in the economy, as catalyzed by the Great Depression and World War II. Rand's championing of self-reliant self-interest in opposition to the intellectuals' social engineering schemes struck a resonant note with the non-intellectual reading public. At least it did so in the McCarthyite 1950s and in the early 1960s, by which time Rand's favorite social grouping—big business—had re-gained heights of popularity not experienced since the roaring twenties. Rand's advocacy of selfishness versus government demands for sacrifice (as exemplified by the Vietnam draft) kept her philosophy alive as a significant strand of Sixties anti-authoritarianism.

The resurgence of Rand's movement in the mid-1980s tracked consolidation of public disgust with overtaxation and government by deficit financing, the return yet again of private enterprise to public favor, as well as a kind of nostalgia for the 1950s era of black-and-white cold-war morality. More broadly, one could view Objectivism as but one attempt to find new certainties to replace or revitalize those of religion, in decline as a totalist set of beliefs since the close of the Victorian era.

Kramer and Alstad maintain that moral certainty and its concomitant inner and outer controls mean more emotionally than do the particular beliefs providing the ballast for that certainty, and that how certain one is of a belief dwarfs the importance of its truth or falsity. A fundamentalism maintains that all current problems result from falling away from a once-revered set of truths. Rand thought that nineteenth-century American capitalism—founded upon Enlightenment thinking (and held in place by Victorian morality)—was *the* golden age that we must return to.

Science destroys myth, but doesn't create the kind of personal values or meanings that myth provides. So even when a worldview fades, for most former believers the sustaining morality it produced lingers, while for others, a replacement myth or religion is sought, even a cult or some ideological 'ism'. But just as the 'isms' of the twentieth century from communism to feminism and environmentalism—all at-least-partly irrationalist reactions against the transformations wrought by industrial capitalism—have been found spiritually wanting by a great many adherents, so too psychoanalysis and other pseudoscientific therapies and new religions rose up against the overwhelmingly dominant ethos of lingering nineteenth-century rationalism. Objectivism is a reassertion of the beliefs and values of industrial capitalism and rationalism in response to so much negative fallout from the ideologies, pseudosciences, therapies, and religions that pretended to replace them. In other words, Objectivism is the proffered cure for the side-effects of prior failed cures for capitalism-rationalism. It consists of what we began with, though with presumed impurities removed, and is propagandized with the same fervent religiosity as characterized those creeds which once had success in *opposing* capitalism-rationalism.

Here Rand is reminiscent of Ernest Haeckel, an influential early Darwinian in Germany. Haeckel founded a new, supposedly scientific religion he called monism, an aggressive rationalism targeting the last vestiges of a superstitious Christianity for elimination. Its proposed monist replacement, a kind of national ideology glorifying science, was the product of a religiously anti-religious sensibility.

Weakness and confusion don't feel anywhere near as good as power and certainty. Cults burgeoned after the fall of Rome, the French revolution, and the industrial revolution. Onetime Objectivist inner-circle member Phil Smith concedes that he and others were simply vulnerable young people looking for a coherent way of looking at the universe, who got sucked in. Of course Objectivism was hardly the first new philosophy of living to offer a coherent way of looking at the universe. America's social history teems with authoritarian figures offering sustenance to hungerers for a more spiritual or motivated life.

A decline in religious affiliation left a spiritual vacuum filled by cults in the 1950s, 1960s, and 1970s. Gurus came with different styles and answers. L. Ron Hubbard's Dianetics, Maharishi Mahesh Yogi's Transcendental Meditation, and Ayn Rand's Objectivism were all launched in the mid-to-late 1950s. The Moonies and Guru Prabhupada's Hare Krishna movement arrived in the 1960s, Rajneesh in the 1970s. The cry 'To be human is to be creative' arose from all of them, creative intellectual work being the focus in Objectivism.

Liberal theologian Harvey Cox in *Turning East* writes that, "Eastern mystics came teaching Enlightenment but what happened was yet another spate of American self-improvement sects as their religion passed through the prism of American consumer culture and psychological individualism." Most of the star gurus, certainly Reverend Moon, L. Ron Hubbard, Rajneesh, and Werner Erhard, were partly innovative and partly syncretic, all to a significant extent breaking with traditional religion, but all offering doctrines which were amalgams of pre-existing traditions. Rajneesh claimed to be initiating a new tradition, like Jesus. Or like Rand, though as Tibor Machan and others have pointed out, bits and pieces of Objectivism had been around for ages before her. Rand's—and Branden's—contribution was to select them, string them together and package them for mass consumption. The aim of all these new religious movements is usually one of experiencing God by finding the Self. Objectivism's aim is experiencing the joyful mastery of Objective Reality by asserting the Rational Self.[3]

The second half of the twentieth century generated conditions particularly conducive to cult growth. Mass media spread the leader's reputation and message far and wide, and provide income via sales of audio-cassette tapes, books, videotapes, guru-portraits, and such. The advantages usually outweigh the bad press most cults draw.

By way of explaining the Rand phenomenon, novelist Mary Gaitskill suggests that the complex interaction between a not very literary writer and millions of Americans occurred because she purported to have resolved the conflict between self and society in a culture steeped in contrary beliefs about individualism, about money, and about power. Rand's solutions may have been neither original nor even workable. Yet her projected world served as a "fun house mirror for a society that is one part sober puritan and one part capitalist sex fiend," a focal point for "American anxieties, and how they manifest themselves in mass culture."

Objectivism as a Religion

Skeptic Martin Gardner confesses that having himself been a Protestant fundamentalist for a youthful stretch, he knows what it's like to be a true believer. Since then he has never ceased to be intrigued by how easily forceful charismatic personalities such as Moses, Jesus, Saint Paul, Mohammed, Joseph Smith, Ellen White, and Mary Baker Eddy can assemble a set of beliefs that seems ridiculous to outsiders, and yet have millions adhering to it. On a smaller scale (so far), he might have cited Ayn Rand. Curiously, while it debunks passionate ideologues, Eric Hoffer's *The True Believer* became one of Rand's favorite books. Perhaps she thought it could not apply to her because *her* ideology was rational, or perhaps it convinced her that some unappetizing features of ideological movements were essential to their effectiveness.

Why do these figures win such allegiance? Answers Ron Merrill, because human beings need fundamental ideas to organize their lives around and need to believe in them strongly, the only way they can function as biological entities. Hegel once explained that "men are so hungry for certainty that they will readily subordinate consciousness and conscience to it; men need great ideals to move them, and the passions created outlast the struggles they served." In fact the same passion can switch allegiance to the once-opposed ideas of the enemy, with ease. Ted Goertzel notes that turncoats like Peter Collier and David Horowitz, former leftists now evangelically promoting neoconservatism, persist in looking at the world in black-and-white terms that provide more or less a mirror image of the New Left ideologies they once rooted for but now despise. A new cause refreshes the turncoat's zeal, after a pause for disillusion. Jerome Tuccille observed in 1971 that Objectivism appealed especially to would-be escapees from regimented Judaism or Catholicism secretly hungering for a religion-substitute.

Like leftists-turned-neoconservatives, Rand too had once been on the other side of the trenches, not as a verbal *proponent* of communism but as a real-life *victim* of a civil-war communism and its aftermath. Rand received her university education at what had become a communist institution and then took a job with the communist state. She knew her enemy first-hand, like an insider.

Bidinotto asks rhetorically what systematic alternatives there are to Objectivism and answers: only theism and communism! He insists that the human mind needs the kind of mooring that only a chain of principles provides. Philosopher Antony Flew disagrees with this perspective, insisting that it's simply not true that everyone needs or wants a system in which everything is connected to everything else, this constituting a rather *peculiar* orientation, in contrast to simply wanting to eliminate inconsistencies in one's beliefs.

Most true believers miss the parallels between their own ideological mindset and that of their opponents. For example, an Objectivist doctor discusses his opponents' resistance to criticism precisely as others would characterize that of Objectivists: "Especially with certain reinforcing, complex belief systems (like Christianity or Marxism), what would be a glaringly obvious error to me may not be quite as obvious to someone immersed within the system, which contains its own self-supporting, semi-stable network of rationalizations to prop them up." Likewise a true-believing Objectivist's mastery of and commitment to his Objectivist system will make him largely impervious to criticism. His emotional and intellectual investment is too great, the glib rationalizations too readily available.

Carl Jung saw the search for something greater than oneself as the dominant need of humans upon reaching maturity. Neo-Objectivist Robert Bidinotto writes that individuals desperately seek out whatever will lend their lives meaning, direction, coherence and purpose. He elaborates, unaware how comfortably the phenomena he cites fit Rand and Objectivism, that this explains is why they "will follow any guru who promises to bring order to their inner chaos. This is true precisely to the extent of their intelligence since minds with more advanced abstract capacities have even greater need than most for the guidance of principles. That is why we see the rise of pop-psychology [Branden?], fanatical cults [Randians?], pseudosciences [Rand's epistemology?], the occult [Objectivists' absolute faith in Rand's robust but slipshod arguments?] and the return to religious fundamentalism [Peikoff's orthodox Objectivism?]."

The pronouncements of traditional moralities resist challenge largely by virtue of having supposedly been transmitted from a superhuman intelligence. Orthodox Randians believe Rand to have been the greatest intelligence on earth in the past millennium or two; so who are we to challenge her well-thought-out pronouncements? Fundamentalist ministers argue that when humans start reinterpreting God, human subjectivity displaces God's objectivity. Fundamentalist Peikoff argues that once Objectivists like David Kelley reinterpret Rand, what remains is subjectivity, not Rand's objectivity. Peikoff considers his dispute with Kelley to be all about objectivity, but it is really all about God's, or rather Rand's, Word, equated with Objectivity itself. Fundamentalists have no illusions about the presumption of revising the word of God. Revision pulls the rug out from under authority and its sustaining structure. Like Rand-Peikoff, American fundamentalists have worked themselves into a lather over fears of a collapse of the social order, a collapse avoidable only if we agree upon essential absolute truths.

Fundamentalism divides the good from the bad parts of the human soul. Seemingly impeccable fundamentalist values mask an 'ethical cleansing' whereby, Kramer and Alstad suggest, the 'goodself' approved of by one's belief system generates a highly-motivated but 'less human' being, becoming the inner authoritarian responsible for keeping the 'badself' disapproved of by one's belief system suppressed or on a very short leash. Living a life of superior righteousness requires and legitimates a severe inner authoritarian. The goodself relies upon external authorities to reinforce its power over the badself and over other people. So while it submits to authorities, it is also "dictatorial, judgmental, structured, often a puritanical harsh taskmaster; and above all it is fearful—fearful that without always maintaining control, one's life would unravel. . . . it suppresses spontaneity, creativity, and enjoyment for their own sake because these expressions often undermine the goodself's control mechanisms." In Objectivists, the division of goodself-badself prevents the integration of rationality with *élan vital*. Such division of human nature serves not to divine and express that nature, but instead to rule it.

Without intending to be pejorative, Ron Merrill compared taking up Objectivism as one's philosophy of life to a religious conversion. One takes all one's habits, associations, friendships and ethical principles, calls them into question, and then exchanges them for something else. It's a tremendous intellectual, emotional and social transition. A lot of people get only so far and say, 'I can't live with this. It's too different. I just don't have the strength'. Such strength didn't necessarily come from Reason.

In most religions, the highest good is equated with the selfless, and the worst evil with the selfish. Rand also orients herself toward the selflessness-selfishness polarity, opting to start off her morality at the opposite end. By bringing in rational considerations, she works her way toward the middle, the only place people and societies can actually live. In effect, Rand simply takes up as a solution what other religions consider as the initial problem. And the controlling dichotomy continues.

Warns David Kelley, "Christianity and Marxism have founding documents that are regarded as canonical [As does Objectivism]. They have well-developed orthodoxies to which adherents are expected to swear allegiance [As does Objectivism]. Each has an institution—the Church and the Party, respectively—that defines the orthodox interpretation of the system and rules on who can be admitted to the ranks of the believers [As has Objectivism with the Ayn Rand Institute]. Christianity and Marxism come closest to fitting Peikoff's description of a philosophical system." Kelley states that only religions and totalitarian ideologies exhibit the features Peikoff ascribes to Objectivism. Bear in mind that Peikoff's Objectivism was the *only* official Objectivist movement from Rand's death in 1982 through 1990, and that it remained the *dominant* part of the official Objectivist movement throughout the 1990s.

Kelley claims that cults are rooted in religious or other nonrational doctrines, while Objectivism is not. To neo-Objectivist George Smith, while it's true that Rand's theories become entangled in rhetoric and prejudice, to insist that her philosophy is inherently religious or dogmatic is false and foolish. But surely it would be false and foolish to accept Objectivism as rational, rooted as it is in *Atlas Shrugged,* a novel infused on virtually every page with angry emotions, and filled in later with sketchy arguments, or to suggest that Objectivism alone among various systems of belief could be purged of dogma and religiosity. It could very well be that there is a core within Christianity, within Marxism, within Rajneeshism, *and* within Objectivism which could be stripped free of unfounded dogma, but what would be left would be neither vibrant nor original.

Write Kramer and Alstad, "Cults become religions whenever they build up traditions, a body of myths, parables, scriptures, and dogmas that are interpreted and protected by specialists (priests, etc.) who see themselves as the guardians of truth, not the bringers of it." The Objectivist movement now consists primarily of just such guardians of truth, centered around Leonard Peikoff and the Ayn Rand Institute. They don't *do* anything else; that is their life.

Religion justifies the ruler's right to rule; rulers legitimate religion's right to justify. Objectivism justifies the business sector's right, in effect, to rule; and the business elite, in Rand's view, *should* legitimate Objectivism's right to justify. Noll regards the Jung cult as a Nietzschean religion. The Rand cult could be regarded as an Americanized Nietzschean religion justifying *laisser faire.*

In Eastern religion, it is Karma one cannot escape. In Western religion it is the judgment of the One God one cannot escape. And in Objectivism it is a monistic Objective Reality whose retribution one cannot escape. Ultimately reality itself, even without Rand's help, will illuminate, if perhaps too late, the self-destructive nature of one's acts.

For R. there is no humanity, only individuals. Being "antilife," all religions are based on fear. R. was contemptuous of politicians and called them parasites. R. insisted that, "we *can* create a super-capitalist world." A follower of R. complains of how the U.S. constitution is being prostituted, how the Moral Majority is setting up the country to go back into the Dark Ages, and how R. was the only balance against fundamentalist religion. This R., however, is not Ayn Rand but Baghwan Rajneesh. Said Rajneesh, "All other religions will disappear into Rajneeshism, as all the rivers disappear into the ocean." David Kelley has stated that he likes to think that everything that is true is part of Objectivism.

The Objectivist movement's implicit prophecy was that Nathaniel Branden would be Ayn Rand's worthy and exemplary heir, spearheading her dynamic movement into an exciting future. Instead, almost overnight he became *persona non grata*, practically an anti-Christ. With the Break in 1968, the more one perceived the world as unacceptably chaotic and the more one had invested in the Randian set of beliefs, the more one would desperately cling to the wreckage. After the Break, the loyal Objectivists became tougher hardliners than ever.

3

The Cult After the Guru's Death

The Guru as Ultra-Genius

Who is the greatest mind since the year A.D. 1000? According to Objectivists, it's not Einstein or Newton or Beethoven or Shakespeare or Leonardo Da Vinci—but Ayn Rand. Most orthodox Objectivists go further: they regard Rand as greater even than her beloved Aristotle, and thus as the greatest thinker who ever lived.

You might think this awesome over-rating of a person's achievements would be highly unusual, and an indication that there must be *something* of substance underlying the claim, albeit exaggerated. In fact, this is so common as to be virtually the norm in cults, as well as in totalitarian regimes. Behind the masks of the various gurus of this century lurks the notion of a far greater intelligence than ours, which knows better than we do what is best for us. Often the implied intellectual and moral superiority presumes infallibility. Followers of Rajneesh saw him "as the planet's main enlightened figure." Christian Science acolyte Adam Dickey referred to Mary Baker Eddy as "the most wonderful woman that the world has ever produced." Stalin, Mao, and Kim Il Sung were officially viewed as super-geniuses in every branch of human endeavor. So we shouldn't really be surprised when Nathaniel Branden refers to Rand as "the greatest mind on the planet" and Harry Binswanger deems her "a once in a millennium genius," nobody having come close to her achievements in either art or philosophy, let alone both.

Rand, who never tired of quoting from her own novels, made it clear she shared the following lament of the once-great scientist Robert Stadler in *Atlas Shrugged:* Oh, "The loneliness for an equal—for a mind to respect and an achievement to admire . . . you'd give a year of your life to see a flicker of talent anywhere." Oh, the "boredom—the terrible, hopeless, draining, paralyzing boredom. Of what account are praise and adulation from men whom you don't respect?" Standing in for Rand, Dagny responds to Stadler: "I've felt it all my life." Having come to believe that there was no one operating on her intellectual level, Rand got her followers to believe it and assert it publicly.

Nathaniel Branden established his status as a judge of literary matters with his characterization of *Atlas Shrugged* as "the climax of the novel form," with "not one extraneous word." To non-Objectivists, or to anyone with a sensitivity to literature, this judgment is comical. (See the *Atlas Shrugged* word-counts in Chapter 11 below.) Even in the 1990s, Branden was still saying that *Atlas Shrugged* was "the greatest novel that has ever been written," better than anything by Hugo, Dickens, Tolstoy, or Dostoevsky, and that Rand had fully deserved the Nobel Prize for literature.

Nor do *today's* orthodox Objectivists damn her with faint praise. Forget about Rand's two major novels; even *We the Living* is one of the greatest novels in world literature, according to Harry Binswanger. Commenting on Objectivist economist Northrup Buechner's proposed new Objectivist axiom, that all Objectivists should reread Rand's novels once a year, Binswanger says: "I very much endorse that." Given that we all should be Objectivists and that Rand wrote more than 2,000 pages worth of novels, ideally then every human would be reading or rereading an average of several pages of Rand's fiction per day.

"The traditional 'Big Three' in philosophy—Plato, Aristotle, Kant—are now the 'Big Four', with the addition of Ayn Rand,"

writes orthodox Objectivist Andrew Bernstein in 1993, with
Objectivist philosopher Allan Gotthelf concurring. Northrup
Buechner announced breathlessly, "If Ayn Rand is able to save the
world, she will save economics too." For, after all, Rand's "concept
of objective value . . . changes the science of economics from the
ground up." Executive director of the Ayn Rand Institute, Michael
Berliner, states categorically: "If this culture survives, she'll get the
credit for it."

John Ridpath repudiates the charge that Rand's alleged *ex post
facto* infallibility implies cultism. Philosophy, he tells us, is
another branch of human knowledge, another attempt to discover
the truth. And there's nothing to say that a comprehensive discovery of very broad principles which make a whole range of other
discoveries, every one of them true, is impossible, that reality or
the human mind in its nature makes that impossible. "There just
never has been advances in the understanding of reason that Ayn
Rand has made. And there is no reason why in the nature of the
human mind and the pursuit of human knowledge that flaws *necessarily* must exist. . . . Ayn Rand was a genius. . . . There is an
enormous amount of knowledge that she had which she didn't
write out," and to unfold all of that is a legitimate form of filling
in any so-called gaps in her philosophy. Another form is to apply
her discoveries "to many of the issues we're faced with, given the
state of philosophy today." But neither of those exercises are
"exercises in continuing the building of the essential edifice . . .
she *has* in essence named the principles in all the major branches
of philosophy that we need as guidelines to proceed." Binswanger
tells us that "like a philosophical Midas, any area she touched
turned to knowledge." She "formulated an invincible philosophic
system . . . what is most distinctive about Rand's philosophy" is
that "it is true."

In *Atlas Shrugged,* we are told that "it would take the sort of
mind that's born once in a century" to complete the abandoned
remnant of Galt's motor. Galt's revolutionary motor is a metaphor
for Rand's philosophy, its actual inventor requiring the sort of
mind that's born once in a millennium. On a 1991 Second
Renaissance taped lecture on intelligence, business-school

psychologist Edwin Locke rates Rand as having "genius-level intelligence. . . . Genius is something that comes along once a century at most, and in this case we're talking once in a millennium." An audience member obligingly requests that Locke estimate Ayn Rand's IQ. Way, way beyond the 150 level at which borderline genius begins, he responds enthusiastically, "OK . . . genius level intelligence. I'm not saying this from having tested her but just from observing her in action. Add to this, genius-level creativity, which doesn't go together with intelligence necessarily . . . virtually perfect psycho-epistemology . . . a totally rational philosophical framework which was her own . . . fantastic sustained effort for many many years . . . and complete . . . dedication to her values in action. . . . You have here a stupendous mental power, the power to change the course of world history, and with our help I hope she does. . . . You could almost look at her as a more advanced species of humanity than the normal person. . . . Imagine solving the problem of concepts, that has puzzled philosophers for 2,500 years, with half an hour's thought!" No one outside Objectivism regards Rand's work on concepts as making any important contribution.

Even *neo*-Objectivists rate Rand in terms incomprehensible to non-Objectivists familiar with her work. Journalist Robert Bidinotto informs us that she is the greatest novelist and thinker of the twentieth century. Ron Merrill predicted that by the year 2100, Objectivism would be recognized as a major contribution to philosophical thought with its ideas accepted as true, and Rand would be classed among the top ten writers of the twentieth century. A letter to the editor of *Liberty* proclaims, "In the centuries ahead she will be recognized as one of the seminal thinkers of the western world, possibly even shining brighter than her beloved Aristotle. I feel fortunate to have lived in her time." Another letter reads, "The achievement of Ayn Rand may be compared to a skyscraper built in the midst of . . . mud-thatched huts."

Ron Merrill so wished to see Rand as without equal that he began his tome on Rand by stating that apart from *Atlas* very few among 1957's crop of new books are in print today. Actually dozens are, several acknowledged as classics such as Jack

Kerouac's *On the Road*. He called her a genius doomed by her gender, despite acclaim during Rand's era for female thinkers such as Simone de Beauvoir, Hannah Arendt, Karen Horney, Suzanne Langer, Jane Jacobs, and Margaret Mead. She fought alone against the world, he informs us. But consider all the major figures in Chapter 12 below, whom she *could have* counted as allies.

Following publication of *The Passion of Ayn Rand* (1986), Objectivist Peter Schwartz attacked Barbara Branden's credibility and impugned her motives. Peikoff asked rhetorically, "What kind of soul do you think it takes to write *Atlas Shrugged*? And what do you want to see in a historic figure?" Responded Bidinotto, "What about the truth?" Bidinotto agreed with the lavish praise for Rand's achievements, only differing in his insistence that those achievements do not justify suppressing the facts about her personal life. Although Barbara Branden's book disclosed discreditable aspects of Rand's character and behavior, other former Rand associates, such as the Blumenthals, maintain that in stopping short of the awful truth, it constitutes a whitewash.

A sympathetic critic will credit Rand with one fairly good pop-novel of ideas *(The Fountainhead)* and a volume's-worth of provocative essays. That achievement is less than one of genius. Rather it is the achievement of a very smart, obsessed philoso-fiction or propaganda-fiction writer, whose literature may be third-rate and whose philosophizing may be third-rate, but whose obsessions elevate the hybrid product to the level of the highly intriguing second-rate. As the founder of a movement which for decades has had some small input into discussions of social philosophy and policy, Rand has additional historical importance. Though Rand will certainly never be ranked among the twentieth century's top novelists or philosophers, she may well rank among its top 'pop-novelists of ideas' or 'non-technical, non-innovative pop-philosophers with an intelligible and marketable vision'.

Attributing genius to one's guru has its own rewards. It can be presumed to rub off a bit, thereby elevating the undistinguished to the absolutely brilliant. Binswanger says of Peikoff's *The Ominous Parallels:* "After Ayn Rand's works, this is the single most important book of our age." It implies that *Ominous Parallels* ranks within the top dozen books of the twentieth century, all the rest of which are by Rand.

This exasperates philosopher Antony Flew, politically an advocate of free-market capitalism, who dismisses the claim that Ayn Rand is a great philosopher, perhaps the greatest since Aristotle, as "simply grotesque . . . just preposterous." Flew commented that the attitude of Objectivists to Rand reminded him of a Jehovah's witness who completed a mortis and tenon joint and was rather proud of it but then remarked that the only perfect mortis and tenon joint ever made was made by Jesus. It's the notion that your hero in one area must be of comparable stature in any other area in which they happen to engage. Philosopher Douglas Rasmussen, far more sympathetic to Rand than Flew is, forecasts that by the end of the twenty-first century, interest in Rand will probably have long since faded out.

Binswanger expresses amazement that Rand wasn't a better scrabble player. Yet astute readers of *Atlas Shrugged* and other Rand novels will note an alarming repetitiveness in her vocabulary, doubtless due to how little she read, in turn partly due to her being, as Barbara Branden has pointed out, "a painfully slow reader." One could also easily imagine Rand scoring not particularly high on an IQ test, and Binswanger being equally astonished at this.

For those doubtful of the enduring value of what is original in Rand's novels and essays, that Objectivists should insist upon her status as a genius, or, in Peikoff's words, "a super-genius," is outlandish. Possibly to convince doubters, in 1986 Peikoff issued a second edition of Rand's *Introduction to Objectivist Epistemology*. It includes 170 pages of Rand answering questions at seminars in 1969–71 on her theory of concepts. The Ayn Rand Institute even sent a free copy to any college philosophy department which requested one in response to ads ARI took out in philosophy journals.

The questioners are "Prof. A" through "Prof. K." But if any are professors, editor Harry Binswanger doesn't say. Rather, they are 'professionals' of some unidentified kind, most in philosophy, a few in physics and mathematics. Perhaps they're mainly graduate students, recent Ph.D.s, and instructors at undistinguished colleges. According to Peikoff, "questioners, myself included, had not yet had the time fully to absorb so revolutionary a theory or, therefore to know what to ask . . . we were thinking aloud, groping to identify our confusions . . . some of us being relatively advanced in the study of Objectivism, others having only a sketchy impression."

Thus what the reader might have thought was Ayn Rand taking on an array of distinguished philosophers in the realm of epistemology turns out to be something else. It is Ayn Rand, Guru, talking down to some nameless, low-ranking academics, who, though also 'students of Objectivism', had not yet absorbed the several essays on epistemology she had published years before in the *Objectivist*, essays she felt were the heart of her philosophizing and which Peikoff had written an addendum to, implying that at least *he* must have absorbed them.

In attendance with Peikoff and Binswanger were George Walsh and Allan Gotthelf, all Ph.D.s in philosophy and Rand acolytes. Walsh relates that there was a section left out because she had misunderstood the question. Among goofs inadvertently left in, Walsh points to Rand on physics: contradicting herself in saying one can't claim that the ultimate constituents of the universe were spatial but then on another page stating that philosophy should absolutely veto the idea that a particle could travel from state A to state C without going through state B. Rand-admirer and neo-Objectivist philosopher Tibor Machan rates *Introduction to Objectivist Epistemology* as too polemical to qualify as scholarship.

A better sampling of Rand in philosophical discourse is Hospers's account of his numerous all-nighters with her in the early 1960s. Hospers was already a professor and, though in accord with many of Rand's philosophical conclusions, was by no means convinced of the soundness of her arguments for them. He was a sympathizer still quite a ways from being an Objectivist. Because he obviously had so much respect and affection for her, it is all the more shocking to discover how philosophically ignorant, narrow-minded, and slipshod her thinking was and the extent to which their discourse was limited by her violent emotions. Few readers could come away from these Hospers articles saying, 'Well, *there's* a paragon of reason in action'.[1]

Rand had three years of university, but Peikoff insists that attending the University of Leningrad in the early 1920s afforded her an excellent university education. How could that be? The revolution and civil war had thrown the universities into chaos. Her history department lost several professors before she enrolled. Nearly 300 prominent Russian professors in the humanities went into exile in 1922 alone. Non-Bolshevik instructors streamed out of the system every year she attended.

The Ayn Rand Institute and its Affiliates

Extra ecclesiam nulla salus (There can be no salvation outside the Church)

Papal dictum

Given Rand's stringent standards of ideological correctness, little by way of organizational innovation in Objectivism could survive Rand's scrutiny in the wake of NBI's demise in 1968. David Kelley observes that for the people who were in school in the 1970s, there was really nothing going on, and that no one who came in during that era figures among Objectivist intellectuals in the 1990s. After her death in 1982, it was a different story, and in 1985 her staunchest advocates were ready. Hoping to initiate a second Renaissance, they launched the Ayn Rand Institute (ARI) in Los Angeles, its funding guaranteed by Philadelphia Flyers owner and Spectacor chairman Ed Snider, with official heir Leonard Peikoff having a veto over policy decisions. Today it operates with an annual $1.8 million budget. Snider was determined that Objectivism make an impact within the universities. Ironically, had it not been for Big Government's post-war GI Bill and the consequent expansion of existing colleges and proliferation of new state colleges, the number of college teachers would not have increased five times faster than the population, and most Objectivist academics currently employed would have had to find a different livelihood.

Since 1985 ARI has helped originate and sustain hundreds of Ayn Rand clubs on college campuses, predominantly in the U.S. and Canada. Some have staying power while others are more transitory. Typically 75–100 are in operation in any given year. ARI provides campus clubs with materials, speakers, debaters, and videotapes. Binswanger conducts graduate training seminars in epistemology and ethics with several students by phone. Some of these students now have tenure track positions in philosophy departments. ARI helped set up an 'Ayn Rand Society' within the Eastern Division of the American Philosophical Association. It has conducted ad campaigns in philosophical journals for books such as Peikoff's *Objectivism: The Philosophy of Ayn Rand* and the expanded edition of Rand's *Introduction to Objectivist Epistemology*, having assembled the latter and distributed it to 900 philosophy departments. ARI regards its main job as overcoming Rand's reputation in academia as, at best, a pop philosopher. It has arranged translations of Rand's books for eastern Europe, including a collection of her essays on egoism in Russian titled *The Morality of Individualism*, whose first printing of five thousand copies sold out in Moscow within two days in 1993. ARI also sponsors two-week conferences every summer by for-profit affiliates at sites alternating between west and east coasts, with an average attendance of 250.

Executive director of ARI, Dr. Michael Berliner, has stated that to increase the number of people in Objectivism "requires some very basic advertising and publicity targeted at young people. That's really one of the basic ideas behind the *Fountainhead* essay contest for high school juniors and seniors, to try to reach young people before their minds get destroyed by the irrationalism they're going to run into in the universities." He even thinks that the recent increase in sales of *The Fountainhead* may be attributable to the contest, which started in 1986, eliciting 3,000 entries in 1990, with a $5,000 first prize. "*The Fountainhead* really hits high school kids where they're living," says Berliner. ARI soon began a similar contest for *Anthem*, both books eliciting 55,000 essays by 1998. Now $10,000 is awarded in all, to those entrants most capable of giving ARI what it wants to hear. Berliner told me that if readers send in the card from inside an Ayn Rand or Peikoff book they receive information from ARI, an Objectivist book service, Objectivist periodicals, and all kinds of other organizations involved in spreading Objectivism. ARI is the only one that is a not-for-profit institution. It receives a thousand or so cards a month, mostly from the more than 150,000 copies Rand's novels sell annually.

In the late 1970s Schwartz's *Intellectual Activist* newsletter evolved into the successor to the *Objectivist*. Having published repeatedly in the *Intellectual Activist*, Bidinotto can confirm that "every word Schwartz printed was first read and cleared by Peikoff." Howard Dickman, neo-Objectivist and a senior editor at *Reader's Digest*, describes the *Intellectual Activist* writing style as rigid and formalistic, very stiff. As per Schwartz's requirements, says Bidinotto. Dickman confirmed that whereas in 1986 Schwartz, Peikoff, and Binswanger were ranting and raving about Barbara Branden being a discredited witness, a liar, and a moral leper, later they admit in passing that her biography's account of Rand's sexual affair with Nathaniel Branden was factual after all.

As for Objectivism's focus on infiltrating the universities, Bidinotto objects to this as a caste-system notion of spreading ideas. Bidinotto also objects to its us-versus-them approach, recommending that Objectivists use Rand's thought as one would any other philosopher, not treating her "as some guru. . . . it would not be a bad idea to have some thoughts of your own!" It is ironic that a leading spokesman for a philosophy that purportedly champions the heroic individual should feel obliged to say this. He does so partly because attempts by followers to initiate books, magazines, or organized activities that would spread Objectivist ideas are typically condemned by Objectivist leaders. Bidinotto is disappointed that so few Objectivists are addressing the individualist American sense of life through novel-writing, painting, or other artistic endeavors. Perhaps he is not sufficiently aware of Objectivism's history of paralyzing rather than catalyzing the creative impulse. The official Objectivist movement continues to be top-heavy with Ph.D.s in economics and philosophy (despite its official disdain for these degrees), as well as with MBAs, lawyers, and medical doctors. Entrepreneurs and scientists are relatively scarce.

Why *has* so little of Objectivism penetrated academia? Neo-Objectivist Chris Wolf says it's partly because more commentary on and elaboration of Objectivism is out on audiotape than in papers and books. He urges Objectivist scholars to halt this trend by writing up their research to publishing standards. David Kelley agrees that generating publishable work is more difficult than generating lectures for audiotape. As it is, reads an internet posting, Objectivism has all this work locked away in tapes that aren't susceptible to scanning and review by readers. Another Objectivist newsgroup post complains that for many years the only way to hear a non-fiction presentation of Rand's philosophy was to take Peikoff's taped lecture course on Objectivism (1976). That way he could always keep them coming back for more, and likely he was making more money lecturing than writing anyway. However, it's impossible to "listen to a tape, integrate the material, AND take notes for future reference . . . tapes were not even available to individuals; you had to wait for a 'business representative' in your area to offer the taped course, and there were damned few reps." Reps played the course tapes through, just once, "not quite conducive to reflection or anything other than furious scribbling." Other frustrated individuals transcribed tapes, "and passed them around, quite surreptitiously (and illegally)."

Peikoff did finally produce his synthesis, *Objectivism: The Philosophy of Ayn Rand*, in December 1991. Neo-Objectivist Eyal Moses worries that because Peikoff is regarded as Rand's intellectual heir, the tome is likely to be accepted without question as the final word on Objectivism by the orthodox. In the old days unauthorized efforts to explain the philosophy were denounced by Objectivist headquarters. Now it is the neo-Objectivists who are angry about what orthodoxy is passing off as the definitive 'integration' of Rand's philosophy.

A recent organ of orthodox-Objectivist education is the Objectivist Study Group (OSG), an ARI-affiliated conference on the internet run by Robert Stubblefield, a former editor of the *Intellectual Activist*. We are informed that "If you do not understand something Ayn Rand said or wrote, OSG provides a medium to ask for help in understanding. If you believe Ayn Rand was mistaken or 'illogical', you will not find a receptive audience in OSG. We are reassured, however, that this "is not an issue of faith, appeal to authority, or dogmatism." He also refers to Objectivism as "Ayn Rand's property (and now her estate's property.)" OSG's motto is: "We don't speak for Objectivism; we study it."

Second in command to Peikoff in the orthodox Objectivist movement is Harry Binswanger. Remarks Kay Nolte Smith, "What's so sad . . . if you had heard how Ayn Rand talked about Harry Binswanger before he got to be one of the few people left . . . you know it's pathetic, really pathetic." Despite her extolling of excellence, like most cult leaders Rand's bottom-line demand was loyalty. Loyalty rather than brilliance is what predominates among her designated intellectual descendents. Binswanger doesn't think there were *any* negative elements in Rand's character. Well, "she spoke with an accent," but "that's not a moral issue. . . . Hypothetically, if you have a great figure, whom the fate of the world depends on, and they have a few minor character flaws, and the world is against that person, I wouldn't put them into a biography until that person had, perhaps a hundred years later, gained the recognition that they deserve." ARI has said that it would publish its own official, and evidently sanitized, Rand biography by 1999.

David Harriman, editor of *Journals of Ayn Rand* (1997) informs us that he deliberately omitted two-thirds of the material from 1955–77 that was of a psychological, non-philosophical nature, written "to understand the people she knew, many of whom baffled her." Nathaniel Branden's name is delicately sidestepped here, Barbara's too. Indeed, the undisclosed notes might have revealed more of Rand's character than theirs. Harriman tells us that among other political nuggets, her critique of Harry Truman's firing of General MacArthur was omitted, a firing widely condemned then, much admired today. Rand scholar Chris Matthew Sciabarra has found that a three-sentence paragraph from Rand's journal had been published years earlier. Comparing the two versions, 1984 and 1997, of this very brief passage, there were no less than six alterations, at least four of them significant and tendentious, none of them indicated to the reader. This suggests that *Journals of Ayn Rand* may be completely unreliable and, if that expurgated paragraph is representative of many others, may have been thoroughly twisted in the interests of the present-day cult.

Randian Loathing for Libertarians

Libertarianism is eighteenth- and nineteenth-century classical liberalism reinvigorated in the twentieth century by mostly economics-oriented thinkers such as Ludwig von Mises and Friedrich Hayek, their major point being that when government intervenes in the economy in an attempt to improve upon market outcomes, it can only do so by exceeding its basic legitimate mandate of outlawing physical force, instead becoming itself an initiator of physical force, with corrupting results, as well as a major economic player whose baleful ineptitude will ultimately drain vitality from the economy as a whole. Libertarians have rallied around the 'non-initiation of physical force' dictum, attracting all sorts of people with varying and conflicting philosophic rationales.

Rand insisted that until libertarians in general adopted her metaphysics, epistemology, and rational egoism as that dictum's necessary and sole underlying philosophy, engagement in politics under a libertarian banner would be premature and deceitful— deceitful given libertarianism's pretense of acting upon principle when in fact its main principle has no philosophic roots. From its formation in 1972, Rand repudiated and condemned the Libertarian Party (LP) for not explicitly grounding its non-initation of force principle in Objectivism. Keith Edwards, once NBI representative in Detroit, and then long-time LP activist, comments that he had never heard of any political party promulgating an overtly philosophical base in metaphysics, epistemology, or ethics.

Whence her aversion then? Rand's ego may have loomed larger than any ideological principle. Murray Rothbard's high profile in the LP's early days, Nathaniel Branden's endorsement of the party, and John Hospers becoming its first presidential candidate would have appalled her, each being an excommunicatee from the cult. Edwards notes that the libertarian movement took off like a shot just as the Objectivist movement was collapsing following the Break, so suddenly there was a whole new bunch of people talking about liberty who had no allegiance to the Rand cult. Perhaps horrified that anarcho-libertarian thought might either taint Objectivism or that libertarianism might make significant inroads independent of Objectivism, Ayn Rand herself erected a Berlin wall of hostility between the two, a wall that since her death has been maintained and fortified by Peikoff-Binswanger-Schwartz.[2]

In 1997 New Zealand neo-Objectivist and talk-show host Lindsay Perigo recalled reading "correspondence among some members and ex-members of Ayn Rand's inner circle dating from the late fifties, in which the word 'libertarian' was used quite freely and uncontroversially to describe the society that they were all fighting for.[3] Now in the orthodox Objectivist sanctum of the Unholy Trinity, the word is more blasphemous than 'fascist' or 'communist'! It's just plain bloody stupid."

David Kelley acknowledges that there has been a lot of bad blood between Objectivists and non-Objectivist free-marketeers, but that among libertarians, once they are shown a willingness to engage in dialogue, he himself has found not a trace of hostility. He dismisses Peter Schwartz's berating of all libertarians as irrational for not accepting Objectivism at one swallow as "unwarranted, self-defeating, and, frankly, stupid."

Orthodox Objectivist Robert Stubblefield has described the world's largest libertarian book service, Laissez Faire Books, as having "an evil intellectual agenda." One might wonder if much Objectivist condemnation of the libertarian movement serves mainly to encourage free-market types to buy their books from Second Renaissance, the orthodox Objectivist book service, rather than from its competitor, Laissez Faire Books.

Roy Childs recalled that most Objectivists he knew in the 1960s and 1970s were in transition to libertarianism, many scuttling Objectivist morality and becoming drug-rock types. The morality was all that Rand *really* had to offer of any apparent originality, philosophically, and was all that might make her seem indispensable to some libertarians.

The Peikoff-Kelley Break

Leonard Peikoff once thought highly enough of David Kelley as an Objectivist philosopher to ask his assistance in updating an Objectivist study guide and to approve Second Renaissance's distribution of Kelley's Objectivist epistemology treatise, *The Evidence of the Senses,* a book that another respected Objectivist philosopher, Allan Gotthelf, felt established Kelley as second only to Peikoff as a Rand scholar.

Kelley announced in 1989 that at Peikoff's insistence, "the Ayn Rand Institute has ended its association with me, and is warning the college groups with which it works not to invite me as a speaker." Agreement with Peikoff's article condemning Kelley "has been made a loyalty test for participating in Objectivist conferences or working with ARI. This is the behavior of religious zealots." At the 1989 ARI-sanctioned Objectivist colloquium, Peikoff pleaded with the "unadmitted anti-Objectivists": "if you agree with the Branden or Kelley viewpoint, . . . drop Ayn Rand, leave Objectivism alone. We do not want you." Kelley later elaborated: "I have been declared an enemy of Objectivism, and my writings, like those of others before me, have disappeared down the memory hole of the official movement." The writings of all those who sided with Kelley against Peikoff disappeared likewise.

So just what were Kelley's sins? In the post-heroic epoch of Objectivism, refusal to recommence trysts with the aging Guru is no longer the occasion for schism. First, Kelley had condoned Barbara Branden's *Passion of Ayn Rand,* though he also stated important disagreements with it. Peikoff had decried the book as soon as he found out that Barbara Branden was writing it, let it be known that he himself as a moral exemplar would refrain from reading it, and proclaimed that the very least a true Objectivist should do, if unable to resist reading it for biographical details unavailable elsewhere, was to refrain from buying it. Second, Kelley accepted an invitation to address a libertarian supper meeting. For Peikoff, these two actions were repudiations of objectivity, since Kelley was openly tolerating objectively evil views.

Neo-Objectivist lawyer Murray Franck felt "deeply saddened" as "another independent thinker" was "made an unperson." Neo-Objectivist Paul Szpunar commented on the Peikoff-Kelley schism that, "I've lost good friends over this issue, I've been called all sorts of names both to my face and behind my back." Another neo-Objectivist reports that a number of people "started this back-patting session of 'who can say the worst things about David Kelley', with very little regard for the truthfulness of the claims."

George Walsh recounts that after he had read *Fact and Value* (1989), Peikoff's delineation of the philosophical principles requiring Kelley's expulsion, "Objectivist economist Northrup Buechner called and told me that unless I assured him of my substantial agreement with *Fact and Value*, I could not lecture at his Poconos Conference. . . . this was a loyalty test. . . . when I refused, . . . he replied that he was breaking off all personal relations with me." Walsh then consulted with Peikoff, up till that point a presumed friend. "I was to resign the positions I had held up to that time in the official movement. This included the Ayn Rand Institute. . . . I have not seen or talked to Peikoff since."

Neo-Objectivist newsletter editor Karen Reedstrom writes, "When George Walsh wrote his letter of resignation from the editorial board of the *Intellectual Activist*, its editor Peter Schwartz asked him if he could edit the letter. Walsh instructed him to print it unedited or to not print it at all. Mr. Schwartz edited and then printed it anyway." Walsh had insisted upon the unacceptable wording, "I wish to declare my opposition to the use of an elaborate philosophical statement"—Peikoff's *Fact and Value*—"as a loyalty test, a means of 'quality control', or worse, as an instrument of a 'purge'."

Petr Beckmann, a pro-nukes physicist associated with Peikoff in the 1980s would later dismiss them as "religious. . . . The Harvard Objectivist club had the audacity to invite somebody for a debate who was a libertarian . . . ARI said that they could debate . . . anybody . . . but nobody from Laissez Faire Books . . . they're behaving like Ceausescu and the Communist Party. This is the party line and if you don't toe it, you will be sentenced to eternal damnation. They have gone crazy with self-inflation. They all behave like little Stalins." Beckmann predicted the "Peikoff-Schwartz despots" would ultimately "get nowhere" with a few hundred people applauding them and no debate.

Just as the Rand-Branden Break in 1968 shook the Objectivist movement worldwide, so did the Peikoff-Kelley split in 1989. Doctoral candidate in English literature at the University of Oslo, Kirsti Minsaas, reported that there had been an Objectivist campus club there since the early 1970s. Its activities were seriously disrupted by the new schism. Minsaas said she was no longer involved in the club, "since it chose to take an official stand for Peikoff and ARI." New Zealander Lindsay Perigo opines, "I think the ARI's behavior is pathetic." He had received a letter out of the blue from Objectivist philosopher Gary Hull, a Peikoff loyalist, relaying the rumor of Perigo's pro-Kelley tendencies and "would I please explain whether I was a person of integrity or not!"

Bidinotto tells us that Peikoff in the late 1980s was being pushed by both *Intellectual Activist* newsletter editor Peter Schwartz and Harry Binswanger to take a much more hard-line stand on issues of moral judgment. He felt torn between their position and a more tolerant line he had been advocating in an anti-rationalism lecture course. The former won out. Behavior typical of the ugly NBI era—demands for loyalty, moral denunciations, excommunication, judging books without reading them, and so on—suddenly came back into fashion. According to Bidinotto, Peikoff's and Schwartz's Kelley-denouncing articles in 1989 "expose (for the first time so explicitly) the premises, motives, and methods which have warped and sundered the Objectivist movement from its beginning, and have reduced it to an object of public ridicule." So for one of *the* highest profile neo-Objectivists, the orthodox movement has gone from promising beginnings at NBI in 1958 to the status of public joke three decades later.

Bidinotto views Peikoff's *Fact and Value* paper as "a summary effort to shrink the realm of honest 'errors of knowledge' to negligibility, to inflate the realm of 'immorality' to include errors of knowledge, . . . and thus to transform every incorrect philosophical statement (save, perhaps, for the babblings of children and idiots) into a moral failing." Peikoff's new hard line actually contradicts what Rand says on a video of the TV program *Day at Night* (with interviewer James Day), namely, that one can judge people by what they preach *only* if one knows that what they preach is not a product of errors of knowledge on their part, and that people should be judged mainly on their actions, given that most people speak so imprecisely. Morality demands only, states Rand, that a person "struggle to the best of their ability to do good and never to do evil consciously. If a man does that, I would regard him as completely good."

And since for Peikoff it is ideas rather than actions that are "the real basis for moral evaluation," continues Bidinotto, "evil intellectuals are far worse, ethically, than mere thugs and killers." The intellectuals know better; they must be evading the truth. In this, says Bidinotto, "Peikoff simply makes an unsupported psychological assertion, and treats it as a self-evident truth." Peikoff and Schwartz morally equate libertarians with the Soviets, David Kelley with Armand Hammer (an American oil baron who dealt extensively with the Soviets), and Kant with all of Hitler, Stalin, Mao, and Pol Pot combined.

Who qualifies as an Objectivist, for Peikoff? Suggests Bidinotto: "those whose talents are sycophantic nodding, agreeing, and obeying." Bidinotto explicitly refers to Peikoff's following as his "cult." Keith Edwards, former Objectivist turned Libertarian Party activist, states that "Leonard Peikoff and Peter Schwartz have proved that if you act snarky and abuse the people who want to learn your philosophy you are going to lose them . . . . You cannot communicate by excommunicating." Bidinotto draws a cruel parallel with *Atlas Shrugged:* Objectivism's best brains are draining out of it. The Peikoffians, Bidinotto points out even more cruelly given their anti-Khomeini ad in support of Salman Rushdie in *The New York Times*, "view Objectivism as a mental refuge . . . a door to slam shut against a threatening, revolting world," yet Objectivism "emphatically does not need a secular

Ayatollah, who props up a shaky self-image with denunciations instead of deeds . . . an ideological policeman, whose only evident gratification is the bitter, endless, self-righteous pursuit of 'evildoers'—no matter how petty their alleged offenses, no matter what their contexts of knowledge." Crueller still, Bidinotto compares Peikoff to the villain of Hugo's *Les Misérables*, Inspector Javert, driven by a petty bureaucratic moralism.

David Kelley started up his Institute For Objectivist Studies (IOS) in 1990, not long after his expulsion. Says Kelley, "It was very hard in many ways because we had no access to the organized instruments of the Objectivist movement, mailing lists, or visible names. George Walsh, Jim Lennox, and I were the only three intellectuals who came over and had any kind of visibility in the Objectivist movement." Meanwhile, it's the Peikoff camp that effortlessly corrals thousands of Rand's readers each year, a permanent, built-in advantage. Embarrassingly in retrospect, George Walsh had introduced Peikoff at a lecture just months before the Peikoff-Kelley fireworks as the finest lecturer inside or outside of Objectivism.

Kelley's IOS mandate in 1990 was to develop the philosophy (via research, weekend seminars, and week-long summer seminars), to serve Objectivists (via a newsletter, and courses in, for instance, thinking skills), and to get ideas 'out there' (via books and tapes, debates and radio shows). A non-Objectivist philosopher would comment in 1994 that "David Kelley has succeeded in creating an Objectivist forum characterized by toleration and open discussion." It took this philosophy of reason from 1958 until 1993, 35 years, to do it. As of 1995, IOS literature was listing 16 campus or off-campus Ayn Rand clubs unaffiliated with ARI. Reflecting Objectivists' reliance on a small stock of clichés, a blurb of a student at the summer seminar week effervesces, "Really amazing. It's like the University of Atlantis." The weekly radio program *In Focus* with David Kelley and Raymond Newman aired on 37 stations each Sunday afternoon for 39 weeks in 1994–95, but IOS pulled the plug on it, feeling it involved too much effort to reach too few listeners. Peikoff has had more luck with an ARI-supported daily talk-radio show of interviews and call-ins on KIEV Los Angeles. He began it in late 1995 and by 1997 it had been picked up by stations in New Mexico, Arizona, and North Carolina.

According to Kelley, subscribers to Stubblefield's internet newsgroup, the Objectivist Study Group (OSG), are prohibited by contract from actively participating in the neo-Objectivist news-group favored by Kelleyites. Some orthodox Objectivist would evidently be monitoring that forbidden site to catch transgressors. Kelley also regrets that OSG members, with Stubblefield's approval, have "engaged in various psychologizing efforts to impugn my character." Stubblefield dubs Kelley and his supporters as "snarling wimps," which Kelley in turn dismisses as "adolescent name-calling."

Of this kind of judgmentalism, Bidinotto says: "that mindset, and the behavior to which it leads, have persisted within the Objectivist movement for three decades now. . . . Future generations will spawn new representatives." Peikoff foresees no peace either, saying that the "cause of all the schisms . . . is not . . . differences in regard to love affairs, or . . . anybody's personality" (he means Rand's love affairs and personality) and the warfare "will continue for many years to come."

One wonders sometimes just *how* different Kelley's perspective is from Peikoff's. In the talk before a libertarian audience which provoked his excommunication, Kelley concluded by saying he would bet that in the ideal society, if it comes, "most people will have read *The Fountainhead* and *Atlas Shrugged.*" Yet surely, say, in the year 2029, the vast majority of the buyers of the 22 million or so copies of Rand books sold as of 1999 will be dead, their *Fountainheads* and *Atlases* dilapidated or discarded, and the Rand-reading subset of that era's doubtlessly small set of serious readers will not even remotely approach half the adult population. In the fall of 1991, after starting up his alternative institute, Kelley asserted that Objectivism "is a crusading set of ideas . . . This is not armchair stuff, where we . . . debate and then . . . go out for a drink afterwards." God forbid should such philosophical differences arise between parents, between parent and teenagers, or between friends. And curiously, while there exist texts on logical thinking by the dozen and one of the more widely used ones is Kelley's 582-page *The Art of Reasoning* with its companion 325-page *Readings for Logical Analysis,* in neither Kelley tome will you find an extract from the works of Ayn Rand by way of exemplifying either impressive or shoddy reasoning.

Kelley may have been brave enough to cross Peikoff, but apparently he had been unwilling to risk crossing Rand herself. Tibor Machan relates that after Binswanger had denounced Machan's *Human Rights and Human Liberties* (1975) as pure mush, Machan had written David Kelley at Princeton "asking whether he was forbidden to communicate with me, and he replied that we had better not talk."

Peikoff's Break with Reisman

Five years after the Kelley expulsion, Peikoff's ARI generated another major rift and a new faction by excommunicating the Reismans, who had long run the Thomas Jefferson School (TJS) summer sessions in affiliation with ARI. At one time an activist for Joe McCarthy, Roy Cohn, and HUAC, when George Reisman became an Objectivist, "I truly thought that *Atlas Shrugged* would convert the country in about six weeks; I could not understand how anyone could read it without being either convinced by what it had to say or else hospitalized by a mental breakdown." He eventually became an economics professor at Pepperdine University's business school.

In 1997 a neo-Objectivist newsletter announced that Reisman and his psychologist wife Edith Packer had had their relationship to the Ayn Rand Institute severed by Peikoff, Schwartz, Binswanger, and Berliner. It anticipated a repetition of the exodus of people and money from ARI to IOS that the Peikoff-Kelley rift had precipitated earlier. The Reismans were first expelled from ARI's board of advisors in 1993 for indelicate criticisms of ARI policy, provoking Schwartz to accuse Packer of "sheer stupidity," and Binswanger to label the Reismans as irrational troublemakers and as "entities" (a choice Randian epithet). Then Schwartz's Second Renaissance Books discontinued sale of Edith Packer's pamphlets and audiotapes. Next, ARI executive director Berliner for the first time declined to advertise TJS's next summer session in any ARI literature or to offer TJS tuition scholarships. Finally, during an October 1994 ARI conference phone call that the Reismans dubbed a "kangaroo court," Peikoff deemed them immoral. That stigma would likely encourage scheduled lecturers to bow out, so the Reismans were obliged by the specter of a financial fiasco to cancel the 1995 TJS session, incurring the loss of a hefty deposit for pre-booked hotel facilities.

Linda Reardan, asking for evidence of the Reismans' immorality, was expelled from Peikoff's Objectivist Graduate Center seminar. A disgusted Jerry Kirkpatrick, Objectivist author of a book on advertising, concludes that the ARI directors' attitude toward its graduate students in philosophy seems to be one of creating clones of themselves, not 'New Intellectuals'. Rick Sanford, having headed the ARI-affiliated Society for Objective Science (SOS) for five years, found himself cut off from ordering pamphlets SOS needed from ARI. *The Intellectual Activist* (TIA) now refused to publish Sanford's years-in-preparation article on the ozone layer. Why? Because Sanford refused to join, on ARI's say-so, the chorus condemning the Reismans as immoral. TIA publisher Stubblefield wrote him that TIA would never publish the article unless Sanford ceased to be agnostic on the Reisman versus Peikoff matter.

Peikoff responded to Genevieve and Rick Sanford's objections to the Reismans' excommunication, not personally, but via an Objectivist conference half-hour lecture in San Francisco in 1995, a tape of which Peikoff sent to the Sanfords accompanied by the proviso that should they not agree completely with the epistemological views expressed therein, any further discussion of the Reisman controversy would be pointless. The tape was all about the evils of being 'agnostic' amidst such a controversy, Peikoff implicitly comparing the Sanfords' refusal to condone ARI's summary conviction of the Reismans (based on absolutely no evidence made public) to the O.J. Simpson criminal trial jury's failure to convict Simpson (despite a towering pile of evidence).

Two years after the Reismans' expulsion, the following announcement was circulated: "The leadership of the Society for

Objective Science and Richard F. Sanford . . . no longer consider
Dr. Peikoff and the directors of the ARI as spokesmen for
Objectivism." Peikoff and Co. had consistently "refused to provide
any facts to back up their charges" of immorality against Reisman
and Packer, and had instead "resorted to intimidation, evasion,
and *ad hominem*."

Sanford warned fellow–ARI financial contributors that "ARI
requires Objectivists to condemn the Reismans or be ostracized.
Objectivists who maintain their silence for whatever reason are
punished as enemies of ARI anyway . . . for refraining from attacking ARI's perceived enemy." ARI-Peikoff have demanded "blind
loyalty or *else*." Genevieve Sanford concludes that at ARI, "a
drone's blind approval is welcomed over a thinking person's honest disapproval. . . . Approval of ARI's leaders has taken primacy
over their avowed mission to spread Objectivism."

What has long been obvious to everyone else, erstwhile-orthodox Objectivists now recognize. A disgusted Jerry Kirkpatrick
calls ARI's directors "self-appointed guardians of Objectivist
purity" and "a cult of mediocrity." An equally disgusted Linda
Reardan now says, "Leonard regards himself as somehow equivalent to Objectivism, and Harry and Peter as his designated lieu-
tenants in this respect."

After the break with ARI, George Reisman's monumental work
Capitalism appeared in 1996. His introduction modestly informs
us that, having been a student of both Rand and Mises, his is the
highest possible "intellectual pedigree" possible for any thinker in
any period. In his chapter on environmental issues he notes that,
in the unlikely event of global warming, "Even the prospective
destruction of much of Holland, if it could not be averted, . . .
could be dealt with by the very simple means of the rest of
Europe, and the United States and Canada, extending the freedom
of immigration to Dutch citizens. If this were done, then in a relatively short time, the economic losses suffered as a result of physical destruction in Holland would hardly be noticed, least of all by
most of the former Dutchmen." For the rest of us, "the only appropriate response" would be "more and better air conditioners."
Similarly, if there were some reduction in the ozone layer, the
answer would be "more sunglasses, hats, and sun-tan lotion."

Neo-Objectivists Confront the Reality of Objectivist Cultism

According to psychiatrist Dr. Alan Blumenthal, and to Joan Kennedy Taylor (co-author of *When To See a Psychologist*), students flocked to Objectivism from orthodox religions and guru-led cults, and flocked *from* Objectivism to orthodox religion and guru-led cults once again after the Break in 1968. For many, Rand's Objectivism was a way station between L. Ron Hubbard's Dianetics and Werner Erhard's *est*. This company isn't as surprising as it might appear at first glance. For not only has the Objectivist movement been a classic cult as defined in the dictionary, it may arguably be viewed as a destructive psychotherapeutic-religious cult, and as much a corruption of the humanist ideals of reason and individualism as was Marxism.

Kelley reminds orthodox Objectivists that the Enlightenment bid good riddance to the many guises of intolerance, such as adherence to authorized doctrine, the notions of blasphemy and heresy, culture-bound intellectuality, hostile sectarianism, constant schisms, savage denunciation of turncoats, and other tools that a rational philosophy would dispense with, but which Rand's-Branden's-Peikoff's Objectivism has gleefully wielded.

Philosopher George Walsh cautions that the French Revolution's bloodshed "was due to the association of extreme fanaticism with a kind of secular religion. It was very irrational; but . . . they thought they were being rational. They instituted the worship of the goddess of reason . . . Of course, there's nothing worse than an irrationalist who thinks he's advancing the cause of reason."

Kelley, uncomfortable with the word 'cult', speaks of tribalism instead. He concedes that in addition to the rational element in the Objectivist movement there has always been a tribal element, brought about by dogmatic attitudes on the part of Rand and Branden, and then Peikoff, the last expressing a truly tribal view bound to generate an insular authoritarianism.

For Kelley, a tribe sees the beliefs shared by members as uniquely epitomized by its founder, lending a transcendent value to the founder's person, acts, and perhaps otherwise unpersuasive assertions. Attacks upon the founder are as profoundly evil in character as the founder is profoundly good. Kelley deems this "idolatry, or worshipping the concrete symbol in place of what it represents, and Ayn Rand has been its object." Kelley explains tribalism as a social-psychological syndrome. One's personal identification becomes dependent on membership in the tribe. One is lost without it. All one's friends are in the tribe. The tribalist shuns outsiders, fears expulsion. It's us against them. The tribalist avoids questioning and substitutes the leader's authority for his own judgment.

While it's true that Rand explicitly advocates independent judgment, she also implies that one's independent judgment should never conflict on any important matter with that of Ayn Rand. Independent judgment, then, can easily come to be equated with the seconding of Ayn Rand's views.

A former *est* follower recalls an insider saying, "Do you know that no staff person ever says anything negative to any human being about Werner?" (Werner Erhard). A follower of Rajneesh, writes one biographer, was "likely to lose contact with the critical intellect" and suffer eventual disillusionment. Whatever NBIers learned of critical thinking was offset by suppression of critical thinking about Rand and those sanctioned by her.

Cautions George Smith, "Randian clones can mimic her writing style, regurgitate her ideas, and denounce heretics—but that is all. . . . There is more than one excuse for being an Ayn Rand, but there is no excuse whatever for being a disciple of Ayn Rand. Her admirers should heed the words of Aristotle: I love Plato, but I love the truth more."

According to Kelley, Peikoff's approach means keeping one eye on reality and the other on Ayn Rand's words, consistency with her writings being the ultimate value, and even abandoning apparent rationality if need be. But no philosophy of reason could endorse such a stance.

Kelley also writes that often we *can* judge an author's rationality from his writings, but not from contextless excerpts or from paraphrases by enemies. Yet on the sole basis of the latter,

Objectivists have been known to denounce Kant as history's most evil figure. Sadly, Rand is their role model here. She read little or no Kant, but excoriated him. She didn't even look at John Rawls's *A Theory of Justice,* yet slammed it on the basis of a review of it in *The New York Times.*

Kelley maintains that a closed system such as Peikoff's version of Objectivism is defined by specific articles of faith in some canonical text, with internal debates highly constrained, short-lived and settled by a ruling from some authority. Peikoff implies that just as new laws must contradict nothing in the U.S. Constitution, new Objectivist writings must contradict nothing in Rand's works nor in works she sanctioned, such as his own *Ominous Parallels*! In contrast, philosophy professor Tibor Machan acknowledges that the "closed nature of Official Objectivism remains a problem. I was very glad I was blackballed from it. I might have become a dependent like so many others."

Kelley adds that if Objectivism wants to be known as a philosophy, not a body of dogma, then Peikoff's Marxist- or Freudian-like treatment of abstractions as perceptual concretes cannot be allowed to stand. In that regard Peikoff insists, "The most eloquent badge of an authentic Objectivist" is that in "his soul, he is essentially a moralist. . . . he judges every fact within his sphere of action—and he does it passionately, because his value-judgments, being objective, are integrated in his mind into a consistent whole, which to him has the feel, the power, and the absolutism of a direct perception of reality." Branden in contrast, with NBI and ARI in mind, urged Objectivists in 1996 "to give up the . . . self-righteousness and the intoxication of speaking in . . . broad global generalities with one's cape fluttering behind one in the wind."

Judging others may often assume a very low priority when one is too busy acting to bother with reacting. And typically information is lacking, which makes Peikoffian Objectivists, in Kelley's words, "liable to judge people *without* investigating all the facts: to judge unfairly, nonobjectively, on insufficient evidence."

Has Objectivism been turning out Howard Roarks? Bidinotto suggests that as for "demonstrated positive effects upon the lives and characters of its proponents, . . . Objectivism has a long way to go. A philosophy which upholds reason is too often perverted into its counterfeit—rationalism. An epistemology which extols independent rational judgment is too often promoted by self-righteous authoritarians and self-doubting yes-men. An ethics which advocates productivity and happiness is too often trumpeted by people with short résumés and long faces." Ironically, Objectivists and neo-Objectivists often claim, as Nathaniel Branden did recently, that it is within the culture at large that there are almost no appropriate role models for young people

Former "boy Objectivist" (as his friend Roy Childs once tagged him) George Smith now deplores the religiosity of so many Objectivists. He writes that the religious Objectivist seeks out the nastiest conceivable motives to explain so-called immoral acts, savors them and gleefully recounts such 'discoveries' to fellow religious Objectivists. Such a pedant is "a walking caricature of moral rigor," that rigor applied to himself as well. He treasures the key to the gates of happiness but wouldn't even know where to look for the keyhole. Caught between fear of Randian disapproval and the fact that exuberant living always threatens to break past the bounds of rationality, these Objectivists opt for emotional safety. Still: private thoughts, feelings and actions betray evil premises, and thus the sense of sinfulness among so many of these pedants.

Bidinotto complains that the individual is of passionate concern for individualist ideologues only as a faceless abstraction, a principle, a cause. As a real live flawed human being, his appeal evaporates. Bidinotto argues that one shouldn't let the apex of one's value hierarchy be a platonic abstraction, an end-in-itself replacing individual human life. He seems to overlook that it is built into Objectivism that the apex of one's value hierarchy shifts from the concrete 'one's own personal individual life' to the abstract 'concept of individual human life', altogether skipping the intermediary concrete consisting of 'the individual lives of actual others'.

For Peikoffians, Bidinotto continues, "relevant facts, motives and contexts are arbitrarily excluded from moral judgments." This makes for an ethics "retooled into an indiscriminately, gleefully wielded moral bludgeon." Bidinotto adds that it is impossible for people-haters to concern themselves with individuals, and certain Objectivists were cornering the market on misanthropy. The 1986 space shuttle *Challenger* catastrophe actually had certain 'individualists' gloating, one letter from an Objectivist even using NASA's status as a government agency to hurl insults at the dead teacher Christa McAuliffe.

And it all goes back to *Atlas Shrugged*, where the word 'evil' turns up on average once every 4.9 pages! Says Nathaniel Branden, "I don't know of anyone other than the Church fathers in the Dark Ages who used the word 'evil' quite so often as Ayn Rand." But once again, by the standard of partly-altruistic moral codes, it is Rand's-Branden's-Peikoff's advocacy of selfishness that is evil. Bidinotto recalls that upon reading *Atlas*, he became outraged and indignant and dwelt on Rand's condemnations. In the late 1960s his manner "became sarcastic, caustic, denunciatory."

Neo-Objectivist Marti Penn writes on the internet that many Objectivists assume any failure of communication in proselytizing must be due to evasion on the part of the listener. Bidinotto cautions proselytizers that failure to shout 'Eureka!' upon finishing *Atlas Shrugged* is hardly proof of evasion or irrationality (implying he believes it *is* such proof for many Objectivists). He warns that Americans will respond with hostility when hostility is the public face of a philosophy of supposed benevolence, especially when they are denounced as moral barbarians by condescending intellectual bullies. Philosopher George Walsh too cautions that the Objectivist ethics' distinctness and unwavering stands can be used as a kind of weapon by judgmentalists against friends and relatives.

Peikoff relates that Kelley once "accused Ayn Rand and me . . . to my face" of being "dogmatic moralizers" or "angry emotionalists," "his standard accusation against anyone . . . who pronounces moral judgment, . . . and I broke off all relations with him." He continues, "Up to now" (1989), "I could explain these attacks only psychologically, in terms of the attackers' *cowardice* or *psychopathology*. But *now* I understand the basic cause. . . . Such people have literally no concept of 'objectivity' in regard to values."

Apparently then, for 30 years he had been misinterpreting critiques of the Objectivist movement: Those critiques he now sees, not as outgrowths of poor character or psychology, but as philosophical mistakes. People he had written off as gutless or mentally ill he now pities as simply baffled about objectivity in the realm of values.

As for critiques from former students of Objectivism, Peikoff says that typically "the accuser started out in Objectivism as a dogmatist, cursing or praising people blindly, in obedience, as he thought, to his new-found 'authorities'. Then at last his pent-up resentment at this self-made serfdom erupts—and he becomes an angry subjectivist, denouncing the 'excessive anger' of those who make moral judgments. They swing from intrinsicism to subjectivism." ('Intrinsicism' is basically Objectivese for 'naive realism' in the ethical realm.) Peikoff is saying that *his* is properly righteous, objectively-based anger. Inappropriate anger comes from unobjective subjectivists and intrinsicists.

Peikoffians complain that Kelleyites not only separate values from facts, thus rendering objective values an empty category, but ideas from reality or concepts from percepts—making objective truths equally impossible. Peikoff insists that, "if cognition implies evaluation, then non-evaluation implies non-cognition." In other words, if an Objectivist is not invariably prepared to judge someone at the drop of a hat as per Objectivist doctrine, then he can't be said to really *know* whatever it was that he would have based his judgment on.

Intellectual Activist newsletter publisher Robert Stubblefield reviews several of the ruptures between Rand and various followers, not explicitly named (I name them): Leonard Liggio "sees Ayn Rand's evaluation of religion as an attack on him—or" as Murray Rothbard saw it, "on his wife." The Smiths "see Ayn Rand's rage when they tolerate changes to her play as a moralistic attack on them. Still others," like John Hospers, "see Ayn Rand's failure to tolerate (even innocent) insults as judgmental."

He explains that ideas must be evaluated morally and that ideas are more fundamentally important than actions. Yet Rand viewed others as not much more than repositories of and enactors of ideas. If so, blasting away at a person's ideas is still an attack on his core humanity. Stubblefield is also saying that moral outrage is indeed appropriate to the discussion of facts and ideas, for they inevitably have moral import. So, emotion *should* mix with reason, once reason has objectively analyzed the data and arrived at conclusions. This actually sounds a bit like: 'Use simple Objectivist principles to cut through the B.S. ASAP, so you can throw yourself all the more quickly into emoting'.

Stubblefield insists that certainly ideas themselves *can* be evil because they are the most human of products. If values are a type of facts and facts are (potential) values, then one's values can be false, not just evil, and facts can be evil, not just false. If false ideas are arrived at through evasion or mental drifting, their evil adheres to whoever expresses them; it doesn't if the ideas are arrived at via honest errors of rational thinking. Nonetheless those ideas are false and must be condemned.

So when Rand is shouting in a colleague's face, apparently she is often merely calling attention to a false idea which will necessarily have evil implications. The colleague should not take it personally. That it *is* taken personally, concedes Stubblefield, is why "the seemingly better ones leave" Objectivism. In other words, a high self-esteem person misinterprets a Randian assault on his ideas as an assault on his person, and leaves the Objectivist movement. But for both Rand and Peikoff, any sane adult—after a Peikoff or a Rand has shown him the error of his ways—can hold irrational and hence immoral ideas only by deliberate choice. For Peikoff, if an idea is false, it is evil, its consequences are necessarily evil, and its advocates, ultimately, are evil.

Peikoff provides an example which he believes supports his case for the existence of inherently evil ideas and of the evil of those who buy into them. He cites an employee who comes up with an idea and presents it to his boss, only to learn that the idea is bad and would harm the company. The badness of the idea suffices for Peikoff as evidence of the irrationality of the employee and the immorality of his thought processes and character. It's an approach that would be definitively excluded from the 1997 business book, *If Aristotle Ran General Motors*. One can only gasp at what a creativity-destroying CEO Peikoff might make—or apparently does make as immovable boss of the official Objectivist movement.

4

Sex, Art, and Psychotherapy

Totalism for Anti-Totalitarians

All questions have already been answered, all decisions made, all eventualities foreseen. The true believer is without wonder and hesitation.

Eric Hoffer, *The True Believer*

In 1954 Gilbert Highet summed up the twentieth century as a war for the command of men's minds. Its totalitarian ideologies were forms of state-worship, "attractive ideologies, attractive to simple minds . . . imposing in their boldness and clarity, and claiming to give a complete explanation of the problems of human life." This, thought Rand, is what communism offers and what she thought she had to formulate an alternative to. However, to her totalistic alternative one could apply the same description that Highet applies to the totalitarians: They contrive a single explanation of the world, one system of thought and action that they insist covers everything, which they then expect everyone to embrace.[1]

Communism and Objectivism: two totalisms, the former— massive in extent and impact—generating the latter, its cultic inverse, whose historical importance lies in its role as a catalyst for the revival of classical liberalism in the closing decades of the twentieth century. Cockett remarks that only when renewed economic liberalism had developed an all-embracing world-view did it mesmerize a critical mass of young people, just as the comprehensive ideology of Marxism allured students in the 1930s with its compelling and simple solutions for complex problems. In reality it was classical liberalism and not just one proffered doctrinal basis for classical liberalism, Objectivism, which constituted, in Cockett's words, "a complete replacement for Marxism, a straightforward meta-narrative that would explain almost everything."

Searching for one key to resolve all perplexities can yield only ideological madness, warned Karl Jaspers. And Isaiah Berlin, who in 1958 published *the* definitive essay on negative individual rights, counselled that reducing the world to one unitary theory, to a simplistic ideology, is a horrendous error, pluralism being fundamental to human life. Rand's work attempts to do this and, ironically in this context, her big idea is the absolutizing of negative individual rights, by way of protecting the smart and civilized few from the stupid and barbaric many (typically manipulated, in Rand's view, by the smart but uncivilized intellectuals).

Philosopher Karl Popper wrote that Hegel's and Marx's totalistic worldviews were products of their effort to eliminate the dualism of facts and values. Far better to retain that distinction, for it may prevent people from shoving their pet normative prescriptions down the collective throat of society using the excuse of divine or quasi-divine authority. (Totalism also erodes the public-private distinction, both communism and Objectivism expecting even private matters to conform to one's public commitment to the ideology.) Like Hegel and Marx, Rand wanted to obliterate the fact-value distinction. For her, reality objectively dictates any organism's basic values every bit as much as it presents the organism with the relevant facts (be they apprehended or not), because values are a type of fact. One may freely choose to ignore the facts, but at one's peril. If one chooses to survive, one *must* adopt the values that maximize one's survival chances. In her philosophy, objectivity extends out from the personal life-or-death choice to a set of inter-related abstractions determining the make-up and behavior of whole societies, and rejection of any part of this whole package means rejecting human survival. We must adapt to reality and Rand is there to interpret what reality is telling us.

This isn't enough for Peikoff, who insists that a great many Rand enthusiasts, though bright, never do uproot *all* the contradictory ideas guiding the formation of their souls and minds. Nonetheless reality's message is that "they must conform to reality 24 hours a day and all the way down." Reality here is actually an emotionally-charged ideology to which one's complete conformity is demanded. Consider the absolutist qualifiers Rand herself deploys in the definition of rationality that she expects us all to adopt: "total," "full," "full," "all," "all," "all," "must," "precise and scrupulous," "ruthlessly strict," "fullest." So many demands—in two sentences![2] Yet the world is already teeming with billions of human beings, very few of whom are Objectivists. The species is an enormous success in biological terms. Does it really seem likely that Reality is broadcasting any message to all these people that they *must* conform 24 hours a day all the way down to the philosophy of Ayn Rand, for the sake of their survival? After all, these people did get rid of Communism without the help of Ayn Rand.

Relating the hopes of students of Objectivism, Greenberg says: "If they learned all the justifications and integrations, if they gained all the requisite knowledge of principles and concretes . . . then they could . . . rid themselves of all conflicts, immoralities, and problems—just like Ayn Rand. By holding the 'right' ideas . . . , they would feel the right things (since emotions proceed from value judgments, which would then be based on valid views of the good, of 'man's life') and . . . focusing . . . on the subject at hand, they would thereby be moral and rational, be motivated to do the 'right' things, gain self-esteem, and, social conditions permitting, be happy." It is reminiscent of Rand's description in her notes for *We the Living* of the Marxist-Leninist affliction as "An unbearable propaganda . . . that makes the atmosphere choking, airtight, until people get to a state of mental scurvy."

Rand's view, as Nathaniel Branden now facetiously formulates it, was that "Everything I say in philosophy is absolutely true and any departure necessarily leads you into error, so don't go mixing your irrational fantasies with my immutable truths." Branden adds that this posture "turned Ayn Rand's philosophy, for all practical purposes, into dogmatic religion."

Objectivists do not like it if people critically examine each particular claim of Objectivism, one by one. They rely on the assumption that Objectivism is a package. You have to take it or leave it as a whole, and if you take it, you have a ready-made Objectivist line on every conceivable issue. Objectivism reminds Antony Flew of the Marxist-Leninist milieu of his youth. The notion of a unified world outlook in which one's ideas are not merely consistent with one another, but in which one has a line on everything, a line derived from the world outlook, he regards as implicitly totalitarian.

Randian Sex Crimes

Objectivism demanded of its 'students' total compliance in every facet of their lives, especially their artistic and romantic preferences. For Rand, one's values are most graphically displayed in the kind of art (including music and literature) and the kind of romantic partner one responds to. The extent to which the whole gamut of Randian values is expressed or not expressed by the object of art or of love should be the measure both of its attractiveness and of the appraiser's character, for the whole point of art and of love is to mirror one's fundamental values (having a benevolent rather than a malevolent view of the world, being highly achievement-oriented and so forth) so as to fully celebrate them.

Branden tells us, "A man falls in love with and sexually desires the woman who reflects his own deepest values." This would simplify everyone's love life, were it true. He also maintains that we appreciate others primarily insofar as they provide us with a reflection of our psychological selves. Rajneesh, similarly, would see sex as "a meeting of you through the other." For Rand and Branden, romantic love is practically reduced to admiring how Randian ideology is expressed in another. Like Rand, Branden will not admit to being attracted physically to a merely human mate; Rand's theory of sex *demands* that one's mate be a mirror of one's soul. He labors to portray his second wife, Patrecia, as having astute, well-articulated insights into people, though others who knew her sadly concede that she was not particularly bright nor a poster-girl for mental health.

Only a man extolling love without sex would be so depraved as to desire sex without love, Branden informs us. (Frightful puritanical rot, comments Albert Ellis.) Ironically, a 1997 newsletter of the Institute for Objectivist Studies, with which Branden is now affiliated, relates with seeming pride that "in *The Playboy Book: Five Decades of Centerfolds,* a dozen of Mr. Hefner's models have declared that their favorite reading was Rand's work." *Playboy,* which ran an interview with Rand, now approved and distributed by ARI, has always been devoted to the depravity of sex without love.

Neo-Objectivist Karen Reedstrom asks how realistic it is in *Atlas* for Francisco to go twelve years without any sexual outlet in the hope that he will one day get together with Dagny again. (When the first d'Anconia copper mine blows up, one wonders if it was simply that Francisco was doing a pit-inspection there when his testicles finally exploded.) Stephen Cox, a libertarian professor of literature who rates Rand's novels quite highly as works of literature, comments that if one took it as a literal ethical imperative to forgo any romantic relationship until one met the ideal soul-mate who represents one's highest value, that would be a mistake, not the fulfillment of some admirable ethic. Yet Rand's heroes were upheld as real-life role models within the Objectivist movement.

Ex-Objectivist Sid Greenberg too wonders *what* in the souls of Francisco and Galt impels them to go without sex for over a decade. (In real life both likely would periodically masturbate while fantasizing about Dagny; however Galt the Onanist probably would not fit with Galt as Rand's Ideal Man.) But it's not just them. In a 1944 letter Rand writes that before meeting Dominique, Roark is a cold and total virgin because he is just too highly sexed, exactly like Dominique, selectivity being in Rand's view the hallmark of the highly sexed person.

Rand claims that only those who are fully rational are capable of love, a view for which she presents no evidence. And she insists that there are no conflicts of interests among rational men even in the issue of love. In *Atlas Shrugged*, Francisco doesn't mind being dumped for Rearden, and then Galt, assuring her that "if I'll see you smile with admiration at a new copper smelter that I built, it will be another form of what I felt when I lay in bed beside you." Nor does Dagny feel too badly for the spurned Francisco. During sex with Hank Rearden Dagny "felt Francisco's presence through Rearden's mind . . . as if she were surrendering to both men, to that which she worshipped in both of them." When Rearden in turn is dumped for John Galt, right after a month spent risking his neck for Dagny's sake owing to Galt's refusal to notify Rearden of her safety, he instantly gets over his romantic loss and even launches into a pages-long speech about how wonderfully things have worked out for all concerned. So determined is Rand to present her world of Reason as one of harmony that she gets carried away, as utopians do, with wishful thinking. It is a Harlequin Romance view of male sexuality, for readers who would otherwise take themselves as too cerebral for that genre. Rand's own squalid affair with Nathaniel Branden and its aftermath of loathing and vengeance is a better guide to human nature, or the actual behavior of Objectivists, than is Rand's theory.

Nathaniel Branden suggested that a happily married man would lose his sexual desire for a new neighbor who has taken his fancy, as soon as he places that desire in context. This man can even blithely confess to his wife that he has been fantasizing about having sex with the neighbor, and his wife will be reassured by his candor and restraint. Don't try this at home.

In *Judgment Day* Branden points to Rand's unreasonableness in trying in the mid-1960s to re-ignite their affair of the mid-1950s. He recalls her shouting at him that his admiration for her should suffice to preserve her sexual attractiveness even were she 90 and in a wheelchair. This echoes what a former student recalls Branden saying at his lectures: that even were Randian superhero John Galt four foot six and in a wheelchair, a woman would have to be out of her mind not to be in love with him. Branden has stated that for Ayn Rand, "in 1960 Nathaniel Branden was the closest thing on earth to John Galt." (She had dedicated *Atlas Shrugged* to husband Frank *and* to Nathaniel Branden. The dedication was shortened in printings subsequent to the Break.) Handsome and brashly assertive, Branden projected something of the Galt image from the NBI podium and young ladies in the audience were smitten. He was certainly ambulatory and a foot taller than any wheelchair-ridden mini-Galt.

Roy Childs recalls that the main influence Rand's theory of sex had on a lot of the rank-and-file teenage Objectivists was that they would force themselves into relationships based on their shared values. More than anything else, endless talking is what relationships became for them. Former student of Objectivism Sid Greenberg recalls that, non-Objectivists typically being scorned, fellow students initiated romances with each other but many did so on such an 'intellectual' basis that they remained unexposed to the everyday experiences and problems of romantic-sexual relationships, to the point of its being comical. If only they'd known the background details of Howard Roark's sex life that Rand planned but left out of *The Fountainhead:* "Until his meeting with Dominique, he has had affairs with women, perfectly cold, emotionless affairs, without the slightest pretense at love. Merely satisfying a physical need and recognized by his mistresses as such." (This was the story in Rand's mind most of the time she was working on the book. Close to the time *The Fountainhead* was completed, she evidently switched to thinking of Roark as a complete virgin prior to Dominique, though this is not stated in the book.)

Shared basic values can take a relationship only so far. Rand's novels also place a high premium on good looks. Apparently one admirable motive for pursuing a lucrative career, among orthodox Objectivists at least, was to be able to afford the plastic surgery required to upgrade one's sexual attractiveness, though Rand herself wrote nothing about plastic surgery. Announced Edith Packer, number one psychologist in the official Objectivist movement in the years up to her excommunication in 1994: "My answer is the same one Dr. Locke gave in his lecture." (Edwin Locke was the number two psychologist.) "Any time a young or not-so-young lady comes into my office and says, 'I am really unattractive, I have a long nose', I say, 'Fix it'. . . . some doctors make a lot of money from my practice. Ha ha ha. So, there are certain objective reasons why you may not find someone. . . . If there is something you can fix, by all means fix it." Doubtless breast implants too are objectively instrumental in attracting a man, who of course shares one's fundamental values.

What if the new nose and breasts are in place and everything is OK between oneself and a prospective romantic partner— except that the latter believes in a supernatural supreme being? According to Packer, as for Rand and all orthodox Objectivists, "everything *isn't* OK" because believing in God is a fundamentally irrational way of looking at life, not just a symptom of some little thing that can be corrected. So, if one's lover adheres to even the vaguest notion of a Creator: goodbye lover.

Do Children Exist?

In his scathing review of *Atlas Shrugged*, Whittaker Chambers writes that "from the impromptu . . . matings of the heroine and three of the heroes, no children . . . ever result. The possibility is never entertained. And, indeed, the strenuously sterile world of *Atlas Shrugged* is scarcely a place for children." The closest Rand comes in her fiction to acknowledging the possibility of unwanted pregnancy is when Marisha in *We the Living* asks, "Citizen Argounova, what do you use to keep from having children?" "Kira looked at her, startled." In a 1995 *New Yorker* piece, Pierpont insightfully quips: "Rand was childless, and her work stops just short of proving that children don't exist."

High-ranking Objectivists thought that having children would get in the way of their careers and, except for historian Robert Hessen and his wife, those who did have children were not gener- ally the intellectuals of the outfit. Though Rand officially held that it was perfectly all right to become a housewife with kids if under- taken as a serious profession, this was not the message her largely childless intellectual intimates picked up on.

Karen Reedstrom grants that many fellow Objectivists have decided not to have children. She is reminded of seeing a poster showing a young mother and a baby, with the caption: "You've now been sentenced to 18 years." Neo-Objectivist composer Eric Nolte wishes that Rand had been a parent, and says of raising kids, "I think the biggest problem is how much time kids consume . . . You can't take a kid back to the store for a refund—except to give it up for adoption. . . . I do think there's a role for duty with respect to a parent's obligations to the child. . . . The frustration comes from not having the control over a child that you have over a hobby." Even someone as critical of Rand's theories of sex and family as neo-Objectivist Laura J. Rift—divorced mother of a young boy—can manage only: "if I had to risk my life in order to save his, I *think* I would do so" (my italics).

Notes that Rand wrote in 1928 toward *The Little Street* present a view she never relinquished, that of family life as the glorification of mediocrity, as a dull and purposeless existence of ridiculous pettiness, bovine contentment, and stupid, prison-like monotony. Rand barely recognizes producing offspring as a significant part of human life. Neo-Objectivist Scuoteguazza admits that this is a huge gap in her theory and asks how one justifies having children as a selfish rational being trying to enhance one's personal survival chances. One would have to stretch the concept of Randian selfishness beyond recognition. Obviously much that parents do for their offspring drains time, money, emotions, and physical well-being, putting many of the parents' other values on hold. Only in Objectivism do parents feel guilty about not having purely selfish reasons for having children.

Nathaniel Branden provides an additional nudge away from parenthood, arguing in *The Psychology of Romantic Love* (1980) "against having children without awareness of the potential impact on romantic love." Indeed, who *would* have children were they to dwell on that downside? In *Taking Responsibility* Branden guides an unhappy client with children to the realization that she "never especially wanted to be a mother." In *The Art of Living Consciously* (1997), Branden cites the "tragedy" of Elena, a management consultant "sad" because the exorbitant fees for the private schooling of her *four* children—a few too many, Branden implies—meant that she couldn't risk devoting work-time to writing the follow-up to a book she'd published a decade earlier. One can't help but wonder whether all this is mere rationalization for Branden's compulsive if lucrative churning out of one rejigged version after another of his basic self-esteem pot-boiler, in lieu of having family and posterity.

Branden has, via his third marriage, acquired grandchildren to dote on. But for couples sensitized to the possible negative impact of parenthood on romance, independence, free time, or disposable income there would be no children and no windfall grandchildren either. Branden in 1996 said that "children would spread me too thin." But what of equally work-focused men who have fathered large families? He now regrets the rationale of those Objectivist couples who chose not to have children merely because the Brandens (and Rand herself) didn't, the difference between them and him being that "I got lucky in the end."

Espousing the kind of perfectionism that clients of other therapists are typically counselled to drop, Packer pronounces on the 'rational' reasons for having children: "A couple has to be psychologically, romantically, *and* financially ready for a child . . . *if* they want another value that they want to share . . . a child *can be* a very high value . . . it's *just another way* of cementing their romantic relationship by having something that is part of them both . . . but *it requires a very unusual couple I'm sorry to say*" (my emphases). Objectivism regards perpetuation of one's own genes and posterity in general as so peripheral to selfish concerns that only a small percentage of couples should risk endangering their romantic happiness by creating progeny.

According to Scuoteguazza, still an Objectivist after a quarter century, things haven't worked out so well for Objectivist loyalists. "Loneliness is all too often the Objectivist trademark," he laments. "I have never encountered a group of people who have relationships as volatile, quarrels as bitter, or friendships as fragile and vulnerable to sudden violent breaks as do Objectivists. While the average person is typically married, has children and a supportive network of family and friends, the typical Objectivist is single, or if married, has no children. Too many Objectivists I've met are lonely. They have a difficult time getting married, staying married or having children . . . For a philosophy that champions the bold fearless hero and heroine, there is an astonishing number of timid young bachelors and desperate aging spinsters. Of all the phenomena I have witnessed, this has to be the saddest."

Rational Bondage for Emancipated Women

I am a male chauvinist.

Ayn Rand

The American popular culture which greeted Rand on her arrival in 1926 offered a 'modern' and 'emancipated' model for women. Henceforth women were to wear pants, smoke cigarettes, look like men, and think like men. The chain-smoking, cape-swirling Rand, with her independent females as fictional heroines, may seem at first to fit this picture. Rand announced that women were the equals of men and, in general, she said she was all for women pursuing the same careers as men. But as so often with Rand, on this issue she seems to have been overwhelmed by her own blind emotions, and then to have rationalized these as the voice of Reason.

The movie *Female*, which Rand, at that time a passionate movie fan, may well have watched shortly after its release in 1933, has a Dagny-type heroine successfully running the car factory she had inherited from her father (but unable to find a man who will dominate her romantically, while letting her dominate in business). All of Rand's major fictional heroines are eager to be possessed and treated roughly by their ideal man. They are all sexually submissive borderline masochists. They all experience rapes or near-rapes, which, naturally, they really want all along. When Rand was in her mid-thirties, she depicted Roark's quasi-rape of actress Vesta Dunning in a chapter of *The Fountainhead* later deleted: "What she saw in his face terrified her: it was cold, bare, raw cruelty. . . . When he threw her down on the bed, she thought that the sole thing existing, the substance of all reality for her and for everyone, was only to do what he wanted." And even thereafter, Roark's love for Dominique, Rand wrote in the planning stages of the novel, will be "merely the pride of a possessor." In *Atlas Shrugged* Rand tells us that the diamond band on Dagny's naked wrist "gave her the most feminine of all aspects: the look of being chained."

Pierpont points to Rand's use in *The Fountainhead* of "the boldest example yet of that essential component of the best-selling 'woman's novel': the rape." While adhering to the "school of flushed-pink prose," Rand manages to deliver the "scraping together of these fleshless bones." Though it may be tame and unexplicit by today's Harlequin standards, Mary Gaitskill writes that lots of girls fell in love with "Definitism" (Objectivism) "because of the erotic power of the books." Nathan Blumenthal was first drawn to the novel only when his sister, who had read it, couldn't help giggling with friends over the sex scenes. Screenwriter Nora Ephron recalls that even in the wider culture, "thousands of fat, pudgy non-architects . . . could not get dates during college because of the influence *The Fountainhead* had on girls like me."

Mary Gaitskill reports interviewing a male Objectivist who told her he knew a lot of guys who felt after reading Rand that they had to slap their girlfriends around first and pretend they were raping them in order to have correct sex. Karen Reedstrom, editor of a fairly sophisticated, unaffiliated Objectivist newsletter, comments on Roark's ravaging of Dominique that some Objectivist women don't appreciate such scenes. At the opposite extreme, Bidinotto tells of young Objectivist men more influenced by Rand's philosophy than her fiction, who, from the Randian premise that the initiation of force is immoral, deduced that one must ask permission to kiss a girl on a date.

Rand wrote in a letter that "an ideal woman is a man-worshipper, and an ideal man is the highest symbol of mankind." Ron Merrill conceded that despite Rand's stated opinions, her novels do suggest that she regarded men as inherently superior to women. She was certainly contemptuous of housewives, and in her novels, whenever she wants to convey the nauseating dullness of the average unheroic citizen, she generally makes references to drab and ugly women. Nathaniel Branden remembers her telling him that as a writer she was interested in her women characters only in relationship to the men. In real life, however, she was sometimes unusually drawn to beautiful women. Before the Break, she kept in her desk a photograph of Nathan's eventual second wife Patrecia.

Even in the purely occupational sphere, Rand drew limits to how far women can go in competing with men. In the 1950s, when asked if she had considered making one of the train-drivers in *Atlas Shrugged* a woman, she replied with reference to Dagny, "Having a woman operating vice president is bad enough." In the 1960s she surprised most of her followers when she explained that, for a rational woman, assuming the presidency of the United States would be "unbearable" and "excruciating psychological torture," producing "the most unfeminine, sexless, metaphysically inappropriate, and rationally revolting figure of all, a matriarch." A woman who would seek the presidency would be psychologically unworthy of the job.

"I am a male chauvinist" were the last words Rand spoke in public at Ford Hall, in 1981. Thirty-six years earlier she had written: "Am not a feminist." On *Donahue* in 1979, Rand responded with disgust to the suggestion of a female U.S. president: "I wouldn't vote for her." What if she were better qualified than any man? "If we had fallen that low, I might." But "it is not to a woman's personal interest to rule men. It puts her in a very unhappy position. I don't believe that any good woman would want that position. . . . A commander in chief of the army, a woman . . . unspeakable!"

Peikoff assures us that if Rand had had a choice between Jimmy Carter and Thatcher, she would have voted for Thatcher. Yet this would still be Margaret Thatcher the revolting matriarchal figure, psychologically unworthy of the job. Peikoff has attempted to downplay Rand's view as merely a preference in symbolism, in line with the psychology of romantic surrender by females to males expressed in her novels, but constituting neither a principle nor a philosophical issue. This interpretation is difficult to sustain. Rand does seem to be saying that her fundamental value, Reason, applied to certain facts of reality—human psychology—rules out women as national leaders. Ironically, had this view prevailed since Rand wrote her piece, the coals of economic liberalism in the U.K. might never have caught fire.

Randian Individualism Meets the Gay Man

Are homosexual feelings—as Branden implies in *The Psychology of Self-Esteem* (1969)—neurotic, unhealthy, and so non-integral to anyone experiencing them that one should be able to put some distance between those feelings and the core self, as a first step toward identifying and eradicating the thoughts that generated them? He implies that adolescents flee into homosexuality because they are taught that sex is evil. Here, changing one's sexual orientation from homosexual to heterosexual is just another psychological problem to target and resolve.

It is likely that Branden's view of homosexuality had repercussions. Former colleagues recall Branden's policy during his New York City days of changing his seat in a restaurant if an evidently gay man sat down at the next table. That aversion was unfortunate given the disproportionate number of gays among political libertarians, many out-of-the-closet, and within the Objectivist movement, all very much closeted.

Gay libertarian Roy Childs went to Branden as a client in 1971. By that time, recalled Childs, Branden was no longer blatantly homophobic, but was still of the opinion that homosexuality resulted from some sort of neurotic turn in the personality and could be corrected. In 1971 Branden told the libertarian magazine *Reason* that it remained his view that homosexuality was *not* a valid option. This would have been a source of distress for homosexual Objectivists. As Branden himself wrote in 1994, "When we behave in ways that conflict with our judgment of what is appropriate, we lose face in our own eyes."

At her Ford Hall appearance in 1971 Rand was asked whether she considered homosexuality immoral and if so, why. She blurted, "Because it involves psychological flaws, corruptions, errors, or unfortunate premises, but there is a psychological immorality at the root of homosexuality. Therefore I regard it as immoral. . . . It's proper among consenting adults, . . . legally. Morally, it is immoral. And more than that, if you want my really sincere opinion, it's disgusting." In Rand's view then, five percent of U.S. males should dis-esteem themselves for having engaged in at least one such disgusting, inhuman, immoral, and irrational behavior. Whereas Rand regarded homosexuality as consciously chosen behavior contrary to man's nature, New Zealand's leading neo-Objectivist Lindsay Perigo, himself gay, offers: "From intro-spection and observation, I don't believe volition plays a part in sexual orientation at all."

Some of Rand's favorite artists and writers such as Chopin, Tchaikovsky, Saint-Saens, Michelangelo, Terrence Rattigan, Oscar Wilde, Noel Coward, and Rudolf Nureyev were homosexual or bisexual. But in the interest of art, Rand turned a blind eye. Once, at a Nureyev ballet, friend Joan Blumenthal whispered that she wished Rudolph would quit telegraphing gay signals to other male dancers because it was detracting from the performance. Rand, shocked at her implication that Nuryev might be gay, cited as contrary evidence the prominent bulge in his leotard.

In a 1983 talk before a libertarian audience a full dozen years after the *Reason* interview, Branden depicted Rand's position on homosexuality—a subject on which "she was absolutely and totally ignorant"—"as calamitous, as wrong, as reckless, as irre-sponsible, and as cruel, and as one which I know has hurt too many people who . . . looked up to her and who assumed that if she would make that strong a statement" condemning homosex-ual behavior, "she must have awfully good reasons." In an obscure 1996 interview Branden would retract his view of homosexuality as, in part, a moral problem.

In the late 1970s and early 1980s Peikoff declined to respond to questions from students about homosexuality, preferring to wait until he could have an Objectivist psychologist on the podium to back him up. In 1983 he did have Edith Packer with him for a seminar, and they jointly concluded that "homosexuality is not a rational option," meaning that while past influences and actions may have made one's present homosexual feelings inevitable, to act on those feelings would imply giving in to irrationality. In recent years Objectivist lecturers have been more reticent, cautiously conceding that for some, homosexuality may be either biologically based or at least too ingrained by early adulthood to reverse. But even as late as the mid-1990s, Peikoff was still placing qualifiers on the morality of gay sexuality *per se.* "I've said many times that I think gays are *abnormal* and that in many cases it's *incurable.*" But "let's say he's tried to solve *the problem,* he's gone to *experts,* he's *tried for years* and he can't." At some point he is justified in saying, "It's my life, maybe I've made some *terrible mistakes* somewhere, but I can't seem to get out of them." Once again though, "I *don't think it's an optional lifestyle. . . .* I think it's a *tragic* situation" (my italics). So homosexuality is: an abnormality, an incurable disease, a problem to be confronted by experts, the product of terrible mistakes, and a tragedy. In maintaining such a perspective, as in his *Atlas Shrugged* view of the world, Peikoff has yet to take his leave of the 1950s.

Rand's Eccentric Take on Art

Because Rand's definition of Romantic *art* is based on the principle of volition, it is pretty well restricted to literature. What other art forms can embody the choosing and pursuing of values? This is typical of Rand. Romantic literature is *her* art form, so it should set the standard for all the arts. Kay Nolte Smith and Phil Smith suggest that her aesthetic theory emerged directly from what she happened to be best at, such as plotting, and that *The Romantic Manifesto* is a justification of *her* books.

Ultimately, Rand sees art's only justifiable function as getting the mental abstractions constituting *her* view of existence 'out there' to contemplate and to emotionally fuel one's drive to master one's environment. Joan Blumenthal now concedes that if she were an aesthetician she would accept Rand's definition of art, but would start from scratch everywhere else. But Rand's definition of art—the selective recreation of reality according to the values of the artist—is obviously questionable. Just how is Beethoven's Seventh Symphony a recreation of reality? To say that a work of art selects rather than tries to include everything or that it reflects the artist's values is, of course, to say nothing that is news to anyone.

Much is made in Objectivist circles of Rand's notion of 'sense of life'. Neo-objectivist art theorists Louis Torres and Michelle Marder Kamhi have emphasized that the term itself has a long history before Rand, though not employed in a sense precisely like hers. In his *On Love* (translated in 1957), Jose Ortega y Gasset defined his equivalent term, 'metaphysical sentiment' as "the essential, ultimate, and basic impression which we have of the universe" which "acts as a foundation and support for our other activities, whatever they may be." Rand did read Ortega, and she did own a copy of Unamuno's *The Tragic Sense of Life*. Then there is Thomas Carlyle's term 'a man's religion', or alternatively 'his no-religion'. It is the prime thing that a man takes to heart, believes in practice and feels he knows for certain, though often never put into words, with regard to his place in the universe, and which then shapes the rest of his life.

For Rand, perhaps the most moral landscape is a vista of skyscrapers. Reproductions of Joan Blumenthal's painting *The Kingdom of the Earth*, which features skyscrapers and towers at sunset, were sold through the *Ayn Rand Letter*. Objectivism did have some effect on her subjects. Blumenthal concedes that she painted a lot of cityscapes right up until her break with Rand in 1978, mainly because students of Objectivism bought them. She had come to feel they were empty, a symbol, but to her not interesting in themselves.

Rand makes no distinction in her trashing of 'modern art' between art that rejects conventions and art that rejects the basic premises of art. For her, to truly innovate would be to bring back elements of an unjustly-rejected past. She wrote to silent-era actress Mia May that "the style and spirit of the pictures you made . . . does not exist in the world any longer—and part of my battle is to bring it back." Even Frank Lloyd Wright's heresies had become part of American architectural tradition by the time that Rand got around to championing him.

Blumenthal explains that what Rand liked personally in painting she elevated to the good, especially what she labelled the conceptual style, that is, having clearly demarcated edges and clear demarcations within the form without gradations. In other words, she liked and elevated above all other forms that art which reflected the either-or, yes-or-no, in-or-out thinking style she expressed in her own novels and essays. In some cases though, she simply responded to a given artist and then invented a plausible rationalization, perhaps about how his benevolent metaphysics outweighs stylistic shortcomings or how his romanticism outweighs his malevolent metaphysics, to accommodate that preference. Rand liked the silent movies of Fritz Lang, but she couldn't deny that their 'metaphysics' was objectionable, so she said she admired them for their 'style'.

Torres and Kamhi remark that Rand's implication that all 'painterly' art is irrational is ridiculous. She was merely assigning the label 'rational' to whatever few styles she happened to like. She disliked Rembrandt. Recalls Blumenthal, "What Ayn held against him was the 'side of beef painting'—which is absurd! . . . I walked out of the lecture in which Leonard Peikoff was saying something unpleasant about Rembrandt. I just couldn't stand for it any more." Joan Blumenthal relates that Rand very much disliked impressionism, believing as she did that the juxtaposition of colors into non-defined areas and the intrusion of atmosphere indicated a 'poor psycho-epistemology', a favorite term of opprobrium. But Torres and Kamhi suggest that she was even mistaken about who the impressionists were. She took them for the 'dots and dashes' pointillists of Neo- or Post-Impressionism, led by Georges Seurat, who were actually *against* Impressionism for having sacrificed form to an obsession with color and light.

Rand names Vermeer as the greatest of all painters, but has so many gripes about him that one wonders why. She regrets that he didn't choose better subjects to express his theme of light itself. Torres and Kamhi point out that Rand's nasty reference to 'kitchens' as being typical of Vermeer's subjects suggests that her factual recollection of his paintings was very hazy. Most Vermeers celebrate creative endeavor, whether writing or reading, playing an instrument, painting, or engaging in scientific research. Vermeer's extant paintings are so few that all of them can be found reproduced in single volumes on Vermeer, which Rand could easily have consulted. Rand wanted to see volition glorified in all the arts, and somehow saw in Vermeer's work a denial of free will.

As for dance, Rand sees dancers 'performing the music' with the assistance of a choreographer, completely missing the point that what they perform is choreography which is usually, but not necessarily, accompanied by music. She manages to make no mention of rhythm, one of the central features of dance. All modern dance for Rand is "random contortions, arbitrarily thrown together, signifying nothing." Yet she saw little modern dance and while she implicitly trashes Isadora Duncan, Torres and Kamhi observe that in abandoning staid traditions for more natural kinds of movement, Duncan not only helped pioneer modern dance but revitalized ballet. Rand even insists that ballet cannot project sexuality or any strong passion.

Asked if Rand would get mad at any suggestion that there might be a non-rational element in any of her tastes, Joan Blumenthal replied, *"You could not* suggest to Ayn that anything was non-rational in her; that was impossible." Was there for Rand no non-rational area between the rational and the irrational? No, everything was either rational or irrational.

For Rand, visual art must represent entities. 'Abstract' art can at best be decorative. Peikoff takes the same line: "All art must recreate reality according to certain value judgments, but it must actually recreate a perceivable, graspable reality. A bunch of blobs or intersecting lines on a canvas denotes nothing. It's contrary to the human form of perception and consequently it's outside any category such as art. If it gets woozy enough that you can't tell, 'Is this something, or blurs and blots?', it's out."

Among other anti-modernisms it is the socialist realism of the Stalinist era to which most critics compare Rand's romantic realism. But Norwegian neo-Objectivist literary scholar Kirsti

Minsaas also claims that the Nazi ideology's "cult of an ideologizing art," typified by Leni Riefenstahl's films such as *The Triumph of the Will*, bears a "disconcerting resemblance to the Objectivist esthetics." Rand's ugly commentary on modern painting and sculpture is indeed scarcely distinguishable from that of the Nazi art authorities quoted in Peter Cohen's documentary, *The Architecture of Doom*.

The Mortal Sin of Irrational Taste

How did supposedly rational individualists come to believe that if you like works of art they don't like, then you are evil? Rand's basic definitions of art and of sense of life do not imply this, but tacitly, 'sense of life' came to be narrowed to mean a person's moral philosophy, as felt intuitively rather than articulated formally. For Objectivists, sense of life came in only two flavors: benevolent or malevolent, neither of which may apply in any meaningful way to the real content of good art, which is too subtle and diverse for such crass labelling.

Rand announced that any artist "reveals his naked soul in his work—and so, gentle reader, do you when you respond to it." In this argument by intimidation, the reader is to worry as to whether his response to a movie, novel, play, painting, or symphony might expose something immoral in his soul. Being moved by a tragedy, for example, might be taken as evidence of a tragic sense of life, implying a belief that heroic purpose and effort come to nought, from which it follows that one might as well mooch around and collect welfare.

Fulminates Rand, "The composite picture of man that emerges from the art of our time is the gigantic figure of an aborted embryo . . . who crawls through a bloody muck, red froth dripping from his jaws, and struggles to throw the froth at his own nonexistent face, who pauses periodically and, lifting the stumps of his arms, screams in abysmal terror at the universe at large." Consequently, "I am not willing to surrender the world to the jerky contortions of self-inducedly brainless bodies with empty eye sockets, who perform, in stinking basements, the immemorial rituals of staving off terror . . . and to the quavering witch doctors who call it art." While entertaining in an unintended way, this sort of thing must have led some Rand enthusiasts to look elsewhere for incisive critiques of the art world.

If a student of Objectivism loved Mickey Spillane's *The Girl Hunters* (1963), that was an expression of good literary taste, Spillane's proper metaphysics and style transcending the limitations of his genre. However, none of Rand's associates would dare give any Tolstoy masterwork a thumbs-up. Painter Joan Blumenthal said that while Rand knew much more than she did about literature, "she didn't know much about the other arts . . . She thought that Mozart was 'pre-music'. . . . She thought Michelangelo was malevolent."

Addressing an audience of neo-Objectivists, Kay Nolte Smith suggested that many of Rand's published statements on art imply that to be an Objectivist in good standing one must damn a whole range of artists and works of art, and constantly police one's own responses for symptoms of irrationality or evil. And indeed, improper aesthetic appreciation did become grounds for moral condemnation within the movement. Consequently a great many people found themselves denying, repressing or faking their responses. They saw themselves as thereby championing romanticism or Objectivism, but often were simply dodging the stigma of responding irrationally or having a malevolent sense of life. She relates that a leading Objectivist (probably Peikoff) once confided to her that he liked a popular not-at-all-romantic author, but begged her not to tell anyone.

Smith recalls that Rand regarded Beethoven as a malevolent composer, "and if you admired Beethoven as I and all kinds of people did, she wouldn't come up to me and say 'Kay, you are a bad girl, now go and do something about it', *but* it would be clearly known that 'you like Beethoven, you have a malevolent streak in your soul', and the implication would be that you should be tending to that." Phil Smith adds ironically: "If your ideal is benevolence, there's something *wrong* there."

Taylor recollects that even Rand's dislike for certain minor classical composers like César Franck was copy-catted, one NBIer rebuking his girlfriend for liking Franck, saying *"That* says some-thing about *your* psycho-epistemology." Comments Taylor, "If lik-ing César Franck is an indication that there's something wrong with your head, there would be fertile ground for people to feel 'Yes, I really ought to go check myself out'. There was a very self-critical element to Objectivism, which Ayn fostered. When you'd crossed some line, you'd be told you had crossed it and why. So if you wanted to stay in Objectivism there was a great deal of, 'Oh I see I made a mistake, what was the mistake, how can I correct it?'" And since self-criticism is a good thing, "guided self-criticism under a therapist would be an even better thing."

In 1986 Barbara Branden recalled seeing people who loved Mozart or some other artist on Rand's blacklist "wondering 'What was the matter with me? What have I not yet understood? What's lurking somewhere in my soul that makes me have an irrational response?' It's clearly nonsense now. It wasn't nonsense then. It was a source of incredible pain to so many people. . . . if people had the wrong aesthetic response, something was wrong, their souls were suspect. If they doubted something that was told them as part of Ayn Rand's ideology by one of the teachers of her phi-losophy, it was time to see a psychiatrist and find out what lurked in their soul. I am delighted to see smiles" (among an audience of mostly neo-Objectivists or former Objectivists). "Many people would not have been smiling 18 years ago. I wasn't."

Scuoteguazza observes that because the Objectivist ethics so extols romantic art, all too many Objectivists stifle their real pref-erences to avoid being labelled irrational and, at least publicly, play it safe by sticking to officially-approved works. Result: "a dis-maying uniformity of artistic tastes among Objectivists." In the early 1970s many Objectivists thought they'd found a kindred artistic spirit in the paintings of Maxfield Parrish. At a Ford Hall Forum "someone asked Ayn Rand for her assessment of his work, to which she curtly replied, 'Trash!' One could almost hear the bonfires raging across the country."

Today painter Joan Blumenthal can say that she likes taking a mundane subject as the vehicle for expressing what is not mun-dane. This was anathema to Rand, who dismissed with contempt 'folks next door' literature which presumed to find something extraordinary in ordinary lives. Her appreciation of John O'Hara and O. Henry must have been tempered by disgust at the squandering of their particular literary gifts on non-entities.

Rand claims that the choice of painting beauty rather than ugliness is a moral one. For her, a painting of an otherwise beautiful woman whose face is marred by a cold sore would inspire revulsion and outrage. But surely aesthetics must not be reduced to a sub-field of *any* ethical theory. Even neo-Objectivists Louis Torres and Michelle Marder Kamhi, who basically accept Rand's theory of art, suggest that she errs in citing a cause-and-effect relation between one's implicit view of reality and one's moral values. Sense of life, consisting of subconscious emotions, cannot directly shape one's morals. So Rand's frequent attempts to tie every passing 'irrationality' to a 'malevolent sense of life' or to 'depravity' is wrongheaded. Neal Peart, a strong admirer of Rand, is drummer and lyricist for the Objectivist movement's favorite rock band, Rush. Peart came to reject Rand's dichotomization of the rational Apollonian sense of life, embodied in the Apollo moon missions, and the irrational Dionysian sense of life, embodied in the Woodstock rock festival. "I stayed up all night to watch the Apollo moon landing, and at the same time I was just as excited by Woodstock." Rand was wrong: "There is no division there."

Contrary to Rand's opinion, the fact that one person gives a thumbs-up and another person a thumbs-down to a movie, painting, or novel, actually gives one barely a clue as to their capacity for 'efficient thinking'. Rand insists that anyone who likes non-representational art does not want to think. Yet a criticism others have levelled at abstract art is that so often its sole function is to embody in paint or stone some quite complex verbal theory. Rand wrongly implies as well, remark Torres and Kamhi, that an artist's global take on existence is embodied in and can be surmised from any single work of art.

Rand also insists that an artist's style projects his view of human consciousness, which is certainly true of Rand's work by intention. But Torres and Kamhi object that despite not having proven this as a universal principle of art, she nonetheless deploys it to render judgment upon this or that style or artist, and upon one's response to them. For Rand, from sharp focused thinking come sharp focused paintings, whereas, from fuzzy feelings-driven thinking only wishy-washy unintelligible paintings can result. She cavalierly dismisses all painting from Rembrandt on that blurs or distorts its subject.

Rand dismissed all cultural artifacts of civilization unattributed to individual artists. "All folk art is essentially similar and excruciatingly boring," she explained: "if you've seen one set of people clapping their hands while jumping up and down, you've seen them all." She scorned medieval art as malevolent, stilted, and gargoyle-ridden. To this perspective neo-Objectivist Madeleine Pelner Cosman, author of *Fabulous Feasts: Medieval Cookery and Ceremony* and various books on medical law, responds that "she was just plain wrong." Her understanding of the Middle Ages was superficial. She was apparently ignorant of the medievals' magnificent sensuality, their wonderful flair for the ceremonial, their astounding engineering feats, and their many great philosophical and literary works, not to mention their absolutely spectacular stained glass, pottery, weaving, embroidery, and wood carving. Perfectly normal for the Middle Ages, for instance, were stained glass panels where exquisitely erotic figures in hilarious peripheral sex scenes counterbalanced the Christian central motif. "In fact," concludes Cosman, "medieval medicine, food, law, architecture, and sexuality were stunningly exhilarating."

Her Heart Ruled Their Heads

An emotion that clashes with your reason, an emotion that you cannot explain or control, is only the carcass of that stale thinking which you forbade your mind to revise.

John Galt's speech in *Atlas Shrugged*

In *Atlas Shrugged*, Dagny remarks that "she had always known that an emotion was a sum totaled by the adding machine of the mind" and Galt informs the world: "Your emotions are estimates

of that which furthers your life, or threatens it, lightning calcula-
tors giving you a sum of your profit or loss." Our emotions are
profit-and-loss statements produced by an adding machine. Rand
tells us that her exact view of human psychology can be summa-
rized as: "The head has its reasons which the heart must learn to
know."[3] In *Atlas Shrugged*, composer Richard Halley serves as
mouthpiece for Rand when he asserts, "I do not care to be
admired by anyone's *heart*— only by someone's *head*," and as those
few who live by the Objectivist code, "we are, in fact, the only people capable of feeling." With those statements in mind, Rand's
bizarre utterance on *Donahue* in 1980 becomes intelligible: "I
don't think President Carter has any ideas, *and if so, he has no feelings.*" Rand holds that only admirable ideas can generate
admirable feelings, and since the only admirable ideas are her
own, her ideological enemies can't experience admirable feelings.

Sciabarra remarks upon Rand's tendency to look at the relation between reason and emotion strictly from the side of reason,
as if conflicts between the two could be eliminated by considering
emotion as mere unarticulated thought awaiting articulation and
then manipulation. It was extremely uncomfortable for Rand to
feel something strongly while not being able to defend it 'philosophically'. She boasted that no emotion would clash with her
intellect for more than a day, which may well be true, but this
compulsion to find an intellectually convincing reason for any
emotion could sometimes cause her to turn up facile rationalizations for any idiosyncratic or obscure feeling she might have.

In a letter Rand declares: "*Either* man's emotions are the
effects of his cognitive faculty *or* they are not. There is no middle
ground." In reality there is nothing but middle ground here. Albert
Ellis, who since the 1950s has been developing techniques for
changing thinking in order to alleviate unhealthy emotions, has
always rejected the notion that it is feasible to 'control undesirable
emotions out of existence'. Ellis points out that, for example, if we
dearly want something and look forward to pleasurable feelings of
satisfaction when we get it, it is unavoidable that we will experience some feelings of frustration or disappointment should we fail
to get it. Many emotions have biological roots, tracing back to

primitive pleasure-pain reactions. Our emotions are joint effects of thinking and innate tendencies, so while we can indeed change our emotions by changing our thinking, we cannot do so to an unlimited extent.

Rand in effect restricts her interest in the brain to what makes it unique, the neocortex. In so doing she neglects the fact that the neocortex is a thin veneer on top of two ancient brains, the reptilian and the mammalian. Those two are no less active today than they were aeons ago, measuring every scrap of input from eye and ear and issuing orders. Rand never understood how even percepts are not immaculate data awaiting transformation into concepts, but data pre-shaped by each interacting part of the triune brain. All sensory input is routed through the limbic system, the very seat of the emotions.

Neo-Objectivist Connie Fawcett has concluded that while emotions lie at the very heart of motivation, Objectivism downplays their role in our thinking and tends to neglect the role of subjective experience. The notion that people's motivations can be completely reduced to rational thought disregards how the brain functions. Brain research indicates that when emotional centers in the brain are disabled by disease or injury, rational decision-making becomes severely impaired or impossible. This is perhaps because the limbic brain provides our emotional feelings of conviction—even the conviction that Objectivism is absolute truth.

Eric Mack contends that while Rand rightly rejected certain roles for feelings as self-destructive, her personal fear of emotions yielded "a disastrous view about the ultimate sources of human action." She believed that desires are based on thoughts, when not on rational thoughts then on irrational thoughts. Mack counters that natural desires, interests, capacities, and propensities arise in early childhood simultaneously with or even prior to thinking.

Former student of Objectivism Sid Greenberg recalls that Objectivists were supposed to analyze rather than evade emotions. In practice this meant that they were constantly interrupting their emotions in flight to consider their consistency with the dictates of Objectivism. Greenberg reports that eventually pleasures and spontaneity dissipated or became repressed from the weariness of dealing with them analytically and trying to change them. In Objectivism, pleasures pale in importance next to character and self-esteem building, achieved via rationality.

Greenberg, who questions whether a young adult can be expected to know the source, nature, and meaning of every emotion he is guided by, suggests that those hurt most severely by Objectivist self-examination were the most conscientious, who applied unremitting rationality via excruciatingly intense emotional self-monitoring, expecting to emerge happier, only to find ever-mounting guilt, fear, anxiety, and alienation.

Rand loathed the idea that anyone—especially herself—should ever act on a whim, because this implies acting without thinking. But if, as she insisted, all emotions spring from the kinds of thoughts called valuations, and whims are obviously a species of emotion, then the whim is not thoughtless at all but merely sudden and unexpected. It is not so much whims that Rand cannot abide, but spontaneity. There are few things as sad about Objectivists as their touting of individualism while simultaneously being too afraid of the label of 'whim worshipper' to occasionally indulge in caprice (or to admit that this is what they're doing). Because Rand, and Rand alone, was 100 percent rational, any action of *hers* could be justified by Reason in retrospect, whereas the students of Objectivism would be in trepidation of later finding out that their act was not Reason on auto-pilot but emotional kamikaze.

Neo-Objectivist Walter Donway says that he keeps re-discovering that so much more in life is fixed than most young Objectivists presume, such as temperament (whether one's personality is basically ebullient or mellow, and so forth), one's looks, one's intelligence (before one can do much about it), the upper limits of one's creativity, not to mention the personalities of one's parents. It flabbergasted him how quickly his son's personality was formed in detail by age six. Donway points out that Objectivists have a powerful sense of control over their destiny. "That's fine, but I spent incredible time and energy battling the fact that I wasn't a genius. I wasn't a bold, heroic young man. I wasn't a creative prodigy either. . . . My emotions and drive and a lot of my decisions just kept fighting those battles." Donway says he unnecessarily failed to pursue many promising avenues which didn't seem to fit Objectivist requirements, and almost passed up having a child.

When, in *Atlas Shrugged*, Hank Rearden comes to after being knocked out, he feels "a distant pain in his head, which would have been violent had he cared to notice it." Rand's heroes can reduce pain to the periphery of awareness by ignoring it. In a letter Rand wrote that "no matter how much pain one may have to endure, it is never to be taken seriously . . . as the essence and meaning of life." Rand herself took psychological pain so seriously that she typically repressed it rather than face it, and when she finally experienced acute physical pain, after her cancer operation, she found it so all-consuming that she made others miserable vociferously complaining about it. The word 'pain' occurs an astounding 207 times in *Atlas*, 'suffering' 109 times. Rand disowned pain and suffering—perhaps to deny Russian Communists, liberal critics, or Nathan as of late 1968 any satisfaction in knowing that their evil had hurt her.

'Think and you shall feel', is the old Objectivist line, still maintained by Leonard Peikoff , while Nathaniel Branden has moved on to 'Feel deeply to think clearly.' Peikoff appears to regard emotions primarily as aids to learning and doing, by readily providing meaningful examples of abstract concepts or by motivating productive output. But in actual practice, the Objectivist cult is very indulgent of unanalyzed emotions, as long as they reinforce adherence to Objectivist dogma. William O'Neill points out that for all their talk of Reason the air is thick with emotional commitment around Objectivist utterances.

Passionate writers draw passionate readers. Rand was a predominantly emotionally-based person, suggests Gaitskill, her emotionality like a huge Wagnerian thunderstorm that she tried to fit inside her constricted ideas. Objectivists weren't comfortable with their own emotionality so they viewed it in terms of Rand's ideas, and all disturbing conflicts of reason and emotion were to be resolved by eliminating premises unworthy of a Randian hero or heroine.

Neo-Objectivist Ron Merrill notes that repression of emotions can lead to denial of facts, for an Objectivist a cardinal sin. In the 1960s Rand was already demonstrating an unwillingness to face unpleasant emotions. In her last several years, she seemed to have repressed so much pain as to begin losing touch with reality. Allan Blumenthal asserts that she was "repressing massively."

Barbara Branden, knowing that her husband was sexually servicing Rand intermittently while carrying on another affair full time behind Rand's back, found that the price of living with this secret was overwhelming repression because "you can't repress about just one issue, it spreads. . . . I ended up cut off from everyone . . . there was very little of a personal kind that I could discuss that didn't have strings to the subject I could not discuss." But this was only the most extreme form of everyone else's difficulties in living Rand's philosophy. It couldn't be done without massive emotional repression, that is, the eventually-automatic wholesale stifling of those emotions that a good Objectivist is not supposed to feel.

From *Therapist* to 'The Rapist'

Rand endorsed Nathaniel Branden as official therapist to everyone in the Collective, to root out irrationalities incompatible with the perfect Objectivist character expected of those closest to Rand. In imitation of this model, practically everyone in the wider circle of New York City Objectivists was soon seeing an Objectivist psychotherapist—Allan Blumenthal or someone sanctioned either by him or Nathaniel Branden.

Nathaniel Branden was Barbara's psychologist as well as spouse throughout their marriage. And "what a nightmare," she shudders. "He was. . . . going to help me reach the exalted state where I would be fully in love with him. Confession was supposedly in the interest of my self-esteem" yet "he morally flayed me every time." She says that in the last years of their marriage he was blaming on her poor self-esteem her suspicions of his sexual interest in Patrecia, already on the way to becoming his second wife. Moreover, he kept telling her that, "if I doubted his honor and truthfulness the cause was my own insecurity . . . this while he was having an affair with her," using Barbara's "respect for him as a psychologist to cause me to doubt myself instead of him."

Barbara's best friend from Winnipeg, Joan Blumenthal, says that she exacted from Nathaniel Branden the promise that he would not practice therapy when he moved to California, so many patients like herself had he adversely impacted in New York. Murray Rothbard writes sardonically that while researching *Judgment Day*, Branden wanted his help "in discovering the names of those whose lives he had wrecked."

Joan Kennedy Taylor recalls that in the Objectivist movement there were a number of psychotherapists. There was "a very strong atmosphere of, 'Oh, what a good thing it is to go to an Objectivist therapist and get your premises straightened out'" and "even quite a bit of pressure, . . . mostly from Ayn. She just sort of accepted that this was an appropriate thing to do."

Greenberg relates that the New York City contingent had access to several Objectivist psychiatrists or psychologists, who stressed the building of character through constant self-monitoring of one's emotions in order to determine whether feelings were founded on rational or irrational premises. Taylor recalls that these therapists had gone through the NBI course in Objectivism, among them Roger Callahan and Lee Shulman, who were the only already-established therapists. The younger therapists were more students of Allan Blumenthal. Blumenthal protégé Lonnie Leonard, much to Blumenthal's disbelief and then dismay, wound up seducing female clients. It was Ellen Plasil who eventually took Leonard to court and won a settlement from him. Leonard was last spotted as a Florida beekeeper, his taste for honey presumably still intact.

Dr. Allan Blumenthal—Branden's estranged first cousin from Toronto, who sided with Rand during the Rand-Branden break in 1968—later made a clean break with the brand of therapy Branden had pioneered. Fellow Collective veteran Hank Holzer says sympathetically of Blumenthal's plight, "I would not like to be in that position of having counselled people for years and then change my mind about the value of what I was saying." (The number one therapist with Rajneesh would have a few followers commit suicide on him.) Blumenthal had been slow to see what was plain to Albert Ellis back in the Objectivist movement's 1960s heyday, namely that "if Objectivist views are strictly followed in the course of psychotherapy, they will tend to help the majority of patients feel more worthless and hopeless (if that is possible) than when they first come to see an Objectivist therapist."

Could one say flat-out then that the spread of Objectivist philosophy was thereby creating a ready supply of patients for Objectivist psychotherapists? When I asked Branden this inevitable question, he coldly terminated our interview. When I asked former members of Rand's inner circle Kay Nolte Smith and painter Joan Blumenthal, Smith replied, "Self-evidently yes," and Blumenthal, "Objectivism drove *everyone* to need psychotherapy!" In fact, the reverse was true as well. Libertarian feminist Joan Kennedy Taylor says that most of the 28 people in the first 'Principles of Objectivism' course, with the exception of herself and perhaps a few other friends, were patients of Nathan. Taylor adds that Branden was obliged soon after to stop practicing as a psychologist because of a change in the regulations that left him officially unqualified.

New York City was not unique in funneling 'psych' patients into Objectivism. Keith Edwards, Detroit area business rep for NBI from 1964 until it closed at the time of the Break, recalls that when he first took the basic course on tape, local psychotherapists Roger Callahan and Lee Shulman, who were interested in Branden's theories, had their patients attending the class.

Former Objectivist Ellen Plasil describes New York City's therapist-rife Objectivist subculture in the early 1970s as intense, when one might have expected the Break to have enervated it. Not only were there right kinds of politics, morals, music, painting, interior design, dancing, party decorum, party guest lists, therapists, and so forth, there were books, plays, records, and movies whose creators were not to be rewarded with the dollars of Objectivists. "And on everything, absolutely everything, one was constantly being judged, just as one was expected to be judging everything around him; and, if one was not judging everything that was around him, one was judged on that too. It was a perfect breeding ground for insecurity, fear, and paranoia."

Plasil's book *Therapist* is a memoir of sexual abuse as meted out by Lonnie Leonard. Hank Holzer recalls that other people cited similar experiences with Leonard, and "we know of one case, personally, where, *qua* therapist, he was involved with a patient." Plasil recalls of her Objectivist years that nearly all her new friends were patients of Dr. Leonard, all united by their respect for him. Therapy was the most important part of their young lives and they were proud of it. Objectivism, Objectivists, and Objectivist psychotherapy were becoming Plasil's entire world. In therapy cults, Margaret Thaler Singer suggests, "patients became like siblings, bonded together to admire and support their common therapist."

Leonard's clients echoed his claim that he would revolutionize the entire profession with his contributions, itself an echo of Nathaniel Branden in the 1960s. Plasil confirms something Albert Ellis has wrist-slapped Objectivist therapists for doing, that is, lecturing patients. Often the lectures consumed the whole hour, all patients getting the same lectures. Any negative reactions she had to Leonard, Plasil blamed on herself. This further undermined her trust in the validity of her own emotional responses and judgment, thereby reinforcing dependence on her therapist.

Not only did Leonard reveal the confidences of one patient to another, he used their trust to obtain sexual favors in the guise of therapy. Plasil says of the root of her sexual abuse that perhaps it was Rand's infusing of hero-worship into romantic love, the healthy woman naturally responding to the man most worthy of her admiration and obtaining her sexual pleasure from pleasing such a man. Feminine sexual psychology entailed seeking fulfillment in being used. Following Leonard's first self-presentation to her in the buff, he chided her that a healthy woman would have at least been tempted to have sex with him. If a woman couldn't respond erotically to a healthy productive man, she must have psychological problems. This degenerated into criminally unprofessional 'therapy' summed up by Leonard's adage that "a healthy woman can experience orgasm at the moment the semen hits her palate," definitely not a part any ideological doctrine, Objectivist or otherwise.

When Plasil took him to court, her friends turned on her. One tells her indignantly that Leonard is the best psychiatrist in the world, and because "contradictions cannot exist" (an Objectivist cliché), Plasil's story must be a lie. Another accuses her of destroying the closest man ever came to a god. Plasil concludes that Rand "unwittingly laid the foundation for a cult" in her "separation of Objectivists who were fit to provide the answers, from the students of Objectivism who were qualified only to ask—and the acceptance of both groups of their assigned function."

For several years during the 1980s, a private institution called the American Renaissance High School, where a quarter of the staff were Objectivists, operated out of a Unitarian church in White Plains, New York, 30 miles north of Manhattan. Teachers included Objectivists Andy Bernstein, Herb Grossman, Freddy Schorr, and Louis Torres. Rand's novels were taught in English; philosophy culminated in a class on Rand. Lee Stranahan, a former student of the American Renaissance High School, recalls that when he attended he was required to see a therapist, "which relates to the Objectivist therapy-worship thing." His therapist was also the therapist for some of the school's founders. "Objectivists in New York City, especially at the time, were very *very* much in therapy. . . . Nobody there thought it was abnormal at all. The weirdness of it only occurred to me recently." The last time Stranahan saw a certain instructor currently affiliated with ARI, that instructor was still in therapy. That was when he began to have "that 'the more I change, the more they stay the same' feeling . . . like seeing someone in suspended animation." The number two man in orthodox Objectivism today, philosopher Harry Binswanger, in 1994 sent Leonard Peikoff a fax (purloined and made public by someone), which explained that he (Binswanger) had moved onto Edith Packer's shit list as soon as he had stopped therapy with her.

Psychotherapy for the
Insufficiently Rational

If Dr. Allan Blumenthal, the psychiatrist whose close friendship with Ayn Rand endured for a quarter century, is right, Objectivism as a philosophic system was a kind of self-administered psychotherapy for Rand. This doesn't, of course, rule out the occasional happy coincidence wherein the world actually *was* just as Rand needed to see it. "It could happen," Allan's wife Joan concedes, tongue-in-cheek.

The Objectivist *movement* too began as a kind of therapy for Rand, a kind of group therapy in reverse. The many students of Objectivism in effect treated, through Nathaniel Branden, the singularly depressed Rand of the late 1950s. She had been devastated by the intellectual world's rejection of her vision in *Atlas Shrugged* but was amenable to reanimation by a young people's crusade inspired by that vision. Gradually, the Objectivist movement as therapy for Ayn Rand was transformed into Ayn Rand designating everyone else for therapy.

In a very early journal entry, Rand had written that what is needed "is an 'arithmetic of the spirit'. . . . Show that humanity is utterly illogical, like an animal that cannot connect together the things it observes. . . . The future, higher type of man will have to perfect just this ability" to achieve "the clear vision." Later she would add the conjecture that the root of all psychology "is really logic, and psychology as a science is really pathology, the science of how these psychological processes depart from reason. This departure is the disease." The other half of psychology would then be the return to Reason.

Leonard Peikoff related in 1991 that Rand did believe that whatever the psychological difficulty, it was possible for anyone to eventually identify the source of his problem and resolve it. And even though a certain reaction may be ingrained in your brain, Peikoff insists today, "what is not ingrained is that you should act on it." The point of therapy is to uncover ideas that led to the immoral-self-destructive reaction, eliminate them, and replace them with ideas serving your new (Objectivist) code of behavior.

This isn't so distant from recycled New Age fare that to change how we feel and act, we must dredge up destructive beliefs from our subconscious and replace them with affirming ones. Are you gay but want to be straight? Certainly Objectivism *used to* say: change the mistaken thoughts that underlie your mistaken sexual orientation, and thereby change *it*.

Rand accepted that if one got oneself sufficiently snarled up psychologically, it would be next to impossible to fully understand oneself and professional help might be required to untangle the knots. Nevertheless, Rand oversimplified the process of understanding one's own emotions, and didn't think much of anyone who had allowed himself to get so snarled up. Allan Blumenthal recalls being "appalled by her contempt for those with psychological problems. She would say, 'I don't know how you can work with such people, how you can deal with depravity all the time.'"

Kay Nolte Smith and Philip Smith recall that if you did not agree with Ayn's aesthetic views, that was a blot on your character. They knew "people who were chastised, including by Rand herself, for malevolent aesthetic responses and told to go off and fix their psychologies. . . . You could either agree with her full-out and say, 'My God, I'd better change my psychology' and go to a therapist for fifteen years, or you could hide it, saying to yourself, 'I've got this horrible thing in my soul that I'm not going to let the world see.'"

5

Nathaniel Branden: The Godfather of Self-Esteem

From Nathan Blumenthal to Nathaniel Branden

He began life as Nathan Blumenthal, the adored son in a family of sisters in Brampton, Ontario, on the outskirts of Toronto. Branden depicts his youth as intellectually and emotionally stultified at home and at school, priming him for the opposing extreme of exhilaration he would feel upon reading Ayn Rand's *The Fountainhead*. "When I was a child, I felt at times I had been born into an insane asylum," he would later say. Family life was "bewildering." Rand would later depict family 'irrationality' ('dysfunctionality' in today's terminology) as sadly prevalent and Branden appears to have superimposed that view on his own unremarkable upbringing.

His sense of rootlessness and disorientation, of having no sense of belonging in Toronto or anywhere and of the void seeming normal were feelings fairly common among children of recent Jewish immigrants living in a goyish milieu. He remembers that at age 14 he was socially inept, friendless, and often lonely. Inspired as young Nathan would be by *Fountainhead* hero Howard Roark, like so many adolescent readers Nathan would also absorb the novel's subtext that alienation from unheroic, average people was a virtue and that a longing for human intimacy could only mean that one was lacking in independence. His pre-existing alienation was rationalized, even heroicized. During his teens, Nathan was a bit of a disaster with girls. He recalls endlessly rereading *The Fountainhead*, "with the dedication and passion of a student of the Talmud," 40 times by age 19. He would go on to marry at age 22, at Ayn Rand's personal urging, the wrong girl because she was the first person from whom he didn't feel alienated. She was, indeed his first close friend, female *or* male, an indication of either an anti-social nature in general or an active disinterest in associating with non-Jewish neighbors or schoolmates.

Nathan's 20 years of confusion and alienation ceased the evening he met Ayn Rand in her California home for their first marathon conversation. "As far as I am concerned, I have come home," he remembers feeling. "I am in the first place I have ever felt at home in my entire life . . . a place where only good can happen and no harm can possibly come." Cult literature abounds with such experiences of novitiates when first drawn into the magnetic field of their guru. But there's no denying the simple impact that a female celebrity author might have made on any intellectually-curious young man. Her best-selling novel of ideas had recently become a movie starring Hollywood idol Gary Cooper. And here she was exhibiting respectful interest in Nathan's opinions. Rand would later say, several years prior to excommunicating him as a fraud, that she thought he was a genius from the first evening, and "I really mean genius."

Earlier, in her initial letter of response (2 December 1949) to Nathan's letters, Rand castigated him for his total ignorance of capitalism. "I thought that a man who was sincerely interested in economic and political questions would have studied something besides Marxism before he attempted to argue on the subject." On 1 September 1950, she writes him, not only to bemoan "the present breakdown of America," but also to ask him, "How can I cure you of screaming at collectivists in political arguments when I am still suffering from the same ailment myself?" He had gone from defending to literally screaming at Marxists in nine months. Rand added that whenever she uncovered irrationality in someone she previously had believed to be rational, she became angry at "their betrayal of their standing as human beings . . . the thing which works best in such cases is contempt."

He would soon go so far as to legally change his name to Nathaniel Branden. On his first published piece of writing, a letter-to-the-editor in his student newspaper, he scrawled, "To my father—Ayn Rand," but he would later deny that he'd chosen 'Branden' because it anagrams 'ben Rand' (ben = 'son of father named . . .'). Among personal associates he continued to be known familiarly as Nathan.

Despite his self-depiction as swimming against the political tide at that time, he was actually beginning his university career and alliance with Rand in unison with a deafening crescendo of anti-communist sentiment in the culture around him. In 1949 his own University of California imposed a loyalty oath on faculty— 26 members then being dismissed, 37 others resigning in protest, and 47 scholars turning down academic appointments there. Two decades later Rand would be imposing an anti-Branden loyalty oath on the movement *he* had created around her.

Branden as Cult Leader

By the 1960s, Branden was beating the drums for Rand's fighting creed of 'reason', 'egoism', 'individual rights', 'capitalism', and 'heroism' in their purest, if eccentrically Ayn Randian, versions. It was Branden, already Rand's lover and protégé during the mid-1950s, who took the philosophic ideas scattered throughout her novels and systematized them in lecture format under Rand's guidance. He was the entrepreneur of Objectivism, setting up in 1958 the Nathaniel Branden Institute (NBI) in New York City, where he, wife Barbara, Mary Ann Sures, Leonard Peikoff, and Alan Greenspan would lecture to spellbound Rand admirers. Rand would often help out by being available to answer questions after lectures, and by speaking at more than a dozen colleges.

Affiliated with NBI were the *Objectivist Newsletter,* which became *The Objectivist,* and a book service selling recommended free-market oriented books. This core sprouted Ayn Rand clubs, regional newsletters, and Objectivist social cliques throughout North America and abroad. It was Branden, far more than Rand, who was responsible for widely disseminating her ideas as an explicit philosophy of living—via essays, talks, radio broadcasts and a stable of busy Objectivist psychotherapists whom new Objectivist patients sometimes waited years to see.

Soon Branden, both as Rand's designated intellectual heir and as spearhead of the movement, achieved a guru status only slightly less exalted than Rand's. As R.W. Bradford reports, "Within the movement, his powers were tremendous: he was Rand's partner in *The Objectivist Newsletter,* controlled access to Rand, carried Rand's messages to her followers, and played the part of inquisitor." Branden grants that as Ayn's bodyguard, protector, and defender, "I made myself as ruthlessly implacable as she." It was as if, in the wake of the critical drubbing *Atlas Shrugged* had received, Rand had hired Nathan as publicist and promoter in order to forge alternative structures for articulating the value of her work. Branden then shaped those structures to form his own power base.

Similarly, in the first phase of Bhagwan Rajneesh's movement during the 1970s, it was Laxmi's vision of Rajneesh's mission and her selfless devotion to it that commenced the validation of his guru status. Laxmi was his loyal vehicle, who in addition furnished him with very important organizational ideas. As was the case for Rajneesh himself, writes Mann, it is common for charismatic male figures to get themselves well launched or promoted by one or several women. Rand launched Branden, and, prince of the Blumenthal family that he still was, his sisters came on board as stalwart Objectivists, Elayne as circulation manager of the *Objectivist* and inner circle member, and Reva, as associate lecturer with NBI. It would certainly be a philosophical achievement to convert Florence, his older sister, Rand wrote him. Luckily he did; she being the only one of the three sisters who would not take Ayn's side against him following the Break in 1968.

Contrary to what is really required for independent thinking, Nathaniel Branden points out in retrospect that with anyone who wanted to be truly close to Rand, "enormous enthusiasm was expected for every deed and utterance." This automatized deference at the top served as model for the rank-and-file. Indeed, the real revelation in *Judgment Day* wasn't Branden's love affair with Rand. It was the extent of the belief and behavior-shaping within the cult of personality that Branden wove around Rand. While not *official* doctrine, Objectivists were nonetheless expected to believe that (1) Ayn Rand is the greatest mind since Aristotle and the greatest human being who ever lived; (2) *Atlas Shrugged* is not just the greatest novel of all time, but the greatest achievement in human history; (3) Rand is the ultimate authority on what thoughts, feelings, and aesthetic tastes are appropriate to human beings; (4) Nathaniel Branden is worthy of only marginally less status than Rand, his name ranking with Aristotle's.

The late Murray Rothbard eventually dismissed Branden as "this creep" and "a *potz!*" Of the whole inner circle he writes that "we came to look at these trumped-up jackasses as figures of ridicule." In fact, his own 'Cercle Bastiat' of libertarian associates tape-recorded a spontaneous skit mercilessly satirizing them: There was "George Reisman, playing Branden perfectly, down to his pretentious sing song Russo-Canadian accent, . . . Ralph Hamowy, playing a 'Tina Zucker' character (a rank-and-file Randian female). One of the pervasive themes, of course, was money: Reisman-Branden: 'Be sure to bring your checks and money orders, your dollars or quarters forward,' with Hamowy-Zucker shrilly complaining: 'You've taken all my money'—in therapist's fees—'Mr. Branden; I have no more money.' Reisman-Branden informs her that she can also pay for her therapy sessions by typing and performing domestic service for Nathan." Branden heard about the tape and demanded an explanation: "After all, you wouldn't mock *God*."

Rand approved Branden as therapist for the Collective. Robert Hessen recalls typical sessions with Branden who, today an advocate of a relaxed therapeutic approach, would pace back and forth like a caged panther. Hessen describes these as "hideous sessions," where, at least with others if not himself, Branden "got away with murder, through bullying and intimidation." Hessen still has gruesome flashbacks from those Kafka-esque encounters, where the last thing he would have done would be to divulge anything truly personal. But such reticence was an exception. As Barbara Branden suggests, "Nathan had the power that only a psychologist had. . . . Because you open yourself up wide. When he then starts flaying you alive, . . . that's the most painful, destructive thing in the world."

Nathaniel Branden was the number one teacher in Objectivism as well as its number one psychologist. It's exceedingly difficult to question the beliefs that build up one's own power, and these beliefs became for Branden, as they might have for anyone in his position, a vested interest. What was his NBI power base in New York City like for his students in the mid-to-late 1960s? Sid Greenberg testifies that NBI lectures "had an atmosphere peculiar to church masses, an air of hushed sepulchral solemnity and a sense of worshipful reverence and awe for the leaders and preachers of the philosophy."

For Nathaniel Branden and other ardent exponents of Rand's philosophy, inappropriate behavior was, so they said, an offence, not against a moral system, but against the patient's own life and happiness. In actuality they so vociferously intimidated and denounced alleged perpetrators that it doesn't make sense that what rankled was the harm done to the self. What rankled must have been the perceived offence against the one true morality and by extension its originator and exemplars.

Some ex-students claim that Nathan consciously emulated not Galt but another *Atlas Shrugged* hero, Francisco D'Anconia, whose laid-back aristocratic bearing disguises a soul as tough as steel. From the podium, Branden would point to his beautiful wife Barbara, who managed both NBI and *The Objectivist Newsletter* (which became *The Objectivist* journal). They paraded as a stable version of the Francisco and Dagny match, even as Nathan's double dalliance propelled him toward divorce from both wife and guru.

"It was certainly profitable," recalls Barbara Branden. The 'live' lecture-course fee in 1961 for about 160 students was $70

($350 in 1999 dollars. Werner Erhard's Forum seminars would be twice as expensive). A taped lecture-course, given in 500 cities, was half that price. Many took live or taped courses more than once. By the time the student has "scribbled half a sentence, he rarely can remember the rest of it," one scribbler put it, adding forlornly, "I've taken this course four times already and my notes are *still* a mess." The average *est* Forum participant in the 1980s spent nearly $2,000 (in 1999 dollars) on introductory and further courses, the former akin to buying a razor, the other spin-off seminars like blades for it. The *average* enrollee for Nathaniel Branden's introductory 'Principles of Objectivism' course—the razor—would take that course again and then some supplementary courses like Barbara Branden's 'Principles of Efficient Thinking' or Peikoff's 'History of Philosophy', would subscribe to the official newsletter or journal and would purchase several books from the book service—the blades—perhaps ultimately spending more than $1,000 (in 1999 dollars) before moving on to other enthusiasms.

Barbara explains that during their last 14 years years together, Nathan increasingly became a cipher to Ayn. This man *she* loved with all her heart was always insisting he loved her passionately and couldn't live without her, while blaming on his own elusive psychological difficulties the non-resumption of their sexual relations. For Rand, the situation generated endless conversations with both Nathan and Barbara, and even countless papers to clarify her thinking on the matter. "That he was a liar and a cheat— never occurred to her," observes Barbara. "The whole process was excruciating and heartbreaking, and when the truth finally came to light, it came close to destroying her." However the cover-up did allow Nathan to stay on for additional profitable years as the leader of her cult. He recalls thinking, "I can't let it go. I don't want to. I love it. . . . This was my first and only sense of 'home'. I was not prepared to give it up."

Nathaniel Branden suggests that the 1968 rift in the Objectivist movement parallels historic rifts in other intellectual movements, as with behaviorism's leader Joseph Wolpe versus *its* 'crown prince' figure, Arnold Lazarus. However, in such rifts intellectual disagreement figured at least as prominently as personality conflict. In Objectivism the split occurred because Branden had reneged on what *National Review* hyperbolized as his 'gigolo' duties. Unless he continued to profess romantic love for Rand, and either had occasional sex with her or contrived plausible excuses for failing to, his job as head of NBI was in jeopardy.

Unmistakable cults rather than serious intellectual movements most often provide parallels to the Objectivist movement. When Branden's affair behind Rand's back finally exploded in his face, former admirers cursed him and pinned psychiatric labels on him, Rand accused him of financial improprieties, and he was actively shunned or verbally abused as was anyone who took his side. When Rajneesh's second-in-command at their communal-ranch in Oregon left after being squeezed out, the rank-and-file cursed her and accused her of mental illness and of having stolen hundreds of thousands of dollars from a Swiss bank account on which she had been a signatory. Followers walked across the street to avoid her.

Of the New-York-era Branden, Kay Nolte Smith in 1991 remarked, "He had a lot of enemies, and still does, with good cause." One former student at NBI claims, "He created a living hell in everyone's heart and mind. . . . He wrecked everyone that I knew." She blames Rand and Branden for transforming one friend of hers, an aspiring actress, into an emotionless "mummy." Former inner circle member Robert Hessen, currently at the Hoover Institution, says of those who underwent therapy with Branden in his Randian days: "Everyone was worse off because of it." Former inner circle member Edith Efron, author of *The Apocalyptics* (1984), insists that though Objectivism was ostensibly pro-self-esteem, the Objectivist movement under Branden's leadership and therapeutic guidance was "a destroyer of self-esteem that left a trail of emotional cripples behind it."

Who Created the Cult?

"Despite a lot of lousy motivations, the one thing Ayn never wanted was power," says psychiatrist and longtime friend of

Rand's, Allan Blumenthal. According to Joan Kennedy Taylor, though it may look as if Rand wanted to control large numbers of people, "that wasn't what it was all about. I don't think she thought in terms of influencing." Taylor thought that Rand would never have started up an NBI-type organization on her own. Barbara Branden insisted, "Insofar as Objectivism became a cult, it was Nathan who did that, not Ayn." He certainly had power, "and it doesn't fall into someone's lap." Cult expert Singer notes that most cult leaders *are* male.

Branden in fact sought full credit for what so many in retrospect regard as a cult phenomenon. He informed everyone on the Objectivist mailing list in late 1968 that Rand "repeatedly told me that the creation of an Objectivist movement was *my* achievement," that early on she had been "enormously skeptical about . . . the whole undertaking" and "that no one had ever done for any thinker in history what I have done for her."

While Rand excoriated others for breaches of her morality, according to Collective members, it was Branden who could be really hurtful, sometimes even attacking in group settings weaknesses that patients had exposed to him in private therapy. He had a knack, partly from knowledge he had gleaned in therapy, of knowing peoples' most vulnerable, most painful points, and he would often publicly make some crack, supposedly humorous, that hit right where it hurt most. "He was constantly denouncing," recalled Barbara. "Oh boy, I remember it, loud and clear. Ayn seemed like a pussycat in comparison."

Nathaniel Branden describes in *Judgment Day* just one example of his stormy star-chamber denunciations of wayward students of Objectivism. But as Barbara Branden points out, he neglects to mention that the brutally-dismissed girl was a client of his in therapy. And "Nathan was expelling right and left . . . These kangaroo courts didn't always mean expulsion, but . . . they were agony . . . twenty years later . . . with some people the scars remain . . . It was horrible what was done to people. Awful." Yet during the savage cruelty of those years, Barbara later admitted, she "sat passively, hating what was being done to people, and did nothing."

According to Branden, anyone whose notions of what life is all about have been absorbed secondhand from people rather than firsthand from Objective Reality, is a practitioner of 'social metaphysics'. 'Social metaphysician' became a label the student of Objectivism wanted to avoid at all costs. The irony is that Nathaniel Branden, in his dependence on and uncritical hero worship of Ayn Rand—in his 30s, not in his teens—was as much a social metaphysician as any errant student. Non-Objectivists are typically eclectic in their secondhandedness. Branden worshipped Rand as a sorceress of reason and envisioned a steel cable connecting their souls: "I had come to Ayn out of the void—and I imagined that without her a void was all that awaited me." Resenting Ayn for the problems arising from this self-imposed dependence, his consequent rage at her had to be and was rechanneled toward others, reinforcing the "moral ruthlessness" she encouraged in him and which he redoubled on her behalf to compensate for his diminishing romantic passion for her. Could anyone that destructively obsessed with staying in sync with Rand's assertions so as to stay in her good graces even be capable of an independent take on reality?

"He rewrites his own past," maintains Barbara Branden about her ex. "He talks, on one of his tapes, about how he argued with Ayn about her theory of sex" (that eros is generated by affinity for the other's fundamental values) "in the old days. Not only did he not argue with her, he was shoving it down people's throats in therapy. He was all for it." In consequence, "I have seen too many people castigate themselves morally for an attraction to someone who is less than a hero." This, despite how the theory was helping to create absolute havoc in his own life, ever since Rand had asked him at the supposed end of a planned two-year affair, "Can you think of any good reason why we can't go on this way forever?" and he had responded, "No, I can't," because he knew this was what she longed to hear. Privately, not only did he regard Barbara as something other than a heroine, he came to believe that if being erotically drawn to Patrecia and repelled by Rand was inconsistent with Objectivism, then in that respect Objectivism was wrong. If only his students and clients had known one could pick and choose among one's Objectivist principles as he was doing. Instead, he concedes, "I was betraying what I taught my students. . . . I was learning to lie expertly."

To Edith Efron, "Branden turned into a sort of con man, which is sad because he didn't start out as a con man." She finds it sad too that Branden himself appears to be unaware of how little he really has to say apart from what he had learned from Rand. Says onetime associate Ralph Raico, "Everything he's accomplished has been built on the crumbs from Ayn Rand's table." Even many of his quirks, like saying that though he is an atheist he can't resist sometimes using the word 'God', are inherited from Rand. (Rand wrote to editor Archie Ogden: "I'm not religious but I say: 'God bless you'.") Opined Hank Holzer, "*His* problem is that he believes he's Nathaniel Branden, that he *is* the person he tried to create," though his wife Erika interjected, "I don't think he believes it any more." Common in cults, writes Margaret Singer, is the "formation of a pseudopersonality (or pseudo-identity), . . . a superimposed identity, a cult self, or a cult personality."

We have seen something of Branden's impact on the keenest Randians. But what did Rand inflict upon Nathaniel Branden? Efron feels "something most unusual was done to him." Since "you couldn't go near the woman without being damaged," and as Barbara Branden says, the people who were close to Ayn "were really desperately hurt in so many ways at so many times," Nathan as closest to Rand was by far the most undone by her. In Efron's view, Branden was "murdered by flattery," Rand exhorting him, 'Think of yourself on the same level as Kant and Hegel'. (Freud once called his crackpot friend Wilhelm Fliess "the Kepler of biology.") Branden conceded in 1996 that Rand had so overpraised him that "it was really harmful—and seductive. So long as I was 'her' man, everything I did was 'genius'." He recalls Rand telling him that but for a few minor flaws he was John Galt.

In 1962 Nathaniel and Barbara Branden published *Who Is Ayn Rand?*, a book so gushingly adulatory toward Rand that Branden felt obliged to repudiate it in his 1971 *Reason* interview, a few years after Rand had turned on him with a vengeance. "Miss Rand is very ignorant of human psychology," he confessed. "In *Who Is*

Ayn Rand?, I compliment her psychological acumen. I was wrong to do so. . . . I wish that book had never been written. The portrait of Miss Rand's character it presents is false." But he doubtless believed most of it at the time and it added luster to his status as her protege. Dimitri Volkogonov observes that "in raising Lenin to the very summit of historical justification, Trotsky was surreptitiously also placing himself on the pedestal of history, since he had so often been named as the second man of the revolution." Branden was very much the second man of the Objectivist revolution, and his close association with Rand was such that the higher he boosted her prestige the higher his own would rise.

The psychiatric syndrome *folie à deux* barely exaggerates the nature of the Rand-Branden interlock, or their relation to the tens of thousands within their movement. While Branden did eventually leave all this behind in 1968, it was not because he had outgrown it. Rand *expelled him*, for having concealed from her an affair he had been carrying on for four years to the detriment of their own extramarital affair. Had she been more an exemplar of reason and less vengefully jealous, Branden might have continued to lead an expanding Objectivist movement indefinitely.

Breaking Free?

> It is doubtful whether the fanatic who deserts his holy cause or is
> suddenly left without one can ever adjust himself to an autonomous
> individual existence.
>
> Eric Hoffer, *The True Believer*

When Rand expelled Branden she declared that he would return to nothingness once bereft of her sanction, something Branden himself feared. However, things turned out much better for him than either expected in 1968. Rand had praised his essays on psychology in *The Objectivist* as being "brilliantly original and of revolutionary importance." They became Branden's self-pronounced "major treatise," *The Psychology of Self Esteem*, released in 1969. In yet another surprise twist in the story of the Ayn Rand cult, Branden's book became one of the most enduringly successful of all pop-psychology self-help books. It is still going strong today,

33 printings later, and a dozen or so subsequent Branden books on self-esteem have also sold well.

The word 'self' in the title of Branden's book resonated in an increasingly self-obsessed culture, and his declamatory tone appealed to Rand's readership, only a very small portion of whom were plugged in to the official Randian movement that now officially scorned him. So Branden rode into the 1970s on Randian and Me-decade coat-tails, preaching the self-absorbed message whose time had come. Though initial sales were slow and the book's first, small publisher, Nash, went belly-up, Bantam then re-issued it as a mass-market paperback, and as the 1970s became increasingly 'self'-oriented, the book sold steadily, topping one million copies a quarter-century after publication.

In his answer to a question at a talk publicizing his memoir *Judgment Day*, Branden says he kept from Rand the truth that he was no longer romantically interested in her and had in fact long been having an affair with a beautiful model, out of sheer pro-crastination and the hope that a happy solution might conceivably materialize. However, some observers now tell a different story. Barbara Branden relates that "Ayn had originally intended to write an introduction to his *Psychology of Self-Esteem* in which she would be calling it a work of genius. . . . When I kept telling him she has to be told the truth, and that if he doesn't, I'm going to, he said, 'Just wait until she writes the introduction.'" Confirms Joan Blumenthal, "He was extremely anxious to stay put there until he got that book out." Grilled on this point in 1996, Branden responded lamely that he had believed the introduction "was owed me, after all I had done fighting for her work and all the compliments she had paid my book." Former colleagues also suggest that Branden was carefully cultivating his west coast contacts during his last years with Rand in preparation for a move there following his inevitable expulsion.

In 1950, Ayn Rand wrote Nathan that "I thought I should really adopt you—but I changed my mind when the postcards stopped abruptly and I realized that motherhood involves worry. . . ." One is reminded of Christian Science leader Mary Baker Eddy who, after her husband died, legally adopted as her son the 41-year-old homeopathic doctor Ebenezer Foster, called the 'young puppy' by an associate for so adoring Eddy and obeying her every whim. Eventually Foster was accused of falsifying account books and having an affair with a married woman, and Eddy booted him out of her church.

Branden is working on his third marriage and never started a family. His second wife Patrecia drowned in their swimming pool as a result of an epileptic seizure, Branden not having made sure that she renewed her depleted supply of anti-convulsant medication when she told him she'd run out. He states that they didn't know that going off such medication dramatically increases the probability of a seizure. Yet even back in the 1970s only a very negligent doctor would have prescribed an anti-convulsant without conveying the standard warning about its sudden discontinuance. In *Judgment Day* Branden minimizes the severity of his wife's condition, as if losing consciousness for a few minutes every three years or so weren't dangerous enough. But the autopsy report indicates she had previously experienced a *grand mal* seizure, making even a temporary absence of medication potentially life-threatening.

In the 1980s, Randian workaholic careerism and pure capitalistic acquisitiveness came as close as they ever had to general cultural acceptance. That atmosphere was most conducive to a resurgence in the popularity of Rand's novels and philosophy—as well as their pop-psychology counterparts, to which Branden offices on Malibu Beach and in Beverly Hills, and a lush home in Beverly Hills, would soon attest.

It is perhaps appropriate that Branden and Werner Erhard once appeared together on a talk show. Both are fallen gurus who once created and shaped ostensibly non-religious cults extolling personal responsibility. Many followers of Branden, dispirited in the wake of his excommunication in 1968, figured among Erhard's *est* graduates in the 1970s. Branden has adopted elements of Erhard's self-presentation on stage—such as sitting on a high-legged stool unshielded by a lectern—and verbal Erhardisms such as 'empowerment', 'making oneself right', or preferring to be 'right' than to be 'happy', and having to 'own' one's feelings. Whereas Erhard went into exile on the other side of the world, Branden has staged a successful comeback from ousted guru of the Objectivist Movement to self-proclaimed guru of self-esteem.

Branden as a Professional

Robert Hessen, who became a member of Rand's inner circle in the 1960s, recalls as typical an instance during NBI's first year of operation. Cash-flow problems abounded and assistants like himself were receiving a pittance, 'free' therapy from Branden making up for it. With scant regard for the position of the institute or its employees, Branden went to one of the most expensive men's clothing stores in Manhattan and bought for himself a dozen or so blazing-blue ties for $500, equivalent to $2,500 today. It was a time when, Rothbard recalls, there were 'NB' monograms on every piece of Brandenian clothing, inspired by the 'HR' on Hank Rearden's robe in *Atlas Shrugged*. Branden's signature had expanded to fill a whole third-of-a-page, so perhaps it was not unwarranted that a power-look wardrobe consume a comparable proportion of NBI's operating budget. Tibor Machan was amused by Branden's enormous signature, which effectively announces, 'I want you to know that I think a whole lot of myself.'

Following his excommunication in 1968 and his subsequent move out of New York City, Branden obtained a licence in California to practice *not* as a psychologist but as a 'marriage, family, and child counselor'. It all goes back to his master's degree from New York University. NYU has become a prestigious, world-class school today, due to recent massive infusions of cash allied with a ruthless raising of academic standards, but in Branden's day it was a third-rate place. Branden relates in his memoir that he wasn't even required to write a thesis. Seemingly, such was his brilliance that his advisor felt obliged to remove an obstacle that would needlessly delay his inevitable revolutionizing of the profession. A curious reader might wonder what reputable department of psychology would waive an integral element of its master's program—the original research thesis. Branden doesn't mention that this master's degree is not from the university's Department of Psychology but from its School of Education, a less demanding degree and not much by way of preparation for a career in a clinical psychology. Paul Fussell has depicted the Education degree as "virtually empty of intellectual content," as befits "its dull aspirants." This of course wasn't the reason why the New York State psychological board denied Branden a licence. It did so because it thought Branden had an insufficient number of hours of practice as a (pre-psychologist) therapist *and* was running a psychologically damaging cult. Branden's high-powered lawyer couldn't sway the board.

But what about Nathaniel Branden, *Ph.D.,* and why has he never become licensed as a psychologist in California? Branden's Ph.D. is from the California Graduate Institute (CGI), which many incorrectly assume is part of the University of Southern California. It is no mere diploma mill, for it does have classes and full-time instructors. One could do worse. Sheela, Rajneesh's second-in-command at his ranch commune in Oregon, gave herself honorary degrees from Rajneesh International Meditation University (RIMU).

CGI's repeated pleas for accreditation have been rebuffed because it lacks a sufficient number of full-time staff, a decent library, and other features that students of the thousands of accredited albeit mediocre colleges throughout North America take for granted. In prestige this Ph.D. is, aside from the mail-order variety, rockbottom. Of the 60 U.S. states and Canadian provinces, only California and Illinois recognize it (California recognizes a similar institution in Illinois). CGI is presumably not what Branden has in mind when he refers to the new global economy's "demand for higher levels of education and training than were required of previous generations." Because his doctorate is from an unaccredited school, Branden is barred from full membership in the American Psychological Association.

Branden didn't have to produce a real Ph.D. thesis for his California Graduate Institute doctorate in psychology. CGI let him bypass the authentic research that an accredited Ph.D. program would have demanded. Albert Ellis recalls that Arnold Lazarus, who has headed up departments of psychology at both Harvard and at Rutgers, once met Branden and was favorably impressed with him as, among other things, a fellow atheist. However, after inviting him to speak at Rutgers, Lazarus had a colleague check on Branden's thesis "and found out it really consisted of a group of recordings that he had done years ago on romantic love." The invitation was revoked.

In tiny print inside the paperback of Branden's *The Disowned Self* (1972) the author acknowledges: "The material in this book was presented as a lecture course at the CALIFORNIA GRADU-ATE INSTITUTE in the fall of 1971, and the book was prepared under the auspices of that INSTITUTE." In fact, Branden is CGI's star graduate. As an indication of CGI's pedigree, page 3 of the 1992 course catalog is devoted to a photograph of CGI's vice-president Jordan Packer, Ph.D. One can peel that photo off the glue strips holding it in place to expose another photo underneath, this one of a graying, unsmiling, rather seedy-looking Dr. Packer. CGI has perhaps made less than giant strides toward credibility during the decades since Branden was enrolled there.

A 'witchdoctorate' is what Branden and Rand might have called his diploma if they saw it framed on the office wall of an enemy. Why doesn't Branden use it to obtain a California psychologist's licence? It seems that clients of late have become much more inclined to sue their psychologist or psychiatrist for making them worse off. Insurance against this kind of thing is difficult to obtain for psychologists in Branden's position because insurers quite reasonably believe that sub-standard training in clinical psychology is the factor most likely to trigger such a lawsuit. So why study long and hard to pass psychology board exams for a license to practice that suspect academic credentials would render prohibitively expensive?

Health critic Kurt Butler writes ironically, "Would you like to get rich in a relatively low-risk business? . . . get yourself a Ph.D. from an unaccredited school; there are a dozen or so in the country. With the degree you can call yourself 'Doctor'. Few publishers, reporters, or talk-show hosts will question the validity of your credentials if their source has an official sounding name." Branden flaunts his Ph.D. credential wherever his name appears. Coincidentally, in a Learning Annex catalog promoting Branden's 1997 seminar in Toronto, an ad for the following seminar appears: "Earn Master's or Doctorate Degrees at Home (Faster Than You Ever Dreamed Possible): Were you aware that the average Ph.D. makes an extra million dollars in a lifetime? . . . discover how you can reap the same big financial rewards . . . Profit from even unaccredited graduate degrees . . . enjoy the elevated social status you deserve."

Branden is not licensed to practice as a 'psychologist' in California, where he has lived and worked for three decades. After continually being refused a psychologist's licence in New York State during his final ten years in Manhattan, he got licensed in New Jersey (and Washington, D.C.) in 1969. Because of a limited reciprocal agreement between state psychological boards, Branden is allowed to practice as a *bona fide* psychologist for 30 days a year even though he doesn't live in New Jersey. This allows him to lead his self-esteem workshops around the U.S. and Canada, and to call himself a psychologist on those weekends. The California Board of Psychology disapproves of this ploy but locates it in a legal grey area resistant to court challenges.

A Learning Annex ad for a Branden workshop touts him as an "acclaimed psychologist" and "one of the great psychologists of the century." But the California Board requested that Branden desist from styling himself 'psychologist'—usually "a practicing psychologist" or "a prominent psychologist"—in his books, particularly on the covers. His subsequent books, beginning with *The Power of Self-Esteem* (1992), complied. The awkward term 'psychological theorist' usually stands in now for 'psychologist' on his book covers. Yet Branden found ways to comply technically with the request while defying its spirit. Some of the cover blurbs refer to him as a 'psychologist'. And inside *Taking Responsibility* (1996), he indirectly refers to himself as a psychologist: "Not that this behavior is peculiar to psychologists. I mention my own profession because . . ."

Branden regards himself primarily as a theorist. Therapy, "my best means of doing research," is a means to that end. In 1971 he described how he used early 'psychological dependence workshops' "to see if I could test, or even refute, my own theories on the subject, as presented in *The Psychology of Self-Esteem,* or perhaps find some significant errors. It was the kind of intellectual exercise I like to do whenever I can. In that case, I failed. The theory stands." While such an amateurish exercise may indeed be the CGI way to test a hypothesis, it isn't science's.

Branden's scholarship-to-self-promotion ratio can be judged by the bibliography appended to *How To Raise Your Self-Esteem.* He lists all of his own books with a paragraph description of each, as well as the audiotapes available through his 'Institute for Self-Esteem'. No professional journal articles or books by anyone else are cited.

Branden claims his books are used as texts in universities. This may be true for continuing education classes, where even Shirley MacLaine can turn up on course reading lists. A Branden essay on self-esteem-based romantic love *did* appear a few years ago in a semi-respectable if obscure anthology called *The Psychology of Love.* He claims to do research at his Institute, but the normal business of therapists seeing clients is not construed as research by professional psychologists.

When state legislator Joe Vasconcellos initiated the California Task Force on Self-Esteem in 1987, Branden's proffered services were not enlisted. In 1990, Branden *was* granted a position on the 24-member advisory board, if not the board itself, of the National Council For Self-Esteem. However, it had no government funding and its newsletter even advertised Branden's self-esteem workshops. The Council gave him its award in 1991.

In *Judgment Day,* Branden takes to task two named old acquaintances (now sworn enemies) for their psychological shortcomings, described in detail, not telling us they had been clients in therapy with him. Then in his self-improvement book, *Taking Responsibility* (1996), he takes to task two unnamed clients, described in detail, for exhibiting precisely the same psychological shortcomings. The two are conjoined, in the same order and to illustrate the same point in both volumes. From *Judgment Day* alone, we do not know enough to fault Branden professionally, because he does not reveal that the two acquaintances had been his clients. From *Taking Responsibility* alone, we cannot fault him for unprofessionally divulging confidences from his therapist-client relationships because the clients' names are not published, not in this text. Yet the names of Leonard Peikoff and Joan Blumenthal will jump out at anyone who has read the other book. And most readers who have read both are neo-Objectivists or one-time followers of Rand, people who do know that Peikoff denounces Branden from the orthodox Objectivist perspective and may know that Joan Mitchell Blumenthal is also an enemy. Branden certainly objects when he is the victim of such treatment, as in Rand's published denunciation of him in 1968: "In her article Ayn hinted that I had dark psychological problems about which I consulted her . . . if it were true then it would have been a terrible ethical breach for her to disclose this information publicly." But all the more terrible an ethical breach, surely, when it's a professional therapist publishing confidential information on former clients.

Man of Science?

Lavish praise for anyone regarded as a friend was one of Rand's oddities, and it remains one of Branden's. His involvement with therapists Roger Callahan and Lee Shulman tell us something about Branden's intellectual and professional scruples.

Callahan, from Detroit, is a psychologist with a real Ph.D, who came under Branden's spell in the early 1960s. He sided with Branden during the Break, rallying Branden's spirits but losing most of his own Objectivist clientèle. This support was crucial to Branden, for he was left with almost no friends at all, now that even the strictly cerebral friendships within the Collective had been terminated. Callahan also demonstrated to Branden the lucrative possibilities of group rather than individual therapy.

Branden has incorporated at least one of Callahan's 'New Age' techniques into his own practice. It's a technique that Callahan promoted in an obscure 1985 book, *The Five Minute Phobia Cure*, and since 1992 on a video distributed both by Laissez Faire Books and by the resurrected *Psychology Today*, now a very New Age magazine. Both book and video present some of the silliest pseudoscience ever captured by either medium.

It seems that Callahan borrowed the basic idea for his technique from a chiropractor. The chiropractor had borrowed it from *applied* kinesiologists. Applied kinesiologists should not to be confused with legitimate kinesiologists. Callahan incorporates what might be called the 'tried-and-untrue' applied-kinesiology method for testing sensitivities, and now phobias: one presses a subject's raised arm down before and after introducing some stimulus, such as thinking about a fear, and then monitors any change in resistance offered between conditions.

The actual phobia treatment consists of: tapping 35 times on the inside of the second toe or just under the eyes or on the fifth rib while either humming Yankee Doodle or rolling one's eyeballs, and thinking about one's phobia. I am not making this up. This *is* his treatment, literally. One *could* perhaps look at it as a very crude relaxation therapy, whereby all the tapping during the contemplation of say, a snake, might distract one from responding to it as anxiously as before, thereby weakening the 'snake-anxiety' association.

The process supposedly eliminates perturbations in one's personal energy field, perturbations brought about by some trauma and which in turn generate the phobia. Callahan boasts an 85–90 percent success rate. This claim is based not on clinical trials but on anecdotes from his own and colleagues' patients. Doubtless hundreds of placebo-type cures and spontaneous remissions may have resulted. Branden makes regular use of the Callahan technique to treat and, allegedly, to cure his clients with irrational fears, a major part of his therapy practice.

Callahan's follow-up book *Why Do I Eat When I'm Not Hungry?* relates how Branden convinces skeptical clients they really did have a phobia prior to his administering the Callahan cure, "Dr. Nathanial [sic] Branden . . . has his patients make an audiotape describing the depth of their problems just *before* beginning the Callahan Techniques. That way they can listen to the tape *after* the treatments work if they don't believe what caused the change." In

Tinsel Town specifically and California generally, alleged phobias are often as much an ornament of personality as therapy is,
so naturally when a phobia dematerializes so easily as to call its
prior existence into question, some clients might prefer to label
theirs a *passing* phobia that faded away on its own. But when
your therapist has recorded you inventorying your symptoms
before all the Callahan tapping and rolling begins, it becomes
difficult to deny that you had a serious problem. "The number of
people I have treated is astronomical," boasts Callahan. "I've
seen more people and helped more people than any doctor in
history."

One would expect a self-styled spokesman for rationality like
Branden to distance himself as far as possible from these all-too-
common kinds of claims, even if promoted by a friend. This, however, is the testimonial Branden provided for the book: "Having
witnessed you demonstrate your phobia treatment technique on a
number of occasions, and having *utilized it with my own therapy
clients*, I must tell you that *I am overwhelmingly impressed* by its
speed and effectiveness—*far surpassing any other phobia treatment*
of which I have knowledge. I think your innovation in this field
will stand as an enormous contribution" (my emphases). On the
flyer accompanying Callahan's video, Branden's blurb reads, "A
practitioner who does not test this technique first-hand does a disservice to his clients." Finally, in *Six Pillars* he describes Callahan's
techniques as "revolutionary," "groundbreaking," yielding "extraordinary results" and having "profound implications for all the
healing arts."

Yet how impressed could Branden have been were Callahan
not a close friend? And when Branden says of Rand, "I think her
achievements in epistemology are stupendous," does he mean just
as stupendous for philosophy as the Callahan phobia cure is for
psychotherapy? Another old friend of Callahan's, Albert Ellis,
reacted differently: "Roger came out with this crap about the five-
minute cure for phobia and I told him what I thought of it. He
wanted me to endorse it! It would be the easiest thing in the world
to do a study to see whether it really works."

Branden's other good psychologist friend, Lee Shulman, knew Callahan in Detroit. He too was a therapist to the emotionally afflicted within Branden's Objectivist movement in the 1960s. He also is a Southern California resident and earned a non-accredited Ph.D., as did wife and co-author Joyce, from Wisconsin's Walden University which later did gain accreditation.

In 1990 the Shulmans published *Subliminal: The New Channel to Personal Power,* which pretends to examine the claims of the subliminal persuasion audiotape industry. The industry pushes the notion that inaudible messages such as 'Don't eat any desserts this week' will bypass conscious resistance by virtue of their inaudibility, instead going straight into the unconscious, from where they will influence behavior. In the words of holistic medicine critic Kurt Butler, "It's a sort of homeopathic theory of psychological persuasion; the weaker the message, the more powerful its effect."

Alas, *Subliminal* is as intelligence-insulting and as poorly-written a pop psychology book as Callahan's. It promotes tapes by the Shulmans themselves and by a company called Alphasonics— whose catalog features a full-page advertisement for the Shulmans' book. Alphasonics claims that the basis for its subliminal tape products is some "very important research . . . conducted in Brazil, using new psychological and electronic technology far beyond anything developed in this country." Timothy Moore, professor of psychology at York University, Ontario, and the leading scientific authority on subliminal persuasion, pointed out that the 25 pages of journal article references at the back of the Shulmans' book actually have nothing to do with the thesis that subliminal tapes can change attitudes or behavior.

Branden's blurb on the cover of *Subliminal* reads: "Lucidly written, informative, and provocative, this *valuable book* takes the reader on a guided tour through the world of subliminal teaching devices, *reviews the salient research,* and *brings badly needed light to a subject of great potential importance*" (my emphases). Coincidentally, *Subliminal* gives Branden's tapes and books three gratuitous pages worth of plugs.

Branden has long been drawn to pseudoscientific methods. He advises *every* therapist to become a hypnotist skilled in age-regressing and questioning his patients in that supposedly altered state. Research on hypnosis suggests that it is *not* an altered state of consciousness, as Branden contends. Neither is it reliable: hypnotic subjects often lie or confabulate. Recalling Branden's hypnosis demonstrations, Philip Smith opined that Branden "enjoyed the theatricality of it, . . . There was that thin veneer of scientific jargon around it, but I just think he enjoyed it and . . . liked that relationship"—this referring to the relationship of controller and controllee.

Branden calls his brand of psychology 'biocentric psychology', which sounds very scientific. Yet its emphasis on individual survival and its reliance on Randian assertions unsupported by any empirical data must make it one of the least biology-based of all approaches in psychology. Until the self-esteem fad swept the continent 17 years after Branden's first self-esteem book, he called his practice 'The Biocentric Institute'. It then became 'The Branden Institute For Self-Esteem', and later 'The Branden Institute'.

Current wife Devers, though without psychology qualifications when they met, is now credited by Branden with innovative work in the field of subpersonality psychology and with illuminating the importance for self-esteem in integrating subselves such as the child-self, teenage-self, opposite gender-self, mother-self, father-self, outer self, inner self and higher self. One could imagine countless other subselves requiring therapy. The reader won't find papers by Devers Branden in any journals of clinical psychology, nor by her husband save one in the *Journal of Humanistic Psychology*, where various pro-Rajneeshism articles have also appeared.

Branden's claim to innovation in therapeutic technique is his sentence-stem completion technique, his elaboration upon the 'Sentence Completion Test', a standard diagnostic tool for a half-century. Branden has stated that his technique is a "uniquely powerful tool for raising self-understanding, self-esteem, and personal and professional effectiveness." It has impressed few other practitioners, but Branden's own confidence in it often impresses clients.

Branden's Ideas

Nathaniel Branden, whose summing-up work *The Six Pillars of Self-Esteem* was published in 1994, bills himself as "the father of the self-esteem movement." A review of *Pillars* in *Booklist* asserts that "Branden practically invented the concept of self-esteem and was probably most responsible for promoting it in this country." Over three million copies of his assorted self-esteem books have been sold. Recent tomes include *Taking Responsibility: Self-Reliance and the Accountable Life* (1996), *The Art of Living Consciously* (1997) and yet three more self-esteem books in 1998, relating to daily affirmations, business, and women.

Branden did not invent self-esteem, and his work has not been influential among psychologists. Stanley Coopersmith's *The Antecedents of Self-Esteem* (1967), predating Branden's *The Psychology of Self-Esteem* by two years, is that era's most often cited book on self-esteem within the professional literature. Another influential work is Matthew McKay's *Self-Esteem: Paradoxes and Innovations in Clinical Theory and Practice* (1989). The concept, under the same or different names, was being marketed before Branden came along. Early proponents of self-esteem included Alfred Adler, Gardner Murphy, Gordon Allport, and neo-Freudian Karen Horney. The concept appeared as 'self-confidence' in the popular writings of Norman Vincent Peale and Dale Carnegie. Dorothy Corkville Briggs was writing *Your Child's Self-Esteem* (1970), at the same time Branden was polishing his first self-esteem book. This and Briggs's other book, *Celebrate Your Self: Enhancing Your Own Self-Esteem* (1977) are recommended by a Branden-free Ayn Rand Institute lecture tape on "rational parenting." The essential idea of self-esteem goes back through the centuries. Immanual Kant discussed what he called "rational self-esteem." And Friedrich Nietzsche, employing the terms 'self-confidence', 'self-estimates', 'self-respect', and even 'self-esteem', long preceded Branden in tying romantic love to egoism, as well as low self-esteem or pseudo-self-esteem to altruism.

Branden has benefitted immeasurably from the the self-esteem movement, which has kept alive even his first foray into psychology. And yet that book in some ways represents the exact reverse of the concept of self-esteem which became so popular. The self-esteem which became influential in education and elsewhere means giving a child trophies for playing on a baseball team, despite a winless season and a lack of individual talent. Getting people to like themselves *prior* to any improvement in performance is the popular trend.

By contrast, Branden's first book is a predictable development of Rand's ideas. In the early 1940s Rand had written in letters that competence is "the test virtue which determines the whole character of a person . . . the only thing I love or admire in people. I don't give a damn about kindness, charity, or any of the other so-called virtues." Branden latched onto ability as the core of character and the term 'self-esteem' because it was a key virtue Rand was pushing in *Atlas*. To Rand self-esteem means career accomplishment without apology. Rand saw poor self-esteem as a result, not of extending oneself past one's level of competence, but of not extending oneself or not being duly rewarded for having done so. Within Objectivism, the assumption seems to be that self-esteem can only be earned by performance.

Some of the positions taken in *The Psychology of Self-Esteem* would certainly jar with the popular ethos of the 1970s and 1980s. Branden blames the psychological ills of children from deprived backgrounds on the children themselves, by virtue of their evident choice not to think clearly about reality. (The Brandens faced no such challenge: their expensive U.S. college educations were lavishly subsidized by wealthy parents or relatives, so much so that they had the time and money to often play hookey and go see four movies in a day). As for adults, "an *unbreached* determination to use one's mind to the *fullest* extent of one's ability, and a refusal *ever* to evade one's knowledge or act against it" is "the *only* possible basis of *authentic* self-esteem" (my emphases). A hectoring and perfectionist tone pervades all 254 pages.

Political correctness aside, one might well ask: Are Branden's *types* such as the "dope-addicted dwarf," "the crippled lesbian," "the helpless scatterbrain," and "the frightened slut," really deserving targets of Rand-style tirades against human depravity?

There's even, "the vicious little sadist browbeating her troop of girl scouts." (She will reappear in another Branden book 26 years later.) Do parties at which people get over-refreshed serve "no other purpose than the expression of hysterical chaos, where the guests wander around in an alcoholic stupor, prattling noisily and senselessly, and enjoying the illusion of a universe where one is not burdened with purpose, logic, reality, or awareness"? Are all picnics, coffee klatches, charity bazaars, and lying-on-the-beach vacations deserving of his utter contempt as rituals of mindless boredom? (Branden's Objectivist parties were desiccated, joyless affairs, everyone intent on expressing nothing that might be construed as 'not rational' by Rand's definition of rationality.)

Apart from the tone of *The Psychology of Self-Esteem* and its dogmatism, what especially bothers Albert Ellis, founder of REBT, is the book's theme that true self-esteem can accrue only from intellectually-centered achievement without which no true self-acceptance is possible. For Ellis, a life of any kind of achievement, if that's what a person prefers, would obviously benefit from the launchpad and refuge of basic self-acceptance—in order to defuse otherwise paralyzing anxieties and failures along the way. After Ellis scolded Branden in print for this omission, Branden began emphasizing self-acceptance as crucial. In fact, in *Six Pillars*, Branden concedes that, "Without self-acceptance, self-esteem is impossible."

Branden's first solo effort, is so Objectivistic that the Ayn Rand Institute, which adheres to every sentence of Ayn Rand as gospel and despises Branden for besmirching Rand's reputation in *Judgment Day*, reluctantly grants that *The Psychology of Self-Esteem* contains little if anything to complain of. As Branden's later efforts become less and less judgmental, less and less Randian, they became increasingly banal. *The Romantic Love Question and Answer Book* (1983), later re-titled *What Love Asks of Us*, was co-authored with wife Devers and could be mistaken for a collection of Ann Landers columns.

In 1993 *New Woman* magazine ran a series of columns on women and self-esteem by "Nathaniel Branden, Ph.D." He begins his column in the September issue with a Randian

Nietzscheanism: "The first love affair we must have is the love affair with ourselves." This he puts in even more extreme form in *Taking Responsibility* (1996): "The first love affair we must consummate successfully . . . is the love affair with ourselves. Only then are we ready for a relationship with another."

Today Branden treads a fine line with respect to Ayn Rand's admirers. He must disown enough of Rand to justify their Break, but not so much as to alienate his readership and clientèle or pull the Randian rug out from under his own theorizing. He has assimilated just enough New Age vocabulary to stay au courant, without going too far for his Randian-libertarian following; *Pillars* is peppered with 'toxic', 'dysfunctional', and 'empowerment'. He has also picked up Hubbard's and Erhard's penchant for referring to their respective therapeutic techniques as 'technology'.

Branden is often confronted by monsters of his own making. He bemoans with exasperation that his present-day clients with an Objectivist background sometimes "speak to me with guilt of their desire to be helpful and kind to others." Yet this is precisely what he should have expected: it's the inevitable fallout from Rand's *The Virtue of Selfishness* (1964), which has sold more than a million copies. Branden wrote five of the 19 essays in that book. Whether or not he receives royalties from its sales, he has profited from the resulting familiarity with his name.

Branden is the originator of what he terms 'the Muttnik principle'. This is his idea that the fundamental pleasure we receive from other living beings, for example from his dog Muttnik, derives from their capacity to reflect back to us some of our own preferred (and hopefully real) characteristics, like trustworthiness or friendliness. Is it pure narcissism that Branden sees so much Branden even in the eyes of a pet? The Randian source of this idea is obvious, and it may have been suggested by her theory of art. As art mirrors an abstract philosophy of life in its concrete representations, so others mirror our abstract conceptualization of ourselves in their concrete responses. "Every aesthetic choice made by the artist, every aesthetic experience of the responder, is a psychological confession," Branden taught in 1967 (lecture 11), as is our every choice of lover, friend, or acquaintance, our every response to worthy or unworthy persons.

Nathaniel Branden, official Objectivists, Scientologists, Christian Scientists, Neuro-Linguistic Programmers, and sundry New Age therapists all believe that ameliorating one's emotional life and personality is almost entirely a function of rooting out self-defeating cognitive content and replacing it with life-affirming content. Recent research suggests that biological heredity contributes at least as much to personality as do environmental factors that are at least in principal manipulable. So a large proportion of clients of 'think better thoughts' gurus may actually find their self-esteem diminished by inevitably failing at 'proven' programs to raise it.[1]

Peter D. Kramer suggests that "a person with a visceral sense of low self-worth will take on negative beliefs about the self, in order to make sense of the bad feelings," the reverse of the usually assumed causality. Evidence for this is the striking success of the drug Prozac in turning low self-esteem to high self-esteem practically overnight by elevating serotonin levels and in maintaining that change for as long as the drug is taken. Kramer concludes that the "the efficacy of medication is evidence that low self-esteem exists as a state of the neurons and neurotransmitters."

Can there be there such a thing as too much self-esteem? Branden replies that like "health, or happiness, or well-being of any kind. . . . You can't have too much of it." But there must surely be optimal levels for any biologically-based value, and even glowing health, happiness, and well-being may be inappropriate to a wide range of unfortunate circumstances, so it must be possible to have too much self-esteem. In 1989 the late Murray Rothbard remarked upon the quandary this presents in the case of Branden himself: "Old Branden or New Branden, Randian shrink or Biocentric shrink, student or Ph.D., young or old, he's still the same pompous ass, the same strutting poseur and mountebank, the same victim of his own enormously excessive self-esteem."

What Has Branden Learned?

"I am not kind, Vesta," warns Howard Roark explicitly in a chapter dropped from *The Fountainhead,* and implicitly elsewhere in the novel. Young Nathan read the book more than 40 times, all but memorizing it, and adopted Roark as a role model. Branden does imply it is his own character that makes him resistant to the idea of sometimes putting another's interests ahead of one's own, a practice he and Rand castigate as self-sacrifice. He confided in 1994 that current wife Devers has informed him that he never learned "kindness that is not a matter of mood or convenience, . . . kindness as a basic way of functioning."

There is evidence that Branden is constitutionally selfish in the dictionary sense. One example is a personal anecdote Branden tells in *The Art of Living Consciously.* He intends it to illustrate how heightened consciousness can resolve problems, but it really only draws attention to how Brandenian selfishness generates them. Branden admits that for 17 years every morning he had been spilling coffee on the kitchen floor, leaving often-difficult-to-remove stains, despite 17 years of complaints and importunings from his wife about her having to clean up after him. Only when she finally summoned up enough nerve to shame him into cleaning up after himself and agreeing to pay a huge fine every time she has to do it does he bother to take a few moments to consider why he's always spilling. Almost instantly comes an Archimedian 'Eureka!': coffee displaced onto the floor = coffee in mug past the three-quarters-full mark. Branden doesn't have a steady hand. Ingenious solution: fill the mug only three quarters full! He concedes that he never drank more than half a cup anyways. Not lost on alert readers is a glaring lesson, but it's about how some people are so intransigently selfish that they are all but incapable of even momentarily setting aside their self-preoccupation to resolve an elementary but aggravating problem that *they* have been creating for a supposed loved one on a daily basis for decades.

Rand's view, and thus Branden's view, was that a benevolent neutrality should prevail pending one's judgment of another person's character; upon judgment, one can knowledgeably deal with the person according to one's own long-term self-interest. But true kindness is never so calculating as this, nor so ready to become its opposite. One wonders if Branden's lack of kindness helped drain his Objectivist movement of even a non-self-sacrificing benevolence, which he concedes in 1995 was rarely evident in NBI teachers or students. He would write in 1997 that leaders don't realize the extent to which they are role models. "Their smallest bits of behavior are noted and absorbed by those around them . . . and are reflected throughout the entire organization by those they influence." NBI absorbed and projected its leader's core unkindness and unbenevolence, producing a cultish atmosphere of, as Branden put it later, "us giants against all them pygmies."

One might think that an adherent of an egoist philosophy that celebrates self-esteem would be likely to encourage high self-esteem. Not so Rand's moralizing egoism, according to both Edith Efron and Allan Blumenthal. Even Branden confides that sometimes "it breaks my heart a little when I get an Objectivist for a client, and he says, 'I've got poor self-esteem, I'm immoral: I must be or else I'd have good self-esteem.' . . . nobody ever improved by telling himself he was rotten—or by being told he was rotten. And boy, is that something Objectivists need to understand." As Branden notes, it is bad enough to suffer from low self-esteem without piling onto it the self-reproach that comes from positing one's own immorality as the cause.

Referring to his second book *The Disowned Self* (1972), Branden revealed in 1984 that it was partly an attempt to get former NBI students to reconsider the ideas about mind and emotion he and Rand had instilled. He avers that his now more-human approach "is already present in *The Psychology of Self Esteem*," but in 1989 he conceded the inappropriate moralism underlying his entire argument in that book. As early as 1971, in a *Reason* magazine interview, he had granted that in spite of his past claims to the contrary, there *is* a "very powerful bias against emotions in Objectivism. . . . I encouraged my own students to fear their own emotions, to distrust themselves," thereby inflicting psychological damage. He apologized to readers of *Who Is Ayn Rand?* and former students at NBI "for perpetuating the Ayn Rand mystique" and "contributing to that dreadful atmosphere of intellectual repressiveness that pervades the Objectivist movement," its members "endlessly worrying about whether or not they are being 'good Objectivists', endlessly watching others for signs of 'deviation'." Yet 18 years later in *Judgment Day*, Branden, as former leader of the Objectivist cult, surely missed an opportunity to take *full* responsibility for Randian attitudes *he* had adopted and passed on to his followers, after having condoned the expression of those attitudes in Rand herself. *Taking Responsibility* is the title of a Branden book, yet in 1996 he would seek safety in numbers, declaring that "we were *all* both meat and meat-grinder—victim and executioner" (my italics).

In the 1980s Branden revealed that even long after Objectivism's heyday, Randians were still coming to him for therapy so as to "become the masters of repression needed to fulfill the dream of becoming an ideal objectivist." When he refused to aid and abet that goal, and observed his patients' resulting confusion and dismay, he found it "hard to keep from smiling a little." His admission is unnerving, despite the benevolence he imputes to it. It was he, after all, more than anyone, who by treating Rand's novels as sacred texts transformed her inhuman and absolutist heroes into explicit role models.

Branden's former colleagues point to how little of his dark side he exposes in *Judgment Day*. Robert Hessen suggests that what he does expose is just enough to convince readers that he is self-critical, thereby lending credibility to his attacks on former associates. But while he drowns self-criticisms in a bubblebath of elaborately-detailed mitigating circumstances, he completely drains the tub on those he knows don't like him. "In even the smallest of his failures, he presents a lengthy and presumably understandable and rational context for his own actions," observes Barbara Branden. "For anyone else, and most especially including Ayn, there's no context whatever . . . only *he* has context. And that was always true of him."

A similar exercise in 'self-criticism' took place in the journals *Liberty* and *Free Inquiry* where he reviewed the 1985 book *Therapist*. Its author Ellen Plasil was sexually abused at the hands

of Lonnie Leonard, the most charismatic Objectivist therapist in
the 1970s. Naturally she concentrates her indignation on him, but
she expresses some anger as well at Dr. Allan Blumenthal, senior
Objectivist therapist. Blumenthal apparently hadn't been able to
believe that Leonard was capable of the sexual predation he was
accused of and so didn't intervene on her behalf. Branden pro-
ceeds to compare himself, not with Leonard or Blumenthal, but
with Plasil—who, in accusing Leonard, is herself accused by
Leonard's other clients of "causing irreparable harm to a great
man" (just as Branden had been accused of harming the great Ayn
Rand). Branden grants that he and Rand did "help to create the
kind of subculture in which irrationality and inhumanity could
exist," but mainly inasmuch as he helped "to launch Dr.
Blumenthal's career." And *that* is what constitutes Branden's
admitted "bad judgment." But if Blumenthal trained and mis-
judged Lonnie Leonard, it was Nathaniel Branden who drafted,
founded, and built the therapeutic cult of Objectivism. And as he
observed in 1996, "The culture of an organization is determined
more by the Chief Executive Officer than by any other force," the
CEO constituting "the ultimate role model."

It had been Branden who promoted the idea that Objectivist
women should hero-worship and fall in love with living male
paragons of Objectivism, a line Lonnie Leonard simply pushed
somewhat further. Rand's concept of woman as man-worshipper
"always made me want to crawl under a rug," groans Barbara
Branden. She remembers Nathan "telling people, in therapy and
out, that if a man wasn't half in love with Ayn Rand it was a serious flaw of self-esteem. And a woman who wasn't half in love with
him also had a serious lack of self-esteem. It was excruciatingly
embarrassing."

Branden eventually confessed that, in having prescribed *Atlas
Shrugged* to young people for more than a decade, he had been
inadvertently condoning its "heroic vision of emotional repression," and its depiction of "an adversarial relationship to one's
emotional life as admirable." He would write in 1994 that "running through Objectivism was a strong but unadmitted condemnation of emotions (which I denied . . . vigorously . . .)." He now

advises instead that one "feel deeply to think clearly," an unacknowledged paraphrasing of Samuel Taylor Coleridge's, "Deep thinking is attainable only by a man of deep Feeling."

On the part in *The Fountainhead* that has Roark ruthlessly suppressing the emotional pain wrought by having to work as a quarry driller because no one wants him as an architect, Branden comments in *Judgment Day* that his adolescent self *longed* to be capable of that. And sadly, by his late twenties, he had become a master at it. He also believed that the rest of the Collective should follow suit. Ignoring his own suffering, he had little patience for theirs. Branden elaborates in 1996 that having had so many Objectivists as therapy clients, he knows that "this paragraph or its emotional equivalent, is written into the psyche of a great many people." Especially since the novel is first read almost exclusively during adolescence—a fragile stage whose tumult of changes virtually guarantees everyone a share of profound emotional hurts—to absorb a Randian contempt for one's own unheroic feelings and compassionate impulses can be psychologically damaging. Branden confesses that the above passage led quite naturally to an awful lot of later problems in his life and probably did so for many others. In *Atlas Shrugged* Rearden forbids himself any expression of the emotional pain in his life whenever he's with his lover, Dagny, because that could only be a contemptible plea for pity. When Dagny temporarily quits her job in angry frustration and retreats to her cottage, she adamantly refuses to indulge a scintilla of her emotional agony, which she contemptuously likens to a wounded stranger dragging her down. Branden, the therapist who long upheld such Randian heroes as role models for real life, now concedes that they do make an unhealthy impression on readers.

Branden's love affair with himself continues. In November 1996 he gave a talk in California to young neo-Objectivists, taped and marketed by Laissez Faire Books. For those interested in the various historic arguments for the existence of God as well as the humanist refutations thereof, Branden manages to recommend the only philosophy textbook in the world that quotes Nathaniel Branden (on Randian egoism), *and* has a chapter on the arguments pro and contra God. It's by John Hospers, who had come to his aid following his excommunication by Rand. Cited second rather than first—only out of modesty, quips Branden—is his own 24-hour-long audio-tape set of *Basic Principles of Objectivism*, the infamous 20-lecture 1960s course, now sold by Laissez Faire Books for $197. Surely his California audience and later tape purchasers would be mainly students who would likely prefer to spend $5–20 for one of the dozens of books devoted exclusively and more authoritatively to the subject, also thereby avoiding the crippling moralism which, Branden concedes, pervades his work prior to 1971.

In a trade journal article publicizing *Judgment Day*, Branden speaks of how his publisher insisted upon looking at his life as non-stop theater. Barbara Branden boils over at the very idea. "I don't know what dimension he lives in where shattered people" including Ayn Rand, are theater. ("Ayn wants you dead!" Barbara melodramatizes during the time of the Break. Ayn was "plotting my annihilation," hyperbolizes Nathaniel Branden in return.) Kay Nolte Smith suggested that his view of his life as theater may help compensate for his playwright manqué status. Rand once wrote in a letter that Nathaniel Branden was going to write the film script for *Atlas Shrugged*. In 1968 he tells *Objectivist* subscribers in a post-Break letter that he had intended to found an organization NBI Theater—that "would pave the way for the production of . . . future plays of my own," after first establishing an audience with Rand plays.

Says Kay Nolte Smith, "Nathan is a great showman. That's his real talent." According to sociologist Ted Mann, describing Rajneesh: "The man was clearly a master showman; many saw him as a master therapist." Barbara Branden writes that on several Saturday evenings in 1967, despite his whole existence at that point having become a tissue of lies, her estranged husband was rehearsing his role as John Galt for a recording of the Galt speech, with Ayn and Patrecia and the Collective as audience. In *Two Girls, Fat and Thin,* Mary Gaitskill could not resist the farcical, and in their climactic confrontation, Anna Granite (Ayn Rand) dresses down Beau Bradley (Branden): "You have betrayed the principle of matching components!" she screamed. "Unless you can give me a rational reason for this treachery, you are my enemy for life—for life!"

Branden seemingly still can't find much other than Rand's work to inspire him. In 1983 he told a neo-Objectivist and libertarian audience that he doesn't have a very happy view of American culture and spends time feeling badly about it. "I wish *desperately* that I knew more people that I could like or respect or admire than I do," he laments. "I wish *desperately* that there were more cultural and artistic events that I could personally get excited by." In *Six Pillars of Self-Esteem* he decries the absence of worthy models in contemporary society, declaring that we are "living in a moral sewer." This is pure Rand, after 26 years of separation. He and Rand, his epochal work and hers, tower over the rest of a pitiful American culture like a two-legged colossus over a moral and artistic wasteland.

Still,what would the Nathaniel Branden of the 1980s and later say to Randian true believers who maintain that they can prove all Rand's propositions? "The hell you can! . . . I know where the gaps are. And so can anyone else—by careful, critical reading. It's not all that difficult or complicated." But it's not as if Branden experienced a revelation upon rereading Rand's texts following his expulsion. He is in effect conceding that he knew all along that a number of Rand's propositions were dubious and that there were significant gaps in her philosophical 'system'. This, however, is the opposite of the impression he had left his NBI students with.

When the Association of Objectivist Businessmen (AOB) reconstituted itself several years ago to promote Objectivism in the business community and to foster business support for the Ayn Rand Institute, Branden joined, perhaps for the mischief of it. This belated and perhaps only half-serious attempt to re-forge old ties foundered when AOB published its membership list. The resulting howls of outrage from hardline Randian loyalists exacted an apology from AOB's president, who promptly refunded Branden's dues and barred him for life. The Objectivist cult mentality of the 1960s was still monstrously alive and kicking in the 1990s, and ready to turn on its Dr. Frankenstein (Ph.D.).

6

Leonard Peikoff:
From Serf to Pontiff

Finding His Guru

When Leonard Peikoff first met Ayn Rand in 1951, he says he experienced "total awe, as though I was on a different planet." He thought to himself, "There can't be such a person as this! This is inconceivable!" Rand convinced him that very night that philosophy is a science, with objective, provable answers to its questions. He gave up his pre-med studies and decided on philosophy as a career. The future Objectivist Pope was 17.

Nathaniel Branden claims to have correctly predicted in 1968 that only Leonard would stick by Rand to the end, never having developed a post-adolescent identity apart from her. Barbara Branden speculates that if he had not found Ayn Rand, "he would have found another guru. He needed a guru and he still has one." In 1998, the maroon convertible parked at his suburban brick ranch house in Irvine, California, sported vanity licence plates that read "AYN RAND."

A *roman à clef* by Kay Nolte Smith, *Elegy for a Soprano* (1985) tells of a tyrannical diva with cult followers who worship her. She winds up being murdered by an old friend whose daughter, under the opera great's spell, has redirected her life to musicianship, which she actually has little talent for. The likely parallel with Rand's circle is Rand's redirecting of Peikoff's life from medicine to philosophy, that is, to Objectivism (plus other philosophies as bent through the Objectivist lens). *Elegy:* "It's wonderful to make a child think music [philosophy] is better than any other career, isn't it? More worthwhile? The only thing to do? To convince her she has real musical [intellectual] ability when she doesn't . . . She knew perfectly well that Jenny [Lenny] was just an ordinary piano student [intellect]. But she convinced her she was special anyway."

Philosopher John Hospers was a college professor in his early 40s writing philosophy texts when he first met Rand. In contrast, Nathan was 19, Barbara was 20, and Leonard Peikoff only 17. Peikoff was introduced to Rand by Nathan and Barbara. Starstruck and with a far more malleable philosophic standard than Hospers, Peikoff and the Brandens were all hypnotized by Rand's charismatic intellect. As Barbara Branden put it many years later, they learned to stifle reservations about her seemingly rational arguments rather than suspend judgement pending further inquiry.

Nathaniel Branden recalls how close Peikoff came to the abyss on occasion, suffering two or three temporary 'excommunications' across the years. In effect he was placed on probation, but his worship of Rand never faltered, and he was always readmitted. One near-excommunication resulted from his not having adequately stood up for Rand in his philosophy classes. Branden recounts that it was treated as a moral offence "more serious than I can begin to communicate to you now. He went away in a semi-exile to Denver for a year or two to teach. I'm not very proud to say that I was present and participated in the evening when he was read the riot act . . . after communicating to him what a disgrace and a failure he was . . . he was so crushed . . . it's horrifying to tell you this. . . . someone suggested to Ayn that maybe she's underestimating how seriously Leonard is devastated and we don't know what he might do in this state, and that I should go to his apartment to comfort him and help put it in some kind of perspective." Psychologists hold that membership in a group is all the more highly valued when one has to go through hell to obtain it.

Professor of philosophy Tibor Machan to this day acknowledges a great intellectual debt to Rand despite the way he was treated by her, by Nathaniel Branden, and by Peikoff. Machan, in a fit of youthful peevishness had mailed a not-very-nice letter to Rand because of her curt response to a prior letter. He apologized, but his excommunication was final. Then in 1965, not realizing that Peikoff was still tied in with NBI despite his teaching far away at the University of Denver, Machan phoned Peikoff to ask if they could meet during spring break to discuss a philosophy paper, and he agreed. With a friend, Machan drove 1,100 miles from the west coast to Denver, whereupon he called Peikoff, only to be told that "he would not see me because I had deceived him by not telling him that I was persona non grata with NBI." The last thing Peikoff wanted while on probation with Rand and Branden was to incur their wrath. Thus did Machan's 2,200 miles of driving go for naught.

In contrast to Ayn Rand's first choice as designated intellectual heir, her second choice does have a recognized Ph.D. (1964), in philosophy from New York University. And in contrast to older cousin Barbara Branden's experience at UCLA, Leonard Peikoff encountered no persecution from Rand-hating philosophy professors. "I spoke in college very loudly for my views at the beginning, and got thoroughly known," he explains. "Therefore I sailed through with high grades, sometimes undeserved." Professors "were standing on their heads trying to prove how fair they were." One was philosopher Sidney Hook, a dedicated anti-Communist but equally as dedicated a social democrat, for whom Leonard became a favorite student.

An Objectivist student once asked Peikoff what he had learned from his graduate school marathon. "It's hard to put in ten years and gain nothing," he replied, "but it's minimal relative to the time and the money involved. I learned, you know . . . *something.*" In 1995 he took a harder line still, declaring that "A Ph.D. today, and in the last half-century, is a means of destroying the minds of the students."

When asked to compare philosophical conversations with Ayn Rand to the experience of studying philosophy at a large university, Peikoff indulged his habit of sprinkling philosophical conversations with references to Nazi atrocities, replying, "How would you compare . . . going to the Metropolitan and watching a ballet versus living in Auschwitz?," a witticism to appall ballet enthusiasts and death camp survivors alike. Moreover, "in one evening of conversation with Ayn Rand," he elaborates, "I would learn more than in an entire semester." Taking Peikoff literally here, as Randians take everything, if the average doctoral program in philosophy requires ten semesters, and he experienced, at minimum, 360 once-a-month evenings of truly philosophical exchanges with Rand during their 30-year acquaintance, then Peikoff has accumulated an impressive 36 times as much philosophical knowledge as his fellow doctors.

And "if you took the total of my mind," he continues, "whatever rational knowledge I have is 98 percent from her, and one or two percent of simply historical data from 14 years of universities." Once again, assuming that what other philosophy doctorates have absorbed in their training is the same "simply historical data," but without the benefit of its clarification via discussion with Rand, Peikoff by this calculation comes off with 49 times their real knowledge, an extraordinary advantage, comparable to Einstein's over a high school physics teacher of his day. Equally extraordinary is his admission of all but total intellectual dependency upon a single source. Most totalistic cults and totalitarian regimes wouldn't dare hope to occupy all but one or two percent of the mental space available to them. Indeed, according to Nathaniel Branden, with respect to *Atlas Shrugged* Leonard identified "very happily and very proudly" with Eddie Willers and Willers's embrace of "feudal serf" status within Dagny's Taggart Transcontinental. Leonard likewise fitted himself into Ayn's Objectivism.

She had a mind that could read just one book on the history of philosophy and "know the ins and outs of each philosopher," Peikoff explains. And while he might enlighten her "on the details of a given philosopher that she hadn't known, . . . they would always be details." It took Peikoff years to understand what certain philosophers were really preaching, "and *she* had picked it up from one or two books."

Another philosopher—University of Southern California professor John Hospers, who spent many all-nighters at Rand's apartment talking philosophy in the early 1960s—has written memoirs of those talks. He takes pains to show Ayn Rand in a good light. Yet the reader is left with the distinct impression that Ayn Rand was not just under-schooled in the subject but largely incapable of dispassionate philosophical conversation.

For her part, Rand sensed that Hospers's analytic approach was wrongheaded. That, combined with Peikoff's insistence that modern thought did not recognize Rand's fundamental tenet that 'Existence is Identity' and that her ideas on epistemology would revolutionize philosophy, is what convinced Rand to undertake the writing of her more philosophic essays. What did Hospers think of Peikoff? "Scared to think on his own . . . he dared not say anything contrary to what *she* had to say; he didn't want to be excommunicated."

Rand and Peikoff never ceased to decry the mind-body dichotomy, depicted as a false choice between living in reality versus living for some fantasized heaven, or between unachievable ideals set up by one's heaven-side versus the practical moral compromises of daily life. But for most, the mind versus body split means the cerebral versus the visceral. Peikoff too was victimized by that split, being at home in the realm of abstractions while lost in the down-to-earth zone where practical thinking meets intuitive feel. "This guy can't even figure out how to make a martini in the real world," remarks Philip Smith. "It's nasty but true." Adds Kay Nolte Smith, "He had a hard time getting around in the world. It's such a contradiction." Rand, expounding "the union of the moral and the practical, was at a total loss in the practical world and to a significant extent so is Leonard."

Her Best Student

Mary Gaitskill's novel *Two Girls, Fat and Thin* (1992) incorporates a send-up of the Objectivist movement. Attending a Peikoff lecture in the mid-1980s was part of Gaitskill's research. Her Anna Granite character is very explicitly Ayn Rand, as Granite's intellectual protégé, Dr. Wilson Bean, is Peikoff. Writes Gaitskill: "Wilson in particular seemed to sit in a patch of personal cold, his thin limbs held stiffly, his comments merely affirmations or repetitions of what Granite had said." Perhaps having absorbed Rand's Russian-pogrom orientation, Bean at the podium "spoke as though describing something that had been done to him recently at the hands of a mob." That quality lends a forcefulness to Peikoff's presentation one might not otherwise expect.

Peikoff"s first book *The Ominous Parallels: The End of Freedom in America* (1982) had been intended for publication in 1968, to help defeat the Democrats. But America was to see the Nixon, Ford, Carter, and Reagan administrations before Peikoff's warnings of impending Naziism appeared. "Since he was checking it with Ayn, . . . every paragraph of every chapter" Barbara Branden explains, "in a sense she was . . . sitting in his head . . . he had no . . . freedom to express *himself,* rather than . . . what he thought Ayn would believe." Philip Smith relates that "We were always hearing Leonard had finished a chapter and was going . . . to talk to Ayn about it," only for him to come back and say it all had to be rewritten. "That went on and on and on and on until it became almost an inside joke." It recapitulated his relationship with his mother, who insisted she edit all Leonard's writing homework.

Rand's attorney Hank Holzer and his wife Erika (author of *Eye For an Eye*), both formerly part of Rand's entourage, say of Peikoff in a joint interview that he's "been under intense pressure forever. First when he was at her feet as a kid. Then when he was her editor" at *The Objectivist*, following the excommunication of the Brandens, as well as her "hatchet man with all the rest of us. . . . And then when he wrote his book which took him 13 years. . . . To go back to her with pages" endlessly, for editing, must have been "a nightmare . . . I would have preferred to be in a POW camp; I *mean* that. But probably the worst of it was when she died, . . . an enormous relief *and* . . . an enormous burden because now he was the keeper of the flame." With Rand's personal imprimatur, *The Ominous Parallels* became an instant classic within Objectivist circles, only a rung less exalted than Rand's works. "One day soon, . . . Dr. Peikoff will have a national reputation in the field of the philosophy of history," Rand predicted in a letter of reference in 1980. Decades later, he does have even an *inter*national reputation, of sorts, as the fellow who writes introductions to new editions of her novels.

Ominous Parallels is almost indistinguishable in style, tone, and even content from Rand's essays. And it *is* very much a collaboration with Ayn Rand, her protestations to the contrary. Despite having mercilessly subjected Leonard to her editorial lash during a decade and a half of excruciating hard labor, she graciously disclaims, in its introduction, any co-authorship. The introduction ends with her blessing, quoted from *Atlas Shrugged:* "It's so wonderful to see a great, new, crucial achievement which is not mine."

The book's main thesis, that the unreason preached by German philosophers led directly to the Nazi regime, had already been explored by two other Jewish writers. One was Frankfurt School philosopher Max Horkheimer in *Eclipse of Reason* (1947). The other, George Lukacs, was a communist writer with experience as Commissar for Education during the Hungarian Soviet Republic's brief life in 1918. His *The Destruction of Reason* (1954, original German version) is as marred by polemical Marxist-Leninist cliches as Peikoff's is by their Objectivist counterparts. Peikoff goes beyond Horkheimer and Lukacs in his somewhat pessimistic prognostication, which he had first issued in 1969, that *America* "is now moving toward the establishment of a Nazi-type totalitarian dictatorship."

Rand died in March 1982, so Peikoff delivered her Ford Hall Forum address the following month, first announcing that he had "decided not to do editing at all." No wonder. Several minutes later he intoned shamelessly, "I urge you to read *The Ominous Parallels* by Leonard Peikoff," a *"brilliant* book. . . ."

Early drafts of the book's chapters appeared in the *Objectivist Newsletter's* successor. "I remember once we went to a meeting where she tore off Leonard's head for an innocent little observation," Kay Nolte Smith recalls. "Ayn was saying, 'the newsletter is going to cost the subscriber X amount' and Leonard looked at her and said, 'Do you think you can get away with that?' The response was a thunderstorm of indignation. 'GET AWAY WITH THAT!!! What am I? Some kind of shyster?' She was pounding on her chair . . ." Having read *Atlas Shrugged* many dozens of times, Peikoff should have recalled that villainess Lillian Rearden exclaims to her husband: "You don't really imagine that you can get away with it!" Villain Wesley Mouch asks, "But can we get away with it?" Confronting Mouch's gang, Hank Rearden "saw the getting-away-with-it look in their faces." For many reasons, including Leonard's bouncing back and forth between the philosophical perspective he was learning at school and the one he absorbed from her, Rand-Peikoff was always, as Barbara Branden put it, "a troubled relationship."

Peikoff writes that one of his most treasured memories of Ayn Rand is an afternoon back in the mid-1970s at her apartment not long after her hospitalization for surgery. To cheer herself up she put one of her favorite 'tiddly-wink' tunes on the record player and went marching about the apartment with a baton in hand, conducting the music, with dear husband Frank looking on lovingly. But the full context of this 'happy' event lends it an aura of the pitiable. Rand had been in hospital for an operation to remove her lung cancer. The tumor had been detected in time only because Rand's stalwart friends the Blumenthals had pressured her into undergoing a physical. But after her operation she so antagonized the Blumenthals about trivia that they simply could endure her no longer and dropped out of her life, knowing full well they would in turn be dropped from her will, leaving Peikoff as sole beneficiary.

Another striking aspect of Peikoff's anecdote is that it revolves around Rand's eccentrically circumscribed tastes in music. Ex-follower Joan Kennedy Taylor recalls the evening Rand asked her devotees for their opinion on a certain piece of musical fluff, perhaps a march and conceivably the same one as mentioned above. Not tipped off that this was the piece Rand loved to play and march around the room to after completing a book, Peikoff opined that he didn't care for it. Rand of course exploded in indignation and Leonard 'had to stay after class' for a lecture on Objectivist aesthetics and the murky condition of his soul.

As for her husband, although Rand loved Frank O'Connor and a photograph of him even went, on her breast, into her coffin, being cuckolded by her over several years with his grudging con sent had transformed him from drinker to drunkard. Karen Reedstrom says, "The empty booze bottles in Frank's studio, according to Peikoff, were used for mixing paints." Reedstrom, herself a painter, notes that the necks of booze bottles are too nar-row for that purpose.

In the last few pages of his *Objectivism* synthesis, Peikoff depicts literary standards over the past century or so as having declined "from the rapture of Victor Hugo to the tongue in the ass-hole of Molly Bloom." One is brought up short by this statement, not just because of its bizarre take on culture, which merely echoes Ayn Rand. It's the swearword, the obscene image. In the Objectivist canon, this is unique. A philosophy of life that focuses constantly on always being 100 percent rational doesn't give humor much room to manoeuver, especially ribald humor. Official Objectivism's prissy neo-Puritanism is ironic though, given that the daring sex-ual innuendoes in Rand's novels, daring by 1940s–1950s standards at least, contributed greatly to her appeal.

Neo-Objectivist Robert L. Campbell writes that back in the early 1970s, Peikoff became quite upset when the Objectivist newsletter at M.I.T. recommended *The Psychology of Self-Esteem* (1969). Not that Peikoff had read Branden's book. He hadn't. But he thought nobody else should read it because Branden had hurt Rand. The same mentality prevailed throughout the 1970s. One neo-Objectivist recalls that when he inquired about renting a taped Peikoff course, he was told that one of the conditions of renting the tapes was for him to certify that he was not a member of any libertarian organization.

Keeper of the Flame

Rand's ideal man would have to be an overtly masculine and virile heterosexual, something of a stretch for intellectual heir number two. His sensibility has him saying on radio that if some-one "ripped out all the roses in her gorgeous rose garden . . . a monstrously corrupt act" or "took a whole set of wonderful Tiffany dishes and smashed them to pieces in a fit of rage, . . . I wouldn't have anything to do with" such a person. He sprinkles his lectures with cooking similes and references to ballet, offers that "I was in tears at the end of that movie *(ET),*" reserves his most ecstatic enthusiasm in art for Greek and Renaissance sculp-tures, underwent psychological treatment for a fear of spiders, and had two marriages go on the rocks despite Rand's high hopes for them. This is no John Galt, but then again, neither was Rand's husband. And yet, it is Peikoff alone among the heaviest intellects of Rand's Collective who got around to fathering a child.

A year and a half after Rand's death, Peikoff would tell student Objectivists that, "Speaking for myself, the actual guidance of day-by-day life is entirely a function of philosophy. Any hope I have for the future depends on philosophy." (When he says "phi-losophy" he very clearly means Objectivism, period.) "It is like the invisible shield of self-protection, protecting you from the slings and arrows of the world by constantly giving you the means to deal with them. . . . I see philosophy wherever I look, whether it's methods of thinking, or value judgments, or art, or politics, or people, or books, or newspapers, or you name it. I would actually be helpless, I would feel I couldn't function at all without it." Since he suggests elsewhere that were any principle of Objectivism found to be untrue, the whole system would collapse, his demon-strated reluctance to investigate any seemingly cogent critique of any part of the philosophy is understandable.

He excuses his dependence by adding, "I think that is true of everybody on the face of the earth" (with regard to *a* philosophy if not Objectivist philosophy). "The difference is whether they admit it, and whether they do it in terms of a deliberate conscious set of principles or whatever hash they have automatized." Peikoff insists that like himself we all need, not just such feeble approxi-mations of a philosophy, or even the philosophizing spirit, but a particular philosophy—Objectivism—without whose guidance individuals are impaired and civilization is ultimately doomed.

In 1991 I asked Peikoff what he thought of *The Philosophic Thought of Ayn Rand* (1984), an anthology of serious critiques of Rand's ideas by respected libertarian or quasi- libertarian philosophers. "I never read it," he replied curtly, "I only read books which I have advance reason to believe would merit the time." Peikoff's entire adult life has revolved around Rand: "I have one mission in life," he declared in 1989—"to entirely understand Objectivism. I have been doing that full-time since I first met Ayn Rand in 1951, . . . and I have not yet entirely achieved my goal." Yet *The Philosophic Thought of Ayn Rand* is a book that finally accords Rand a modicum of the recognition as a philosopher that she sought in vain, and her supposed intellectual heir now refuses to read it. There *are* indications that Rand, forewarned of the volume, might have litigated to keep it off the shelves were she still alive. Peikoff's attitude may be that the least he can do is not read a book she wished to remain unpublished.

In the late 1980s Peikoff hired Hollywood screenplay writer John Hill for *Atlas Shrugged*. Hill describes working with Peikoff and wife Cynthia, from whom he had not yet separated: "He simply didn't see the problem in doing what Ayn Rand wrote. 'Where's the problem?' he'd say. They didn't understand why you couldn't have a good movie about . . . what we call 'talking heads' in the movie business." Today audiences at screenings of *The Fountainhead*, "laugh at some of the dead serious stilted scenes. And I did not want that to happen to *Atlas*." But for Peikoff the top priority was preserving the sanctity of Rand's dialogue. Suggestions for overcoming its limitations were treated "as if I was trying to rewrite the Bible," Hill recounts with exasperation. "Peikoff had built into the contract very specific examples about how little the dialogue could be changed. . . . It was an extremely delicate, tricky matter" to get agreement. "There would be endless seminars on one sentence, on a single word. . . . Brain surgeons are sloppy compared to the intensity with which the details of the dialogues and scenes and characters were discussed."

So on it went, an endless series of conversations, meetings, and memos amongst Peikoff, his wife, Hill, Ed Snider, and other people involved. Somehow Hill got the job done. However, he groans, "even though we . . . were all simpatico, I turned in a script" to Peikoff's group and "never heard anything. That's the final irony. They were afraid *I'd* be too Hollywood. *This* is Hollywood."

In the 1980s Ed Snider had paid a $800,000 fee to Peikoff for the rights to the film until 1992. By that point all the pieces of the film-development puzzle had fallen into place, says Snider, but instead of paving the way for the planned production Peikoff "just yanked the rights, after giving me his word that he would not." John Agliaro, chairman of United Medical Corp., then acquired a 15-year lease (1992–2007) on the rights for $1.1 million. Snider subsequently dissociated himself from Peikoff and ARI and began backing David Kelley's Institute for Objectivist Studies. (Agliaro soon did likewise.) "What about Ed Snider's threat to crush you in court?" Harry Binswanger would write in a leaked ARI memo to Peikoff a few years later.

Nathaniel Branden recalls that just prior to the publication of *Atlas Shrugged*, embodying "the excited child in us all . . . Leonard's projections were so extravagantly wild that they bordered on hysteria. He spoke of the conversion of the country to *laissez-faire* capitalism and the ideals of individualism 'within a year '. He even wondered what there was left for him to do in philosophy, since Ayn had said everything." He would alternate from inordinate optimism to inordinate pessimism and back. December 1983 had him confessing that there are "times and situations where despite my knowledge of philosophy I feel overwhelmed by the evil in the world, isolated, alienated, lonely, bitter, malevolent," once so much so that he thought, "I'm going to retire and stop lecturing and let the whole thing blow up."

A kind of depression-to-mania pendulum swing appears to have ensued, for by 1985 he was declaring that Ayn Rand's philosophic legacy "will overturn the reign of evil and save the world. . . . Objectivism will triumph ultimately and shape the world's course . . . and today's culture will be remembered in the end only for what it is—which I refrain from saying." To most Americans, who would not rate the works of Rand or Peikoff as among the finer products of recent American culture, the latter remark, if unpacked, would be unbelievably insulting. Peikoff believes that "what it is" is a Kantian sewer, with all the contemporary output of the cultural industries carried along it like so many turds.

Though Objectivist philosophy experienced something of a renaissance in the mid-1980s, Peikoff's manic optimism proved short-lived. "I *have* a bleak view of the future," he announced in 1989. "You may think this is needlessly apocalyptic" but "in the recent meetings with the publishers, one of the demands I made to which they agreed is that there's going to be at least 50,000 copies of every one of Ayn Rand's works printed on acid-free paper within the next ten years. I want the feeling—and it's reached this stage of practicality in my mind—that if civilization does go under, there'll be 50,000 copies of each of her works on enduring paper, which I'm going to promptly see are disseminated to the most far-out spots in the world—New Zealand, and India, and Africa, and in caves and in you-name-it, 'cause I don't know what will be left if there's an ultimate holocaust, with the hope that one of these 50,000 will be dug up somewhere."

In 1989 the Berlin wall and East European Communist regimes came crashing down. One suspects that the worst of all worlds for Peikoff would be the persistence for centuries of the continually self-modifying postwar political-economic systems of Western Europe, North America, Japan, and assorted other democracies or quasi-democracies, joined recently by increasingly democratic and capitalist former Soviet Bloc states. (These were all forecast by Peikoff in 1991 to be headed for dictatorship, among them Poland, Hungary, the Czech Republic, Estonia, Latvia, Lithuania, and Slovakia.) Government jurisdiction would sometimes expand spurred by populist rhetoric, and sometimes contract spurred by pro-business rhetoric such as Rand's. The pattern has repeated itself in numerous variations in civilizations throughout history, and now that so many nations are evolving toward democratic capitalism, the pattern may shed much of its violent character. Peikoff wants to terminate that systole-diastole with a final victory—made possible by the

Objectivist ethics—for the Ideal Man, largely in the collective guise of big business and its allies in the arts and sciences. But the gradual conversion of the world to the kind of predominantly self-oriented ethic that varying cultures can adopt in practice is well under way. Rand's draconian either-or version may have become superfluous.

Ex Cathedra

Presumably to secure a measure of respectability among contemporary philosophers, Peikoff did at last in 1984–1985 have one paper each on Plato and Aristotle published in the third-tier philosophical journals *International Studies in Philosophy* and *The New Scholasticism*. His preferred activity, though, is to excoriate the philosophy professors who publish in the first-tier and second-tier journals. His two books, one shaped by Rand's heavy editorial hand, the other a synthesis of her philosophic essays, were all but ignored by reviewers and academics, the latter despite copies mailed gratis to 900 philosophy departments. Perhaps they were unimpressed by the introduction to *Objectivism: The Philosophy of Ayn Rand*, which cautions us that "this book is written not for academics, but for human beings (including any academics who qualify.)"

At the 1989 Objectivist summer conference Peikoff revealed that he'd read *The Fountainhead*, whose theme is independence, 60 times, but found himself floundering intellectually for weeks trying to write his chapter on independence for *Objectivism: The Philosophy of Ayn Rand* until suddenly it struck him that a 61st perusal of *The Fountainhead* might clarify matters. Lo and behold, it did. (More precisely, the theme of *The Fountainhead* is being independent in the sense of having your own ideas and sticking to them, not taking your self-valuation from any source other than yourself. If there is an irony here, it escaped Peifoff's notice.)

While Rand never assembled an up-to-date systematic presentation of her philosophy, at the insistent prodding of Edith Packer, Rand's "best student," as Peikoff designates himself, got the job done. The resulting tome could be a millstone around the necks of less dogmatic Objectivists, if not Objectivism's tombstone.

In one of the best Objectivist newsletters unaffiliated with the ARI, co-editor David Oyerly notes in his review of Peikoff's synthesis the author's "constant, unending need to indulge in polemical attacks," most of which are "pointless, insulting, and for non-Objectivists, confusing," and his "repeated displays of anger, petulance, and frustration, as if modern philosophy, Adolf Hitler, and the welfare state existed just to bother him." In most of Peikoff's illustrations of any given point, there is an "emphasis on negatives, on disaster scenarios, and on condemnation instead of examination."

David Ramsay Steele, reviewing Peikoff's *Objectivism* for *Liberty* was even less impressed. "He seems to think that the most effective strategy is to issue a succession of hot-tempered incantations, often abusive (demeaning all who disagree with him), slovenly in logic (. . . there are dozens of appalling non-sequiturs), and so constructed as to head off thoughts subversive to his position, before these thoughts can be looked at closely. If Peikoff has ever . . . seriously wondered about any philosophical question, he has taken great pains to conceal the fact in this book, which has the tone of an encyclical against heresies." For Steele, Peikoff is now to philosophy what William McGonagall was to poetry; that late-nineteenth century Scot wrote poetry so exquisitely awful that it has never gone out of print. "Some of Peikoff's positions could be given a respectable defense by others, but in this book the most elementary standards of competent argument are flouted on every page," groans Steele. "Peikoff cannot seem to cite anyone without misrepresenting them."

Peikoff could have looked at the thousand or so pages of critiques of Objectivism that have appeared over the years so as to anticipate and address the kind of objections raised, not by devotees terrified of incurring Randian wrath, but by educated critics not so constrained. He did not. And *this* is the magnum opus of Objectivism integrating the best of both the oral and written Randian traditions. *This* is the sophisticated and complete version of what Branden was proclaiming in his lectures for a decade and which ignited a movement in the 1960s.

The Grand Inquisitor

Barbara Branden's *Passion of Ayn Rand* provoked the wrath of cousin Leonard and other hardline Randians. Peikoff was particularly incensed because of the book's account of Rand's prolonged affair with Nathaniel Branden. Peikoff believed that Barbara Branden had fabricated that account. But he had to change his tune. Barbara remarks, "All these years he has been in a rage with me and Nathan, because we were telling this horrible lie. Then he announced one day . . . that his wife had been going through some of Ayn's papers and had discovered it was true." Adds Joan Blumenthal, "I constantly thought from the time of the Break that it was *impossible* that Leonard didn't know. And yet . . . if you won't know, you *won't* know." Announced Peikoff: "I certainly do not recommend this book. . . . I have not read it and do not intend to do so." (Peikoff comes across no better in *Passion* than does the Ayatollah figure in Salman Rushdie's *The Satanic Verses*.) Peikoff dismisses *Passion* as non-cognitive, prompting libertarian David Brown's sarcastic inference that closing one's eyes to the evidence while pronouncing judgment represents cognition at its best.

In 1983 Peikoff was damning some early draft of Barbara Branden's 1986 biography. There are "willful falsehoods motivated by malice mixed into the text," he told his students, and he would *never* comment on it. "I would consider it immoral on my part to . . . to even get to the point of distinguishing that this page was true and this page was false, on exactly the grounds that I would not take some libel from the Nazi party against the Jews and say, 'Well now on page 34 maybe he made a good point, but the first 12 pages are dishonest.' In its inception and by its method it's corrupt." He was defending his idol by implying that to write or read unflattering material about Ayn Rand is as morally repugnant as writing or reading the most grotesquely evil anti-Semitic propaganda ever printed.

According to a source Robert Bidinotto deems reliable, the publication of Barbara Branden's biography "brought Peikoff to a value crisis. . . . He was emotionally distraught during that period." It "terribly distressed him. One's response to the book soon became for him a moral litmus test," reminiscent of the stormy old NBI days, and provoked him to revert to that state of mind. Bidinotto, journalist and pillar of the official movement until the late 1980s, suggests that any supposed intellectual "who, in the name of objectivity, publicly denounces a book . . . he has not bothered to read—and who then expels from his movement serious scholars" like David Kelley "for having voiced insufficiently negative opinions of it—has abdicated any claim to reason, objectivity and justice."

Peikoff's loathing of both Brandens continued unabated into 1998, when Randian Michael Paxton's feature documentary *Ayn Rand: A Sense of Life* was released. His access to Peikoffian and ARI archives had been conditional upon agreeing not to interview the Brandens, and apparently, not to give them more than the most perfunctory mention in the film. Defending that stance Peikoff declares, "I haven't the slightest interest in supporting those who disseminate falsehoods about Ayn Rand any more than I would ask Hitler to appear in a documentary about George Washington." As Hitler is to Washington, the Brandens are to Rand. Of the Brandens and David Kelley's Institute For Objectivist Studies he adds graciously, "I'd rather blow up the whole movement than ally myself with this slime."

Barbara and Leonard, whose mothers are sisters, are obviously no longer *kissing* cousins. Despite their being L.A. neighbors for a decade, and despite trips to Winnipeg to visit their interconnected families, Peikoff has refused to speak to Barbara since the Break, even skipping family reunions he knows she will attend. Though *who* introduced Peikoff to Rand is common knowledge today among Objectivists, Peikoff says now only that it was "an acquaintance," which has Nathaniel Branden shaking his head at the "the implicit contempt Leonard and his friends must have for their own audience."

Of Leonard, Barbara says, "He hasn't added a word to what Ayn explained to him at agonizing length." Even the organization of her philosophy "he learned from Ayn. . . . His approach is very cultish," especially in declaring incessantly that everything Rand wrote is true. "It is so self-defeating and so harmful to the ideas of Objectivism." More importantly Leonard and his ilk "do their own brains a great disservice by saying Ayn Rand must be perfect and her philosophical system must be without flaws. They have to convolute their thinking in some very dangerous ways in order to arrive at these conclusions, and they come across as they are: fanatics not to be taken seriously, . . . people who are in search of someone to answer all of life's questions for them," it being almost chance that for them it was Ayn Rand. Allan Blumenthal confirms that "Leonard's position is that if you do not agree with Objectivism *in toto*, in every aspect, you cannot be an Objectivist. Sooner or later anybody who has any thoughts of his own will be excommunicated." Does that mean agreeing with every single sentence that Ayn Rand wrote?, I asked Blumenthal. "Yes, it does. This is without precedent." By 1998 Barbara Branden would be dismissing Peikoff and Co. as a cult of "little Ayn Rand parrots."

Peikoff appeared before an Objectivist audience in 1989 to explain why he had excommunicated philosopher David Kelley. "There are too many subjectivists posing as Objectivists and, not to put too fine a point on it, *we need a purge.* I don't use the methods of purging of a dictator. . . . I have no armed troops and no physical forces. Nor do I regard Objectivism as a religion. But I sympathize with the idea . . . that you have no patience for people who repudiate it." When Catholic priests and nuns, who teach, deliberately depart from essential Catholic doctrines, they're *out.* The same applies to Objectivism, which has "a completely systematic integrated viewpoint. Therefore, when I hear an outright assault on . . . the very concept which gave it its name, namely 'objectivity', that is the end of my patience."

Kelley had committed the sin of daring to make a supper-club speech to libertarians—libertarians stigmatized by Rand as moral lepers for demoting the Objectivist ethics to optional status—and then defending that action as tolerating mistaken views in the hope of persuading their holders of the correctness of Objectivist views. Peikoff characterized his own decision as irrevocable and unappealable: "When I make a decision on a matter of ideology, that is *it* for me. I do not read anything further, *ever* . . . in support of that viewpoint."

In 1992 Peikoff would declare that Objectivism "is a small movement but is growing, especially in quality." Yes, excommunication by excommunication—according to Lenin's dictum, "Better fewer but better." Peikoff claims that he would much prefer to lecture at Objectivist conferences to upfront non-Objectivists than to 'doctrinally soft' pseudo-Objectivists like Kelley's supporters. Perhaps, but no non-Objectivists would spend their two-week summer vacation attending expensive lectures by a dwindling 'old guard' reiterating its frozen dogma.

I told Peikoff in 1991 that the Canadian Broadcasting Corporation (CBC) radio program for which I was interviewing him would be "more or less" a tribute to Rand to mark the tenth anniversary of her death. It did turn out to be a tribute, according to the dictionary's broader definition, featuring a balanced range of views on Rand, critical and supportive. Several of my neo-Objectivist interviewees, such as Barbara Branden, Phil and Kay Nolte Smith, Allan and Joan Blumenthal, and Ron Merrill, wrote or phoned me after the broadcast to tell me they enjoyed the show and thought it was fair. Peikoff however was livid. His post-broadcast 1992 letter to the CBC fumes: "Let me say that in nearly forty years of dealing with the American media, I have never seen so dishonest and vicious an action as the one you people have perpetrated in this instance. Please be assured that I will do everything in my power to spread the word among my friends and associates that the CBC has finally lost the last vestige of objectivity and has degenerated into a socialist sewer."

Seven months later a letter arrived from a New York City law firm hired by Peikoff, threatening legal action if the CBC didn't furnish written assurance that there would be no further dissemination of the program via Laissez Faire Books, which had obtained a licence from the CBC to sell the two-hour program on cassettes. The letter concluded with, "most importantly, our client requires a formal written apology." Instead, I wrote them a letter refuting the allegations, and that was the end of it. Laissez Faire continued to sell the tapes for years. (Litigiousness is a characteristic of most cults, as it was for Rand personally and for NBI.)

By late 1994, Peikoff had officially excommunicated the purveyors of the orthodox movement's summer seminars, the Thomas Jefferson School's George Reisman and Edith Packer—for immorality. The dispute leading to that decision was a rather arcane intra-ARI one, a matter of personality clashes and turf wars dignified as matters of principle. Linda Reardan, co-editor of *The Intellectual Activist,* took the Reismans' side and resigned from that newsletter of orthodox Objectivism. She blasted as "irresponsibility" Peikoff's refusal for years on end "to be bothered with any complaints about his associates at ARI" despite Peikoff's having told her: "I have complete veto power, by charter, over everything ARI does." He eventually did intervene, on the side of his closest pals at ARI—Michael Berliner, Harry Binswanger, and Peter Schwartz—against orthodox Objectivism's number one economist, Reisman, and its number one psychologist, Packer.

Reisman denounced Peikoff and ARI for acting like "Spanish Inquisitors, claiming the right to level charges and conduct proceedings in secret, whose nature their victims are not allowed to reveal . . . we reject any such claim with the profoundest contempt." Reisman supporter and former ARI stalwart Genevieve Sanford called it a "grotesque and catastrophic purge." Peikoff's action "directly led to: the dishonor of two life-long Objectivists, the destruction of the first school that advanced Objectivism, a world-wide split between Objectivists as well as old friends, the withdrawal of support for ARI among contributors, . . . and the erosion of respect" for Peikoff himself.

It was indeed a repeat of the Branden and Kelley splits, the faithful everywhere expected to rally to ARI's side on the basis not of evidence but of authority, and to personally shun their Objectivist friends and acquaintances who didn't do likewise. Reisman, whose credentials were then on the verge of substantial enhancement via the long-awaited publication of literally the heaviest volume of orthodox Objectivist thinking since

Rand's death, the thousand-page *Capitalism* (1996), would go on to form yet another splinter organization within the Objectivist movement.

Perks of the Pontificate

Being a cult leader has not been without its rewards. Peikoff inherited some $750,000 from Rand when she died. (She could have been a multimillionaire but was neurotically averse to investing.) He has sold options for the *Atlas* film rights for nearly two million dollars. He receives the royalties from the quarter million or more copies the Rand titles sell annually, which include *The Early Ayn Rand*'s never-before-published stories, plays and *Fountainhead* out-takes. Karen Reedstrom has commented that she was embarrassed for Rand that it was in print, to which Barbara Branden replied that it "was wastebasket stuff for her, the material from *The Fountainhead* . . . He had to know that the reason she never published it was because she didn't *want* to publish it." He did it simply "to make money." According to libertarian author Justin Raimondo, Peikoff "is cashing in on her corpse. . . . what he wants is a monopoly on the lucrative Ayn Rand industry that has grown up after her death." Would Schwartz's and Peikoff's "second- and third-rate scribblings have attracted the least amount of attention if they hadn't managed to sneak them into books like *The Voice of Reason*, with Ayn Rand's name plastered all over the cover?" Peikoff's two books are part of a Penguin USA series called, not 'The Objectivist Library' but 'The Ayn Rand Library'. Says neo-Objectivist Steve Reed, "If anything confesses, quite purely and simply, to how Peikoff is borrowing the unearned prestige of Rand's name for his own work, this does."

An instructor at some small college, as Peikoff might have become, could never match the remuneration of the sole inheritor of Rand's estate. Nor could such an instructor match the status Peikoff automatically acquired as designated spokesman for a once-vibrant-and-still-kicking movement, nor the corresponding guaranteed market for his books and his very expensive taped lecture courses on grammar, communication skills, the history of philosophy, moral virtue, great plays, and contemporary issues. And then there's his annual $40,000 fee for lecturing at those two-week Objectivist summer conferences (now organized through ARI rather than by the Jefferson School).

For any given individual to uphold Objectivist philosophy is not enough. A student asked him in 1983 if one could be an Objectivist philosophically yet not care for Rand's fiction. Peikoff said he found the question "bizarre . . . in the realm of aesthetic judgment Ayn Rand's works are to the good what Hitler is to the evil. . . . I do not see any legitimate ground on which *anyone* could say 'I find this boring or unenjoyable' . . . anybody who says that is simply wrong." So it is objectively wrong and consequently immoral for even a non-Objectivist not to relish *We the Living, The Fountainhead,* and *Atlas Shrugged.*

His perspective hasn't altered in 40 years. Nathaniel Branden recalls of the 1957-to-mid-1960s era that Rand's entourage would "hear of somebody who liked the ideas in *Atlas* but wasn't especially fond of the novel, and we had no interest in such a person whatsoever . . . we found such a person psychologically incomprehensible, which did not prevent us from having a very negative view of his psychology. . . . We couldn't understand how anybody could read *Atlas* and not fall in love, not be 'converted' . . . and want to sign on for this world and its vision."

Peikoff asserts that her fiction "is such a thorough embodiment of *everything* that matters to me that if someone can . . . say I don't like it, they may as well tell me we are opposite on everything. . . . I have no further interest in that person." This surely is unprecedented: that one *must* love a philosopher's fiction writings if one accepts the philosophy it expresses, otherwise one is not worth dealing with and one's espousal of the philosophy is phony. (A counterexample is philosopher Douglas Rasmussen who, though an Objectivist true believer around 1970, never enjoyed Rand much as a novelist.) Peikoff is implying that because everyone ought to live by a true philosophy—the only such philosophy being Rand's—everyone in the world is morally obliged to read her novels. As noted, the royalties from these go straight to Peikoff himself.

Even Peikoff has had to admit the presence within his ranks of an undesirable element consisting of those who relish denouncing others. "I know perfectly decent people who won't call themselves Objectivists although they agree with and understand Objectivism," he confided to his students in 1989, "on the grounds that so many people have called themselves Objectivists that they think are wrong and no good that they don't want to be identified with."

He elaborates, "Many, many people with good intentions come to Objectivism and are completely programmed . . . from childhood, to be receptive to an alien philosophy," alien from Objectivism that is. "And then they take Objectivism and put it as the filling within the categories already established. The typical person who is too harsh in moral judgment, . . . brought up religiously or not . . . , inclines to think in his deepest subconscious of moral judgment as being a series of rules: You must not sanction evil; you *must* hold a job . . . so he takes the ten commandment approach but he just substitutes the Objectivist content."

If so, it is still hardly the fault of religion that Objectivism's instructors fail to take account of the contexts their students are coming from. Moreover, surely there have been no worse professional denouncers, excessively harsh in moral judgment, than Rand herself, the Brandens, Peikoff, and others among Rand's closest associates. Their high-minded contextually-applied principles typically deteriorated in practice into a ranting rule-mongering no more edifying than that of the plebeian Randroid contingent.

Continues Peikoff, "I don't think you should give the term Objectivism away to the wrong exponents of it. You should . . . say" of the rule-monger, "'He isn't an Objectivist, but I am.'" Yet while dismissing rabidly denunciatory Objectivists as not true Objectivists, it is never these so-called 'Randroids' that Peikoff asks to leave town, but rather the insufficiently judgmental adherents who exhibit a little independence of thought.

Peikoff has stated that of the two main errors—the dogmatic assertion of principles irrespective of context, which he calls 'rationalism' (not to be confused with rationality, which is the highest good), and the jettisoning of principles in favour of a case-by-case approach, which he calls empiricism—the former is preferable. Rationalism at least indicates a serious approach to philosophy, and he grants it is rationalism rather than empiricism which most Objectivists are prone to and many succumb to. That is why in 1983 he presented a 12-lecture course called *Understanding Objectivism,* mostly devoted to overcoming rationalism. It's available on 24 audio-cassettes for $275, a cost so prohibitive that the course's anti-rationalist message could only be reaching a small proportion of Objectivist rationalizers.

In *Understanding Objectivism,* Peikoff concedes this downside to the Objectivist movement in terms he would not use in the presence of outsiders: "I've seen Objectivist parents drive their kids crazy with Objectivist dogmatism. They hammer it down the throats of these kids of just 15 years; every time the kid just wants a Coke he gets a lecture on 'A is A'." Eventually the child revolts in the name of human self-assertion, and for the rest of his life hates Rand and Objectivism as the forces which destroyed his childhood. Peikoff, who says he knows particular kids who as a result of this treatment will never support Objectivism, finds this an understandable reaction.

Chris Sciabarra notes that in a 1983 lecture-tape "Peikoff emphasizes . . . that rationalism," in celebrating reason, "embodies an abiding contempt for emotions. Rationalists equate feelings with subjectivism. They believe that feelings must be ruthlessly suppressed in the quest for objective knowledge. As such, rationalism becomes a *rationalization* for emotional repression that can only distort the objectivity it seeks to achieve." Yet elsewhere Peikoff confesses to having struggled with a particularly acute case of rationalism within himself for nearly 15 years, despite constant tutoring from Rand. This suggests that he was thus afflicted from his earliest encounters with Rand in 1951 until about 1966, two years from NBI's closing. It further suggests that all the lectures on Objectivism Peikoff delivered while in graduate school and for two years afterwards, by which time he was in his thirties, were infused with rationalism. It means that he was passing on to his students, if only implicitly and by his own example, a contempt for one's own emotions and a justification for ruthlessly suppressing them, a stance that he himself admits precludes objectivity, the *sine qua non* of Objectivism. It means that in his early thirties, even though he couldn't live according to the philosophy despite the presumably enormous advantage of regular consultations with Rand herself, he was telling his 19-year-old students that *they* should be able to.

In *Understanding Objectivism* he feels obliged to tell students that there is no Objectivist principle they are abrogating if they simply don't care for skyscrapers, the classic Randian symbol of human aspiration and achievement. And for the first time, he even cites differences in opinion between himself and Rand. Unlike Rand: he didn't care for TV's *Perry Mason* (he found it too hard to keep track of the large casts of characters); he reads a bit of horror fiction; he listens to a bit of Beethoven; and he can't get excited over the achievements of the U.S. space program. Even apart from what is implied by being bowled over by *Atlas Shrugged* while unimpressed by lunar exploration, the space shuttle, and planet probes, such a meager flicker of intellectual and artistic independence would perhaps have been better left unproclaimed.

The 35th-anniversary edition of *Atlas* was published in March 1992, with a new introduction by Peikoff. Each year thousands of new adolescent readers enter that Randian 'universe', and many who send in the attached 'for further information' card to Objectivist headquarters will not return, or at least, not with all their faculties intact. Edith Efron, a veteran of Rand's Collective, recommends that *The Fountainhead* remain unread until age 25, *Atlas Shrugged* until age 35. Younger readers lack the critical thinking skills to filter Rand's onslaught, and are too likely to become completely alienated from their culture and themselves.

Kelley sympathizer Richard Dempsey writes that Peikoff "seeks to establish Objectivism as a monument to Ayn Rand, in effect to preserve the cult of Ayn Rand" whereas David Kelley "is promoting the transition of Objectivism to a growing school of open inquiry and thought." However, the ease with which ARI rounds up recruits may keep the IOS in the shadows for some time. For example, a few years after IOS pulled the plug on its weekly radio show *In Focus* with co-hosts David Kelley and Raymond Newman, Peikoff began hosting a *daily* one-hour talk show on KIEV radio in Los Angeles. Students of Objectivism can obtain audiocassettes of the first year of programs for a mere $750.

It is unlikely, however, that the following KIEV incident will make it onto an audiocassette for sale: In February 1998, a liberal organization ran a pro-affirmative-action ad in *The New York Times* featuring this quotation from Alan Greenspan: "It is good for business. It is good for our society, and it is the right thing to do." Ever since Greenspan's favorable comments on *The Passion of Ayn Rand,* he had been disdained by ARI and its affiliate newsletter, but Peikoff had never personally performed the excommunicatory rites. Now he apparently had a plausible excuse. Within days he announced on KIEV that "it is necessary to set the world straight on Alan Greenspan, once and for all" and in effect "formally excommunicate" him "from any connection with Objectivism." No longer would Peikoff even "regard him as an admirer of Ayn Rand." Unless the quotation was "taken out of context, . . . he is out" and "I will never again say a kind or favorable word about him. . . . That is my obituary on an old friend." Now of course Greenspan *had* been quoted out of context, as anyone bothering to get ahold of the easily-obtainable text of the Greenspan speech from which the quote was uprooted would have discerned. Perhaps fearing that this goof-up might trigger another exodus from ARI, Peikoff bit the bullet and apologized.

7

Alan Greenspan: The Undertaker Takes Over

There at the Dawn of Time

Born the year Ayn Rand arrived in the U.S., the son of a stockbroker, Alan Greenspan graduated from New York University's School of Commerce in 1948. He soon took a dull job at the National Industrial Conference Board, a propaganda outlet for big business, and worked on steel inventories. Through a soon-annulled marriage to Joan Mitchell (later Joan Blumenthal)—not until 1997 at age 71 would he take the plunge again—Greenspan met Ayn Rand, herself a veteran of extensive contact with other business propaganda outlets like the National Association of Manufacturers (NAM). NAM and the U.S. Chamber of Commerce would one day have not very nice things to say about Greenspan's performance as chairman of the Federal Reserve Board.

Business Week refers to Greenspan as a "former Ayn Rand devotee" who became a key member of her original inner circle in the mid-1950s. "He was very much part of the Collective. But he had his own life," recalled lawyer-novelist Erika Holzer. He would come late to every meeting and leave early. Having his own relationship with Rand, which was dignified, he kept somewhat aloof from the others. For his appearance and demeanor, he became known to other Collective members as 'the Undertaker'. Recalls Edith Efron, "He was her special pet," partly "because . . . there wasn't anybody known to her closely who was a business-man who was out in the world of power."

"It was like sitting in on the dawn of time," reminisces Collective member Harry Kalberman, a brokerage-business executive and Nathaniel Branden's brother-in-law. "We would take whatever Ms. Rand had written and read it. And she would watch our faces—to see whether we got it." Nathaniel Branden recalls that Alan "would compliment Ayn on some passage in the novel, saying, 'On reading this . . . one tends to feel . . . exhilarated'. Or 'the reader is inspired here'," demonstrating an early flair for convoluted, depersonalized language. Robert Bleiberg, a business magazine editor in 1961, was sufficiently impressed by a Greenspan lecture that he reprinted a few of his essays in *Barron's*. Why did Bleiberg resist invitations to ally himself with the Collective? "It became evident to me that they were a cult," he explains.

In 1968 Greenspan was one of a gang of four Collective members who at Rand's insistence irrevocably repudiated both Brandens in the *Objectivist*. At the time Greenspan was off working on the Nixon campaign. Barbara Branden suggested later that Greenspan signed Rand's statement about the break because he believed what she told him. "He'd never heard my side of the story and he was the most stunned man on earth when I told it to him."

Roy Childs recalls that an early draft of the Rand biography Barbara showed him contained "some great Greenspan anec-dotes. . . . Ayn took him apart at an elegant elite restaurant, got mad at him, blew her top, called him a coward." Barbara Branden responds, "*Everybody* went through that." A subtle retraction typ-ically ensued.

Master of Greenspam

Despite Greenspan's youthful two-year stint at the Juilliard School for music, followed by a year touring with Harry Jerome's swing band playing clarinet, Greenspan would be greeted by Rand with:

"How's the Undertaker? Has he decided that he exists yet?"—the latter dig referring to his initial philosophic skepticism. This also despite what Barbara Branden recalls, namely that, "It was incredible how he always had a beautiful woman at his side. . . . I think it was the attraction of his intellectual power and probably his reserve." Another Collective member was less favorably impressed by that reserve: "It's simply that he is a very cold person. It's very hard to know what's on his mind. Through those Coke-bottle glasses, you can't even tell he's awake sometimes." Says friend and NYU professor Robert Kavesh, "sometimes you just want to say, 'Damn it, Alan, tell me a dirty joke. Or at least listen to one.'" Decades later, despite having pushed himself to become a decent tennis player and golfer for political schmoozing purposes, his nickname in Washington became 'The Creeper'. Libertarian economics theorist Murray Rothbard, who knew Greenspan in the late 1950s, writes that "Greenspan was supercilious and monotonic; he had the sense of life of a dead mackerel . . . He's a namedropper." According to Michael Lewis, Washington society regards him as a social inept with bad breath, and "known to faint under pressure."

Arthur Burns, Fed chairman from 1970 to 1978, taught Greenspan at Columbia. In 1974 Burns beseeched him to take up the chairmanship of the president's Council of Economic Advisors (CEA) in order to fight inflation. Their friendship would later give Greenspan entree to the Fed.

Despite having no Ph.D. in economics and little esteem in academia, Greenspan was sworn in as, in a sense, the nation's leading economist. And there in the front row at the White House ceremony sat Ayn Rand. Two days before she had told a reporter, "Alan is my disciple." Greenspan did eventually get his Ph.D. from NYU in 1977, but it was apparently for articles he had written that NYU then conveniently lost, notes Lewis, making it the most suspect doctorate since Nathaniel Branden's California Graduate Institute diploma. Comments neo-Objectivist Victor Niederhoffer, author of *The Education of a Speculator,* "As far as I know, no one has ever seen or read Greenspan's dissertation." Niederhoffer places quotation marks around *Dr.* when applied to Greenspan.

Greenspan had a gift for persuading politicians he was so smart they couldn't get elected or re-elected without his number-crunching. Gerald Ford's economic policy coordinator suggests that "Greenspan has an unbeatable way of getting next to the guys in power and getting their attention" and sounding profound "even if you don't understand what the hell he's talking about." A person close to the 1968 Nixon campaign for which Greenspan served as an economic advisor recollects that "Alan came in with the idea that you could have this black box that explained it all—inflation, unemployment, GNP." The language he used was as impenetrable as that black box, his "sentences designed not to be understood." Former top aide to Nixon, Leonard Garment, who played in Harry Jerome's swing band with Greenspan, says of him, "He talked Nepal Kathmandu language." Neo-Objectivist Congressional aide Edward Hudgins comments that "even when he does something right, he has a way of talking that you can't quite figure out what he's saying." Humorously, but inaccurately, Greenspan told an audience on August 11, 1987: "Since I've become a central banker I've learned to mumble with great incoherence. If I seem unduly clear to you, you must have misunderstood what I said." Actually that strategic incoherence, "Greenspam," *Time* calls it, had become second nature to him long ago.

A Dogmatist at the Helm

When Greenspan was not advising politicians, he was providing continuous color commentary on American economic data at Townsend-Greenspan, the firm he took over upon William Townsend's death in 1958. (When Greenspan left to head up the CEA, Objectivist M. Kathryn Eikoff ran the company for him, and, having become a very good friend of Ayn's, spent the Christmas of 1981 with her after buying her a tree.) He was the first to adapt economic forecasting specifically for CEOs. Lewis marvels that "no one seemed to mind that most of his predictions turned out to be wrong." Indeed the forecaster "may be thought of as an important economist by people who don't know better, but his credibility among knowledgeable people is zero." One former member of the Collective points out that despite ample opportunity, he never attended the NYU seminars of Ludwig von Mises, Rand's favorite economist. Mises believed reliable, detailed economic forecasting to be impossible.

Greenspan, writes Steven Beckner, credits Martin Anderson, onetime contibutor to *The Objectivist* and author of *The Reagan Revolution*, with getting him involved in politics, first as director of domestic policy research for Nixon's presidential campaign, after which he did stints with an assortment of Nixon-era task forces and advisory boards. In 1968, writes Lewis, Greenspan landed Nixon in trouble when he masterminded a very Randian and soon-abandoned proposal to set Wall Street free from regulation. Later he helped conduct Gerald Ford's WIN (Whip Inflation Now) publicity campaign, "an ineffectual stunt." Next, Greenspan presided over one of America's worst recessions as chairman of Gerald Ford's Council of Economic Advisors. Many business people thought he worried too much about inflation and too little about growth. *Business Week* depicts him as "the man who, as chief White House economist during the recession of 1974–75, created a furor by suggesting that stockbrokers (his dad had been a stockbroker) "were suffering more from the downturn than the poor." Continues Beckner, he then persuaded Ford to propose a reduction in government spending for fiscal 1977—election time, which was "kamikaze politics. . . . many believe that Ford's budget helped him lose the election in 1976."

President Reagan, relates Beckner, "put Greenspan in charge of his National Commission on Social Security Reform which worked from 1981 to 1983 to produce recommendations, mostly enacted, to restore financial integrity to the troubled Social Security system for the next quarter century." Objectivists *and* neo-Objectivists want Social Security abolished, not rescued. Said Greenspan dryly: it "could be made better. And better is better than not better." He served too on Reagan's Economic Advisory Board and on the boards of directors of several mega-corporations.

In Greenspan's pre-Fed days, there occurred the Keating affair. Charles Keating of Lincoln Savings and Loan in Phoenix, Arizona, would lose three billion dollars of other peoples' money in the 1980s, but, Lewis tells us, "at the time, he seemed like a free-market hero of the sort lionized by Ayn Rand. His only problem was that some government bureaucrats wanted to block Lincoln from diversifying out of home-mortgage lending and into anything it wished to buy. . . . At Keating's behest, Greenspan penned an impassioned plea for savings-and-loan freedom. The letter concluded with an offer to lobby in person on Keating's behalf." Keating eventually served prison time and became a symbol of the corruption that led to the bankruptcies of hundreds of Savings and Loan institutions and to the most expensive government bailout in U.S. history.

Neo-Objectivist economics professor Larry Sechrest suggests that, "Alan Greenspan is either one of the world's most schizophrenic human beings or one of the most dishonest. Anyone who can write the articles he wrote back in the 1960s, while he was associated with Ayn Rand—saying that you never can have a stable economy, you can never have economic freedom, and you can never have justice as long as you have a central bank and as long as you're not on a gold standard—and then turn around and become the head of the most powerful engine of paper money creation in the world has got to have some kind of problem. I don't know if he needs therapy or . . . condemnation." Of the gold exchange standard approximating Rand's pure gold standard, Greenspan would say in the 1990s, "If you have a number of countries who are unwilling to abide by fixed exchange rates then you can't impose a gold standard." A gold standard has to be "the end result of international economic stability—not the cause of it."

He had predicted that inflation would *not* come down in the early 1980s, but was wrong. Inflation had got so out of hand that Fed chairman Paul Volcker had been given a mandate to restore Fed credibility and the unprecedented degree of independence required to carry it out. Volcker did wrest control of the money supply from the politicians and did slash inflation. For Greenspan the Fed chairmanship was now a job worth having.

In Rand's inner circle sessions during the mid-1950s to mid-1960s, inflation threatened freedom, and tying the value of paper money to gold was the only way to avoid the kind of over-expansion of the currency that results in price inflation. Kalberman's view is that Greenspan's hawkishness on inflation "is a necessary outgrowth of a passionate free-market orientation, one nurtured by a 30-year-old bond to Rand." As Fed chief, Greenspan would like Congress to enact his proposal requiring the Fed *by law* to achieve zero-inflation. Historian Edward Luttwak, admittedly a nationalist and protectionist in economic matters, comments that "it takes the absolute faith of religion to refuse even very moderate inflation at the cost of . . . slow economic growth for years on end."

It was in mid-1987 that Greenspan was selected as chairman of the Federal Reserve Board. "He engineered the demise of Paul Volcker," Lewis quotes a senior advisor to President Reagan as saying. Nonetheless, writes Beckner, "Greenspan gives Volcker tremendous credit for defusing what had been a very real threat of U.S. hyperinflation in the early years of his 1979–1987 tenure." When Greenspan arrived at the Fed in August of 1987, "the big job had been done." The federal funds rate had hit 19 percent in early 1981, the prime rate 21 percent, and unemployment 10.7 percent in 1982, but by 1986 inflation was less than 2 percent. Greenspan conceded he was faced with nothing so daunting as what Volcker had confronted.

Greenspan's first several months at the helm were rough ones, for Greenspan and for the financial world at large. In his last speech to Congress on July 21, 1987, outgoing Fed chief Volcker suggested that no more than modest credit tightening was required. But right from the get-go, Greenspan determined to have 1950s-style price stability. Aides to Reagan were afraid Greenspan would out-Volcker Volcker. Even though he compared the 1980s to the 1920s, Greenspan "began in earnest to tighten the money supply, which caused the market crash in October," says neo-Objectivist financial advisor Jim O'Donnell of the USA Financial Group.

Numbers-wise, the Volcker Fed had cut the discount rate in March 1986 from 7½ percent, and then three more times, to 5½ percent in August 1986, where it stayed. The federal funds rate even dipped below 6 percent by the end of 1986 but rose to 7 percent over the next several months. In early September 1987, freshly installed as Fed chief, Greenspan persuaded the Board to raise the discount rate from 5½ to 6 percent. The funds rate rose from 7 to 7¼ percent. Banks increased their prime lending rate a half percent to 8¼ percent. And unfortunately, writes Beckner, Greenspan created a perception that U.S. interest rates were wedded to exchange rates, meaning that interest rates would not be lowered while the dollar was weak and might even be raised to strengthen the dollar, "was to become a source of major disruption for the financial markets." In the week prior to Black Monday, "many were convinced the Fed would soon raise the discount rate from 6 to 6½ percent."

Two monetarist followers of Milton Friedman—Beryl Sprinkel (chairman of Reagan's CEA) and Michael Darby (assistant treasury secretary for economic policy)—went to see Greenspan after the September rate hike. They believed money growth was too slow at less than 4 percent annually and that Greenspan was trying to reduce inflation too fast. Writes Beckner, "They warned the Fed chairman he was risking 'a classic monetary shock situation', where tight money precipitates recession or financial crisis. Greenspan thought Sprinkel and Darby were 'overly concerned' and that the Fed could continue tightening credit without difficulty." Looking back, Sprinkel says that Greenspan "had a misguided policy which did a lot of damage."

Beckner relates that by mid-September, Fed vice chairman Manuel Johnson "had co-authored with Darby a proposal to set up a crisis contingency planning group that would involve the Fed, Treasury, SEC, and Commodity Futures Trading Commission (CFTC) in preparing for a possible stock market collapse." They were sure the market was going to fall gradually or suddenly. Darby recalls that "Greenspan thought we were . . . nervous nellies." Thankfully, despite Greenspan's skepticism, the group was set up.

Writes Beckner, "Sprinkel still thinks the Fed provoked the crash by tightening monetary policy too much, then not easing credit on Friday, the 16th." The market was obviously in big trouble that Friday, but Greenspan did nothing in response. On October 19th, Black Monday, the Dow dropped more than 500 points or 22 percent, and similar stock market crashes ensued around the world.

Luckily for Greenspan, he was credited for ending the panic by pumping the financial markets full of cash in the wake of the meltdown. But as Lewis notes, it had long since been demonstrated by Milton Friedman and Anna Schwartz, among others, that "the correct response to a market crash was to flood the banking system with money." Paul Volcker would have responded likewise. The markets expected nothing less. Beckner writes that New York Federal Reserve Bank president E. Gerald Corrigan had the more hands-on role. To Corrigan the freezing up of securities lending and the importance of ensuring liquidity was "a no-brainer."

The Chairman had initially raised interest rates in order to head off an anticipated rise in inflation. The crash first reversed and then ultimately delayed by several months the implementation of his anti-inflation strategy. The federal funds rate didn't rise to its pre-crash level until 22 June 1988, and the discount rate hike from 6 to 6½ percent, feared as imminent by Wall Street in October 1987, didn't occur until 9 August 1988. This extended delay should have brought on the very inflation that his September rate hikes had been designed to forestall. However, the inflation rate remained unchanged until 1990. He had been wrong. The unprecedented market meltdowns and worldwide financial panic of 1987, of which Greenspan's action and inaction were a necessary if insufficient cause, had been anything but inevitable. The Dow Jones Industrial Average, thought to be so over-valued at its pre-crash peak of 2,700, climbed to 9,300 in 1998.

Ayn Rand's inflation paranoia, impressed indelibly upon the mind of disciple Alan Greenspan in the 1950s, wound up administering a stunning shock to investors worldwide three decades later. The crash even resulted in further regulation of the financial markets, something Greenspan had come to Washington to reduce.

Despite American distrust of central banks and their paper money machinations, the Fed was born in 1913. The Fed is an empire. Lewis explains: "Our nation's monetary policy is made by a body called the Federal Open Market Committee, which consists of Greenspan, six top Fed officials called governors, plus a rotating cast of five regional Fed presidents. The FOMC dictates a couple of key interest rates on which most private lending rates—including mortgages and car loans—are based . . . Regional Fed presidents make the most important economic decisions in our democracy, yet they are not democratically accountable." But of course that is the whole point; otherwise monetary policy might be conducted as irresponsibly as fiscal policy has been since the 1970s. True, Fed governors are appointed by the President but "Greenspan has authority over a staff of some 1,700 permanent Fed employees whose driving instinct is to protect their boss."

A Clinton administration official claims that the Fed has shown "a very conscious strategy to mislead." Greenspan "beefed up the power of the Fed and removed it further than ever from anyone's control but his own," effectuating a "shift in power from elected officials to unelected ones." He even nixed a Clinton administration proposal to consolidate all bank regulation into a single new agency. It would have reduced government and regulatory complexity, but also the Fed's power over banks. So Greenspan lobbied against it, despite bipartisan support in Congress.

The Greenspan Recession

Beckner writes that the Greenspan Fed's goal was not just to whittle away at inflation but to end it. This was rather a quixotic goal, given that Fed manipulation of monetary policy to that end would have to be complemented by enormous fiscal policy changes that were simply not in the offing. Moreover, most Fed officials "frankly admit conducting monetary policy is an imprecise exercise—more of an art than a science. Given the lag times and other imponderables, some would say using reserve pressures and rates to bring about a particular growth rate" without inflationary pressures is more a guessing game.

According to Beckner, from 30 March 1988 to 23 February 1989, the Fed put all thoughts of the crash behind it and—defying the wishes of the administration that had appointed Greenspan—hiked the funds rate from less than 6½ percent to nearly 10 percent. Recently released FOMC transcripts reveal that the Fed was consciously flirting with recession. Even the business sector was displeased. A U.S. Chamber of Commerce economist warned, "All they're going to do if they persist in this is push us into a recession." The head of NAM told Congress on 8 September that it "would not endorse any further restrictive measures that might increase the risk of sharp slowdown." In late March 1989 Greenspan suggested that the economy was pausing, not turning downward. Moreover, "The worst thing that can happen to us . . . is that we are perceived to be easing too fast."

The U.S. Treasury typically worries about trade imbalances and competitiveness; the Fed about how a shrinking dollar imports inflation. Greenspan, continually worrying about the strength of the U.S. dollar even at the 140-yen level and not dreaming that the next administration would let it fall to below 90 yen without inflationary effect, inclined toward supporting the dollar with interest rates higher than would otherwise prevail.

Greenspan's Fed even seriously pondered scheduling the phase-out of remaining inflation, complete with 'sacrifice ratios', a euphemism for "how many people we're going to throw out of work," the chairman conceded. In contrast, Corrigan worried that targeting zero inflation might provoke a backlash against the Fed. It did. Fed governor Edward Kelley warned that in the event of a recession, the cost of the savings and loan bankruptcies crisis might get completely out of hand. It did.

Real GNP steadily slowed in 1989. By keeping the funds rate at 8 percent until November despite collapsing credit demand, the Fed was in effect tightening credit. In August 1990, Greenspan cautioned that, "those who argue that we are already in recession I think are reasonably certain to be wrong." But it was Greenspan who was wrong. Fellow Objectivist and money-man Victor

Niederhoffer opines that, "Greenspan has a million abstruse indi-
cators that are as dated as the dodo." The recession began in that
third quarter of 1990 with a contraction in GNP of minus 1.6 percent. The last quarter saw minus 3.9 percent and the first quarter
of 1991, minus 3.0 percent.

In July 1990 Greenspan had strongly implied any easing of
interest rates would depend on a federal government budget that
significantly reduced the deficit. After the budget deal he supported collapsed, the Fed delayed easing for several weeks, writes
Beckner, "despite the demonstrable needs of the U.S. economy."
Fed governor Wayne Angell complains that had the Fed begun
easing earlier and more steeply in 1989, "it wasn't necessary to
have any recession in '90–'91 at all."

The Greenspan Flat Recovery

A foundering economy would doom George Bush's re-election.
"Given the Fed's oft-stated belief that the effects of its actions are
not fully felt for at least a year or a year and a half," remarks
Beckner, "the administration was not pleased to hear that the Fed
planned to wait to see the effects of past moves, since all but one
of those moves had been made in the past four months."
Greenspan always wanted to be ahead of the curve on inflation;
not so with recession. At a late-March 1991 FOMC meeting, says
Beckner, "preposterous as it seems now," the Fed's easing bias was
overriden by fear that further rate cuts might lead to an overly
robust and inflationary expansion. Luttwak laments, "Greenspan
invariably errs on the side of caution: a million can lose their jobs
because higher interest rates might, perhaps, keep inflation at
one-tenth of one percent below what it might have been."

Lulled by the upbeat mood in the nation following the successful Gulf war, it took until late summer 1991 for Greenspan to see
that the momentum of the recovery was uncharacteristically feeble.
Commentators talked of a double-dip recession and annualized
growth rates for GNP during the last three quarters of 1991 aver-
aged a meager 1.2 percent. *Finally*, on 6 December 1991 came a
major discount rate cut, from 4½ to 3½ percent, with Greenspan

conceding he had misread the economy. Blinded by dread of inflation, he had, writes Beckner, "lowered rates in dribs and drabs in a process one administration official labeled 'Chinese water torture'."

Greenspan further admitted on 10 January 1992 that the economic recovery was anemic, so he would be ready to lower rates again in 1992. Still, Greenspan viewed deficit reduction as a *sine qua non* for generally lower interest rates. But lower interest rates themselves reduce deficits by stimulating greater economic growth. The fiscal 1992 deficit would be "far less than feared," writes Beckner, thanks to the recovery that finally began in earnest in the spring, and the fiscal 1993 deficit would be nearly eighty billion dollars below projections.

The Fed failed to engineer a soft landing for the economy after its duel with inflation in the late 1980s. Worse, its sluggish response to the resulting mid-term recession delayed any sure signs of recovery until after the once extraordinarily popular George Bush had met defeat, ending a Republican dynasty.

True Believer or Traitor?

Former Fed governor John LaWare groans, "I can't imagine, to this day, how Alan Greenspan got himself euchred into sitting in that box"—between Hillary Clinton and Tipper Gore—"for the President's first State of the Union message. I think that was a serious mistake." As a former Fed official put it, "He desperately wants to be reappointed." The desperation was probably unwarranted. As Luttwak has remarked, central bankers "invariably remain in office for terms of papal length often prematurely renewed for fear of disturbing financial markets."

In contrast to the Bush administration, writes Beckner, "Clinton was less clumsy in pressuring the Fed. He orchestrated the most clever campaign to manipulate monetary policy in memory." Regular threats, not from Clinton but from Congressional Democrats, to curtail powers of the Fed or to politicize it were used as leverage to keep rates down.

By November 1993, the once inflation-obsessed Greenspan would remark that "the only country in the world where inflation seems to be a problem is China," and that the Consumer Price Index overstated inflation perhaps by as much as one percent. Two percent, suggests Beckner; three percent said economist Lester Thurow.

Rates remained at 3 percent through 1993 and well into 1994. In response to the economic expansion, the Fed raised rates from 3 percent to 6 percent between mid-1994 and mid-1995. But with each raise, Thurow noted, "Greenspan admitted that the Fed could not point to even a hint of inflation in the current numbers." Then the Fed began to ease. It was part of its new thinking that, in Beckner's words, "Just as the Fed had started raising rates before there were visible signs of worse inflation, it would have to start lowering rates before there was an outright economic turndown." In 1996, it wasn't until Greenspan hinted at the possibility of further 'insurance' rate-cuts that Clinton announced his renomination.

Michael Lewis suggests that Greenspan is on the long road to *laissez faire*. "He has preserved a hard core of fanaticism by encasing it in a shell of pragmatism." Greenspan's friend Barbara Branden asserts that "I do know he believes he is doing the right thing within an Objectivist context," at the Fed, and a number of neo-Objectivists support his incrementalist approach. In *The Nation* Greenspan is quoted as saying, "I have been a strong supporter of the teachings of Ayn Rand." He told former wife Joan, "I haven't changed my mind. About anything." A 1995 televised Senate Banking Committee hearing included Greenspan suggesting both a return to the gold standard and the sunsetting of the Fed. But he then effectively negated each by noting that everyone else on the FOMC would oppose the gold move, and that he was just as ready to sunset the Defense Department as the Fed.

Beckner's view is that Greenspan has held his nose and learned to live with an obscenely oversized federal government that he and most mainstream conservatives would prefer to see on a stricter diet. Niederhoffer provides a harsher assessment. To the question "What do you think of Greenspan?" he responded in 1997 that "when a man gets a hankering for politics, rottenness grows in his soul." Central bankers like Greenspan "are politicians and they are interested in creating the World State and maintaining their power and perks, maintaining their access to the outside world through fantastic multimillion-dollar jobs after they leave."

So in the view of some neo Objectivists Greenspan has become a politician and can now be written off as a rotten human being. After all, Rand herself had stipulated that one should refuse "any job in a regulative administrative agency enforcing improper, non-objective laws"—such as controlling the money supply by creating fiat money and regulating the banks—because "it is improper to take the kind of work that nobody should be doing." A real Randian wouldn't be heading the Fed at all, even while helping contain inflation and government spending. "Central banks are a statist device to finance the welfare state," is the official line from the Ayn Rand Institute.

The ARI position on Greenspan, articulated by economist Richard Salsman, is that, "He is not an Objectivist, but a pragmatic-statist," less economist than bureaucrat. "He does not work in a statist government to rationally reform it. . . . His motivation is power lust." Greenspan is a Dr. Stadler, the scientist who sells out his scientific integrity for political clout in *Atlas Shrugged*. Greenspan "is fully aware of the truth . . . yet leads and promotes the government agency destructive of objective money . . . his public record . . . involves a series of intellectual cave-ins for the sake of maintaining his political standing." Among them, "In 1981, he scared Ronald Reagan and his advisors out of returning to the gold standard by resorting to bogus arguments. He headed the Social Security Commission in 1983 and recommended huge hikes in the payroll tax, even though partial privatization options were available . . . He fought Reagan's tax cuts and supported Bush and Clinton's tax hikes . . . When the banking system failed in the late 1980s, he refused to blame the Fed, or the socialist deposit insurance system. He always argued for more Fed powers. . . . He rejects sound stock-market advances as 'irrational exuberance'."

Although Beckner's account approximates an authorized biography, he acknowledges: "Mistakes were clearly made. The Fed could have done more to head off the banking problems of the late eighties and early nineties. It could have recognized the credit crunch and other economic headwinds" earlier than it did. "It could have eased credit more aggressively during the 1989 to 1992 period. . . . If the Fed proceeded more cautiously in the later period"—when raising rates during Clinton's first mid-term—"perhaps it was because memories were fresh of what happened in the earlier one," namely: a spectacular worldwide stock market crash, additional regulation of the U.S. stock markets, a damaging and widespread recession, an initially anemic recovery, and the premature ending of the Reagan-Bush era.

Even Greenspan, as Dean Foust in *Business Week* recounts, has now become convinced that the financial markets, which can react instantaneously to developments, are playing much of the Fed's old role of stimulating or restraining the economy. And as Thurow suggests, "If the battle against inflation is primary, central bankers" such as Greenspan at the Fed "will be described as the most important players in the game. Without it, they run rather unimportant institutions." However, inflation "died in the crash of asset values that began in the mid-1980s," a crash reinforced by the precipitously declining fortunes of world communism, OPEC, unionism, and nationalist economics, and by a rise in worker productivity made inevitable by ubiquitous computerization. Today, Thurow suggests, "business firms in their planning have to simultaneously plan for a world where there is no inflation, but there will be periodic deliberate recessions designed to fight imaginary inflations."

8

The Mind of the Guru

Rand the Dogmatist

I think I could sell some bumper stickers with a slogan like this: 'Ayn Rand said it. I believe it. That settles it!'

Objectivist Internet newsgroup posting

Rand was friendly for a few years around 1960 with distinguished philosopher John Hospers, who has acknowledged that he was influenced by her. The two had many extended discussions, but her short temper had him pulling his punches. Once when he identified a clear contradiction in one of her arguments, she ungraciously yielded, not with 'Touché,' but with, 'You bastard!' It was a delicate matter to point out a Randian error in reasoning without provoking a firestorm. It had to be done with feigned casualness, as if any such error were merely a minor detail. Often it just wouldn't be worth it. "So what if a few fallacies went unreported? Better to resume the conversation on an even keel . . . and spare oneself the wrath of the almighty, than which nothing is more fearful."

Rand was arrogant and dogmatic. In her later decades, at least, she became incapable of self-criticism. She became equally incapable of having a calm, tolerant discussion on civil terms with intellectual opponents. Unyielding disagreement or even persistent questioning on any significant point would drive her into a venomous rage. Not only did she seem unable to grasp the arguments of thinkers she denounced, she was actually little schooled in philosophy and in most of the intellectual traditions she reviled. Elementary mistakes abound in her depictions of them. Evidently she made sweeping assertions about philosophers she hadn't read.

In arguing, Rand could dish it out but not take it, reports Hospers. She would attack others nastily, but would accept even the mildest of criticism *only if* her interlocutor maintained a tone of complete agreement throughout, gently asking sympathetic questions as though needing to have a few things clarified before becoming a disciple. Then she'd be "sweetness itself," Hospers recollects.

When Rand complained that contemporary philosophers were ignoring her, Hospers suggested that she write up an idea, briefly or at length, publish it in a philosophy journal, and then respond in writing to philosophers' criticisms. But she never did this, so averse was she to submitting her ideas to the give and take of rational discussion. She could not bear to see her own views criticized. Hospers speculates that she wouldn't have lasted ten minutes anyway. She would have gone into the stratosphere with anger, "and that would have been the end of that."

By May 1964 Rand had formalized her policy: "I never engage in debates about my philosophy." Kelley would later say of such a stance that, "I do not see how the danger of partiality and hasty integration can be avoided by someone unwilling to debate adherents of other positions."

Inevitably, Rand fell out with Hospers, as she fell out with nearly all her close intellectual relationships, typically never again speaking to the erstwhile friend or that friend's associates. The break with Hospers came after he had arranged for Rand to deliver a paper at a philosophy colloquium. The paper was 'Art and Sense of Life', which Hospers thought interesting and provocative. Unfortunately he was obliged by academic custom to voice at least some minor criticisms following her address. Rand exploded. She really did take any criticism as a betrayal, and at an Objectivist gathering that evening Hospers was shunned, the unspoken signal of excommunication.

Rand's horror at having her ideas dissected and her hostility to all but obsequious or tame questions have been reported by many, and can be witnessed on videos of Rand's appearances on the *Donahue* show in 1979 and 1980. (Rand complained bitterly to Donahue about hippies' and certain questioners' lack of manners, but the core of manners is consideration for others, and Rand had approvingly written in her journal that her ideal man, Howard Roark, was "born without the ability to consider others.") Though a Renaissance was presumed to be blooming within Rand's inner circle during the 1960s, its model was Galt's Gulch, where as Steele notes, "everyone makes speeches all the time expounding Rand's opinions, the listeners all blissfully nodding their heads in agreement. They are "saved by coming to agree in every particular with Rand."

In 1996 Nathaniel Branden recalled an incident which illustrates Rand's touchiness, the way she was handled by her foremost followers and how unlike a science Objectivism is. In *Atlas Shrugged*, Rand had defined reason as the faculty that *perceives*, identifies, and integrates the evidence of the senses. But 'perceiving what is perceived' is a tad redundant, so an NBI student sent in on audiotape the suggestion that 'perceives' be dropped from the definition. Rand "went almost immediately ballistic, and she began to read the riot act to this poor unknown," informing him that he wasn't a serious student of her work. Months later, Branden found himself rethinking the merits of this spurned proposal and decided to bring it up with Rand. However, he realized he had better avoid mentioning that student. On Branden's suggestion, she instantly agreed to drop 'perceives' from that definition in future writings. Yet she would never acknowledge that this change had been made or specifically repudiate the old definition. "She didn't want to say in print that she'd made a mistake."

Rand told Hospers in the early 1960s, "Today, I am not looking for intelligent disagreement any longer . . . what I *am* looking for is intelligent agreement. That is what any thinker looks for, when and if he knows he has discovered and stated something which is new." I have yet to find any record of Rand's *ever* having sought out intelligent disagreement, something that many original thinkers do indeed seek out by way of testing and honing their new ideas.

Instead we have O'Neill obliged to report that Rand's "favorite type of verification is self-quotation. She never tires of quoting her own eloquent words." *Atlas* "assumes the proportions of sacred writ in her subsequent writings." Readers typically go from Rand's novels to her non-fiction essays for elaboration and real-life application of the novels' ideas. Yet in essay after essay, quotations from the novels are scattered like product placements in contemporary movies.

An Ignorant Oracle?

He had been quick to see that where people were even fifty years ago aroused by miracles, they are to-day attracted by specious reasoning.

Merwin-Webster, *Comrade John*

Rand originated an Objectivist tradition of proudly refusing to read books and articles which she knew to be evil, thereby sparing herself and her successors any exposure to such malignant falsehoods or the exercise of refuting them. The downside of such a tradition, however, is exemplified by the following: in a letter, Rand refers to Whittaker Chambers's review of *Atlas Shrugged* in the *National Review*. Rand, having refused to read the review, instead had it perused by some confidante who told her it claimed that *Atlas Shrugged* advocates dictatorship. Not so, though it *is* one sizzler of a review, imputing to Rand a maliciousness that would gladly urge all her worthless opponents to march themselves off to a gas chamber.

Asked in 1991 why Rand never read William O'Neill's book on her philosophy, *With Charity toward None*, Nathaniel Branden replied defensively that Rand simply "wasn't interested" in that kind of thing. When I asked Barbara Branden if Rand had read either O'Neill or the Albert Ellis book, *Is Objectivism a Religion?*, she replied that "Probably someone would have given her a fast synopsis. Her policy was to not give free publicity to people who were denouncing her." Surely though she could have profited from their critiques without publicly mentioning them.

After college, Rand appears to have read few if any major philosophers other than Nietzsche, whose works are more literary, rhetorical and speculative than carefully reasoned. She reports having bought and delved into the complete works of Aristotle during the 1940s; however one suspects that she may have merely skimmed these selectively. Her review of Randall's book on Aristotle made Aristotle-scholar Jack Wheeler wonder if she had read any Aristotle at all. A number of her published marginal notes show her deciding to check a given point about Aristotle by asking Leonard Peikoff.

Hospers relates that during their two years of regular conversations, he tried to give Rand some idea of the essentials of modern philosophy since Descartes, but failed. It was sometimes almost comical how she persisted in misunderstanding Moore and Wittgenstein, gripped as she was by the ludicrously-mistaken conviction that all such philosophers hold it to be doubtful that there are tables, trees, and other physical entities. Mack points out that in reading Rand's attacks on contemporary philosophy, one is left wondering precisely whom is being attacked. Her sole quotation is Wittgenstein's celebrated remark 'Don't look for the meaning; look for the use', which she misunderstands as recommending opinion polls to ascertain the meanings of concepts. Mack speculates that Rand read no philosophy published after World War II.

Rand sincerely believed that she knew what the well-known philosophers had said and meant. She had taken a handful of philosophy courses in Russia and picked up further nuggets of what given philosophers had supposedly said from the likes of Barbara Branden and Leonard Peikoff, both pursuing graduate studies in philosophy at then-undistinguished New York University, neither of whom would make their mark in philosophy. Being acolytes, both have expressed amazement at Rand's ability to penetrate to the core of any issue, but being acolytes, they should perhaps have considered their limitations in properly presenting philosophical ideas to a guru so appreciative of a spin on those ideas in the direction of her preconceived worldview. In any case, her belief that she could accurately reconstruct the thinking of the great philosophers from such biased, second-hand, and perhaps third-rate reports was an exercise in self-conceit.

On what did Rand base her repeated denunciations of western culture? In the last 30 years of her life, Rand read a slew of mystery novels, but little of a rigorous theoretical nature. She followed the culture, recalls Nathaniel Branden, chiefly through *The New York Times*, television, some movies, and a few plays. Branden claims that reading the newspaper as thoroughly as Rand did and watching as much TV as she did enabled her to draw some fairly meaningful and legitimate conclusions about the culture.

Not only did Rand review books that she plainly acknowledged not having read, such as John Rawls's *A Theory of Justice*, she also reviewed movies she hadn't seen, but without mentioning that detail. In the June 1969 issue of the *Objectivist*, there appeared an eviscerating review of *Charly, Bullitt*, and *2001: A Space Odyssey*, entitled 'The War of Liberation in Hollywood', under the byline, "Ayn Rand and Erika Holzer." Today a successful novelist, Holzer recalls: "I didn't do it up to snuff so she took my movie reviews which were apparently very good—*she* hadn't seen the movies— and then was able to weave a moral out of the whole thing." Rand let her unsuspecting followers assume that her bile had been provoked at first hand.

O'Neill points out that despite the Objectivist lauding of 'the mind', Objectivism actually implies a kind of anti-intellectualism. This emerges from Rand's view that certain truths are self-evident to anyone not intentionally 'evading reality'. So while thought is good, excessive thought—such as critically scrutinizing propositions which Rand has decided are beyond question—comes to be seen as pointlessly morbid, even 'anti-life'. As one follower puts it, "Why doubt that which is evidently and objectively true?"

A number of neo-Objectivists, including David Kelley and Eric Mack, have lamented the way Objectivists cope with criticism and have pointed out, what is a commonplace for non-Objectivists, that we tend to have a bias for self-confirmation, correctable only by exposing ourselves to opposing arguments. In 1996, even Nathaniel Branden finally conceded to a neo-Objectivist audience that *Atlas Shrugged* cannot itself be construed as defensible philosophy. Perhaps he was nudged toward that reassessment by Christopher Faille's *Liberty* article on Francisco's 'money speech' in *Atlas Shrugged*, showing it to be effective rhetoric but lousy reasoning.

The Banality of Ayn Rand's Thought

Another disadvantage of not reading one's opponents is not knowing when their position approximates one's own. Often Rand and Randians suppose that she is the lone voice in espousing a given position when it actually matches the prevailing view, or at least one widely-held view, among scholars. Mack suggests that if Rand had known the actual views of writers such as Ryle, Austin, and Wittgenstein, she would have seen that they were "on her side." Rand was sufficiently unfamiliar with the philosophical literature as to believe that her ideas were new discoveries, rather than mainly derivative. In fact, many of her ideas had long since been elaborated in great detail.

Is there anything original in Rand? Hospers judged her as certainly no great originator of ideas. A number of writers, including the Norwegian neo-Objectivist Kirsti Minsaas, have pointed out that, although owing something to Aristotle, Rand's ideas are in all respects less satisfactory or well-developed than Aristotle's. In political philosophy, George Smith points out that Rand says very little that was not said many times over by classical liberals in the eighteenth and nineteenth centuries.

Philosopher Douglas Rasmussen replied to the question as to what in Rand is original: "In one sense I would say *nothing*, and in another sense I would say *the following* ideas: (1) 'Measurements *must* exist in some quantity, *can* exist in any';

(2) 'Without life there can be no values', (3) 'Consciousness has identity'." Rasmussen holds that no one ever quite *emphasized* these ideas in the way that Rand did. "That is her originality." He adds that to speak of Rand having a philosophic system "is a bit much. . . . Aristotle, Aquinas, Spinoza, and Hegel had a 'system', or at least a body of detailed work that tried to put everything together. Rand did not come close to that." In fact, Rand viewed her epistemology articles "as a preview of my future book on Objectivism," which she never wrote.

To William O'Neill, Rand's philosophy: (1) is simple; (2) is extreme, and thus memorable; (3) is dogmatic, and thus easily classifiable; (4) fills a hitherto empty philosophic category: non-theistic essentialistic realism; (5) is untenable, and thus of use in professorial one-upmanship. O'Neill long ago characterized Rand's philosophy as a "theodicy of capitalism." Her recently-published journals confirm that this was her intention. She attributes Communism's popularity among youth to the fact that it "offers a definite goal, inspiration and ideal, a positive faith. . . . The old capitalism has nothing better to offer than the dreary, shop-worn, mildewed ideology of Christianity . . . the best possible kindergarten of communism." Consequently, "a new faith is needed, a definite, positive set of new values and a new interpretation of life," one more irreconcilably opposed to Communism than its bastard weak-sister—Christianity."

Rand presented her thought to the world as rigorously worked out by relentless logic from indisputable premises. She told an audience of architects, "I use words the way you use a slide-rule." Hospers recalled: "I found her linguistic habits quite sloppy." Non-Objectivist philosophers familiar with her philosophic essays are nearly always appalled by her sloppiness and ignorance. Antony Flew, like Rand an outspoken atheist and a strong supporter of free-market capitalism, rated her contribution to philosophy as "absolutely zilch." Referring to Rand's philosophic *magnum opus, Introduction to Objectivist Epistemology*, he was aghast: "To think of that as a major contribution seems to me just ridiculous. . . . That sort of thing is unintelligible to me. . . . One begins to look for explanations like transference on the analyst." As far as reasoning goes, Rand "committed almost every error that you might look for."

After citing several examples, philosopher Gary Merrill concluded that Rand's "egregiously poor scholarship" is so systematic and so deeply embedded in her work that it is virtually impossible to separate her ideas from the inept or dishonest manner in which they are expressed. "If there is such a thing as pseudo-philosophy," by analogy with pseudoscience, "this is it."

The Virtue of Selfishness

Rand advocated the virtue of selfishness as an ethical guide to life. But she did not mean 'selfishness' in the ordinary sense. As Flew put it, her advocacy of selfishness does not mean 'Do what you want to do!' but 'Do what you want to do when what you want to do is fulfilling a Randian ideal of humanity!'

The person drawn into an Objectivist milieu soon finds that, rather than becoming liberated from prior constraints, he is further constrained by countless new rules. He comes to feel anxious and guilty, fearful of overtly enjoying an unObjectivistic piece of music or art, feeling sexually turned on by a non-Objectivist, or taking an overly active interest in non-Objectivist family and friends. Rand plausibly identifies true selfishness with rational, long-term selfishness. It's a truism that enlightened self-interest requires some measure of self-control and life-planning. But Rand's rigid ideology combines with her arbitrary eccentricity to then generate a whole slate of such measures, which she pronounces will make us profoundly happy in the long-run, as opposed to witlessly sated in the present.

Rand tells us that "the exact meaning and dictionary definition of the word 'selfishness' is: *concern with ones own interests.*" In fact, dictionaries define selfishness as an *excessive* or *exclusive* concern with one's own advantage, in disregard of others. Rand invented a new definition of the word 'selfish', but would never admit it. Barbara Branden speculates that Rand got the definition from a very old dictionary long since gone missing. Sciabarra merely objects that "most" dictionaries define 'selfishness' as concern *only* with ones own interests. Sciabarra's readers might suppose that he knows of a dictionary that defines selfishness as Rand does.

While Rand always insisted that her use of 'selfishness' conformed to the dictionary, following her death, orthodox Objectivist Harry Binswanger revealed at last that one of Rand's achievements was to have shown that terms like 'selfishness' had heretofore been improperly defined. Rand took traditional words and gave them new, rational definitions, says Binswanger, sidestepping Rand's own denial that she was doing any such thing.

Rand similarly changed the definition of 'altruism', the supreme vice in Objectivism. Dictionaries define 'altruism' as an unselfish regard for the welfare of others. This means a regard transcending exclusive or excessive concern with one's own advantage, an uncontroversial virtue in every ethics apart from Objectivism. Rand so redefined 'altruism' as to imply a complete abandonment of one's own interests leading inexorably to self-destruction and premature death. Her purpose was to make doctrines with even one baby toe on the slippery slope to totalitarianism sound as if they too are essentially treating the individual as 'a sacrificial animal'.

Throughout *The Fountainhead* Rand wrongly uses the word 'egotist' when she means 'egoist'—a common enough error and easy to slip into, especially for one whose native language is not English. Two years following publication she would still be describing Roark, in a letter, as "The absolute egotist." Decades later, having at some point discovered the embarassing gaffe, she mentions it and puts the blame squarely on an unspecified, faulty dictionary, which, like the dictionary giving her definition of 'self-ish', has yet to be found.[1] A reasonable reaction to the discovery might have been to apologize for the error, and ask the publisher to make line corrections throughout the book in subsequent printings, if necessary offering to accept deductions from royalties to defray this additional typesetting expense caused solely by the author's blunder.

The Objectivist argument is further complicated by Rand's claim that there can never be real conflicts of interest between two rational humans: if two people apply for the same job, it is in the best interests of *A* that *B* get the job if *B* is better qualified. Nozick observed that Rand never offered a knock-down argument for her harmony-of-interests claim, and if genuine conflicts of interest really are possible, she offers no reason why the rational individual should always exclude the option of using force or fraud to enhance his own values at some other rational person's expense. If there are conflicts of interest, in other words, Rand, who tries to derive all morality from self-interest, is left without any argument for respecting individuals' rights. Dwyer states the obvious, namely that, "Genuine conflicts of interest are ordinary, everyday occurrences." Neo-objectivist lawyer Murray I. Franck suggests that conflicts of interest are inherent in society, and besides, to determine in each case which side was rational or irrational in any apparent conflict of interest would require an impossible approximation of omniscience. Franck concludes: "As Madison argued, and Lincoln perfected, a basic tenet of the American political culture is and must remain a respect for the rights of others *despite* conflicts of interest." In fact, espousing egoism in opposition to altruism *presupposes* genuine conflicts of interest, for these are the very problem for which *any* ethic is the proposed best solution.

Steele remarks that "'The virtue of selfishness' sounds like a serious challenge to conventional thinking, or at least an echo of Stirner, but because selfishness is redefined, most of traditional bourgeois morality comes out unscathed. What Rand adds is the denigration of common decencies." Rand knew something of individualist anarchist Max Stirner's famous 1845 advocacy of unqualified selfishness in *The Ego and His Own*. She remarks in a letter that the head of the National Industrial Conference Board had given a 'pink' acquaintance copies of both *The Ego and His Own* and Nietzsche's *Thus Spake Zarathustra*. At age 23 she had enthused in her journal: "what is good for me is right." She considered this Stirnerist sentiment "the best and strongest expression of a real man's psychology I ever heard." At age 30 she would write: "One puts oneself above all and crushes everything in one's way to get the best for oneself. Fine!" On the other hand, the Stirnerian motto that "Nothing is higher for me than myself"— and here he most emphatically includes any doctrine that does not unreservedly serve even the most eccentric of one's personal interests and whims—might have been helpful to Randians whose grim selfishness came to mean living a life that Rand, or Branden, or Peikoff, would approve of.

Classical liberals since Adam Smith have taken for granted that the pursuit of self-interest, apart from being unavoidable, is also beneficial to everyone when there is competition. But they don't share Rand's rosy view of total selfishness. George Gilder suggests that selfishness, in the dictionary sense, leads to a desire for unearned benefits and to organized pressure on the state to provide them. Ryerson contends that "special favors sought from government by this or that business are driven by selfishness, by contempt for the common good, and are bad not because they fail to serve the selfishness of the beneficiary (which they obviously do), but because they distort fair conditions of business competition." The Randian objection that such perpetrators are hurt in the long run by the resulting distortions disregards the fact that they will often have reaped the ill-gotten gains, comfortably retired, and died peacefully before the larger social ripples their actions have collectively caused can engulf them individually.

In her private journal Rand does rail against what she calls "vulgar selfishness," by which she means sacrificing others to self, "living through others through ruling them." Rand's ultimate aim is *laisser faire,* so she can't abide self-promoting behavior that coercively intrudes upon individuals. But having adopted and revved up the pro-selfishness rhetoric of 1920s business theory, and having insisted that no one can ever truly gain at the expense of anyone else, she felt obliged to expel people-users from the realm of the selfish on the dubious pretext that a worthy individualistic self doesn't need or want to dominate other selves. Objectivists, confronted with all-too-common behavior that anyone would find objectionable and which non-Objectivists brand as selfish, will instead depict it either as irrational in the long term or in its full context, or as indicating an absence of anything worth dignifying as a self and thus self-less, evil, and irrational to boot.

Objectivists excel in contriving arguments for why practically any given conventionally-correct way to behave turns out to be in a person's self-interest anyway. But there are some divergences. Rand was generally contemptuous of charitable endeavors, other than ones that she undeniably benefitted from personally. Although Rand admired Victorian England and America, she evidently did not admire the tremendous outpouring of voluntary charity and social work that was an integral part of those societies and helped to make industrialization bearable. Observes historian Modris Eksteins, "In the ideal moral code of the nineteenth-century middle class, the goal of individual effort was always social harmony, the commonweal, the public good. In the end the interests of the individual, which were to be protected and furthered by the state, were nevertheless subservient to the public good; personal restraint was the hallmark of respectability."

Rand saw a place for what she called 'benevolence', a modicum of general goodwill which could be extended even to strangers. But she considered it morally wrong, for example, to risk one's own life to save a stranger. Hospers asked her what she would do if, while driving a car, she were suddenly faced with the choice of running smack into her own dog or of swerving into a human stranger. She refused to give an answer. Several neo-Objectivists have pointed out that the Randian focus on individual survival provides no rationale for having and raising children. (Had the World War II generation consisted of proto-Randians, the bulk of Rand's readership and royalties would never have materialized.)

Objectivist and neo-Objectivist groups sometimes discuss the pros and cons of situations over which more conventional thinkers would not pause. An Objectivist newsgroup considered the following dilemma. A child has been poisoned, and the only antidote is in a locked drugstore. Some Objectivists suggested that it would be immoral to violate the drugstore owner's rights by breaking into his drugstore to secure the antidote and save the child's life.

A typical dilemma for Objectivists is that of the solo pilot of a small private plane faced with the choice of crash-landing in a schoolyard, killing the children playing there but saving his own life, or crashing into the nearby ocean, which will certainly kill him. Murray Franck opts for the latter by dressing altruism in egoistic attire. Franck argues that when the pilot took off, he could have foreseen the possibility that he might be forced to land away from an airport, and that his life would be at risk. "To claim that it is morally justified to land in the school yard to save his life at the expense of the children . . . is to punish the innocent children for the consequences of his choosing to fly in the first place." Leaving aside the leap from pure self-interest to not harming the innocent, Franck's argument implies that if the pilot had instead been forced by a terrorist to take off at gunpoint (the terrorist soon exiting the scene via parachute), it would then be morally OK to mow down the kids, because he would not then have freely undertaken the risk associated with the flight.

Official Objectivism applauds the Chinese protestors who defied their government at Tienanmen Square in 1989. A poster displayed at the Ayn Rand Institute features a lone pedestrian defying the oncoming tanks. But was risking his very survival motivated by pure self-interest? Surely self-interest would counsel discrete efforts at ameliorating conditions, not staring down a tank. The heroism of the Tienanmen rebels, as stirring for ARI as for everyone else, was self-sacrificing to the core. Randians desperately want to attach to their 'living' philosophy the same sizzle of heroism that Rand contrived in her fiction, despite having philosophically withdrawn the motive force that might light such fires in the first place.

Consider what Rand herself said in the 1960s on the Columbia University student radio station, when asked to consider an ethical emergency wherein an armed *A* says to an unarmed *B*, 'Shoot *C* or I'll shoot you'. Rand's answer is, "Since he is under the threat of death, whatever he decides to do is right . . . you could not blame him for the murder. . . . No rights are applicable in such a case. . . . Once the element of force is introduced, the element of morality is out." The only fiction aimed at strictly embodying

Randian morality is fiction constructed to make that morality look good. Were someone to write a novel depicting the downside of Randian morality, including its application to emergencies, most readers would be appalled.

As Mary Gaitskill suggests, Rand's defense of self-seeking appeals to young people tired of being reproved by parents for *any* assertion of self that disregards how others will feel about it. But such self-seeking is more consistent with modern culture as it has been evolving in this century than it is at odds with it. "A little bravura selfishness has always seemed attractive in American fictional heroes," argues Pierpont, "if only to lighten our perpetual burden of doing good." In any case, "Rand's novels are riddled with syntactical loopholes that permit, in bluffest disguise, just the compassionate behavior she claims to disavow."

Although only Objectivists accept Rand's theory of selfishness, her popularity as a writer and the appeal of Objectivism to many adolescents are consistent with a wider change in the culture. The twentieth century saw the loosening of family bonds and the emergence of the self, rather than the family, as the basic unit of society. When Rand left Russia and arrived in America, she found a culture which has been described as a "cult of the self." American advertisers were promoting cigarettes to women as "torches of freedom." Numerous 1920s fads appear to have left their mark on the impressionable young immigrant from Russia: curves were being abandoned in favor of straight lines, dieting was becoming fashionable, short bobbed hair was giving women a boyish look, and a new International Style was taking hold in architecture, emphasizing those straight lines. Rand became a lifelong dieter via amphetamines, never substantially changed her helmet of short hair, and bought an International Style house near Los Angeles. Even the faces of Rand's male heroes are made up of 'straight lines', and "the fire in a man's hand" is Rand's rhapsodic updating of "torches of freedom." The explicit defense of selfishness and individual rights along proto-Objectivist lines was also a staple of 1920s business theory. (See Chapter 10 below.)

The Crumbling Foundations of
Objectivist Ethics

Criticizing the non-orthodox Objectivists who support David Kelley, Peikoff asks rhetorically, "If value judgments do not flow inexorably from the judgment of truth or falsehood, if the 'ought' does not flow inexorably from the 'is', where do value-judgments come from and on what are they based? No answer. What then is left of the *objectivity* of values, and thus of the whole Objectivist ethics, politics, esthetics? Nothing." That's the trouble. Non-Objectivists find it astounding that the very little Rand wrote about deriving an 'ought' from an 'is' could be persuasive to anyone. But here is Peikoff admitting that upon that persuasiveness rests Objectivism in its entirety.

In Rand's formal philosophy, one's own life, in the sense of biological survival, is the standard of moral value. So it cannot be right to give up one's life. But Rand's fictional heroes are sometimes prepared to die voluntarily for a cause or a valued other. Even the formal philosophy sometimes has survival as a rational being under proper conditions constituting the minimum human standard, not *mere* survival. Objectivists and neo-Objectivists who cling to Rand's ethics disagree on whether survival or flourishing is the foundation of values. David Kelley has stated that every value and every virtue that goes to make up a good life *must* be shown to have a bearing on survival. It must enhance prospects for self-preservation. Kelley thinks that this is a very large task yet to be fully carried out, but an inescapable one. (If so, why should we at present accept the Objectivist ethics, given that this crucial evidence for it isn't in yet, and may never be?) He suggests that there is no way to show that some value is a need except by proving that being deprived of that value would impair an organism's ability to preserve itself. Without the survival criterion, then, ethics becomes arbitrary.

To a non-Objectivist it does not look promising to reduce ethical decisions to a choice between one's own continued existence or non-existence. To take just one example, some people like taking risks. If risk-taking is built into our genes, as it may be, then a purely survival orientation is even counter to human nature. Would Objectivists really prefer a world where adventurous activities are deemed immoral? Other neo-Objectivists, returning to Aristotle, espouse flourishing rather than survival.

Rand had anticipated this impasse in 1945, writing in her journal that the axiom of her morality was *"not* 'Man must survive', *but:* 'Man must survive as *man'*. This is the crucial point; otherwise it becomes an issue of any kind of survival . . ." Crucial, perhaps, but forever fudged.

Individual Rights

For Rand, the implications of recognizing individual rights constitute whatever is good about American culture. Rand's conception of rights owes much to the nineteenth-century liberal Herbert Spencer, though Objectivists rarely mention Spencer. Like Spencer, Rand contends that persons in close proximity to one another require guarantees of non-interference with life-sustaining activities. Neo-Objectivist George H. Smith points out that the crux of Rand's theory of rights (and therefore, I would maintain, the crux of her entire 'system' of thought) comes close to being a paraphrase of Spencer.

Bill Bradford observed in 1990 that natural rights theory has increasingly been questioned and rejected by libertarians. In the 1970s, libertarians mostly accepted a theory of natural rights derived from Rand or Rothbard, but by the 1990s these theories were being discarded. Even those libertarians still attracted by a Randian kind of rights theory usually agree with libertarian philosopher Fred Miller that Rand offered "a sketch of an argument" rather than a complete theory. Rand's erstwhile intellectual heir, Nathaniel Branden, now says that Rand's ethics is "underdeveloped and very incomplete." Philosopher and former Objectivist Eric Mack states that "her arguments about moral rights and their foundation . . . are just bad."

Objectivists have yet to offer a convincing argument for the step from ethical egoism to respect for other people's rights. Kelley acknowledges that if "I understand that your freedom is good for you in exactly the same way that my freedom is good for me, I don't yet have a reason for regarding *your* freedom as good for *me*. But this is precisely the point that *must* be established if we are going to validate rights on the basis of ethical egoism." Kelley is counting on the future success of a theoretical project doomed to frustration in the view of most thinkers. So much for the confident proclamation of certain truth.

Keeping the Government in Its Place

Rand argued that even the minimal government she advocated should be financed by voluntary donations, not by confiscation. Otherwise force is being initiated and the individual's natural rights trampled. Some neo-Objectivists find Rand's notion of absolute rights incompatible with the very constitutional government required to protect individual rights (defined less absolutely than Rand would define them). Lawyer Murray Franck has argued for the necessity of compulsory taxation, contending that any government dependent on the whim of contributors will be a short-lived one. Moreover, "Ayn Rand's position that if sufficient funds are not contributed voluntarily, the nation deserves dictatorship and/or death, is *collectivist* in that it reifies the concept of nationhood and ignores the rights of each individual."

Objectivist philosopher Allan Gotthelf argues that without a *moral* argument for capitalism, even when it is demonstrated in practice that less government intervention means superior results, people will argue that tomorrow's interventions will succeed where yesterday's have failed. Yet surely, to attain agreement on a new morality is a far more unlikely prospect than to attain agreement on the results of free-market versus controlled economies. What Objectivists overlook in their apocalyptic view of the future is that as long as predominantly capitalist economies keep government intervention within reasonable bounds in the long run, then capitalism (despite occasional downturns) will continue to deliver the goods and in doing so will win converts worldwide.

Because socialism was consciously organized and imposed in Rand's Russia, throttling incipient Russian capitalism in the process, Rand came to believe that capitalism too required for its survival an equivalent ideological substructure, *hers*, namely Objectivism. Yet capitalism has arisen in a variety of conditions and triumphed in the twentieth century despite the intellectuals' predominant support for socialism. Paul Johnson depicts capitalism as a morally neutral "organic process," springing from human nature and ingenuity. It will occur of its own accord unless positive steps are taken to prevent it, unlike socialism which has to be deliberately constructed under the guidance of intellectuals and coercively imposed.

Objectivism's Great Satan: Immanuel Kant

Rand once made a marginal note that Kant's defense of a sphere for faith "leads . . . to Hitler and Stalin, as its necessary, logical climax." Peikoff has affirmed that Rand held Kant to be morally much worse than any killer, because Kant unleashed the likes of Lenin, Stalin, Hitler, and Mao. Kant's "evasion of reality . . . makes possible and necessary all the atrocities of our age." According to Canadian economics professor and ARI Objectivist, John Ridpath, "Kant is a hater of man almost unparalleled in western literature." Ridpath agrees that Kant "is as Rand properly characterized him, the evilest man in history."

This view of Kant is so ingrained among Objectivists that even at a 1991 seminar of somewhat dissident Objectivists, that is, neo-Objectivists, half the participants in a group photograph are wearing T-shirts with a red slash through a circled 'Kant'. George Walsh is one of those sporting the latest in anti-Kant leisurewear. Walsh has since stated that Kant should *not* be thought of as the Great Satan of philosophy, and laments the fact that Objectivists typically label as Kantian anything they disagree with, often applying the label 'Kantian' to writers who would not have agreed with a word Kant wrote.

An example of where Rand-inspired anti-Kantianism can lead is Objectivist-cum-John-Bircher William McIlhany, who attributes such evil modern tendencies as Einsteinian relativity, quantum mechanics, and non-Euclidean geometry to Kantian irrationalism. Rand is known to have made disparaging remarks about modern physics, and pro-nuclear-power crusader Petr Beckmann, who was affiliated with official Objectivism in the 1980s, edited an anti-Einsteinian physics journal.

Gary Merrill expresses exasperation that when Rand cites a source for her interpretation of Kant, she quotes from an utterly obscure 1873 book by Henry Mansel. There are many translations of works by Kant and many reputable commentaries on his theories, all apparently unknown to Rand. Merrill maintains that even the quotation from Mansel fails to support Rand's interpretation of Kant. IOS founding member George Walsh emphasized how easily one can "read a primary source under the influence of a secondary source and get thrown off the tracks." Walsh, who knew Rand and her philosophical ideas at first hand, also stated, "I don't think she was primarily a reader of primary sources."

It's hard to see why Kant should have been chosen as the Great Satan. In terms of influence, what Rand found most objectionable in Kant's views has generally been rejected by twentieth-century philosophy in the English-speaking world. Perhaps it is that Rand 'imprinted' philosophically on Nietzsche, and Nietzsche did punctuate his works with sardonic roastings of Kant that resonate with Rand's much later efforts. Adopting Nietzsche's stance on Kant would not have displeased Rand's University of Leningrad philosophy professors. As Sciabarra notes, most Russian philosophers before 1917 rejected Kant for having supposedly detached the mind from reality, precisely what Rand would most hold against him.

George Walsh, who has made a thorough study of Kant's metaphysics and epistemology, points out that Rand not only misrepresented Kant's reasoning, but because she didn't grasp what Kant was driving at, she exaggerated her differences from him, and overlooked how similar their views sometimes are. As against Rand's interpretation, Kant very clearly insisted that his notion of 'appearance' was not to be interpreted as 'distortion'. According to Walsh, Kant's view is that the mind must passively accept both the *a priori* forms of space, time, and causality (coming from within) and the *a posteriori* 'filler' of specific shapes, distances, colors, degrees of heat, and scientific laws (coming from without). Kant certainly does not hold that the mind creates the objects it becomes aware of, or that there can be any primacy of 'wish' in man's dealings with reality.

Not only was Rand mistaken, says Walsh, to attribute to Kant the position that human knowledge was a distortion and a delusion; she was also wrong in attributing to him the argument by which he allegedly arrived at that conclusion. (Rand thought that Kant argued that perception had to involve distortion just because the perceptual apparatus intervenes between perceiver and object.) In Walsh's view, quite at odds with Rand's depiction, Kant hoped to save the Enlightenment by urging a strategic withdrawal to what he regarded as impregnable outposts. Contrary to Rand, wishes and whims are strictly banished from Kant's ethics, the veto of faith over knowledge is never asserted, "and the strict examination of the arguments for God and immortality from the theoretical standpoint are declared a draw."

Like Rand, Kant was a classical liberal, committed to individual rights and limited government. Here again, Walsh corrects the Objectivist party line: "Kant's classical liberalism is, contrary to the statements of some Objectivists, consistent with the rest of his philosophy." While Walsh was an associate of Peikoff's, until 1989, to have made known the above views, had he arrived at them by then, would have meant instant excommunication.

For Walsh, Rand's inaccuracy about Kant provides "a warning to study the primary sources in estimating the place of major intellectual figures in history and get it straight. It is at the minimum very bad publicity for your own point of view if you make accusations that can easily be refuted." This erstwhile-orthodox Objectivist philosopher is citing Rand for setting a bad example in a crucial aspect of critical thinking. Philosopher Antony Flew, though no Kantian, agrees that Objectivists don't fairly portray Kant: "I want to have masses said for Kant's intentions because I think Kant's intentions were wholly good."

Hospers too saw things in Kant which Rand would probably agree with, and recommended her to read Kant's defense of individual rights and the passages in his *Metaphysics of Morals* on duties to oneself. Hospers maintained that Kant was actually decidedly less altruistic than the Christian tradition. Rand refused to read these passages, explaining that they could only be incidental details within a profoundly evil system of thought.

9

The Dark Side of the Guru's Soul

Perfectly Correct in Retrospect

I'll never be such a gosling to obey instinct, but stand as if a man were author of himself and knew no other kin.

William Shakespeare, *Coriolanus*

The mature Ayn Rand always said that her fundamental ideas had been developed in childhood and had never changed. She said, for instance, that her theory of sexuality was in place by the age of fifteen. It's not possible to check this implausible tale against any independent record of her youthful opinions, but knowing her lack of candor about specific issues later in life—her attempts to cover up her vulgar Nietzscheanism of the 1930s, for example—we can assume that Rand did reshape her early history to fit her evolving views.

Alissa Rosenbaum's mother, a high-school teacher of languages, insisted that Alissa learn French, Russia's language of high culture. French led her to the boys' adventure magazine that serialized *The Mysterious Valley*, a typical boys' story of British

India, comparable to the Indiana Jones stories of a later period. Late in life, Rand spoke of *The Mysterious Valley* and especially of its hero, with whom she had fallen in love. Orthodox Objectivist Harry Binswanger notes how Rand, in recollecting an illustrated drawing of the hero in *Mysterious Valley*, confabulates beyond what is there; the actual picture can't carry all the meaning she attributes to it. Yet Binswanger ignores this confabulating tendency when he discusses her alleged age-12 diary entries on the theory behind Communism and other serious subjects, and takes her decades-later paraphrasing of the long-since-destroyed entries at face value.

Rand has said that given her Russian surroundings, boredom was the chief emotion she experienced as a child. She felt there was nothing there for her, nor did she like being a child or part of a family. Her only real source of pleasure was stories and movies.

By all accounts little Alissa was not a very lovable child. It appears that she compensated for rejection by playing from her strong suit. This meant asserting intellectual and moral superiority over those around her. It also meant settling upon values, and arguments for those values, prior to much personal experience of life or facility with rational argument. And it meant concocting imaginary colleagues—heroes appreciative of her exalted intellect and disinclined to reject her.

For Rand "Russia was just a cesspool . . . real life, real intelligence and real people lay abroad." This she recalls concluding—despite having seen almost nothing of Russia outside that most *un*Russian of cosmopolitan cities: St. Petersburg—from her trip abroad at age nine to London, Switzerland, and Vienna. The view that 'real life lay abroad' was probably a commonplace among educated St. Petersburg traders.

She tells us that at age eleven she was already "very contemptuous of faith and mystical beliefs. . . . Reason was always an absolute for me. . . . I held that everything has to be proved and if something cannot be proved by reason, then it's nonsense. . . . If anyone would say anything against logic or reason, I would not care to argue because the feeling of contempt would be over-whelming." She says that by her mid-teens she had already concluded that the views of life of philosophers and other writers were wrong, that they had no arguments to offer and that since reason was on her side, she was right. "Once I could prove any-thing rationally, it was an absolute, there's no doubt about it because I could prove my case," she recalled. Rand would concede that as an adolescent she exhibited too much "violent intensity" and was too quick to draw others into argument.

Rand had no use for her peers as a child, a hostile depiction of what may have been a hurtful situation. She would later often complain about how the sensitivities of the truly talented are abused. Psychiatrist Allan Blumenthal, who knew Rand very well for many years, has suggested that it was "insecurity that led to her ultimate psychological problems . . . I don't think people liked her very much . . ." Joan Blumenthal added, "a very smart little girl . . . expressing her negative opinions about people and things."

During her childhood, things got much worse. John Hospers reports her recounting to him that "when the Soviet revolution broke . . . her father was classified as a capitalist because he had hired more than five people. He was simply cut off," and they would have starved in Leningrad (formerly St. Petersburg) had it not been for an uncle in Kiev with whom they stayed for several years, after first having to walk two thousand miles from Leningrad to Kiev. Rand mentioned "going up hills and walking across rocks in broken shoes, at age twelve or thirteen." Hospers thought this had made an enormous impression on her.

For an unsociable personality, Communism constitutes the nightmare of compulsory sociality in its least attractive form. If Alissa's anti-social nature predisposed her to hating Communism, then expropriation of her father's business and the family's conse-quent suffering would have clinched the matter. Later, a fully 'matured' personality emerging from this personal history would forge a highly-emotional anti-collectivist position, rationalized in completely impersonal terms, no doubt to avoid reliving unacceptable feelings of hurt and humiliation. Here we have a sequence of first being rejected, and responding by becoming anti-social and anti-society in general; second: expropriation and impoverishment, taking her anti-sociality off the back burner and transforming it into a flame-thrower of hatred concentrated on the new politico-economic system, and third, in America, a more fully intellectualized anti-collectivism, deployed not just against the Soviets but against New Deal and Great Society reform liberalism.

On the "About the author" page of *Atlas Shrugged*, Rand tells us that in her early years of struggling to establish herself in America, "No one helped me." This is inaccurate. Among numerous acts of kindness which the struggling Ayn Rand accepted: It was her relatives who arranged to have her expired visitor's visa renewed several times. A cousin translated her first 'screen originals' into readable English. Hard-pressed relatives gave her a train ticket to L.A. and $100, worth thousands in 1999 dollars. An aunt procured from a movie distributor she knew a letter of introduction for Ayn to a woman employed in the P.R. department of the Cecil B. DeMille Studio, and it was her trip to that studio which led directly to both an amazingly lucky meeting with DeMille himself *and* a husband. It was through DeMille that she got a pass to see a famous murder trial, thus providing her the required background for *The Night of January 16th*. When Rand got to L.A. she went straight to the Studio Club, a philanthropic venture offering Hollywood's female aspirants subsidized accommodation. During three years there, while often falling behind in her rent, Rand was never asked to leave. One time its director picked Ayn out to receive a patron's special $50 gift (worth more than $1,000 in 1999 dollars). During the lean years prior to publication of *The Fountainhead*, her friend Albert Mannheimer would lend her $500, worth several thousand today, an enormous help as she once admitted to Nathaniel Branden. In these and so many other respects Rand was the beneficiary of the charitable impulses of others. Once she had exhausted their use to her, she wrote novels and philosophical essays which downgraded such impulses and deprived them of justification.

Absolute Certainty through Total Control

We can be absolutely certain only about things we do not understand.

Eric Hoffer, *The True Believer*

Kramer and Alstad observe that psychological authoritarianism arises from a longing to submit to some near-superhumanly moral or knowledgeable source, *or* to be that source for others. Control was, understandably, for Rand, an obsession. The Bolshevik regime had wrested control of her life from her and she wanted it back. Recalled Nathaniel Branden, "Outside the territory where she felt in full intellectual control, she was utterly lacking in a spirit of openness or adventure."

Her social ideal and personal ideal were forced into compatibility. Rand insisted that everything in a man's life is subject to his mind's control and that the worst tragedies result from willfully suspending that control. She contends, "There is no place for whim in any human activity—if it is to be regarded as human, . . . no room for the unknowable, the unintelligible, the undefinable, the non-objective in any human product. This side of an insane asylum, the actions of a human being are motivated by a conscious purpose," and when they are not, "they are of no interest to anyone outside a psychiatrist's office." Her view is reminiscent of the Soviet policy of packing off to an asylum anyone with a reprehensible political whim. "She knew, as if from inside, how tyrants think," considered Hospers.

Rand hated surprises, even pleasant ones like a surprise party celebrating the publication of *Atlas Shrugged*. "I do *not* approve of surprises," was her immediate reaction. She sat stonefaced through the dinner and was still complaining about it years later. Nathaniel Branden commented: "I have no happy memories of the occasion." Surprise does not reassure. Total certainty reassures.

Rand believed that her rational mind always dominated and guided her emotions, and that this should be the case for everyone. Barbara Branden remembers, "She often said she understood *every* emotion she had and she knew where it came from and what it represented . . . not so. She didn't ,. . . partly because she did think the process is easier than it is." Rand never intro-spected. The Blumenthals say she didn't believe she *had* an uncon-scious, her mind having refused entry to the irrationalities so common to everyone else. So, presumably, her thinking could never be warped by an unconscious bias.

Fired up in 1928 by plans for her misanthropic novel *The Little Street*, she had noted in her journal, "The secret of life: You must be nothing but will. . . . Be a tyrant—no compromises with your-self. . . . You don't exist. You are only a writing engine," dedicated to "individualism, . . . the theme song, the goal, the only aim of all my writing." And so it was. In a 1945 open letter to *Fountainhead* readers she declared, albeit in a romanticizing mode, "I have never had any private life in the usual sense. . . . My writing is my life. . . . My life has been 'single-tracked'. . . . I have no hobbies, . . . few friends." Her whole life is dedicated to writing in defense of self-sufficient autonomy or individualism, or, more specifically, individual rights (the *sine qua non* of individualism), which in her view Christians and Christian philosophers like Kant had philo-sophically undermined to the point where the Bolsheviks could in good conscience and with plaudits from western intellectuals extirpate those rights, and with them the happy prosperity of Rand's family.

Rand outlined in her journal the basic character traits of her most famous hero, Howard Roark: "His emotions are entirely controlled by his logic." Two things dominate his entire attitude toward life: "his own superiority and the utter worthlessness of the world." He was "born without the ability to consider others. . . . Indifference and an infinite contempt is all he feels for the world and for other men who are not like him." Other people are merely a convenience for his work. He recognizes only the right of the exceptional (and by that he means only himself) "to create, and order, and command."

Rand writes that "my life purpose is the creation of the kind of world (people and events) that I like, i.e., that represents human perfection." She likes neither reality nor real people, inevitably imperfect as they are, but still thrives upon the company of imag-inary perfect beings who represent variations on what she most loves about herself. Singer compares the fantasy life of a child (like young Alissa) to that of a cult leader (like Ayn Rand): "The difference is that the cult leader has actual humans doing his bidding as he makes a world around him that springs from inside his own head." It's the difference between a Galt's gang and a real-life Collective in Rand's apartment.

Remarks Kay Nolte Smith, "Ayn lived very much in her head. She was a victim of the mind-body dichotomy she decried." Nathaniel Branden says of the long years of writing *Atlas Shrugged* that "Ayn had disappeared into that alternate reality and was not coming back." And *its* mysterious valley was an extension of *the* 'Mysterious Valley', the boys' adventure story that transformed her youth and whose Anglo-Saxon hero, Cyrus, made every Russian a pygmy by comparison in Rand's eyes, just as no Americans outside her own inner circle could measure up to the heroes in *Atlas Shrugged*. Branden recalls that at one point, "I could not shake off the idea of arrested emotional development. Were Frank and I characters in Ayn's storybook?" David Ramsay Steele suggests that *Atlas Shrugged* "has something of the unnerving quality of a delusional system made real" which we find in some of Philip K. Dick's sci-fi novels, but "Dick was doing it on purpose."

According to Allan Blumenthal, Rand "created an entire system, *including her philosophical system, to deal with her own psychological problems.*" To which this interviewer stammered, "*All* of Objectivism was to deal with her own psychological problems?" Blumenthal insisted, "That's my view." Though surely an exaggeration, this perspective reframes the statement she once made: "Objectivism is me. . . ."

Rand's attorney in the 1950s, Pincus Birner, once propelled Rand into a rage with his suggestion that *everyone*, Rand included, at some time or another had done something they knew was ethically wrong. Decades later when asked whether "according to your philosophy *you* are a perfect being," Rand replied: "Have I absorbed and practiced all of the principles of behavior which I preach? . . . I would say—Yes, resoundingly" Philip Smith offers, "I don't think she liked to change her mind because that would mean she made a mistake. I think the problem with Nathan that got her so upset was not that there was a split but that she had to change her mind on something"—which would imply less than perfect judgment. For Rand, moral perfection is not only possible but absolutely essential for man to survive. It's perfection or oblivion. Many of Rand's comments are like this: Things *should* be such and such, so they are. Since any man who occasionally puts faith above reason deserves to be destroyed, therefore he is.

Did Rand admit to the slightest blemish within her final 1,800 pages of fiction? Smith remembers her saying "the only thing she would ever change in *The Fountainhead* is where she's describing a dressing gown that Ellsworth Toohey wore as having Coty powderpuffs. She said, 'I would not use the brand name. I'd take out Coty.'" Adds husband Phil, "And 'Coke', where someone's drinking a Coke." The imperfections here aren't even literary; they consist of two inadvertent unremunerated product plugs. At Rand's private fiction-writing classes, Kay Nolte Smith recalls, Rand projected in manifold ways that to write a novel she would approve of, given the staggering dimensions of her novelistic achievements, would set a task such as would inevitably defeat any human being on earth other than herself.

Rand almost never left her apartment and was almost afraid of going out. Kay Nolte Smith again: "Remember that New Year's Eve party, a big tradition in the circle and which a lot of us dreaded but nonetheless it was the official thing. One year we were giving the party and we decided to get baby pictures of everyone; we were going to have a game and then see who could identify who. And I went over to her house to pick up a baby picture of Frank and she said it was the only picture of Frank that she had and that she was so nervous about my taking this out to have it shot, to make a slide of it for the party. She said, 'Won't it get burned if they take a picture of it? Couldn't the camera burn the picture?' I said, 'No, Ayn, it couldn't do that.' 'Well, maybe if you take it out, couldn't someone cut off your shoulderbag?' I said, 'No, Ayn, no one is going to cut off my shoulderbag.' And she said, 'Well, you could be hit by a taxi crossing the street, couldn't you?' . . . she really was paranoid about practical reality."

Rand confessed, "I have always been a little afraid of riding on trains, . . . thinking that some dreadful accident might happen at any moment." It was only her desperate ego-need for recognition in academia and the prospect of forgoing the honorary doctorate to be bestowed upon her by a west-coast college that got her aboard a plane for the first time, at age 58. She was "deathly afraid of germs," writes Barbara Branden, which made sense in the contagions of war-torn Russia and little sense in 1950s America. Contemptuous of all superstition, she had a 'good-luck' gold watch herself. She never invested the accumulated royalties from her millions in book sales, worrying that the government might somehow get its hands on them; consequently she left an estate worth less than a million dollars. Malfunctioning toasters and blouses with missing buttons seemed "malevolent adversaries whose sole intention was to frustrate and thwart her," eliciting intensely angry exasperation, Nathaniel Branden remembers. Her lack of physical coordination and incomprehension of the mechanical meant that she never learned to drive, guaranteeing a sense of isolation at her California ranch 20 miles from Los Angeles.

Rand suffered from prolonged bouts of depression. The one following publication of *Atlas Shrugged*, recalls Nathaniel Branden, "would last almost without abatement for more than two long years." Writes Barbara Branden, "To spend more than thirteen years on *Atlas* and then to re-emerge" exhausted into the world to awful reviews "has got to be a stunning kind of negative experience . . . the bitterness, the . . . alienation, the sense that the world had nothing to offer her, they just snowballed. . . . By 1968, the negative, angry, moralistic aspects of her personality had become totally predominant." According to Nathaniel Branden, Barbara in 1957–58 was actually copying Ayn's reaction and moaning about how "this world has died for me—the world has become an essentially boring place in which to live." In fact, old 1940s comrade-in-arms Ruth Alexander depicted Rand in the New York *Mirror* review as now "destined to rank in history as the outstanding novelist and profound philosopher of the twentieth century." Faint praise perhaps, but also a hint to think in terms of long-term impact. Rand's despair was largely self-inflicted.

Smith also relates that Edith Efron was over at Rand's apartment one day "and there was a knock on the door . . . it was some person selling magazines to get through college, so Ayn launches into this thundering tirade, 'Do you know what the magazines have done to me? Do you expect me to finance them after the slime they've printed about me?' That poor little student— 'Aaaagghhh!' That was Ayn; *That* was Ayn!" Yet many a writer has put a decade or so into a book, only to have it published to mostly negative reviews. In her case the book sold very well and kept on selling. It was her choice to cease writing fiction at age 52, very young for a novelist to retire, and withdraw into the center of a cult. Rand told Barbara Branden, "My attitude always toward reviews and compliments, since my high school days, was that I expect superlatives or nothing." The unforthcomingness of the kind of rapturous appreciation of her work that she craved from the intellectual world made her generally unhappy. Her accomplishments, in themselves, really *didn't* satisfy.

Rand said later that "the man who saved my life" in the post-*Atlas* period was Nathaniel Branden. "I was almost paralyzed . . . by disgust and contempt . . . for the whole culture." After her split with Nathan a decade later, she never rose much above a depressed state. Her continuing aversion to exercise was so extreme that following her lung cancer operation she refused to so much as move a limb, even though this stubborn immobility was life-endangering. Barbara Branden notes that from the time of her surgery in 1974, Rand was never again without physical ailments. She was probably clinically depressed from her husband's death in 1979 until her own death in 1982.

Joan Blumenthal recollects that in the 1970s, "She didn't say she was depressed. She said she was disgusted with the world. It was a moral issue again." Allan adds: "She was saying 'There's no one to write for any more' and she didn't 'care about posterity'." Nothing gave her pleasure. Nothing was worth a major effort. And as always, it was all other peoples' fault. "Even Leonard wasn't paying her all the attention she would have liked," what with her "constant complaining . . . when we were still there she was complaining bitterly *all* the time. She'd have two-to-three hour conversations with Joan, complaining. She was not a happy woman."

Dr. Blumenthal looks back: "We knew there was trouble for a long long time. . . . As we get older we all become more what we are, and she certainly did. And it became intolerable . . . you couldn't disagree with her about anything." Added Joan: "It's impossible to stay in a relationship with someone when you cannot disagree. She always said it would be monstrously boring to be with someone without any differences but I don't know what her idea of a difference was . . . except that it was in a pretty narrow range, that's for sure." (Rand would soon say on a *Donahue* program: "I want to hold only my ideas. . . . You know what my policy is? I don't deal with those who disagree.")

On Rand's medication-induced hallucination while hospitalized—a reflection of her intravenous pole in the window of her ninth-floor hospital room became for her a real tree—Barbara Branden comments that Rand would grant that medication could cause hallucinations, but the idea that something had affected her brain that she didn't know about and that she had no control over, that would be horrifying to her. For months thereafter she berated the Blumenthals for insisting that her illusory hospital tree was illusory. It was Rand's shouting match four years later with her longtime friends, the Kalbermans, mostly over this diabolical Blumenthal plot to undermine her rationality, that finally drove the Kalbermans to break with her.

The theme of her projected *To Lorne Dieterling* novel that she wrote notes toward between 1957 and 1966, was the problem of remaining "totally motivated" when "alone in an enemy world." In the wake of *Atlas* she had once said, "I hate bitterness. . . . That would be the real victory of pain that I don't want to allow." Her planned ending to the projected novel was the line, "*What* pain?" In fact, her own end was a stifled "*What* pain!"

The Supremacy of Rationalized Whim

Rand was very much constrained by her central organizing conceptions. "She would see something in a thinker or a writer that really hit her very powerfully for good or bad, and that would be her focus." From then on, it was "as if there were nothing else to the person," recalls Barbara Branden. In the flesh, she might be pleasantly surprised temporarily by someone but usually not permanently. Usually after knowing the person she would go back to her original view. Hospers notes that "she opposed Reagan from the beginning because Reagan was against abortion. Everything else that he had—pro-free enterprise and so on—counted for nothing, except that."

As with individuals, so with social systems. Joan Kennedy Taylor recalls that a mistake she made under Ayn's tutelage was to spend a radio program on *Russia and the Big Red Lie*, propagating the view, espoused by Rand, that Sputnik was a hoax. The creativity-killing Soviet system would not be capable of developing something like that.

According to Barbara Branden, Rand's response to the initial batches of NBI students, when they didn't completely understand and completely change overnight, was that "she was very disappointed and felt, 'they're nothing.'" Within a few years though she had gone to the other extreme, declaring that even the least promising of Nathan's students were "infinitely better people . . . even if they certainly weren't Objectivists yet." Nonetheless several years later, highly agitated by Nathan's romantic betrayal, Rand pulled the plug on NBI and on plans for a Nathan-less successor organization. Barbara Branden was aghast at "the peremptory manner in which she abandoned . . . the future of the Objectivist movement."

Barbara Branden also recalls that Rand thought "there were no movies, no painting, no music" that she could respond to, and that "the country was philosophically, morally, and politically" bankrupt, at "a dead-end." Especially following Break, the rottenness of the world was "the one topic that had the power fully to engage her." Rand was inverting the cultural elite's view that it is *her* novels which do not merit a place within America's literary pantheon. Roy Childs commented on Rand's dismissal of everything in contemporary culture as without value: "I always found that a crock. This is a very rich culture . . . to not find any values

in the popular music, the popular culture, the movies, and the arts
. . . you'd really have to have blinders on."

The agony of finding a publisher for *The Fountainhead*, which
she bitterly complained of in later years, Rand brought upon herself quite unnecessarily. Macmillan, publisher of *We the Living*,
had no qualms about publishing her next novel, despite having
seen only the first several chapters, some of which Bobbs-Merrill
would later insist that she drop. It was Rand's insistence that
Macmillan be committed by contract to spend the equivalent of
about $13,000 (in 1999 dollars) on promoting the as-yet unwritten
book, which squelched the deal.

As for the fruitless agony of getting *Atlas Shrugged* to the
screen, this too was entirely self-inflicted. In 1972 producer Albert
Ruddy, fresh from the stupendous success of *The Godfather*, made
an oral agreement with Rand that gave her complete script control for a movie production of *Atlas Shrugged*, which they then
announced at a press conference at the Twenty-one Club. The deal
unravelled a few days later, Rand implausibly claiming that
Ruddy had additionally agreed to grant her control of the final cut
(!) and was now revoking that promise. A good film-version of
Atlas Shrugged would probably have re-animated the foundering
Objectivist movement. The quarter-century of lost opportunity
and frustration that followed was largely Rand's own doing.

She would write that those who properly appreciate *The
Fountainhead* "are the ones who will save the world—if it can be
saved. I still think it can." And "not only is *Atlas* good, you have no
idea how good it is," Rand would say if provoked, Barbara
Branden recollects. But for the most part, as Kay Nolte Smith
comments on the cult's touting of Ayn Rand as the greatest, "That
was for *others* to say, and God knows they did." Rand did believe,
and had her troops believing, that her brilliance was without
limit, and that *Atlas* would one day be admired as the world's foremost literary masterpiece. Still, explains Barbara Branden, "She
wanted someone *of stature* . . . to stand up publicly and say this is
a great book."

Barbara Branden also says, with apparent earnestness, "Ayn
would have given anything in the world to find an equal, and any-

thing in the world—plus the next three worlds, if there are such—
to have found a superior intellect." Yet there is no record of any
effort on Rand's part to commune with any prominent creative
intellects at all, except the quite elderly Deems Taylor, Ludwig von
Mises and (very briefly) Frank Lloyd Wright. For as Barbara
Branden also remarks, "She seemed unable to handle not being
the center of attention."

Since Rand felt she deserved to associate with people of high
status but generally wasn't invited to do so, she attributed gifted
qualities to those with whom she did associate. Her own self-
esteem was enhanced by the idealized value she assigned to those
around her.

To an editor at Putnam's Rand wrote of friend Isabel Paterson's
book: *"The God of the Machine* (1943) is the greatest book written
in the last three hundred years." It could "literally save the world."
It "does for capitalism what the Bible did for Christianity."
Actually, better than *The God of the Machine* in Rand's estimation
was *The Fountainhead,* making it the best book since (at least)
1643. Rand writes in a letter in the 1940s that Albert Mannheimer
and she had been working on "the definition of the nature of
human intelligence—and we have some most startling ideas and
discoveries on the subject." Albert was a screenwriter, and the
world was left unstartled by their discoveries. Her later collabora-
tions with Nathaniel Branden continued in the same amateurish
vein. In her journals she refers to the epistemological methods she
and Nathan had "discovered."

After the first theatrical performance by the woman who
would one day take Nathaniel Branden away from her altogether,
Rand exulted to a puzzled Patrecia: "What is magnificent is that
you have taken the philosophy of Objectivism and applied it to the
art of acting!" Anything good in the world had to ultimately be
connected with Ayn Rand.

Rand wrote in the aftermath of *The Fountainhead*'s publication, "I cannot consider those who are not friends of my book as
real friends," meaning that "I know very few people whom I like."
But even among friends of her novels, recalls Efron of Rand's
post-*Atlas* days, "Lots of well-known, good minds would troop to

her. Within minutes she would alienate them." Her former attorney Hank Holzer put it more succinctly, saying that "she was such a prick. . . . She was a terrible person to deal with."

Sons and Lovers

Rand extolled Barbara Branden, in an inscription in her parents' copy of *Atlas Shrugged,* as "a girl who has the spirit, the ambition and the talent of the best characters in this book." The talent of a Rearden or a Galt? On tape she tells Barbara that, "you're going to be a great writer." Rand writes to Barbara's mother in 1950: "I feel a great sympathy for Barbara because she reminds me of myself at her age." Rand seemed capable of appreciating others only in this narcissistic fashion. For a while during the 1940s she 'adopted a son', Thaddeus Ashby, 21, of whom she says that, "he's a replica of me, as I was at twenty-one, or as near a replica as one person can be of another."

Nathan was the first and last of Rand's young lovers. He came close to being the second or even the third. College student Evan Wright, who was proofreading early chapters of *Atlas Shrugged* for her at the O'Connors' San Fernando Valley home in 1951, implies that Rand would have seduced him had he but given her the go-ahead. Years earlier, their young long-term houseguest Thadeus Ashby had verged on an erotic relationship with her. In 1955 she would take the plunge. By the end she would be telling Branden that if she had a harem of lovers, he should be thankful to be counted among them.

Though Nathan and Barbara would probably have drifted apart romantically, Rand had pushed them to marry in 1953. "It was a relationship that never should have begun and I think we're both clear on that," said Nathaniel Branden in 1996. Rand, with an already unimpressive record of prognostication, told them, "You're going to have a very happy life together." Nathan later reflected that for him to have a wife like Barbara was convenient for Ayn. Who else would be so in awe of Rand as to lend out a husband for Rand's sexual gratification? Scarcely giving the marriage a chance, Ayn and Nathan began their affair a year and a half later, after Rand had pressured her husband and Barbara into accepting its rightness and inevitability. On being romantically and sexually involved with two lovers at same time, Rand declared publicly, "It's a project that only giants can handle properly . . . nothing that most people even need to think about." Historian Paul Johnson observes that "in every case where intellectuals try to apply total disclosure to sex, it always leads in the end to a degree of guilty secrecy unusual even in normally adulterous families."

Barbara Branden relates that Rand, during her disintegrating affair with Nathan, never thought 'Did I do something to bring this on?' or even 'Is there something I didn't mean to do that has some relevance to what's happening?' "Never. *Never.* There would have been some signs of it. . . . Her view of her own actions was that they were objective, that they were rational, therefore the problem had to be in someone else."

According to Nathaniel Branden, once Rand had decided that he should be in love with her if he really were John Galt, "then reality went out the window. . . . She took it as axiomatic that her perspective and mine must be the same." Had Rand not been so self-obsessed and had she not believed her needs were so special and her intellect such an irresistible romantic lure, she would have *expected* Nathan's sexual interest in her to dwindle as she aged, especially with attractive young women among his students. Instead Branden heard, "You have no right to casual friendships, no right to vacations, no right to sex with some inferior woman!" and "The man to whom I dedicated *Atlas Shrugged* would never want anything less than me! I don't care if I'm ninety years old and in a wheelchair! This will always be my view!"

Other People Are Hell

As the dead carcasses of unburied men that do corrupt my air, I banish you! And here remain with your uncertainty

William Shakespeare, *Coriolanus*

Rand wrote in a letter that "all my life I have been troubled by the fact that most people I met bored me to death." In another letter:

"I am becoming more anti-social than I was . . . I can't stand the sort of things people talk about." And in a late 1940s letter Rand asserts that she couldn't care less about the so-called 'average man'? "What I am interested in is the great and the exceptional . . . I do feel something which is probably real hatred when I hear somebody say he believes in the 'middle of the road'."

She declared that she could look around her levelly, but couldn't bear to look down, and had wanted to look up. But she felt there was no one at a higher level than her to look up to. Rand's Kay Gonda in *Ideal* (1934), asked if she really thinks she's so much better than everybody else, responds "Yes, . . . I do. I wish I didn't have to."

Rand asserts that Roark "is the only genuine human being" in *The Fountainhead* "because he embodies precisely those qualities which constitute a human being, as distinguished from an animal. Keating is subhuman." Such remarks go beyond disdain into hate. They also provide a clue as to why her fictional villains are so unconvincing. Their subhumanity puts them beyond foreshortened range of the author's empathy.

In another letter she writes, "A book like *The Fountainhead* cannot be inspired by hatred, nor the things which one opposes." Yet Rand had wanted to call it *Second-Hand Lives*, a phrase to tar the vast majority of her fellow Americans. Had her editor not demanded something more upbeat, that would have been the title. An Ayn Rand *alter ego*, the potentially great writer Henry Dorn in *The Simplest Thing in the World* (1940), futilely tries to dumb down his latest effort so as to produce something sufficiently "dull, stale, sweet, dishonest and safe" that his fellow Americans will read it. "Can't you be stupid?," he berates himself, "Can't you be consciously, deliberately, cold-bloodedly stupid? . . . Dear God, let me be stupid!"

Rand allows that, "I do like people—when they are really human beings." But this was a remarkably infrequent experience. She also wrote, "Frank says that what I love is not the real city, but the New York I built myself. That's true." In parallel she might have said, 'What I love is not real men, but the Man I built up myself'.

Rand's novels were a celebration of the kind of minds capable of producing science and technology, and a denunciation of the kind of freedom-destroying history and politics that suppress such minds. She admired only art which reinforced that perspective. She had boundless contempt for art which wallowed in feelings and for its generative culture of navel-gazing bleeding-heartism. In her journal she observes that the good industrialists she has met are high types of men—whereas the artists (allegedly the 'spiritual' sort) are neurotic or depraved weaklings.

Nathaniel Branden notes that in her writings, Rand even ridicules the physical appearance of political opponents, such as Hubert Humphrey. Rand cracked at her last Ford Hall Forum lecture that creationists are handicapped in debate, because "the looks of some of them could be used to fill certain gaps in the theory of evolution." Scarcely a Rand novel, play, or short story is complete without a gratuitously snide reference to some variation on the 'Vocational School for Subnormal Children'.

Moreover, as Branden relates in 1996 to a neo-Objectivist audience, "She had no real insight into the depth to which her anger contaminated her." He cites the disproportionate frequency with which Rand's characters are described as having negative as opposed to positive feelings. It's "quite depressing," given that the message implied by that imbalance registers with most readers without their realizing it.

In another letter Rand describes how, in detecting irrationality in someone she had believed to be rational, she is angry at their betrayal of their standing as human beings. Does she argue with such subhuman specimens? No, "As a practical rule, I find that the thing which works best in such cases is contempt." Edith Efron said of Rand, "She turned her back on humanity and turned *that* into a virtue."

Did Rand reduce people to their basic premises? Answers Barbara Branden, "She very much did. . . . But her tendency was if, say you said, 'philosophically I believe such and such', she would think that certain attributes psychologically follow from that. Since you believe 'A', you must be a certain kind of person psychologically. She would very much tend to take people at face value and therefore make profound mistakes."

Continues Branden, "It's a failure to understand human psychology, that people are much more complex than that and that often they are not at all the ideas they spout, that what would be consistent with those ideas really has nothing to do with what they are. I don't know quite what she would have done with it if people she considered absolutely different from her philosophically had loved what she loved" such as the music of Rachmaninoff. "Actually, she considered that impossible." Here, what is impossible for Rand is fact for everyone else; one can be sure that all but a tiny proportion of Rachmaninoff enthusiasts have quite non-Objectivist values.

Barbara Branden writes that Rand "did not understand the difference between morality and psychology." She would morally denounce "with no awareness that there can be psychological reasons for what she observed," having nothing to do with morality. Everything was a moral issue, either morally good or morally bad. To Nathaniel Branden she wrote off 'psychology' as "that sewer" and complained, "how I *hate* your profession, Nathan, how I *hate* the irrational, how I *hate* in having to deal with it or struggle to understand it" (my emphases). In other words, she had no real interest in coming to understand human nature. Yet, tragically, the first application of a moralistic Objectivism was to psychology, and, says Nathaniel Branden, "she made it abundantly clear that my task as a psychologist was to develop knowledge that would support her work as a philosopher."

According to Barbara Branden, for Rand "pain happens but we don't give it the importance we give joy." Certainly she didn't give others' suffering the importance she gave her own joy. Her journal notes inform us that John Galt's "joy is all-pervading . . . particularly in the torture scene." However, following her operation for cancer, she gave her own pain tremendous importance and complained bitterly even after being heavily medicated, so antagonizing the medical staff that they started using Allan Blumenthal as a go-between. As for psychological pain, Nathaniel Branden insists, "She was obsessed with not being affected by pain in any fundamental way," and when he rejected her as a lover, "All her energies were . . . mobilized to deny her suffering." The inferior cannot be allowed the victory of having inflicted humiliating pain upon the superior; what is felt as pain must be retranslated into moral indignation. The word 'pain' and its alternate 'suffering' occur between them 316 times in *Atlas Shrugged*.

Nathaniel and Ayn "were alike in their lack of empathy with the suffering of others," writes Barbara. Rand certainly had difficulty recognizing the desires, subjective experiences, and feelings of others. And persistently accounting for others' allegedly immoral behavior or ideas by attributing malevolent motives wrought havoc in her social life. Presenting herself as an explicit role model in all respects made moral condemnation the predominant theme within her Objectivist movement.

Rand *could* empathize with and nurture others, but only in the expectation that the other would 'be there' in return to meet her own needs on demand, and she was prone to sudden, dramatic shifts in her view of others. Sooner or later nearly every member of her inner circle would disappoint her and be excommunicated or would leave in frustration. *And* be reviled from that moment on as if he or she had always been worthless. Acolyte-philosopher Allan Gotthelf defends her angry outbursts as heroic, insisting that Greek Homeric heroes and Ayn Rand shared an intensity such that when happy, sad or angry, they were *incredibly* happy or sad or angry. He recalls Rand's 'warmth' in an odd way: "I told her something about what her novels had meant to me, and there was an expression on her face as we were saying goodbye of the most immense warmth I've ever seen in a human being to this day." Notice what made Rand so radiant: appreciation of Ayn Rand. Renowned screenplay-writer Stirling Silliphant, having collaborated with Rand on a never-filmed script for an *Atlas Shrugged* miniseries, regretted that, "She did not reflect the kind of humanity or warmth I like in people."

In *Elegy for a Soprano*, Smith in the guise of one of her characters says of operatic novelist Ayn Rand, in the guise of opera diva Varda Wolf that she was "a terrible human being. Quite monstrous, actually . . . an evil woman, despite her artistry," turning people "into blind worshipers who stop living for themselves," ending in "unforgivable treatment of people who were devoted to her." Kramer and Alstad write that ultimately a guru "shows little concern for those under him, as they have become mere tools for his ambition." Kay Nolte and Phil Smith have explicitly depicted inner circle members as Rand's tools and Nathaniel Branden has remarked upon Rand's "disposition to use people in the most cold-blooded and hypocritical way." Roy Childs recalls "a six-hour discussion" at the Blumenthals' "about whether or not Ayn Rand was evil, the Blumenthals and Kay Smith saying 'Yes' and Barbara Branden being very defensive saying 'No'." Barbara's former husband recalls, though, "In the early years following the Break, Barbara . . . told me I was refusing to confront the extent of Ayn's evil and of the harm she had done me and her and everyone else."

Joan Blumenthal relates that in the 1970s, "I suggested to her that she should start thinking about writing another novel, and she was angry with me, 'How can you say that to me when you know there isn't a mind out there I can talk to?' I said, 'That's insulting.' And she said, 'Oh I don't mean you, darling.' But she did mean it."

The Husband She Bought

For all Rand's talk of independence, she had a deep need for some-one to always be there for her. Her husband served in this capac-ity for a half-century. Handsome part-time actor Frank O'Connor married Ayn Rand so that she could stay in the U.S. Rothbard recalls Frank, "Mr. Rand," as "the only genuinely nice person in the Randian movement." According to Barbara Branden, "bot-tomless agony" is what Frank endured at Ayn's hands. Laments Kay Nolte Smith, "He was just such a sweet lovely man and yet she drove him to drink."

O'Connor's marriage to Rand endured, if just barely, because it was fine with him that she wore the pants in the family. His nature was such that he didn't need to dominate anyone, least of all his wife. In the movies he never got to play more than a supporting role, and it was the same in his real-life marriage. His financial contribution to the marriage consisted mainly in his urging Ayn to buy and hold onto the ranch house he found in California's San Fernando Valley, which escalated significantly in value over the years.

In a journal entry in June 1945, Rand specifies three categories of "strikers" in what would become *Atlas Shrugged*. She cites Frank as an example of one type: the "gifted men" who "function in some field other than their proper one and produce only enough for their own sustenance, refusing to let the world benefit from their surplus energy." Comments Barbara Branden, "No, he was not what she told other people he was." Curiously, Frank's only speaking role in any film available on video today is in *Cimarron*, named for a town located a morning's drive from Ouray, Colorado, site of Galt's Gulch. O'Connor's character has one line.

"For the ugly duckling to have married the most gorgeous prince was a major issue in their relationship," Kay Nolte Smith suggests. He was so beautiful and always elegant, Smith recalls. Rand wrote that "we think in the same fashion, and everything one of us likes or dislikes, the other always likes or dislikes as well—even music. Our friends say we have an 'ideal marriage'." Phil Smith recalled, "She used to say the proudest accomplishment of my life is my marriage to Frank," to which Kay added, "Which is *so* ridiculous." Barbara Branden saw Frank's financial dependency on Ayn as the only reason this 'ideal marriage' endured. Frank told Barbara that if he could have left Ayn, he would have.

The turning point for the couple was Ayn's decision in 1951 to abandon their California home to follow her soon-to-be-lover Nathan Blumenthal to New York. She would one day puzzle over Frank's talking in a delirium about the ranch, "But he *hated* California." *His* wants were always distorted by the prism of *her* ego needs. Rand's own letters from the 1940s make clear what a trauma the transition from ranch to downtown apartment would later be for her husband. "Frank has gone wild about working the soil . . . out with his chickens and rabbits all day . . . I don't remember ever seeing him" so "chronically . . . happy . . . ardently enthusiastic . . . busy, and glowing . . . a complete gentleman farmer."

Hating the ranch was the least of Rand's delusions about Frank. By the 1940s, because both were so alienated from their emotional lives, they no longer really communicated. Still, in letters to fans she wrote the following accolades: "Who is Frank O'Connor? Howard Roark, or as near to it as anyone I know." Frank is "my best proof that people such as I write about can and do exist in real life." Even with regard to looks, "All my heroes will always be reflections of Frank." Indeed a portrait of Frank captioned, 'This is John Galt', appeared in newspaper and billboard ads for *Atlas.*" If you noticed a certain similarity of appearance" in Roark, Galt, Rearden and Francisco, "the reason is that my husband was the model. And the same is true of their spiritual resemblance." Frank resembled an older brother of Gary Cooper, who played Howard Roark in *The Fountainhead*, but that and the Galt portrait are as close as Frank got to embodying Galtian virtues. Frank was an artist who took up painting as a desperate Manhattan substitute for the landscaping and gardening he had left behind in California, and he took it up too late in life to produce exceptional work.

Rand's following Nathan to New York led to consummation of their relationship a few years later. Rand procured explicit permission from both spouses for the affair. It was only very grudgingly granted and Frank would probably have felt more like a man if he'd been secretly rather than so openly cuckolded. "She loved him, he was the companion of her life. And she betrayed him in a brutal way—a really brutal way," comments neo-Objectivist author Ronald Merrill. As Pierpont writes, when in *Atlas Shrugged* "Dagny finally crashes into Galt, her longtime lover graciously steps aside in recognition of the better man. Frank O'Connor, however, took to drink." Twice a week, for years, Branden would arrive at Ayn and Frank's apartment to have sex in their bed, while the humiliated husband retired to a neighborhood bar. Sometimes, awkwardly, Nathan arrived before Frank could get out the door.

Barbara Branden recalled how mistreatment of Frank and Rand's later preoccupation with Nathan not being the interested lover he had been began to erode what was still left of Frank. "I would see Frank being in the room for conversations that he *should not* have been present at," Ayn's conversations with both Brandens about what was wrong with Nathan. In Kay Nolte Smith's *Elegy For a Soprano,* inner circle members "would watch Scotch slide down" Frank's "throat more easily and more often, gradually coating his eyes with glass and turning his gestures into painful slow motion. . . . There seemed to be less of him than before, not physically, but less of his personality. His self. As if he had a slow leak in his soul."

Frank's drinking buddies regarded him as an alcoholic as far back as the mid-1950s. Barbara Branden relates that toward the end when people came into Rand's apartment, "the first thing they smelled was alcohol, and Frank had clearly been drinking," even in the morning. Now "Frank would fly into rages over nothing." After he died, his studio was found littered with empty liquor bottles.

When Frank had begun to waste away in New York, Ayn projected to all that he was still fully in command of his faculties by sending him as her proxy to casting sessions for a remounting of her play *Penthouse Legend (Night of January 16th).* Recalls Kay Nolte Smith. "He would just come and sit in the corner and nod and sleep," yet "she tried to keep up the fiction that he was an active contributor to the rehearsal process." She would even give him a writer credit for an article in *The Objectivist* about his days in Hollywood, though it was obvious to insiders that Ayn alone had written the piece based on his rambling reminiscences. As he slid toward senility, she frantically tried to delay her *de facto* abandonment by mercilessly subjecting him to interminable but futile exercises in remedial thinking, needlessly "torturing him" in Barbara Branden's words because she "knew nothing of medical science." Rand herself lasted for only a few miserable years after his death.

For Rand to have produced John Galt, Frank had to be nothing like a John Galt in reality but very much like John Galt in her fantasies, not an easy balancing act. Were he not excused for being her husband, Randians would write him off as an unambitious, undertalented, out-of-focus, drunken moocher.

A Great Eccentric

Historian Paul Johnson has remarked that, "massive works of the intellect do not spring from the abstract workings of the brain and the imagination; they are deeply rooted in the personality." Similarly Dr. Blumenthal suggests, "It is thought by Objectivists that one's philosophy dictates one's psychology. I think the reverse is equally true, that one's psychology determines the philosophy one creates for oneself." Indeed, Rand's personality was icily cold, purportedly objective, hyper-rational, and emotion-less on one level, yet hysterically defensive, obdurate, hostile, and sarcastic on another, this combination of characteristics long-predating its crystallization in her official philosophy of life.

Leonard Peikoff insists that all of her individualism, pro-self-ishness, pro-independence, pro-heroism, pro-reason go "back all the way to her childhood." These "broad fundamentals . . . never changed from beginning to end." It could be, though, that these ideas in their incipient form rose to the surface neither because Alissa was an intellectual prodigy, as Peikoff contends, nor even primarily in reaction to the trauma of the revolution. Consider the possible negative origins of these fundamentals: an anti-social nature can be the negative core of individualism, inability to empathize the core of selfishness, unpopularity the core of inde-pendence, contempt for one's acquaintances the core of the heroic vision, and hatred of religious tradition the core of an exclusively pro-reason stance. These were present and already shaping her personality when the trauma of the revolution ennobled and refashioned them as tenets of an anti-Marxist nineteenth-century liberalism, an outlook not dissimilar to that of her father. So not only did her key personal beliefs crystallize at a pre-critical-think-ing stage, that is, prematurely and for emotional reasons, those emotions may have been quite unadmirable ones.

"I do think of her in many respects as a great eccentric," offers Joan Kennedy Taylor, but Edith Efron sees that as euphemism for something far more serious. Efron asserts flat-out, "There is no way to communicate how crazy she was. . . . Ultimately everyone who knew her would ask themselves, 'Is she insane or am I? . . .

She was a profoundly manipulative woman . . . so repressed" that it resulted in a "very complicated paranoia." Once one got a whiff that something was wrong with her, it would suddenly hit home that something was *really* wrong. "What looked before like 'walking reason' was now 'screeching megalomania'. And the flaw it implied in her was not simply a neurosis but a profound disease. . . . Acknowledging her debt to Aristotle and Hugo saved her from total lunacy." Even Nathaniel Branden suggests that, "In her grandiosity and suspiciousness, her behavior bordered at times on paranoia," and that she merited "the most stern condemnation for her hypocrisy, dishonesty, and megalomania." He recalls his second wife Patrecia telling him she had detected bitterness, enormous anger and even madness in Rand's face right from the outset, and his own realization that, "I had seen in Ayn's eyes precisely what Patrecia had seen."

Psychiatrist Allan Blumenthal, who knew Rand intimately for a quarter-century and who was *the* psychiatric authority among orthodox Objectivists for more than a decade, believes that Rand suffered from a veritable cluster of personality disorders: Paranoid, Borderline, and Narcissistic. For those impressed by the American Psychiatric Association's ever-more-inclusive *Diagnostic and Statistical Manual of Mental Disorders,* one could make a very plausible case from anecdotal materials for Rand being thus afflicted. For those *un*impressed by the *DSM,* the exercise might still give one pause before citing Rand as role model or her philosophy as life-affirming in areas where it seems rather to embody the symptoms of such disorders.

Rand portrayed herself as the ideal embodiment of her philosophy and as *the* role model. Yet while the ultimate goal of her philosophy is ostensibly personal happiness, it made neither Ayn Rand nor her most devoted followers happy. How ironic it would be, and unlikely, that a vulgar Nietzschean philosophy formed at the intersection of one unhappy woman's personality problems and a spectacularly aberrant societal disorder (Communism), and which blighted the lives of founders and followers alike, should turn out to provide *the* moral code without which Man cannot survive but with which Man will not only survive but flourish.

Rand despised Bertrand Russell, who once wrote that "always thinking of the next thing," and not letting oneself "be absorbed in the moment . . . is more fatal to any kind of aesthetic excellence than any other habit of mind." Rand recalls of her trip in a locomotive as research for *Atlas Shrugged*, "I have seldom enjoyed anything concrete or in the present tense, I am always in the abstract or the future. That locomotive ride was one of the few times when I enjoyed the actual moment for its own sake." Barbara Branden describes Rand's affair with Nathan as "her one chance to enjoy life in the present . . . To have found it and then lost it was very, very destructive to her."

The copy-editor for *Atlas Shrugged* recalls that with Ayn, "there was never a light moment, . . . no capacity for simple enjoyment. . . . I found that very sad." In a letter Rand writes, "You still tell me to have a good time. I still don't know how to go about it. My good time is only at my desk." But she didn't *really* have a good time there either. Phil Smith remembers her saying that one thing she envied Frank for was that "Frank actually enjoyed the process of putting paint on a canvas, whereas she didn't enjoy the process of putting words on paper." Kay adds, "To be a novelist and not enjoy that, just blows my mind."

Two Packs a Day

Philosopher Jack Wheeler, who regards Rand as the greatest philosopher of vision in this century of technical philosophy, describes her as "a very unpleasant person . . . hooked on Dexadrine, which makes you really unpleasant and angry." Such 'diet pills' are amphetamine-like drugs with psychoactive effects similar to those of cocaine but in some ways more potent and longer-lasting. Childs commented, "I know she took Dexadrine every day for 40 years. Her secretary told me she'd take a couple of five milligram" pills, and if nothing happened in an hour, "she'd take another two, or three, or four. She was taking this on top of pots of coffee," with added caffeine from chocolate after chocolate, and the nicotine from her two packs of Tareytons a day. "I took Dex as a diet pill," Childs said. And that does "produce

things like paranoia, suspicion of other people, and nervousness
. . . that became traits of her character." Nathaniel Branden suspects Dexadrine side-effects if only "because at times her behavior
struck me as bizarre in ways that totally mystified me."

Ayn Rand characterized as irrational and immoral all that is
self-destructive in the long term. Yet she dramatized her smoking
habit in public, flourishing a stylishly-long cigarette holder while
curtly dismissing the dangers as statist propaganda. Recalls Dr.
Allan Blumenthal, "She did not approve of statistics and the only
evidence against smoking was statistics, which she claimed were
put out by people trying to destroy free enterprise and the cigarette industry. She would not accept *any* evidence that smoking
was bad for you."

Frank Lloyd Wright biographer Meryle Secrest relates that
when Ayn Rand finally got to meet Wright in 1945 at his Taliesin
residence-school, she "kept chain-smoking and blowing the
smoke in Wright's face. Finally he took the cigarette out of her
mouth, threw it into the fireplace and walked out. That was the
start of the absolute prohibition against smoking in Wright's
presence." Partly because of his Welsh background, Wright
abhorred tobacco as moral flaw, and he got plenty of exercise. It
appears to have paid off for him. Wright was in his glory in his
80s, executing 300 commissions, 135 being built. In contrast
Rand spent her last ten years unhappily accomplishing very little and spent her 80s dead. Heavy smoking and zero exercise
may have been what prevented her from living to see two cherished dreams come true: a televised miniseries of *Atlas* and the
fall of communism.

Newspaper editor Horace Greeley once described smoking as
"a fire at one end and a fool at the other." Not so in *Atlas
Shrugged*, where the philosophical musings of the kiosk owner
who used to run a cigarette factory link cigarette smoking to
innovative ideas: "When a man thinks, there is a spot of fire alive
in his mind—and it is proper that he should have the burning
point of a cigarette as his one expression." The statement is even
repeated later in the novel. Rand was thinking about herself

thinking about her life-affirming philosophy—in the course of which every cigarette chain-smoked likely subtracted 5.5 minutes from her life. And what is, in Galt's Gulch, the job of the greatest philosopher of the age, Rand's stand-in Hugh Akston? He manufactures the dollar-sign-stamped cigarettes that all the heroes smoke.

Rand loved the whole culture of smoking. Her first public success, the play *Night of January 16th*, centered on the life and death of a Swedish industrialist known as the 'Match King', safety matches—along with the cigarette-rolling machine—being what began the transformation of cigarette smoking from a 40-per-year (on average) indulgence in the 1880s, to the 40-per-day addiction of an Ayn Rand in the 1960s.

Rand loved the 1967 Virginia Slims jingle, 'You've Come a Long Way, Baby' so much that she arranged to have a recording of it sent to her. Several years later surgeons were combatting her malignant lung cancer by removing a lobe of one lung as well as adjacent lymph nodes and a rib. Says Joan Blumenthal, "She didn't do something we wanted her to do. We wanted her to make a statement" about her cancer "because a lot of young people were influenced by her. She was smoking all the time, which made it look terrific, and we thought that if she would say that smoking is probably bad for your health that it would have an influence." I asked her if some significant proportion of students of Objectivism actually took up or kept smoking because of Rand's example, to which Blumenthal replied, "Yes, we thought that maybe this was true." The average starting age for smoking is 15, with 90 percent of regular smokers starting by age 21. This age range was typical of Rand's readership and NBI students, one of whom, Nathaniel Branden's second wife Patrecia, even became a Salem Cigarette Girl in magazine ads of the early 1970s.

Not only did Rand not do what the Blumenthals asked, she even demanded that the nature of her illness and her operation be kept secret. Barbara Branden suggests that this insistence arose from embarrassment. Rand tended to think that cancer

was the result of what she termed "bad premises"—that is, philo-
sophical-psychological errors and evasions carried to their final
dead end in the form of physical destruction." For one blinded to
the obvious by ideology, an undetected mental event had to be
responsible, not four decades of puffing like a chimney.

10

The Roots of Objectivism

A Nineteenth-Century Ayn Rand

There are many parallels between the lives of Ayn Rand and Englishwoman Harriet Martineau (1802–1876). Martineau and Rand were both fiction propagandizers for laissez faire. James Mill was Martineau's Ludwig von Mises. Martineau's magnum opus contains a tale paralleling *Atlas Shrugged,* both books way outselling more critically-acclaimed fare of their times. Martineau's book would sell 10,000 copies a month, beating John Stuart Mill and Charles Dickens.

Martineau, like Rand, wrote a volume of fiction, in Martineau's case a collection of stories called *Illustrations of Political Economy,* justifying and celebrating the entrepreneur and the laissez-faire economy, and advocating the clearing away of government controls. In Martineau's book, looters reduce the society to primitivism, but principled men espousing *laissez faire* arise to guide that society back to prosperity. Along the way, the leading characters discuss various topics of economic policy. Critics complained of the didactic dialogue, wooden characters, inauthentic emotions, and lack of humor.

Even their personal lives were often remarkably alike. Martineau endured an unhappy childhood; came from a minority-religion background; became an atheist; was deeply affected by the destruction of her father's business; experienced years of money worries; suddenly became a best-selling author; sank into a depression for years after publication of her biggest book; gave up writing fiction for the last two decades of her life, turning instead to essays later collected in book form; was not a complete feminist but did generally urge women to pursue advanced education and traditionally 'male' careers; flaunted her smoking habit; and never had chidren.

Both classical liberals, Martineau wrote at the end of a period when classical liberalism had been influential in policymaking, while Rand wrote at the end of the period when socialist collectivism had been influential, a time when classical liberalism was making a come-back.

Three Precursors of Ayn Rand

Edward Bellamy (1850–1898) was a kind of Ayn Rand on the Left. In 1888 he published the million-seller *Looking Backward,* a novel which projected a centrally-planned technocratic Utopia in A.D. 2000. It advocated complete nationalization of all industry, whereas Rand would advocate just the opposite. As a measure of its impact, in 1935 philosopher John Dewey and historian Charles Beard, asked to nominate the most important books of the preceding century, placed *Looking Backward* second only to Marx's *Das Kapital.*

Bellamyist 'nationalist clubs' sprang up across America, a preview of the campus Ayn Rand clubs and NBI phenomena. Bellamy and Rand organizations experienced a similar rise and fall, followed by revival decades later. The Bellamy phenomenon ultimately became absorbed by the theosophy movement, much as the Rand phenomenon was mostly absorbed by libertarianism. Bellamyism influenced the Technocracy movement, American socialism, and feminism. The Franklin D. Roosevelt administration was affected by Bellamyists as much as Reagan's would later be by Randians. Many in Roosevelt's administration had read and admired Bellamy, and Roosevelt appointed Arthur Morgan as Chairman of the Tennessee Valley Authority. Morgan so admired Bellamy that he had written his biography. Reagan's appointee as Chairman of the Federal Reserve Board would be Rand admirer Alan Greenspan, who didn't actually write Rand's biography—his first wife's best friend did that.

Count Alfred Korzybski (1879–1950) was as high-profile in his time as Rand was in hers. Korzybski, founder of 'General Semantics', wanted to impose a linguistic precision that would allow people to deal in facts. George Orwell remarked that it would have been impossible for an intellectual of his time to miss the Korzybski phenomenon entirely. His life and work share some extraordinary parallels with Rand's. His major work *Science and Sanity* (1933) was a massive tome which became the bible of General Semantics. Korzybski believed it was third in a series of great philosophy works, the first two being Aristotle's *Organon* and Bacon's *Novum Organum*.

Korzybski's work oriented itself toward Aristotle's either-or logic, as did Rand's, but while she loved it, he hated it. While Korzybski implied that Aristotelian logic was a form of mental disorder, Rand and her followers saw any departure from Aristotelian logic, and all of modern philosophy, as akin to delusional mental illness. Korzybski too believed that he was a great philosopher being snubbed by professional hacks. He refused an invitation to speak at a University of Chicago symposium on semantics because he wasn't asked to deliver the main address. Korzybski and Rand each placed their own work within a pantheon of great philosophy and in opposition to almost all contemporary philosophy. Korzybski's 'structural differential' gismo has its counterpart in Rand's epistemology, most professional philosophers regarding neither as any contribution to philosophy.

Korzybski and Rand had a whole set of parallel peculiarities, such as he demonizing 'is' and she demonizing 'altruism', as well as blind spots and personal quirks. Both retained their thick eastern European accents and both lectured in eccentric attire—Korzybski in khaki military garb, Rand in a cape and flourishing a cigarette-holder. Each had a big falling-out with their respective heirs-apparent, Senator Samuel Hayakawa and Nathaniel Branden. Both heavily influenced the work of a best-selling psychologist—in Korzybski's case, Albert Ellis, whose REBT borrowed Korzybskian buzz-words like 'overgeneralization'. General Semantics inspired the 'null-A' of A.E. Van Vogt's science fiction novels, Objectivism the comic-book 'Mr. A'. Both movements sprouted parochial quasi-academic journals. Two main rival organizations represent Korzybski's thought today, as is the case for Rand. One of each has or had a corporate sugar-daddy.

Ayn Rand was not the first to propound an ethics for the masses based on survival as a rational being. That honor goes to fellow novelist and cult leader L. Ron Hubbard (1911–1986), the science-fiction writer who founded Dianetics and the Church of Scientology. Dianetics preceded NBI's start-up by eight years and the Objectivist ethics by 11 years. Dianetics groups formed on campuses during the 1950s, much as Ayn Rand clubs would in the 1960s. Many who flocked to Objectivism in the 1960s had previously had some contact with Dianetics or Scientology.

Dianetics used reasoning somewhat similar to Rand's about the brain as a machine. Hubbard's 'analytical' versus 'reactive' mind has its equivalent in Rand's system. Both have a higher mind reprogramming the rest of the mind. Hubbard and Rand were both extremely intelligence- and survival-oriented, in the interest of rational man. They counselled the uprooting of irrational premises (or 'engrams'). Both contended that the resulting enhanced rationality leads to greater capacity for healthy emotion. Perceptual data is immaculate for both. Both regard our often being unconscious of incoming data as the real problem. After many years of working at it, the student of Dianetics becomes a 'clear', while the student of Objectivism becomes a full-fledged 'Objectivist', each typically requiring much therapy (or 'auditing') along the way. Both Dianetics and Objectivist psychology drew fire from the psychiatric establishment.

The philosophy of each relates immorality to decreasing one's survival potential. Each claims to be science- and logic-based.

Both share a benevolent universe premise. Both see real pleasure as that accompanying one's striving toward survival goals, and as the real motivator rather than mere pain-avoidance. Each rejects both subjectivism and determinism. Hubbard and Rand are very much against all rule-by-force. Both assert that rational men have no real conflicts of interest. Each deplores social complexity being wielded as an excuse for introducing government regulation when it is the latter that generates the former in a vicious circle. Both attach mail-in cards inside their books to put readers in touch with each's institutional apparatus. Hubbard and Rand both produced thousand-page-plus novels, treated derisively by most critics but greatly admired by followers (though Scientologists are not required to believe that *Battlefield Earth* or *Mission Earth* is the greatest novel of all time). Each was lambasted by biographers for serious personality problems. And both figures have been denounced by former associates who claim that the leader had feet of clay and the doctrine is detrimental to its adherents' mental health.

Because Hubbard and Rand shared a number of quirks and basic ideas, it does not follow that their complete philosophies are essentially similar—that is hardly the case. What we can see is that those basic ideas were circulating within the culture of mid-century America and that both figures exemplify the growth of a cult preaching 'rationality'.

The Young Nietzschean

Rand read Nietzsche in late adolescence and he made a tremendous and lasting impact upon her, similar to the impact made by Rand on numerous adolescents in the 1960s. Among the elements of Nietzsche's thought which might particularly have struck her were his egoism and anti-altruism, his hostility to Christianity and contrasting admiration for the Jews, his anti-statism, his individualism and anti-egalitarianism, and his dislike of Kant.

To be so impressed by Nietzsche was not uncommon during Rand's Russian youth; the Symbolist artists and novelists, and even the socialists were impressed. Rand's torchbearers try to minimize the importance of Nietzsche's influence on her, but the contents of her journals suggest that it was enormous. In calling Rand a Nietzschean, I don't mean to suggest that she shared all Nietzsche's views, or that those views she thought she shared were necessarily true to Nietzsche. (Some Nietzsche scholars deny, for instance, that Nietzsche really held the common herd of ordinary humans in contempt.) Rand was a 'vulgar Nietzschean': that she adhered to a cluster of ideas, including contempt for the common herd, popularly associated with Nietzsche.

Rand found the common man of the twentieth century, if anything, to be an even more grotesquely botched entity than Nietzsche had predicted. Her first projected hero, Danny Renahan in *The Little Street*, is explicitly Nietzschean in his sense of absolute superiority over and utter contempt for nearly all of humanity, which presumes to dispute his superiority by sheer dint of numbers. He burns with "disgust . . . and with humiliation" at not being able to crush "the mob" under his feet. His superior intelligence "makes the mob feel that a superior mind can exist entirely outside its established morals," provoking "a murderous desire to revenge itself against its hurt vanity. . . . He was superior and he wanted to live as such . . . the one thing society does not permit." And much more along similar lines. Renahan's girlfriend agrees with his outlook, loves him for it, and like Dominique in *The Fountainhead* hates the rest of the world for its active resentment of him. This Nietzschean hero, much more negatively disposed than Roark, is an early prototype of Roark. The theme of the disgustingness of non-heroic average humanity would be a constant in all Rand's novels.

Rand's *Journals* contain numerous explicit and implicit Nietzsche references. (Since these journals as published appear to have been edited to make them conform with Objectivist orthodoxy, it seems probable that many more Nietzsche references have been omitted.) Passages in the 1936 edition of *We the Living*, deleted in the revised edition, indicate that she was still very much a Nietzschean at age 30. Her Nietzscheanism is confirmed by other works she wrote in the mid-1930s, such as the unperformed play *Ideal*, though she later denied this had been her outlook at the time. It is common for cult leaders, eager to emphasize their uniqueness and self-sufficiency, to disown embarrassing early influences.

Material from *The Fountainhead* cut in 1942 mainly because of length restrictions indicates a continuing Nietzschean frame of mind despite Nietzsche's bad press during World War II. (Though Nietzsche was then painted as an anti-Semite, he had been in reality a strong philo-Semite and, if he detested any people collectively, it was his fellow Germans.) Rand even wanted a Nietzsche epigraph for each of her novel's four sections. What did make it to publication in *The Fountainhead* was still so Nietzschean at an unconscious level that many knowledgeable readers assumed that the novel had been designed as a disquisition on Nietzsche's Superman.

Rand is what a European Nietzschean looks like after transplantation to late 1920s America. Especially with their discrediting during the 1930s, Rand wanted to re-vitalize business values by injecting their seemingly dull Apollonian nature with a shot of Dionysian Nietzsche. Actually, depicting the American business tycoon in Nietzschean terms in fiction had already been done long before by Theodore Dreiser. Rand came to see that, luckily, rights in America for the inferior many would also protect the superior few.

Rand exaggerated the importance of her differences from vulgar Nietzscheanism to distract us from their blatant similarities. Nietzsche, in his way, was as pro-reason as Rand, and Rand, in her way, was as pro-Dionysus as Nietzsche. Objectivism absorbed Nietzsche, vulgarized or otherwise, at its core; the wrap-up on Ridpath's lecture-tapes on Nietzsche confirms this in the very language and imagery he uses to deny it.

Ayn Rand's Jewish Context

"Nothing could have been less important to her than that she was Jewish," says Barbara Branden of Rand. Certainly, Rand had no wish to make a public display of her Jewishness or associate her ideas with Jewishness. But there are many little indications of sensitivity to this subject, as when Isabel Paterson remarked "I don't like Jewish intellectuals," and Rand lashed angrily back: "Then you don't like me!"

Objectivism, both the philosophy and the movement, was also very much Jewish at its core, and was at pains to distract attention from that otherwise interesting fact. In Objectivism, non-Jews and well-off unpersecuted Jews got to feel like pogromized Russian Jews. It was actually anti-Semitism in 1940s Manitoba that was ultimately responsible for propelling the originators of the Objectivist movement into Rand's arms: Barbara Weidman left Winipeg for Los Angeles, she says, because of anti-Semitism. And it was Jewish alienation from the non-Jewish American majority culture that motivated the coalescing of the Objectivist movement around a Jewish core. In the second half of Rand's adulthood she was personally drawn back into a Jewish context that she would never explicitly identify as such.

Just as Rand's first intellectual heir's name-change perhaps suggests at least an unconscious desire to retain covert Jewish connotations, the Jewish-Danish critic Georg Brandes having been Nietzsche's first great booster much as Branden wanted to be Rand's, it appears that Rand concealed the Jewish connotations of her chosen *nom de plume*. 'Ayn' derives from, 'Ayin' ('eye'), her father's not-uncommon Hebrew pet-name for her as a child, the diminuative of which is 'Ayneleh', and whose implied meaning is 'bright eyes', an all-too-appropriate sobriquet for one with such arresting eyes as Alissa's. Alissa's adopted surname 'Rand' would ring bells for most Jews of her generation because of that name's well-known association with South African gold—The Rand—and the mostly Jewish entrepreneurs who mined it. The word 'gold' and the imagery of gold saturate *Atlas Shrugged,* and the gold standard plays a prominent role in her ideology. Even 'Galt' is 'gold', pronounced with a Yiddish inflection. (Numerous published accounts repeat the flimsy legend that the name 'Ayn' came from 'a Finnish writer' and the name 'Rand' from Alissa's Remington Rand typewriter.)

Rand took from Nietzsche his withering contempt for Plato, Kant, and Christianity as incubator of socialism. Nietzsche first and then Rand deplored the—typically Christian but typically unJewish—mind-body dichotomy. Rand, having been always repelled by Russian Orthodox Christianity, and never having inquired too closely as to how American Protestantism might be different, doubtless thrived on Nietzsche's evisceration of Christianity. Rand emulated Nietzsche in seeing Christianity as a disease afflicting western culture, by way of squishy-soft liberalism if not Communism. Distortion of reality to further the interests of exploitative mystics at the expense of the honest and productive "is the greatest problem in history, the one that has caused all of human suffering," Rand tells us in *Atlas Shrugged*.

For Nietzsche, and then Rand, a trading-business ethic underlies all ethics, and since Jews became civilization's most business-oriented people, they also became civilization's most ethical people. For Rand, as for Nietzsche, Christian faith is anti-ego and has fostered the sub-human. Christianity *per se* is seen as anti-reason and anti-wealth. Rand could hardly have avoided being aware that Judaism has historically been more pro-reason and pro-wealth than she assumed Christianity had been. The main cultural characteristics of Jews, especially in the last few centuries, steer them in the opposite direction from the bovine mediocrity that appalled Nietzsche. Nietzsche cherished the modern Jewish intellect and this may have favorably disposed Alissa Rosenbaum toward his ideas. Nietzsche celebrated Jewish intelligence and culture, while Kant viciously derided both.[1]

Jewish Influences in Objectivism

The following are some of the traits of Jewish cultural identity embodied in Rand's Objectivism:

1. *Opposing the mind-body dichotomy.* Christianity has always been notably more other-wordly than Judaism, which pays little attention to the afterlife, being more concerned with 'life on this earth' (a typical Objectivist phrase).

2. *The prizing of reason, even in its narrow form of 'logic'*. Logic is a more central part of Jewish than of Christian tradition. The Jewish mindset has been hypothesized to be more verbally and abstractly oriented than that of most gentile communities. Nietzsche lauded Judaism as the most "rational" of religious traditions.

3. *Earthly happiness as a proper goal of conduct*. Judaism has preached a moral obligation for the individual to pursue happiness in this life, whereas Christianity has generally preached resignation in 'this vale of tears', with hope reserved for the after-life.

4. *Emphasis on ability, especially 'brains'*. Education and sharp-wittedness have been traditionally favored by Jews, in lieu of land ownership, exalted rank, or fighting prowess.

5. *The virtue of pride*. Pride and high self-esteem have always been more acceptable to Jews than to Christians, who have often been fond of humbling themselves as 'miserable sinners' in a manner alien to Jews.

6. *Awareness of superiority*. Although Objectivism does claim that the free market will benefit even the least capable individuals, the focus of Objectivism's emotional appeal is on not placing obstacles in the way of the most able. Jewish culture's emphasis on extensive learning and scholarship was especially adaptable to the more science-based second wave of the industrial revolution. Superior Jewish intelligence, whether it be entirely cultural or partly genetic, has been remarked upon by a number of respected observers, as has its proven potential for stirring up resentment among gentiles. 'Children learning' is more highly valued in most Jewish than in most gentile homes. Rand as a *fin-de-siècle* Jew would have internalized her superior intelligence *vis-à-vis* most gentiles as a given. The notion of superior Jewish intelligence is widely held among Jewish Americans today. One Jewish former Objectivist, the philosopher Eric Mack, has suggested that a high

proportion of Objectivists are Jews because the philosophy draws more intelligent and combative people.

7. *Not apologizing for one's merits: not according oppressors 'the sanction of the victim'.* Jews have often felt the need to downplay their own capabilities, such as their business success, in an attempt to defuse resentment by the surrounding gentile community. This must always have irked some Jews, like Ayn Rand, who have felt indignant that 'the good ask forgiveness for being good'. (Rand's very idea of using 'Atlas' imagery could have been sparked by its use in a notable 1947 movie with an anti-anti-Semitism theme, *Gentlemen's Agreement,* starring Gregory Peck.)

8. *Reliance on one's own efforts, fear of government intrusion.* Jews, typically a distrusted minority enclave in a gentile society, have far more often had cause to fear the government than to fear private initiatives. The free market, in which all are equally free to show what they can do to satisfy the customer, has always been the Jews' friend, the government often the Jews' enemy.

    For nearly two thousand years Jewish culture was not oriented toward state formation or state maintenance. Jews' primary role was as economic catalysts in other peoples' states; the downside of this role was being smeared as parasites by religionists. Jews came to contribute so much as economic catalysts to other people's states that they were in practice responsible for strengthening those states more than did certain other sectors resentful of the Jews as supposed outsiders.

    Jewish commitment to the market economy, as opposed to the traditional economy, has both promoted their survival and spawned anti-Semitism, emanating from those within the traditional economy. Objectivism emerges from the fear, a very Jewish one, that the undeserving will undermine the deserving if only by dint of greater numbers, and provides a theory for delegitimizing any such undermining.

9. *Atheism.* This may seem strange, given that Judaism is a
   theistic religion. But whereas a Presbyterian who becomes
   an atheist automatically ceases to be a Presbyterian, a Jew
   who becomes an atheist remains a Jew, since the Jews are
   a cultural community, a 'people', not just a creed-defined
   community. Many non-religious Jews would think twice
   about marrying non-Jews.

   In practice, dating and marrying within the Jewish
   faith became transformed into dating and marrying within
   the Objectivist faith, though even here, most Jewish
   Objectivists married other Jewish Objectivists. Because of
   Jewry's identity transcending religious belief, and the comparatively high incidence of atheism and agnosticism
   among Jews, an identification with Objectivism's forthright
   atheism would not be as disruptive for typical Jewish as it
   would be for typical non-Jewish families.

10. *Preoccupation with survival, and with survival as a special
    being.* Survival is claimed to be the basis of the Objectivist
    ethics. For a Jew, 'survival' has traditionally meant survival
    as a Jew, just as for an Objectivist, 'survival' automatically
    means survival at a fully human, rational level—nothing
    less.

11. *The sanctity of individual rights.* A distinctive and possibly
    mistrusted minority, especially one more capable than the
    majority, has the most to gain from unalienable rights: an
    iron-clad guarantee that the law will treat members of the
    minority by just the same rules as it treats everyone else.
    Rand blends Jewish and American rights-consciousness
    with a Nietzschean take on the trader principle. Her phi-
    losophy sanctifies the American founders' creed of unalien-
    able rights, that creed ensuring the prosperity of
    non-religious Jews, given their values and traditions.

    Historically, Jews have found that legal rights won can
    become legal rights lost, therefore the unalienability of
    rights can become viewed as imperative. Rand doubtless
    experienced anti-Semitism in Russia and encountered it
    in the American conservative movement. It may have

prevented her (by its effects on both her and the American conservatives) from becoming a lasting part of the growing conservative coalition. The Founders' creed of unalienable rights could be appealed to as a weapon against the threat of anti-Semitism.

For Jews, self-interest automatically embraces (extended) family-interest, so an individual-rights-protecting culture becomes for Jews a family- (and ethnic-group-) preserving culture. This is why diaspora Jews have generally been Anglophiles, seeing so much concern for individual rights in English-speaking countries. Rand's views were largely those of her parents and other pre-1914 European Jews, Russia's Jews longing for European conditions.

12. *Wanting to be American.* Rand decided in her teens that she was Hollywood-bound. Once she got to Hollywood, she found other former Russian Jews who combined a worshipful awe of the American public with a resentment toward it. For Rand, this polarity took the form of a profound respect for the Founding Fathers combined with a profound contempt for all those descendents who had strayed from the Founders' wisdom. While the Hollywood moguls strove to recreate America on the screen, Rand tried to do so on the page, their efforts coming together in the *Fountainhead* movie. At Warner Brothers, Howard Roark's character fell right in line with the studio's preferred male type. Like the Hollywood moguls, Rand was obsessed with being *more* American than the Americans. (Exactly this motivation has been identified in the non-Anglo-Saxon support for HUAC and Joseph McCarthy.) Both Louis B. Mayer and Rand concocted idealized fantasy versions of America which they found far more congenial than the reality.

13. *Defending business as morally proper.* Jewishness and money-making have long been associated. The defense of business and trading as morally appropriate for everyone is therefore tacitly a defense of Jews.

14. *Commitment to sound money: opposition to inflation.* For sound historical reasons, acquiring money is equated with survivability for Jews and the fear of inflation is deeply rooted in the Jewish psyche. For Jews, survival is tied to the kind of higher-level operation of the intellect required in business (in contrast to what is required for, say, farming). The resulting economic power can often be wielded successfully against numerically stronger opponents relying upon territorial, cultural, legislative, and establishment-based power. Money-power for Jews has served as a substitute for territory-based power. Jews were seen as capitalism personified long before they became seen as communism personified.

15. *Replacing the cross with the dollar sign.* Instead of the symbol of a traditionally Jew-persecuting religion, Objectivism upholds a general symbol of money-making, at which Jews have usually succeeded brilliantly, given the legal right to try.

16. *Opposition to government welfare.* American Jews have traditionally disdained welfare in non-emergency situations, considering it a humiliation to go on welfare.

    Jews have a history of not being allowed to look to the government for work and instead having to look to the free market to make a living. They have been free-market-oriented for a great many centuries longer than they have been socialism-oriented. Rand took the Enlightenment and German-Jewish-American route to Jewish emancipation: assimilation to free-market principles. Post-Enlightenment Jews, Rand-included, became intent on erasing the cleavage between gentile and Jew, Rand by re-defining Americanism in an even more non-sectarian universalistic way.

17. *A 'light unto the gentiles'.* Jews have traditionally been acutely aware of their specialness. The religious Jewish impulse to teach the gentiles mainly by example becomes, with the secularization of Jews, an impulse to teach them

directly. Many modern movements, highly influential among gentiles, have had disproportionately Jewish leaderships: psychoanalysis (and most schools of psychotherapy), Marxism (and nearly all those forms of socialism which have not actually been anti-Semitic), and numerous more abstract intellectual movements emphasizing certain Jewish values, such as Chomsky's linguistic theory and Michael Lerner's 'Politics of Meaning'.

Jews and the Left

Most American Jews have ancestors who arrived in America well before the Russian Revolution. Jewish-American intellectuals have mostly been quite left-wing, though many Jews did move right toward the end of the twentieth century.

By contrast, Alissa Rosenbaum was a direct victim of the brutality of the Bolshevik regime. The Rosenbaum family was very well off, even by St. Petersburg rather than Russian standards, and the revolution's destruction of this hard-earned well-being, just as the entire Russian population was being further immiserated, must surely have constituted *the* formative influence of Rand's intellectual life—not just something that confirmed previously-held views, as Rand, Peikoff, and ARI would have it.

The reason Alissa couldn't simply immigrate to America in 1926 was the 'Red Scare' that was associated with the Jews. Intellectual Jews moved even further toward sympathy for Communism during the Depression. The writers of Hollywood were mostly Jews, most of them socialists or outright Communists trying to lose themselves in a universalist utopian struggle. A comparatively few Jews were so aghast at the Communism-Jews association that they were actively trying to break it, *Commentary*, for instance, by displaying a vigorously anti-Soviet stance.

Rand saw Franklin D. Roosevelt's administration as merely a slower route to communism or fascism. Both socialism and Communism were rife within the Jewish-American community throughout the 1920s, 1930s, and 1940s, a time of rising anti-Semitism in America. More established socialist organizations were too goyish and not radical enough for many Jewish leftists who flocked instead to the Trotskyite camp, goy Stalin becoming their voodoo doll. Likewise, conservative organizations were too goyish and stodgy and not radical enough for Jewish free marketeers of the late 1950s and the 1960s, so they flocked to Rand and Rothbard, goy Kant substituting for Marx as the Randian voodoo doll.

The left-wing refugee Jewish intellectuals from Nazi Germany who streamed into New York City during the 1930s must have appalled Ayn Rand. They were messianic heirs to Marx and Freud, not the Founding Fathers, intent on re-creating the culture of America to accommodate themselves. Jewish intellectuals in general wanted to forge a culture that Jew and gentile could dissolve into. Marxists tried to switch the Jew-gentile cleavage to capitalist-worker. Objectivists would switch it to rational individualist-mystical collectivist. American culture is bankrupt, said Marxists in the 1930s and Objectivists in the 1960s. Like most Marxists, Rand spoke of and encouraged an alienation from American culture that, left to their own devices, few gentiles felt.

Pre-Marxist socialism had been somewhat anti-Semitic given the association of Jews with capitalism. Then Marx imposed the caricature of the Jewish capitalist on all capitalists, thus sparing capitalist Jews from being singled out for harassment and focusing the workers' anger on a class rather than an ethnicity or religion. Marx projected Jewish alienation onto everyone. Alienation infused the Marxist movement with its Jewish leadership. Jewish Marxists aimed to create a society eliminating Jewish—supposedly universal—alienation. First came universalist socialism and then its inverse, universalist Objectivism.

Marxist revolutionaries, a greatly disproportionate number of them Jewish, had usurped Russia's democratic revolution and then laid the groundwork for a totalitarian state. Russia had been on a dynamic path toward industrialization and democracy before the Bolsheviks took over. Jews motivated to entirely transform the social order for the sake of uprooting entrenched anti-Semitism were even more disproportionately prominent in the Bolshevik coup and resulting civil war and then took up prominent positions in all sectors of the new Soviet government.

Marxism converted Christianity's anti-Semitically-tinged anti-wealthism into a universalistic ideological anti-wealthism. A religiously-zealous Marxism in power led to tens of millions of otherwise unnecessary deaths. Rand was aware of the unprecedented impact of Marx's imposing intellectual edifice upon the world and believed that an equally sophisticated intellectual edifice supporting *laisser faire* was needed to rival Marxism's drawing power for western intellectuals. She was also aware of Marx's Jewish background, and the disproportionate extent to which Jews were involved in the debacle. As a result, she both dis-identified with Jewish culture and pinned the blame for Marx on Kant, whom she saw as the modern philosophic face of Christian mysticism.

Atlas Shrugged was a kind of bible for a 'right-wing' Jewish-American internal exodus. Rand and all Objectivists have been strongly pro-Israel, on the grounds that the Israelis are intelligent, rational, civilized men combatting 'savages'. Rand also defended U.S. support for Israel as promoting America's oil interests in the Middle East and encouraging a more individual rights-oriented culture than elsewhere in the region. The number three man in orthodox Objectivism today, Peter Schwartz, considers a somewhat parochially Jewish publication, *Commentary*, as the only worthy journal outside of Objectivism in the world, even though Rand considered its Catholic Christian counterpart, *National Review*, just about the worst journal (of any kind) in the world. Leonard Peikoff has suggested on radio that American interests are so equivalent to Israeli interests that in retaliation for Iran-sponsored terrorist attacks against Israelis, America should vaporize Tehran's six million inhabitants (including more than a million children) with an atomic bomb, should American demands that such attacks cease not be obeyed.

The main totems of modern Jewish culture are the Holocaust, pro-Israel activity, and anti-anti-Semitism. These are reflected in Objectivism by *The Ominous Parallels*, Objectivism's staunchly pro-Israel stance, and its anti-envy position.

1920s Business Theory

Who is John Gall? He was an influential spokesman for the National Association of Manufacturers (NAM), and he became Rand's attorney. Her correspondence with him suggests a partial model for John Galt. NAM and the Chamber of Commerce were operating, it was thought, at a respectable intellectual level through the end of World War II, but Rand wanted to explicitly undergird NAM-style political and economic teaching with the elaboration of an underlying moral philosophy equivalent to a faith, providing for capitalism what Marx had given Communism.

Rand implicitly drew a parallel between what leading socialist-realists such as Maksim Gorki were doing for Bolshevism and what she was doing for capitalism. "Propaganda is the whole meaning of life and reality," she wrote, frankly and proudly characterizing her writing mission as that of propagandist. She believed her propaganda fiction could be more effective than NAM's educational efforts. Rand explicitly characterized even *The Fountainhead* as pro-business ideology expressed through fiction. She planned *Atlas Shrugged* to be still explicitly propagandistic for the pro-capitalist cause, and even incorporated at least one businessman's suggestions into the novel at the philosophical level.

Business theory of the 1920s affected Ayn Rand in two stages. When she first arrived in America, this ideology was 'in the air', very much in fashion, and echoed in popular culture. Rand picked up some of its language and attitudes at that time. Then, from 1940 on, John Gall and other new-found 'conservative' friends (some of them more classical liberal than conservative), encouraged her to go back to this material from the 1920s, material which was now decidedly out of fashion but familiar to pro-business lobbyists.

The explicit defense of selfishness was a staple of the 1920s pro-business literature. Rand's rhetoric of selfishness and satisfaction in productive achievement is lifted wholesale from such writers as Fay, Hooper, Feather, and Thorpe. To cite but two of a great many possible examples, in *Politics In Business* (1926),

Charles Fay wrote that "history shows that the prime motive of capitalism—namely, *selfishness*—merely reflects the conviction, inborn in every living creature, that it is his natural right to keep, own, and control whatever he himself has made, saved, thought out, bought, or fought for." Ben Hooper insisted that "the dynamo of selfish individualism" had created "its very own Garden of Eden." Prothro remarks upon the tremendous prestige enjoyed by such business dicta in the 1920s, when *Nation's Business* was declaring that, "capitalism is today triumphant" and the American businessman occupies an unprecedented "position of leadership." President Coolidge regarded businessmen as the true leaders of the entire nation, and these true leaders Rand would re-assemble in Galt's 'Utopia of Greed'. In 1926, Charles Fay was writing of the dependence of the untalented many upon the talented few in industrial society. Fay lambasted the anti-trust laws much as Rand would three decades later. While Rand's admirers would one day suggest that Objectivism has shaped business ethics, the reverse was certainly true at an earlier stage. Rand's Objectivism conveyed commonplaces of the roaring 1920s—forgotten in the 1930s—right into the 1980s and 1990s.

By the end of the 1920s, *laissez-faire* economics seemed defunct but *laissez-faire* morality was blooming. Self-indulgence and instant gratification were being accorded a new sanctity. In the 1930s, Rand observed a self-indulgent, vulgar selfishness, offering scant resistance to collectivist demagoguery, just as she had seen in revolutionary Russia a rootless, disorganized liberty, no match for ruthlessly disciplined collectivism. Rand believed in the *mind*-oriented code of self-*productivity* she had imbibed largely from 1920s business theory, and opposed it to the self-indulgent kind of vulgar selfishness she witnessed proliferating in the culture. By the time of *Atlas Shrugged,* the beatniks, fed on the bohemianism of the 1920s, were the spokesmen of the new selfishness. Rand shared their dedication to self, but denounced what she saw as their irrationality. She *detested* 'do your own thing' hippie selfishness, seeing it as ultimately erasing the integrity of the self, and therefore sliding toward collectivism.

In *Two Girls, Fat and Thin*, Gaitskill relates how "the ultrareality theory" (Rand's epistemology) was "the most daring and controversial aspect" of Granite's (Rand's) thinking. Gaitskill has more literally described how Rand "went beyond politics and into a simplistic derivative philosophy in an attempt to nail her theories to the floorboards." It isn't just a question of left or right, "it's reality or unreality." Rand's epistemological enemies, in Gaitsksill's words, "too weak to deal with real existence, try to wish it away by constructing worlds of illusion, claiming that nothing is real anyway, in an attempt to foil the strong people they envy." This too is largely taken from 1920s business theory. Howe wrote that only in business must one confront "unadorned fact" and "the simple facts of life." Fay held that "no socialist, collectivist, or progressive takes the least account of such trifling things as fact and human nature! 'We'll pass a law', say these dreamers, 'and change human nature!'" The likes of Howe and Fay, in Prothro's words, took "pride in the rigorous realism of their theory." In later Objectivist argot, they refused to evade the facts of reality.

At Pat's Feet

Although she had voted for Roosevelt in 1932, Rand participated in the Wendell Willkie for President campaign in 1940, and was drawn into the company of various conservative and classical liberal thinkers and activists. Foremost among these was novelist-columnist Isabel Paterson, known as 'Pat'. At this time Rand played the part of acolyte within a quasi-guru's inner circle. Monday evenings when the *Herald Tribune*'s Sunday book section went to press and Pat was going over the final copy, a handful of fellow conservatives would convene in her office for some high-brow intellectual exchanges into the wee hours. Rand became an enthusiastic member of the entourage, along with journalist Sam Wells, literary critic Will Cuppy, and others. Rand's inner circle would one day have similar sessions on Saturdays nights. Muriel Hall, Pat's heir, told Barbara Branden that Rand would sit at Pat's feet again and again while Pat and others would elaborate on some issue such as the Supreme Court until Ayn had a full grasp of it. Unlike Ayn, Pat was extraordinarily well-read in world history, American history, political philosophy, literature, economics, and science. At the time Ayn knew little of American history, political or industrial. Husband Frank O'Connor's niece Mimi Sutton recalls that when she stayed with the O'Connors one summer, Pat, "the guru and teacher," was often there and Ayn was spellbound by her, "sitting at the master's feet" until dawn. Much like Nathan sitting at Rand's feet in the 1950s.

Rand would later come to adopt many of Pat's more self-destructive behavior patterns. Pat's "hair-trigger temper, her bitter intransigence, her infinite capacity to embarrass friends publicly" eventually alienated her, one by one, from allies such as Rose Wilder Lane, and journalists John Chamberlain and Will Cuppy. The Pat-Ayn break came when Pat exploded at businessman William Mullendore, a crusader for capitalism whom Rand admired and consulted, Pat declaring that the economic climate could ultimately be blamed on businessmen because none of them cared enough about free enterprise to act on its behalf. Ayn later told Barbara that Pat had became "increasingly belligerent toward everyone. She spoke as if no one was really fighting for capitalism except her. Everyone else was a coward or a hypocrite." By the time Rand told Barbara this, in 1961, it had already become a good description of her own posture.

The Death and Rebirth of Classical Liberalism

In postwar America, leftists already dominated intellectual life, but they did not dominate popular culture. And in retrospect it's easy to see that the leftist intellectual hegemony was facing fresh challenges. George H. Nash notes that by the mid-1950s, "a vigorous, if heterogeneous, conservative intellectual movement had arisen" to challenge leftism. "Where, just a few years earlier, only scattered voices of intelligent right-wing protest were audible," by 1957, "a chorus of articulate critics of the left had emerged." Rand was part of that chorus, her jarring contribution coming from the largely abandoned bastion of popular culture.

Rand can best be seen in the context of long historical cycles of opinion on economic policy. She became prominent at a time when classical liberalism or libertarianism was re-emerging from its long eclipse and beginning to fight back against socialism and other forms of collectivism. She played an interesting and important role in the ideological resurgence of *laisser faire* in the second half of the twentieth century, but this resurgence would have occurred without Rand.

Talk of the twentieth century as an age of collectivism was common long before Rand. In Britain, Fabian theory became government policy after a quarter-century of spreading Fabian doctrine. A literature of reaction to Fabian policies accompanied their implementation, both in Britain and the U.S. It was the Austrian school of economic theory which provided the most important source of respectable and powerful critique of socialist theory and policy.

American columnist Walter Lippmann formed a pre-World War II prototype of what would become the Mont Pèlerin Society. Classical liberalism may have appeared dead and socialism unstoppable by 1940 but socialism's intellectual undoing and economic liberalism's re-tooling were already under way. Friedrich Hayek's *Road to Serfdom* made a huge splash in 1944, doubtless helping out sales of *The Fountainhead*. Hayek's book moved American conservatism in a more libertarian direction.

Briton Antony Fisher, inspired by *Road to Serfdom*, would write his own book and then go on, by means of the several influential think-tanks he founded, to become the most important architect of what would later be ideological Thatcherism. The founding of the Mont Pèlerin Society in 1945 marked a decisive point in liberalism's resurgence. Hayek's Mont Pèlerin-based movement became the Fabian Society of renewed classical liberalism. Rand had hoped the Objectivist movement would play that role at a more philosophic level, but Objectivists were neither knowledgeable enough nor civilized enough to make the kind of headway that Mont Pèlerin made.

Post-war American business leaders were willing to embrace an increased role for government and abandoned free-market fundamentalism, thereby also ceding intellectual territory to Rand. Lewis H. Brown made some concessions to government but was also the man behind the American Enterprise Institute, eventually a highly effective think-tank for promoting smaller government. It was William F. Buckley, who, prior to *Atlas Shrugged*, united the diverse strands of conservatism. In the long run, it may have been the very unquestioned simplicity and undeveloped nature of the Lockean dogmas pervading the American mentality that allowed them to triumph over a far more intellectually sophisticated and integrated Marxism. While *Atlas Shrugged* was published when the left was *it* intellectually, a new rightist intelligentsia was already becoming a force to be reckoned with.

11

The Disowned Ancestry
of *Atlas Shrugged*

The Greatest Book of All Time

In summing up the past thousand years of progress, the *Chicago Tribune* gave its nominations for the ten best and ten worst books of the millennium. *Atlas Shrugged* came second worst. The *Tribune* described it as "the most protracted, militant, and demented expression of Rand's Objectivist philosophy." This evaluation is entirely typical of the opinions of well-read people. Yet Gore Vidal has remarked that Rand is the only writer everyone in Congress has read, and Mary Gaitskill observes that Rand's novels are a staple in many high school English courses as well as required reading even in some colleges. Here is a book despised by the literati and beloved by the masses.

Atlas Shrugged is the story of what occurs when a man of true genius decides to halt the spread of collectivism by persuading those with outstanding ability to go on strike. The crumbling economy falls increasingly into the hands of 'looters', 'moochers', and 'parasites', who gladly exploit the economy but require the willing contribution of creative minds in order to do so. Railway magnate Dagny Taggart and steel-works wunderkind Hank Rearden fight valiantly to keep their businesses going, but thereby preserve the remnants of capitalism for the government to loot. The strike's leader, John Galt, withholding his revolutionary motor design from an undeserving world, is eventually captured by the looters. These thugs, hoping to hang onto power by having Galt salvage the economy, try to force him to become economic dictator. Galt is tortured but then rescued by strikers, including Taggart and Rearden, who finally realize that their best capitalist efforts are merely sustaining a collectivist system parasitic on such efforts. They fly to Galt's Gulch, a capitalist utopia hidden in the Colorado Rockies, and await the moment when a collapsed world will welcome back "the men of the mind" on the strikers' terms.

The message in *Atlas Shrugged* is not subtle. Its fans experience the emotional power of the novel without being disconcerted by its zealous propagandizing. It is the starkness of Rand's black-and-white characters that is so seductive to so many readers and is how she draws her readers into her philosophy. Mary Gaitskill maintains that Rand's novels "use emotional manipulation, melodrama, jargon and sexual fantasy to make her points . . . she plugged into a mass psyche, using archetypal characters devoid of real individuality, and having the same vulgar emotional power as the Wicked Witch."

A hostile letter to the editor of the *New York Times* pointed out The *Fountainhead*'s affinity with the comics. It's more pronounced with *Atlas*. Both *Anthem* and *The Fountainhead* were published in comic strip format. Objectivist Steve Ditko has published several issues of a comic book called *Mr. A,* based on Rand's 'A is A' slogan. In 1973 he did *Avenging World,* a kind of illustrated *Virtue of Selfishness* for pre-teens—deliberately crass, caricatured, and didactic. Little of Rand's philosophy is lost when her novels are transferred to comic format. As Mary Gaitskill put it, she succeeded "because her writing was like the broad slashes and gaudy colors of the cheapest comic strip—but it was a comic strip about life and death and everyone knew it."

Science-fiction critic Robert Hunt observes that in twentieth century American culture, "the cartoon increasingly became a release mechanism for the visual imagination . . . the human need to exaggerate. . . . One of the constant themes in these dramatic comics is that Western society is in decline and that its peoples are gripped by an inner fear." Rand was familiar with magazine science fiction, her own *Anthem* appearing in *Famous Fantastic Mysteries* in June 1953. Hunt observes that in its crudeness of characterization, *Atlas Shrugged* "recalls the pulp science fiction of the 1920s and 1930s." Garth Hammond, the planet-smashing entrepreneur of Jack Williamson's 1939 *Astounding* novella, *Crucible of Power,* is close to Hank Rearden. *Atlas's* heroes, though they resemble *GQ* models, "fit squarely into the pulp tradition of the tight-lipped, two-fisted engineer-research scientist-capitalist-adventurer that dominated science fiction until and beyond World War II."

In Galt's static electricity convertor, "Readers of early-1940s science fiction will recognize parallels with the cheap, clean 'broadcast power' that obsessed . . . many of *Astounding's* regular contributors." There are five boffo inventions in *Atlas:* Rearden Metal, Galt's motor, Galt's mountain-scape reflector screen, the baddies' Project X sound-ray (the work of a committee), and the baddies' torture machine. Then there's Dagny's tour of Utopia: "Such tours, a common subgenre at the turn of the century," seemed old-fashioned even by the 1920s. Much in *Atlas Shrugged* that seemed weirdly unfamiliar in the 1950s would have been immediately recognized as pulp cliché a few decades earlier.

In Galt's Gulch the revolutionary scientists "work in isolation, without the need for research assistants or advanced facilities; they are, in short, not realistic scientists or inventors, but versions of the stock 1930s scientist-as-wizard, the genius who steps into the lab to cook up a solution to the latest plot crisis." As for the breakdown of civilization in *Atlas,* Hunt sees it as "a marginally more sophisticated version of the pulp apocalypse."

The setting of *Atlas Shrugged* is deliberately anachronistic, artificial, and self-contained. Though set in the future, the economy is more like that of the 1920s than the 1950s, with railroads predominating, and the few airplanes propellor rather than jet. Hunt points out that there are almost no mentions of real individuals (except Plato and Aristotle), corporations, wars, ideologies, or artists. All the features of the cultural landscape have been made up by Rand, not taken from American history.

Rand "had to dismantle and reassemble the universe in order to make *Atlas* work. Only in the realms of myth and science fiction can human beings exhibit the purity demanded by ideological fiction." And it *is* "a paradigm of ideological fiction" shouting that "Any system that is not based on reason is self-contradictory, absurd, unstable, doomed" as is "modern civilization . . . the novel's imagery, its characterization, its confident projection of a 'universal calculus' to resolve human conflicts by quasi-scientific means are all rooted in the '30s and '40s. . . ."

In trying to account for the book's wide and intense appeal, Hunt suggests that Rand plugs into our feelings of being unappreciated and exploited by others, and meant for something better, and has the reader identifying with the heroes and all their glitzy symbols. Furthermore, the freedom not to give a damn about the weak remains a heady concept for many readers.

Nathaniel Branden recollects of Rand in 1957 that she had come to regard herself as a master of her craft who did not need the services of an editor. Part of the emotional power of *Atlas Shrugged* presumably derives from its continual repetition of a limited number of emotion-laden words. (Where my careful word counts err, it is on the low side.) *Destroy* or *destruction* occurs 278 times. Characters *laugh* on 241 occasions (or are *amused* 123 times, although I count only a dozen genuine laughs for the reader). Fire and brimstone favorites predominate. *Evil* occurs less often in the Bible: in *Atlas Shrugged* it is deployed a staggering 220 times. *Damned* or *damnation:* 213 times. We are numbed to *pain*, which Rand is so intent on relegating to the realm of the unimportant, by its 207 instances. *Suffering:* 109 times. Characters exude *anger* an astonishing 174 times and are *astonished* an almost equally astonishing 173 times. The evil of *sacrifice* or *sacrificial* requires 135 deployments. *Fire*, admittedly without brimstone, lights up the page in 135 spots and characters receive a *shock* to the system nearly every eight pages, 130 zaps in all. *Fear* gives us 110 shivers. When theft is suggested 105 times, *loot* or *looter* is with perfect assurance inserted on each occasion. Characters and things *jerk* hither and thither a hundred times— and also snap (87) or jolt (39) for variety. It is usually the heroes with whom 98 *gold* mentions are associated, and who exude the lofty *indifference* (96) so richly merited by meddling mediocrities. As for *cigarette* mentions, there's nearly a carton's worth—94. *Blood* hemorrhages within the text 92 times; *hell* rekindles 92 times. Other Rand staples include: *desperate* (87), *twisted* (81), *tense* (73), *hate* (72), *resentment* (70), *mocking* (67), *contempt* (65), *torture* (65), *ugly* (64), *waste* (64), *panic* (63), *lonely* (61), *shudder* (57), *violent* (57), *fog* (55), *perish* (47), *terror* (46), *rotter/rot/rotten* (46), and *vicious* (43). Those who find *Atlas Shrugged* a sexy novel rather than a cold one won't be surprised that *naked* (64) edges out *cold* (62), though a lot of that nakedness is naked contempt, naked violence, or being strapped naked to a torture machine.

Not only is it held to be the finest novel ever written, Barbara Branden tells us that "the idea is incredible. The men of the mind go on strike. That's never been done before. That's totally original." The claim of extraordinary originality has been advanced on Rand's behalf by many followers. And yet the book clearly has its precursors, some largely unknown among Objectivists until quite recently. To point these out is not to belittle Rand or to detract from any merits the book possesses. Many fine novels are not particularly original in conception, and where a major writer got her ideas is always interesting. Whether Rand concealed any of these likely influences or forgot them, I will not pursue.

Precursors of *Atlas Shrugged*

1920s Business Theory

By 1940 John Gall was probably familiarizing Rand with the 1920s business-heyday trade journals of NAM, the United States Chamber of Commerce, and other pro-business organizations, and with business oriented books of that era. Not only did these business theorists advance a view of capitalism based on the virtue of selfishness, they openly called for works of fiction which would, as Prothro summarizes it, "recognize the peculiar quality of the American ideal."[1]

The basic idea of the plot of *Atlas Shrugged*, that prosperity, and even civilization itself, depends upon a comparatively few creative minds, and would crumble if those minds were withdrawn, was familiar to 1920s business theorists. A 1920 NAM report states: "History proves conclusively that the only hope of the mass is the development of able individuals. Withdraw the ten thousand best minds from any country and you would atrophy the nation." Eugene Lombard wrote that without great leaders' minds, "the multitudes would eat their heads off, and, as history proves, would lapse into barbarism and die of pestilence and famine." Looking at the unpopularity of the capitalist, Harper Leech wrote in 1926 that "it appears to be a characteristic of some parasites that they seek to devour their host regardless of the fact that . . . their short-sighted appetites will mean their own extinction."

The 1920s business literature was filled with talk about the all-importance of the mind or "brains." Charles Fay dilates on the importance of brains as accounting for the success of great merchants and entrepreneurs, and predicts that, although the envious multitude periodically revolts against the men of brains, ultimately public opinion will come to recognize their value. The notion that technology is an instrument of the mind is of course a commonplace even outside 1920s business theory. Karl Marx wrote: "Nature builds no machines, no locomotives, railways. . . . They are organs of the human brain, . . . the power of knowledge objectified." Yet the young Hank Holzer was greatly impressed by a phrase from *Atlas Shrugged:* "The machine, the frozen form of a mind's ingenuity."

The Businessman as Hero

Active entrepreneurs or captains of industry as heroes of novels are surprisingly rare. Generally, these figures are given little attention, appear as villains, or, as in Henry James, feature in the story only when they are away from their businesses.

One notable exception is Theodore Dreiser's unfinished Frank Cowperwood trilogy, in its two completed volumes, *The Financier* (1912) and *The Titan* (1914). Dreiser had read Mencken's *Philosophy of Friedrich Nietzsche* (1908), as Rand would later do, and imbued his capitalist hero with Nietzschean virtues. Cowperwood's 'private law' is to satisfy himself. In Henry Nash Smith's view, Cowperwood is "by far the most impressive portrait of a big businessman in American fiction." No later writer would bring to the subject Dreiser's commitment or intensity. Yet, according to Smith, Dreiser simply took over "the familiar catalogue of the businessman's vices and presented them as virtues."

Noting that "Rand is one of very few authors who have stood up for business men as decent people and business as being a productive and beneficial activity," Merrill points to Cameron Hawley as a precursor. In Hawley's *Executive Suite* (1952, superbly filmed two years later), the theme is that of "the entrepreneurial businessman as an underappreciated hero who gives society far more than can ever be repaid." And two years prior to *Atlas*, Hawley has his protagonist protest in *Cash McCall* (1955), "We have a peculiar national attitude toward money-making. . . . We maintain that the very foundations of our way of life is what we call free enterprise—the profit system," but when someone accumulates a little profit, "we do our best to make him feel that he ought to be ashamed." It's a Christian precept that "poverty is somehow associated with virtue" and a millionaire has to "expiate his sin" by charitable giving. Where McCall gripes, John Galt will thunder in outrage.

Saint-Simon's Parable via Friedrich Hayek (1941)

Hayek's extraordinarily influential defense of economic liberalism against creeping socialism, *The Road To Serfdom*, was published in 1944. Ayn Rand was already mapping out her post-*Fountainhead* novel by then. Just prior to the outset of that process, a time when Rand had recently forged all kinds of contacts with free-market thinkers who would have been recommending relevant books and articles to her, a 1941 issue of *Economica* featured a Hayek essay that recounted the so-called parable of Henri de Saint-Simon.[2] The latter was mentor to sociologist Auguste Comte, who would found a positivist sect intent on applying science to society, and "in which the material benefactors of mankind replaced the hierarchy of saints." In 1819, Saint-Simon, with Comte's support, started up a journal called *Organisateur,* which attracted wide attention. Hayek writes that "the celebrated Parable with which the new publication opens . . . shows that if France were suddenly deprived of the fifty chief scientists in each field, of the fifty chief engineers, artists, poets, industrialists, bankers, and artisans of various kinds, her very life and civilization would be destroyed. He then contrasts this with the case of a similar misfortune befalling a corresponding number of persons of the aristocracy, of dignitaries of state, of courtiers and of members of the high clergy, and points out how little difference this would really make to the prosperity of France." In *Atlas Shrugged* the most competent in the productive professions, such as scientists and industrialists, would disappear from American society, leaving its leadership to the union bosses, priests, politicians, and bureaucrats whose parasitic ways bring only devastation.

Wells's Things to Come *(1936)*

Britain's famous H.G. Wells sci-fi film epic *Things To Come* (1936) depicts the approaching world war as a 35-year regression into primitivism. Technologically-sophisticated international warfare exhausts itself only to be replaced by technology-bereft intertribal warlordism. It turns out that the world's most technologically brilliant men have abetted this collapse by withdrawing to the birthplace of civilization near Basra. These 'men of the mind' have in effect gone on strike but are planning the rebirth of civilization, as *Atlas* characters will in Galt's Gulch. They regroup as the 'Airmen' of 'Wings Over The World', a self-appointed provisional world government. In the 1970s the Airmen begin flying emissaries out to barbarian strongholds and substituting a new order based on their far superior technology (brains) and morality (war as the initiation of force between peoples is banished).

In one scene, the head Airman (played by Raymond Massey) refuses to place his brainpower at the disposal of his warlord captor, is threatened with torture and in turn warns that his imprisonment will trigger rescue by an armada of Airmen. In *Atlas*, hero John Galt refuses to deploy his brainpower on behalf of his fascist captors, and really *is* tortured before being rescued and returned to safety by a Galt's Gulch air squadron.

Malcolm Muggeridge wrote in 1940 that in this film Wells has endowed prosperity, once viewed as an end in itself, with transcendental qualities, adding to it benevolence and eroticism. Bank balances dissolve into embraces, factory chimneys blossom like flowers. Muggeridge called this 'romantic materialism'. In *Atlas Shrugged* Rand takes bourgeois values and injects them with a heroically Nietzschean *élan*.

Lane's Discovery of Freedom *(1943)*

The year 1943 saw the publication of three important libertarian books by women: Ayn Rand's *Fountainhead*, Isabel Paterson's *God of the Machine*, and Rose Wilder Lane's *Discovery of Freedom*. In November 1945 Rand wrote Lane a letter on the occasion of her glowing review of *The Fountainhead* in the *National Economic Council's Book Reviews*, insisting that "we certainly must" meet. They then exchanged letters on professional and philosophical matters for two years before finally meeting.

Lane's novella *Let the Hurricane Roar* (1932), later made into two TV movies, sells today as *Young Pioneers*. Still in print is her best-selling novel *Free Land* (1938), first serialized in the *Saturday Evening Post*. Her credo, *Give Me Liberty* (1936), was perhaps a model for Rand's never-published *The Individualist Manifesto*. The short stories in her *Old Home Town*, portraying rural America circa 1900 but with a feminist theme, continues in print and her *Little House on the Prairie* series is a perennial best-seller among older children. (Rose was unveiled in the 1990s as its true author, rather than her mother, Laura Ingalls Wilder.)

Rose Wilder Lane's plain language and humanist sentiment transmogrified into the more haranguing style of *Atlas Shrugged*. Dozens of motifs and expressions to be found later in Rand are sprinkled throughout *The Discovery of Freedom*. Some of Rand's favorite words and phrases, like 'sunlit', 'standard of value', 'life on this earth', 'savages', 'stagnation', 'static universe', and others dot *Discovery*'s landscape.

The same goes for Rand themes such as: the counterproductivity of government planning; the case for limited government; the factual nature of morality (though Lane's was religious); that contradictions cannot exist in reality; that words have an exact meaning; that human rights cannot exist without property rights; that more supposed democracy actually means more rule by gangs and less individual liberty; that statist meddling could completely de-industrialize a country; that capitalism does not cause wars; that American intellectuals are being seduced by European intellectuals into fantasies of benevolent state intervention; that we must never forget that effects cease when their causes cease; that governments are inimical to the exploitation of new inventions; that Bismarckian welfare statism, Marxism, and Fascism are all German-styled counter-revolutions against the values of the American revolution; that the enemies of freedom succeed only by appropriating and turning against freedom the technology that only freedom could create, . . . and so on. In fact, one could easily construct an embryonic version of John Galt's radio speech from the ideas in Lane's book.

Twain's A Connecticut Yankee in King Arthur's Court *(1889)*

Mark Twain's burlesque *A Connecticut Yankee in King Arthur's Court* countered the anti-business cult of medievalism. Hero Hank Morgan, is dropped suddenly and inexplicably into sixth-century Britain, secures for himself the status and title of Boss, and sets about putting King Arthur's Kingdom on a businesslike basis. He has no respect for antiquity and tradition; and he takes a commercial view of everything, eagerly seeking opportunities to make money and constantly using figures of speech derived from business, like 'contracts' and 'selling short'. He sets about building factories, workshops, mines, and systems of transportation and communication that will drastically raise the standard of living for the people as a whole.

Henry Nash Smith points out that, in making his protagonist a master technician and interpreting economic development as an increase in productive power rather than as a mysterious opportunity for speculators to enrich themselves, Mark Twain was "taking over a rationale for capitalism familiar in economic and political discussion but previously unknown in fiction." Morgan acts the true capitalist hero until the last quarter of the novel when, unable "to educate the superstition out of them after all," he realizes "they are but 'human muck', chained forever by their own prejudices and fears of authority, unable in a crisis to resist the commands of their masters, the Church, and the nobles." As Smith puts it, Twain "brings out in bold relief the central myth of nineteenth-century American capitalism, . . . the myth of Prometheus, enemy of the reactionary and tyrannical gods of tradition, bringer of intellectual light and material well-being to the downtrodden masses."

In *Atlas Shrugged*, as in *Connecticut Yankee*, capitalists like Dagny make a noble go of the Promethean project but the ignorant workers and incompetent bureaucrats regress the economy to medieval conditions. Eventually the capitalists retire from the scene to allow conditions to deteriorate to the point where people will turn in desperation to John Galt's metaphysics, epistemology, and ethics—in Rand's view the necessary undergirding of a capitalist system. In both Twain's medieval England and Rand's America, the population's irrational beliefs doom its fragile industrial base. And in both novels the heroes aid in the destruction of that base to prevent the forces of unreason from turning technology against them.

Garrett's The Driver *(1922)*

Libertarian writer Justin Raimondo first brought to light similarities between Garet Garrett's *The Driver* and Rand's two major novels, mostly *Atlas Shrugged*. Garet Garrett was a well-known figure, who served as executive editor of the *New York Tribune*, as a financial writer with both *The New York Times* and the *Wall Street Journal*, and as editor of *The New York Times Analyst*, all before the age of 38. He was the author of several novels, now difficult to find. *The Driver* is about a rather shadowy figure on Wall Street who buys up more and more shares of a railway company, which, in the midst of a widespread depression, is sliding toward receivership. "I'm the driver," he says when he assumes control.

The chief male heroes of *Atlas Shrugged* are John *Galt* and *Henry* Rearden. The hero of *The Driver* is *Henry Galt*, a man of mystery whose secrets slowly unfold. Unlike John Galt in *Atlas Shrugged*, there is no mystery as to the *identity* of Henry Galt, but there is mystery as to what he is up to. Eventually he goes from oddball Wall Street speculator to the greatest railroad magnate and multimillionaire financier of 1890s America. The confidence he demonstrates in making enormous investments of capital at the nadir of the 1891–94 depression becomes contagious, which resuscitates the whole economy. "After 1896 the flood tide began to swell and roar. Henry Galt was astride of it—a colossus emerging from the mist."

In the world of *Atlas Shrugged*, the phrase 'Who is John Galt?' has become an everyday expression for resigned hopelessness. In *The Driver*, the question, 'Who is Henry M. Galt?' occurs twice—thrice if you count Mordecai the banker's Yiddish-inflected, "Ooo iss zat Mr. Galt?" (Mordecai is modelled on financier Jacob Schiff, and Galt on the Schiff-backed Averill Harriman.) In both books, the phrase disturbs those who hear it.

There is much in Garrett's depiction of Henry Galt that is heroic in the Randian mold: Galt's is a "solitary serenity." He has a "power to move men's minds." He is "like an elemental force." Galt's "reasoning was always clear. . . . Galt's touch was sure, propulsive, and unhesitating." He held "public opinion in contempt. . . . His mind was not on money, primarily. He thought in terms of creative achievement."

Galt's predecessor as President of the Great Midwestern Railroad sums up the railroads' dilemma as America's: "Prejudice against railroads was . . . irrational and suicidal. All profit . . . had been taxed and regulated away . . . unless they allowed the railroads to prosper the great American experiment was doomed." We watch the Great Midwestern Railroad gradually fall apart, just as Taggart Transcontinental, an emblem of the whole economy, does in *Atlas Shrugged*.

Henry M. Galt, speculator, is a means toward Henry M. Galt, railroad tycoon. His heart—no less so than Dagny's—beats with a love for the country's railroads, its veins and arteries. Garrett hits the reader with as much technical detail about railway operations, by way of explaining Galt's corporate strategy and his major railway takeover, as Rand does to illustrate Dagny's ability to improvise ways of surmounting the problems imposed upon her railway by bureaucratic interference. In three different places Garrett harkens back to the Dark Ages as the fate of a business-hating culture, also a recurring motif in Rand's writings.

The conventional political right does not escape Garrett's censure any more than it would Rand's. One character is overheard saying, "You put the money into the pockets of the manufacturers by high tariffs. The people know this. Now they say, 'Fill our pockets, too.' It's quite consistent. But it's Socialism."

When Henry Galt at the peak of his success is dragged before Committee of the House hearings, he offers a plain-speaking defense of unlimited business profits that anticipates what John Galt will intellectualize more long-windedly. Henry's empire is under attack from the Anti-Trust Act. But the Act, which Rand vilified as the turning point in the collectivist war against capitalism, is itself non-objective. Asks Henry Galt: "Who knew what the law was? It had never been construed." Rand too will denounce antitrust law for its unintelligibility—putting honest businessmen at the mercy of the politically-appointed judges arbitrarily interpreting its ambiguous meaning.

Henry Galt's dramatic day in court galvanizes the nation. The sudden winning of popular vindication by talking past the authorities directly to the people is Henry Galt's, Howard Roark's, and John Galt's.

In 1940 Garrett became editorial-writer-in-chief at the *Saturday Evening Post*. In 1944 he would publish the political monograph, *The Revolution Was*, an uncompromising denunciation of the New Deal that went through many editions. Being one of the few authors of the 1930s and 1940s whom, as an overt anti-statist Rand could call an ideological soul-mate, it's very likely that *The Driver* came to her attention.

Atlas Shrugged contains at least five non-banal uses of the phrase 'the driver'. For instance Francisco tells us that "money is only a tool. It will take you wherever you wish, but it will not replace you as the driver." And of course *Atlas Shrugged* is built around the sustained metaphor of 'the motor'.

Bramah's The Secret of the League *(1907)*

In 1943 Rand mused to her friend Isabel Paterson, "What if all the creative minds of the world went out on strike? . . . That would make a good novel." It already had, nearly 40 years earlier, and Rand may even have read it.

Ernest Bramah (1868–1942) was extremely well-known as a popular fiction writer before World War II, and continued to have some following later. He is best known for two series of stories: those of Kai Lung and of Max Carrados. The Kai Lung stories are heavily ironic tales set in imperial China and remain in print today. The well-known British writer Hilaire Belloc (author of the anti-socialist tract, *The Servile State*) contributed a preface to *Kai Lung's Golden Hours* (1922). Max Carrados is a blind detective who makes up for his lack of sight by the acute sensitivity of his other senses, plus extraordinary intelligence. A Max Carrados yarn is nearly always included in collections of early detective stories, two Max Carrados books were reissued in 1970, and BBC radio aired dramatizations of three Max Carrados mysteries in 1997. Rand, at one time a mystery buff, may very well have read some Bramah.

The Secret of the League was published in London in 1907 and reprinted in 1909, 1920, and 1927. This anti-socialist, quasi-libertarian novel would presumably have been known to some of Rand's libertarian acquaintances of the 1940s. Ernest Bramah expressed in his novel the dread of creeping socialism that many felt in Britain in the early years of the century. His account preceded any American equivalent because collectivism took root in Britain sooner.

The action of the story takes place about ten years in the future—that is, in about 1917. Britain is gradually sliding toward economic and moral ruin as a succession of socialist governments impose increasingly drastic regulations and soak-the-rich taxes. Even the nation's navy is emasculated so as to redirect the savings into social spending. A mysterious, unidentified figure calling himself George Salt—'Salt' is a condensed version of his real name, 'Stobalt'—decides that enough is enough. He devises a plan to swiftly undermine the socialist regime, all those who voted for it in the expectation of receiving its patronage, and the very idea of socialism. He then persuades a wealthy aristocrat and business tycoon, Sir John Hampden, to join forces with him in The Unity League to orchestrate a withdrawal of middle and upper-class purchasing power from the coal market. The coal industry is the beating heart of Britain, pumping energy to all of British industry. A big-buyers' boycott would deliver a blow to the coal industry and eventually bring down all other industries and governments indirectly dependent on coal. Those who join the League will be provided by it with stockpiled coal and oil.

Government revenues fall as businesses fail, and soon the socialist regime finds itself unable to continue funding even basic government functions, let alone its lavish social programs. Finally, economic conditions evoke such universal distress and anarchy that the hapless regime capitulates altogether. The book ends as Sir John and Salt and a slate of League candidates prepare to be swept into power by the humbled electorate.

A number of themes in *Secret of the League* are restated in *Atlas Shrugged*. Both Sir John and G. Salt in *Secret of the League* and John Galt in *Atlas Shrugged* deprive their country of energy sources, the former in disrupting the coal industry by withdrawing the buying power of the productive class, the latter in Galt's withdrawing his revolutionary motor design plus all the most productive minds from society. Bramah writes that there were

League manufacturers, "who in their faith and enthusiasm wished to close their works at once, and, regardless of their own loss, throw their workmen and their unburnt coal into the balance. It was not required." *Atlas Shrugged* takes that extra step. The bosses of the biggest companies not propped up by resources looted from the taxpayers *do* abandon their plants.

There are many parallel elements in *Secret of the League* and *Atlas Shrugged*. *Secret of the League* has Brother Ambrose, who preaches that "it would be as easy for a diver to pause in mid-air as for mankind to remain at a half-way house to Equality. All! All! Every man-made distinction must be swept away. . . . That is the only practical socialism." The Brother Ambrose of *Atlas Shrugged* is Claude Slagenhop, president of Friends for Global Progress, who believes that collective need must dictate all policy. Britain's upper ranks in *Secret of the League* are seen by the lower ranks as "insatiable birds of prey who sucked their blood." In *Atlas Shrugged*, a trendy novelist publishes *The Vulture Is Moulting*, an exposé of the greedy businessman. In Bramah's work, the politicians and those who vote for them are "themselves bunglers . . . in their daily work and life." Rand's book too bemoans a universal decline in worker competence, as workers shift their focus from doing their jobs to collectively extorting special rights and higher wages from employers and taxpayers.

Much of Bramah's sardonic commentary could be mistaken for Rand's. Of the usurping of effective charitable work by ineffective government social workers, Bramah writes that "there had never been a time when men so . . . desired to help their fellow men" or "found it so difficult to do so." A preacher decries "the easy donation of a cheque . . . as frequently vanity." Recipients of government largesse have come to demand it as a right: "they regarded existence . . . as assured, and . . . stirring them to rebellion was not the fundamental . . . 'right to live', but the . . . right to live apart from the natural vicissitudes of life." One pleading deputation to a government minister "included a countess, a converted house-breaker, and an anarchist who had become embittered with life since the premature explosion of one of his bombs had blown off both his arms and driven him to subsist on the charitable." This reads like classic Rand, only wittier.

Rand condemns those who place nature ahead of industry. Bramah writes sardonically: "On the 22nd day of July, seventeen million 'estimated chimneys' ceased to pollute the air." As in *Atlas Shrugged*, government interference doesn't profit its ostensible beneficiaries in the long run, for "with more money the majority of the poor were poorer than before. . . . The lowest depths of human poverty had not been abolished by an Act of Parliament after all."

The following depicts the sort of industrialist John Galt would happily recruit from Bramah's fold: Lomas is a Lancashire colliery proprietor, "a man who had risen from the lowest grade of labour. . . . Positive, narrow, overbearing, he was permeated with the dogmatic egotism of his successful life. He had never asked another man's advice; he had never made a mistake." Lomas is the richest employer in the north central coal-field. "But there were fewer widows and orphans in Halghcroft than in any other pit village of its size, and Lomas spent nothing in insurance. Under his immediate eye cage cables did not snap, tram shackles part, nor did unexpected falls of shoring occur" and "no mysterious explosion had ever engaged the attention of a Board of Trade enquiry."

Then there are the Rand-like depictions of social collapse, brought on by the buyers' strike: "Leicester lay at the mercy of an epidemic of small-pox which threatened to become historic . . . rioting broke out in practically all parts . . . London, in its ice-bound straits, began curiously to assume the appearance of a mediaeval city . . . Thieves and bludgeoners lurked in every archway, and arrests were seldom made." *Atlas Shrugged* also depicts a regression to a medieval level of civilization.

As in *Atlas Shrugged*, Bramah's intellectuals and politicians are ultimately responsible for corrupting the basically good-hearted working man's nature. *Secret of the League* has its socialist officials like Mr. Bilch with his "splendid invulnerability to argument, reason, or fact," and Mr. Chadwing, who "smiled the thin smile of expediency." Failing to thwart the Unity League, the government simply "declined to believe the evidence." Rand's villains too try to cope with reality by evading it.

Salt's character is in the Galt-Rearden-Ragnar-Francisco mold. Where "the ceaseless din of industry made rest impossible; where the puny but irresistible hands of generations of mankind had scarred the face of the earth like a corroding growth, where the sky was shut out by smoke, vegetation stifled beneath a cloak of grime, day and night turned into one lurid vulcanian twilight, in which by bands and companies, by trains and outposts, dwarfish men toiled in the unlovely rhythm of hopeless, endless labour: the lupus spots of nature; there Salt took his holiday." Feeling most at home where industry subjugates nature is characteristic of all Rand's heroes.

When one of Bramah's characters says that he had supposed Salt to have been enjoying wild times at Monte Carlo or some other pleasure resort, Salt replies that "there was an impression of that sort given out. . . . But, between ourselves, it was strictly on a matter of business," that is, planning the buyers' strike. In *Atlas Shrugged*, Francisco deliberately encourages a media image of himself as a cosmopolitan high-society playboy, when he is really working hard for the strike.

In *Atlas Shrugged*, Ragnar, with unfathomable cunning and against all odds, manages to attack and sink countless relief ships and navy escorts while emerging unscathed. *Secret of the League* has a flashback to Salt's career as naval commander Stobalt, when he had been posted a thousand miles from where the Peruvian navy has the British navy on the run. Nonetheless Salt appears "miraculously one foggy night" in his ship the Ulysses, and, accompanied by two destroyers, launches a surprise attack on the Peruvian fleet. It is an audacious move that turns the tide in Britain's favour. It had been planned in a "methodical," "painstaking," and "far-seeing" way. Then, "throwing into the scale a splendid belief in much that seemed impossible—Stobalt succeeded in doing what . . . perhaps no one else would have tried." The heroes of *Atlas Shrugged* also share a flair for audacity governed by ruthless rationality.

Atlas-like incidents abound in *Secret of the League*. Here are just a few of them:

When the government, having banned oil-imports to thwart the League, finds that the League has anticipated the ban and already stockpiled oil, Mr. Bilch "stopped suddenly, jerked his head twice with a curious motion, and fell to the ground in a fit." In *Atlas Shrugged*, when John Galt's torturers are obliged to rely on Galt's technical know-how to restart the torture machine, James Taggart collapses in a fit of utter humiliation.

In *Secret of the League*, "Hampden refused to take office under the existing franchise, and no one but Hampden could form an administration in that crisis that hoped to live for a day." In *Atlas Shrugged* the government eventually insists that Galt save the country, but on *their* terms, so Galt refuses to take power.

With the crisis reaching a crescendo, Sir John communicates the Unity League's page-and-a-half-long manifesto by telescribe (a prediction of fax) and newspapers to the whole country. "For two hours and a half . . . he controlled the reins of the Fourth Estate of an Empire." In *Atlas Shrugged*, using a high-tech intercepting device of his own invention, John Galt monopolizes the air-waves for nearly three hours to broadcast his 60-page speech to every radio in America. "It is a lie—deliberately misleading lie," responds the Premier in *Secret of the League*, "but it was the truth." In *Atlas Shrugged*, America's leader Mr. Thompson responds, "It wasn't real, was it?" At the climax of *Secret's* economic crisis, a member of Parliament announces, "I have found that all communication has been cut during the last few hours." In *Atlas Shrugged*, there's a New York City blackout.

In *Secret of the League*, the Prime Minister is now known simply as Premier; in *Atlas Shrugged* the President is now known simply as Mr. Thompson, head of state. In *Secret*, William Mulch is the name of an important labor spokesman. In *Atlas*, one Wesley Mouch becomes Economic Director of the country. *Secret's* bad guys form an "Expediency Council." *Atlas's* bad guys form an "Emergency Committee."

The following story summary will apply equally well to *Secret of the League* and *Atlas Shrugged:* Disaffected intellectuals and politicos legitimate an escalating exploitation of the talented few by the untalented many that devastates the talented few to the point where they implement a secret plan to remove themselves from the economy in such a way as to let the damaging impact of exploitative policies be felt full-force by the masses, thereby impoverishing them and obliging them to realize the extent to which their survival and well-being depend upon the freedom of, not the exploitation of, the talented few, whereupon the intellectuals and politicos who originated the whole destructive process are themselves discredited.

I certainly do not claim that Rand *plagiarized* from Bramah. But one can imagine the angry charges of plagiarism from Objectivists if a new novel along the lines of *Secret of the League* had been published at any time after 1957.

Wellsprings of *The Fountainhead*

The Fountainhead is the story of Howard Roark, expelled from architecture school for designing buildings as startling as his orange hair. Roark keeps at it, but must draw upon every ounce of his ego, his supreme confidence in his own ability, his independence, and his integrity, to stand up to the envy, mediocrity, conformism, and corruption of the powers that be. Even the love of his life pits herself against him, believing Roark's struggle to be futile in such a world. When Roark secretly designs a low-cost housing project on the condition that his design not be emasculated, only to see exactly that occur, he dynamites the building. In court, he delivers a ringing defence of the individual creator, which moves the jury to acquit. Roark's egoism and integrity triumph.

The book was inspired by, if not strictly modelled upon, real-life maverick architect Frank Lloyd Wright. In fact, a Wright-mania was under way at the time, to be followed by continued fascination with the man and his work, and periodic Wright mini-manias thereafter. *Frank Lloyd Wright on Architecture* edited by Frederick Gutheim was published in 1941. *In the Nature of Materials: The Buildings of Frank Lloyd Wright* by Henry-Russell Hitchcock came out in 1942 and has yet to go out of print. Then came the expanded version of Wright's autobiography in 1943. So *The Fountainhead* was riding the Wright wave.

According to ARI literature, Rand began generalized planning of *Second-Hand Lives* (the working title for *The Fountainhead*) in 1934. Her journal reveals that she made two and a half pages of notes on *Building to the Skies: The Romance of the Skyscraper* (1934) by Alfred Bossom. One of this work's key themes is the reliance of second- and third-rate architectural minds upon outmoded traditional styles, about which Bossom had this to say: "Except from the brains and hands of men who were ready to depart from tradition and to welcome the new and the unknown, the skyscraper would not have come into existence." Louis Sullivan designed the first one, erected in Chicago in 1889. The Chicago Exhibition of 1893, continues Bossom, was a triumph but "not for a distinctively American architecture as most of the structures were a reproduction of European models." The first skyscrapers were often "overladen with incongruous festoons and figures, bulbous maidens and bastard Greek temples, cherubs and wedding cakes, and what might well have been taken for litter from an undertaker's yard." America's European-trained architects tried to imitate the classical styles or adapt them, slow to realize "that the new vertical axis for buildings of an unprecedented height called for" a different eye and treatment. These views are those of Howard Roark.

Literary osmosis may have absorbed the spirit of the following excerpts from Bossom into *The Fountainhead:* The skyscraper is "perhaps America's greatest permanent contribution to the arts . . . . As such it exactly expresses the spirit of her people, . . . the character, the intellectual qualities and the ideals of the nation that produced them. . . . All of those mighty structures proclaim the daring, the inventiveness, the self-confident power of their creators. . . . The Titans might have built them."

As for Rand's attempt to transfer Christianity's monopolized sense of profound spirituality onto the most distinctive symbols of American capitalism, Pierpont observes in her *New Yorker* article on Rand that "there was nothing in Rand's vision of the modern Civitas Dei which hadn't been intended by the architects of modern capitalist theology. Still dominating the skyline in the year she arrived was the Woolworth Building, a sixty-story Gothic tower that had been presented to the world as a "cathedral of commerce" and described as a "battlement of the paradise of God" in a brochure issued shortly after its completion.

The Nietzschean business tycoon played by Warren William in the movie *Skyscraper Souls* (1932) defends the value of the skyscraper he builds as "this marvel of engineering, this spirit of an age crystallized in steel and stone." He waxes, "They laughed at me when I said I wanted a 100-story building. They said it wouldn't hold together. But I had the courage and the vision, and it's mine and I own it. It goes half way to hell and right up to heaven and it's beautiful. I've achieved something big, something worthwhile. Feel it under you. It's solid. Even the fiercest storm can't budge it. It bends but it won't break and it stands here defiant." Rand, working in the movie business at the time, may have seen the film and, inspired by William's spirited oratory, ennobled its sentiments and re-attached them to the character of Gail Wynand.

A favorite bit of dialogue for many readers of *The Fountainhead* or viewers of the 1949 movie version is villain Ellsworth Toohey's importuning Howard Roark, "Well Mr. Roark, tell me what do you think of me?" to which Roark replies, "But I don't think of you." A similar exchange between Peter Lorre and Humphrey Bogart occurs in the 1941 movie *Casablanca*. Lorre: "You despise me, don't you?" Bogart: "If I gave you any thought, I probably would." "A leash is only a rope with a noose at both ends," the almost-a-hero Gail Wynand realizes too late. "How I treasured that sentence," recalls Nathaniel Branden. Long before, Ralph Waldo Emerson had written, "If you put a chain around the neck of a slave, the other end fastens around your own," which for a while became the adage, 'A slave's chains are heavy at both ends.'

Upon his death the *Atlantic* depicted Frank Lloyd Wright in Rand-Roarkian terms as "a Carlylean hero . . . of Wagnerian dimensions . . . forced to breast the wave of ignorance around him." As in Roark's courtroom speech, Wright once declared, "Our tribe destroys on . . . suspicion the man who might impart something of immense importance and value" to it. In the early 1930s the architectural-cultural tide had turned against Wright, so he depicted himself, according to Secrest, as "standard-bearer for a new, quintessentially American vision that owed nothing to European influences, particularly not those becoming admired in the early 1930s. He needed to appear as an individualist." This Rand absorbed during her research for *The Fountainhead* in the mid-1930s, though, asserts Secrest, she misunderstood Wright and his work.

In Wright's eyes, Secrest tells us, Rand's "association with Louis Kahn, the American architect most influenced by Le Corbusier, had already made her suspect." Those chapters of *The Fountainhead* that Rand sent Wright were enough to show him that "her instinctive sympathies . . . were in accord with the rational and geometric purism of the International Style. . . . Her hero ought to have been an ascetic . . . Internationalist. . . . In taking as her model an architect who is rejected by the Establishment and reviled for his genius, . . . she did not understand that the Establishment now seeking to discredit Wright was the one whose ideas . . . she represented." Rand bought a house designed by one of Wright's former students, Richard Neutra, who had become one of the leading practitioners of the International Style on the West Coast. As for the International Style itself, no words could express Wright's contempt for this "evil crusade."

A key plot device in *The Fountainhead* is that of one architect claiming credit for the work of a 'ghost architect'. The device had been used in the 1907 novel *Comrade John*, by Merwin and Webster who also wrote what became Rand's favorite novel, *Calumet 'K'*. In real life, Wright's autobiography relates how he allowed another architect to take credit for designing his Arizona Biltmore hotel. Rand's idea for Roark's 'ghost-designed' low-cost public housing project probably derived from Wright's Usonian house, intended as an affordable yet beautiful alternative for average people.

Rand wrote in her journal, "If I take this book" (the biography of an eclectic traditionalist Peter Keatingish, *Thomas Hastings, Architect* by David Gray) "and Wright's autobiography, there is practically the entire story of *Second-Hand Lives*."

Not just the story. Even ARI in the person of David Harriman concedes that Wright mentor Louis Sullivan "served as the concrete inspiration for the character" of Roark mentor Henry

Cameron, and that, "In his basic architectural principles and in his fight for modern architecture against tradition, Wright served as a model for Howard Roark." But her debt is far greater than that. In her journal she noted Wright's insistence that, "All artistic creation has a philosophy." There too she draws from Wright's *Modern Concepts Concerning an Organic Architecture from the Work of Frank Lloyd Wright* (1937): "Individuality is sacred. Let us dedicate this republic to multiply and elevate that quality in all art and architecture in all men in all life." From Wright's *Taliesin* journal she copies, "We are all possessive and . . . egoistic. . . . But neither 'possessive' nor 'egoistic' need be inglorious. . . . There is probably no suitable economic system not founded upon human egotism."

Architect Peter Reidy inventories apparent sources in Wright's work and life for events in Rand's novels: Roark is kicked out of architecture school for a drawing done "as if the buildings had sprung from the earth and from some living force, completely, unalterably right." This, comments Reidy, is in keeping with "one of Wright's most familiar dicta." Continues Reidy, "Roark observes that the trouble with modern classicism is that it is a steel-and-concrete imitation of a marble imitation of a wooden original"— a point Wright had made in his Princeton lectures of 1934. Roark's Enright House is "a rising mass of rock crystal," with "harmony of formation" and "each separate unit unrepeated but leading inevitably to the next one and to the whole, . . . like a single crystal to the side of a rock." This is more than similar to Wright's St. Mark Housing project as depicted in his autobiography.

Wright asks: "Why not, then, build a temple, not to God" but to man? The horizontality and human scale of Roark's 'Stoddard Temple of the Human Spirit' echoes Wright's Unity Temple. In her journal Rand notes that Wright's autobiography remarks upon a "female model posing for sculptors right in a shanty on the building site," a preview of Dominique in the Stoddard Temple. Reidy specifies that Rand's Stoddard account of "friendly, late-night intimacy of sculptor, model, and architect does recall Wright's account of the Midway Gardens in Chicago in 1914."

The lakeside country house that Roark builds for Wynand resembles Wright's most famous house, Fallingwater, which straddles a waterfall. Roark explains why he is turning down an eclectic 'man with ostrich tail' type commission; Wright, using plant imagery, made the same points in both his autobiography and his Princeton lectures. A later Roark 'lecture' repeats the Wright-Roark 'integrating principle' theme. *The Fountainhead* has Roark camping out one winter building a resort, as did Wright in Arizona at San-Marcos-in-the-Desert, "the resulting building in each case being true to Wright's organic aesthetic."

The Movie of *The Fountainhead*

In an article called 'Movies that Changed My Life', Canadian director John Pozer singles out *The Fountainhead*. He explains that two architectural students invited him to see the video. Having read the book, the film was exactly as he'd imagined it. But what affected him were the students' reactions. Every time a bad design by Roark would come up, they would all cry: "Fail him! Hang him!" The film just came alive for Pozer, seeing it with such a vociferous and knowledgeable audience. Peter Reidy, a neo-Objectivist architect, characterizes Roark's efforts in the movie as "mostly insipid, sometimes ludicrous, modernist designs." Other than at Objectivist gatherings, no public screening of the movie goes unaccompanied by outbursts of guffaws at these monstrosities.

Edgar Tafel, the architect who supervised the construction of the Fallingwater house and many other famous Wright buildings, recalls that as senior apprentice he was delegated the task of evaluating *The Fountainhead*. Unable to get past page 50, Tafel foisted the novel onto a junior apprentice, who later turned in the verdict, "It's a piece of junk." Writes Tafel, "I gave it back to Mr. Wright and said, "Sir, it's a piece of junk." He adds that later, "it made a piece of junk movie." Historian Frederick Gutheim remarks that "Not even Gary Cooper could make Ayn Rand's *Fountainhead* a good movie."

What mattered to Rand was having her words, exactly as written, dominate the movie. Architecture was an afterthought. Pierpont regards the film as "an unintended comedy played at the wrong speed and in a collision of styles, from arch expressionism to dismaying earnestness: Gary Cooper ambling through *The Cabinet of Dr. Caligari.*" Steven Bach has called *The Fountainhead* one of the worst pictures director King Vidor ever made.

Rand wrote in letters, "For the first time in Hollywood history, the script was shot . . . word for word as written . . . the most uncompromising, most extreme and 'dangerous' screenplay" of all time. It would be "the atom bomb of the movie industry." After a preview, she enthused: "a real triumph . . . I am completely satisfied." After it opened she wrote that "there is no actor . . . closer to . . . the right type for it than Gary Cooper." Cooper was two decades senior to a Roark in his 20s. Since Warner Brothers had allowed Rand "the miracle of having my script shot verbatim, without any distortion of my theme or dialogue, I am willing to accept the smaller imperfections and I am happy about the picture."

In the late 1980s, Leonard Peikoff hired John Hill to write a screenplay for *Atlas Shrugged.* Hill warned that, "if you screened *The Fountainhead* with Gary Cooper and Patricia Neal for today's average audience, they would laugh *at* the dialogue. They would laugh *at* some of the dead serious, stilted scenes." They would. They do.

Rand wrote to a friend: "Do you remember your prediction that the picture would give me the kind of 'Hernani' controversy that I envied Victor Hugo for?" It is sad to think of Rand believing this bomb might become the *cause célèbre* to launch her *à la Hugo* into the forefront of national politics. George Reisman recalls that a few years later, in the mid-1950s, "Miss Rand declined" Reisman's invitation "to an upcoming dinner in honor of Roy Cohn, Senator McCarthy's chief aide, at which Senator McCarthy would be present, . . . on the grounds that to get involved as she would need to," she would have to drop writing *Atlas Shrugged* "and do for McCarthy what Zola had done for Dreyfus." The careers of both McCarthy and Cohn ended in utter disgrace.

The Literary Sins of Ayn Rand

Even Rand fans and former Objectivists usually come to accept that Rand's characters are poorly developed. Stephen Cox, literature

professor and Rand admirer, maintains that Rand's novels sometimes suffer from her "insistence on morally idealized characters."
Kay Nolte Smith comments that "the stronger the message you
wish to deliver the harder you have to work to make your characters believable real people, and I don't know anybody who thinks
John Galt *is* a real person." Ron Merrill suggests that "Galt was
explicitly intended to represent man-become-god" but "she could
not make her ideal hero fully male." Barbara Branden confesses, "I
believe that John Galt is two-dimensional." Yet the creation of this
character was the culmination of Rand's fiction-writing career.
Neo-Objectivist Walter Donway says that for him, John Galt
doesn't come close to Tarzan. Cato Institute founder Ed Crane has
referred to *Atlas Shrugged's* stilted parts, one-dimensional carica-
tures, and dialogue that was archaic even when it was written.

Objectivists will say that Rand's characters are not meant to be
everyday mediocrities, but that misses the point. A good novelist
can make an unusual, 'unrealistic', larger-than-life individual
seem real; the complaint against Rand is that she is unable to do
this. Nathaniel Branden has stated that, apart from Rand, "Very
few authors are qualified or competent to write novels about creative geniuses." But many such novels, as well as fictionalized
biographies of real-life geniuses, have been published, and few
readers of this genre think much of Rand's attempts.

Kay Nolte Smith has almost as much a problem with the love
of Galt's life. Dagny "had three men and seems to have chosen the
one she wanted solely because he had more intellect than the others did." Phil Smith comments that Rearden, in stepping aside for
Galt, is in effect saying, quite unrealistically, "Well, of course he's
smarter than I am, so of course you should go to bed with him.
What the hell—I'll just find somebody dumber." Joan Kennedy
Taylor says, of Rand's intention to create morally ideal persons: "I
don't think she succeeded. . . . Dagny didn't have to shoot the
guard when she went to free Galt. I thought that was a very wrong
thing to do." Barbara Branden claims of Dagny that "she's perfection from a feminist point of view." Yet Dagny only gets a chance
to run Taggart Transcontinental because it's a family-owned
railroad company and her only brother is not competent.

Rand's own publisher Alan Collins said of her play *Ideal* that the "characters aren't people at all, any more than they were in *The Fountainhead.*" Cox suggests that Ellsworth Toohey, Rand's most famous villain, is "not really . . . a character but . . . a personification of evil." Even Peikoff during a question period has conceded Toohey's impossibility in real life. To cite but two other examples, does any *Atlas Shrugged* reader accept the plausibility of Ragnar—"It is I against the organized strength, the guns, the planes, the battleships of five continents"—Danneskjold? Or the Wet Nurse's ludicrous at-death speechifying about how "Man is only a collection . . . of conditioned chemicals"?

The protagonists in *We the Living* are Rand's most real, being largely autobiographical, but Ron Merrill rightly points out that heroine Kira's interest in engineering is an artificial part of her characterization, tacked on by Rand to make her more 'unconventional'. When Rand does accurately portray an engineer, the problem is that she is trying to portray an architect. Howard Roark has the stolid linear-thinking mentality of a non-innovative engineer. Yet we are to believe he is a creative genius as an architect, despite biographies of Frank Lloyd Wright, who inspired Rand to invent Roark, demonstrating a mind and personality utterly at odds with Roark's and infinitely more interesting. Rand had told Wright at the outset that her novel could become "a monument to you, in a way, to the spirit in you and your great work." She wanted "your blessing on my undertaking." Wright found Roark "not very convincing." When he had finally read the published novel, he complimented Rand on the extent of her research and the worthiness of her individualist cause, and said he liked Toohey's characterization, but he didn't say that he particularly liked the book. Rand took Wright's comments as her most cherished rave ever.

Famed architecture critic Lewis Mumford did say of Wright upon his death what Rand wanted Roark to project: "He lived from first to last like a god: one who acts but is not acted upon." Pierpont notes that in Roark's as opposed to Wright's life, there are "no family, no mistakes, no uncertainties: this is the ideal man, hewn from the Nietzschean rock face of the author's will to dream," conveyed in a "simplified monumentalizing style" whose only counterpart is Socialist Realism. As for Roark's love, even Barbara Branden concedes, "I don't think she is well realized. . . . Dominique is more a symbol and it doesn't work."

Kay Nolte Smith points out that Rand gives each character "a moral label the first time you meet him," not allowing readers the pleasure of coming to know the characters and making their own observations about them. Roy Childs suggested that Rand's characterizations are not very deep. "People don't change much. She never had a theory of psychological change. So her heroes and villains appear full-blown in their teens. There are occasional figures like Cheryl who struggle. Rearden sort of struggles," but "it's just that he doesn't have the mental tools to understand his own values."

Rand's didacticism differs from that of other novelists in its relentlessness. Stating what is obvious to non-Objectivists, neo-Objectivist literature scholar Kirsti Minsaas remarks, "I would say that Shakespeare was a *much* more openly inquiring writer than Ayn Rand, less dogmatic, closer to Aristotle in fact, less concerned with teaching a doctrine and more concerned with inspiring and provoking the reader to think for himself."

Pierpont remarks that in *Atlas Shrugged*, "A reader can hardly get through a page or two without sniffing the burning fuel of subverted emotion, or seeing political outrage as a mere component of her recoil from the broadest offenses of mankind (and especially womankind) upon her senses: dirt, sweat, fat, sagging breasts, softness, confusion, ill-fitting clothes, ugliness, all endangering the heroic ideal." (The very word *ugly* appears 64 times.) Ideological and physical disgust merge, as do the embattled heroes' ideological and aesthetic purity.

Pierpont suggests that as "emotional science fiction, the novel contains almost nothing related to human experience," except Dagny's pride and sexual longing. Former followers of Rand don't remember it that way though. Erika Holzer says, "I think people who get pulled into ideas through fiction get pulled in by their emotions . . . she hooked me because I cared about the characters and the plot and I entered that world."

Libertarian philosopher John Hospers grants, "She is great in a sort of limited area. . . . The ideas are not just abstract entities that . . . float in and out of a novel," as in Thomas Mann's *Magic Mountain*, "but are totally integrated with the plot. . . . At confrontation of ideas expressed through dramatic characters, . . . she's absolutely brilliant, better than anyone else."

Mary Gaitskill observes that *Atlas Shrugged*'s emotional resonance is delivered in a rather sterile intellectual container. People often respond in "a truncated intellectual manner to authors" playing "an intellectual game that, as technically good as the writing may be, doesn't address the reader at a more emotionally, spiritually, or psychologically integrated level. And in a way the Ayn Rand people are on a much lower level. For instance, when they talk about the intricate plot of *Atlas Shrugged*, well, there is a lot of mechanical moving around," yet "it's poorly done." The characters aren't real in *The Fountainhead* either, "but they *do* have this kind of sticky, gooey, pulpy, drama happening for them that will strike a certain spot on an unsophisticated person's emotional switchboard. . . . *Atlas* doesn't even have that, so I think" for "these people . . . it's like a third or fourth removal of a mental response on a low level."

Rand's novels are all but mere embodiments of her Objectivist theory. Almost. But if that were all, they wouldn't have sold in the millions. Pierpont describes *Atlas* as "a sprawling triple-decker romance that was by turns melodramatic and speechifying, titillating and edifying—a best-seller in a tradition so nearly extinct that it seemed new. Not since the popular novels of almost a century before, bent on refutations of Darwin or God, and offering what George Eliot called 'a complete theory of life and manual of divinity, in a love story', had there appeared so vividly accessible and reassuring a guide for the cosmically perplexed."

Randall Dipert complains that Rand's aesthetic is a "robust but . . . naive and not-well-thought-out romanticism" resulting in "long, strident, blustery tirades by major figures—as if loud, angry speeches were the primary literary mode of being 'moving'. Seen from another perspective, the novels are heavy-headed political-ethical propaganda, virtually lacking in all the niceties of careful character development, plot nuances, and elegant language . . . "

Comedy impresario Mark Breslin, having first read Rand at double the usual initiatory age, 32 rather than 16, regrets that *Atlas* and *The Fountainhead* are "utterly, utterly humorless. There's not even room in her world for any irony, because to admit irony would be to admit the gap between expectation and reality and, for her, there is no gap, or if there is a gap, that's a tragedy. . . . I think in an Ayn Randian universe humor would have no value, humor would have no part in it, and that's why ultimately I could never embrace her philosophy." John Hill, who wrote a screenplay for *Atlas*, says of the novel, "This is a grim, humorless universe that Ayn Rand portrayed people in." (As noted above, *I* found a dozen actual laughs: on pages 73, 101, 131, 146, 371, 374, 548, 665, 670, 762, 1062, and 1066.)

12

Ayn Rand's Legacy

Literary Impact

Claudia Roth Pierpont suggests that "there has probably not been a less respectable novelist among the irrefutably enduring writers of our time than Ayn Rand." A freshman class at Berkeley recently voted *The Fountainhead* its favorite novel. Most writers would kill to be able to sell the quarter million or so books Rand sells annually, decades after their publication. (In Britain, novelist, essayist, and Christian apologist C.S. Lewis is perhaps a similarly cultish figure with comparable sales.)

Pierpont notes that Rand had wanted to publish a novel with the force of Chernyshevsky's *What Is to Be Done?*—"the Russian *Uncle Tom's Cabin,* which converted Lenin to revolutionary socialism at the age of fourteen." *Atlas Shrugged* hasn't exerted that kind of force—neither in politics nor in literature.

"It's a shame," said Kay Nolte Smith. "I'm sure she would have liked to be remembered as a novelist much more than she will be because people tend to think about her as an ideologue. After all, she devoted most of the years of her productive life to writing fiction." And Rand had wanted to spark what she used to call 'a new romantic revolution', getting rid of the minimalist tradition, the fragmented non-linear narrative, and the hopelessness and degradation of the human spirit.

A hefty proportion of her adolescent readers desert her in adulthood. Remarks Erika Holzer, "I cannot tell you the people I have encountered throughout my life in all the years since, everywhere you look, people who loved her books when they were younger, and now they say 'That was a long time ago and she's old-fashioned and she's a fascist', and all that awful stuff. . . . 'Oh yeah, I used to like her when I was young but that's kid stuff'. Ask yourself how many times you've encountered that." Holzer interprets this change of heart as lost idealism, against which the books stand as a reproach. A simpler interpretation is that often literature that appeals mostly to adolescents will not appeal to these same people as adults.

As a mature adult, it's harder to take the sneering contempt for people in general exhibited by the heroes of *Atlas Shrugged*. Smith observes, "They talk about their enemies that way, and . . . people who take the philosophy seriously pick that up. And if you saw Ayn on the platform, that was her platform style, and certainly if you knew her personally that was her style."

The literary historian of the future will be hard put to it to find any discernible influence of Rand's literary example upon contemporary writing, but instead will find traces of an awareness of the cult and its ideological ripples.

Mary Gaitskill's *Two Girls, Fat and Thin* (1991) is a novel that mercilessly satirizes Rand, her books and her movement. Spoofing *We the Living*, she writes, "In the meantime, Katya had perished on an ice floe in an effort to escape to America, Captain Dagmarov had killed himself on realizing that he was philosophically in error, and Rex, having been broken by the collectivist society around him, was writing pornography for a living." In her *magnum opus* we read, "Solitaire D'Anconti, oil magnate and lonely woman, paced the room in her black plunge-necked jumpsuit, one arm wrapped around her own slim waist, the other holding the cigarette which issued the snake of smoke that was coiling around her." Ayn Rand becomes Anna Granite, and her literary characters—from *The Last Woman Alive*, *The Bulwark*, and *The Gods Disdained*—become Bus Taggart, Skip Jackson, Eustace Kwetschmer, Asia Maconda, Frank Golanka, Captain Dagmarov, Rex, and Jesus Delorean Dilorenzo Michaelangelo. Granite's philosophy is called Definitism. Her protégés are Beau Bradley and his wife Magdalen, until their expulsion, when Dr. Wilson Bean takes over. Explains the novel's narrator about its journalist protagonist, "Justine was morbidly attracted to obsessions . . . She could not help but be drawn to the spectacle of flesh-and-blood humans forming their lives in conjunction with the shadows invented by a mediocre novelist."

Gaitskill isn't ready to write Rand off altogether: "I don't think she's a genius, no, although she did have something . . . to evoke *that* kind of response from people. . . . I think she addressed things, however badly, that don't get addressed very often and it meant a lot to people culturally, as almost a survival issue." Entrepreneur Mark Breslin grants, "There is something nostalgic about the one-man-against-the-world structure and ethos of her novels and you can get really turned on by this. It's a good source of energy to read them and say 'Yes I can, I can do this, I have the will, I have the energy'."

In Nancy Kress's sci-fi novel *Beggars in Spain* (1993), the philosophic guru for the smartest people is Yagai, who says: "No, the only dignity, the only spirituality, rests on what a man can achieve with his own efforts. To rob a man of the chance to achieve, and to trade what he achieves with others, is to rob him of his spiritual dignity as a man. This is why communism has failed in our time. *All* coercion—all force to take from a man his own efforts to achieve—causes spiritual damage and weakens a society." And so on, all mere paraphrasing of Rand, though Kress goes on to illustrate the unviability of certain aspects of a thinly-disguised Objectivism.

Real Impact

The late Roy Childs recalled the excitement of the 1960s for those young people who were picking up the pieces of *laissez-faire* economics and classical liberalism. Rand's talks at the Ford Hall Forum and various universities were broadcast live on National Public Radio. "Zillions" of little groups of people got together in apartments to listen to these broadcasts. Childs himself went to two of Rand's Ford Hall Forum presentations, with thousands of people crammed into the auditorium or listening via loudspeakers outside. Some waited in line for two days to get tickets.

In the 1960s, said Childs, "there were two radicalisms, not one." In the lesser-known radicalism were people like Childs, who were busy reading Rand and Mises, Hayek and Friedman, and all these others "who were individualists and pro-reason and pro-capitalism and anti-war, pro-legalizing drugs." This individualist philosophy had been reconstituted, starting in the 1920s and 1930s, by people like Albert Jay Nock, Rose Wilder Lane, Isabel Paterson, and Ludwig von Mises, then later by Hayek, Rand, and Rothbard. "But they had no public organ. They had no *New York Times* magazine or *New York Review of Books* or anything else. And by and large everyone was aware of the left-wing radicalism but not the libertarian-individualist radicalism. . . . We didn't have any Abbie Hoffmans." Furthermore, the libertarian individualist radicals tended to be five to ten years younger than the headline-grabbing leftist radicals.

First Presidential candidate of the Libertarian Party John Hospers had met Rand in 1960 and would devote pages to her ideas in his ethics text *Human Conduct*. He recalls that in reading *Atlas Shrugged*, "I had never thought much about the effect of government intervention. . . . Her economic message in the book hit me like a ton of bricks." Says Smith, "An awful lot of people have been turned on to libertarian politics by *Atlas Shrugged*. What amazes and amuses me is this whole movement practically was launched by a novel, only none of the people in it read novels . . . like, that was *the* novel, that and science fiction." Joan Kennedy Taylor suggests that Objectivists, though not Rand herself, really founded the contemporary libertarian movement, which in her view "is three-quarters based on Objectivism." Hospers agrees: "There would be no Libertarian Party today were it not for Rand. Ed Crane, Ed Clark, . . . many people have said that to me."

Taylor recalls that until the late 1960s, "the Democrats were the party of intellectuals and the Republicans had no ideas . . . It's considered to be *now* [1991] that all the heavy thinking is on the Republican side and the Democrats have no ideas. And Ayn had a lot to do with that." Richard Cockett writes that in Britain, the younger Conservative students who began to exert an influence in the late 1970s were "mainly 'libertarian' in character, and many owed as much to the writings of the American 'anarcho-capitalists' Ayn Rand and Murray Rothbard as they did to the Institute of Economic Affairs," a very influential organization promoting free-market thinking.

Rand's ideas receive a fair hearing in academia. For example, in the mid-1990s, Rand's essay 'The Ethics of Emergencies' was included in new editions of both Nina Rosenstand's *The Moral of the Story: An Introduction to Ethics* and Joel Feinberg's *Reason and Responsibility*, the most widely used introductory philosophy textbook in North America.

In her fiction, Rand did something for American culture similar to what anthropologists Ruth Benedict and Margaret Mead did for other cultures: caricaturing rather than characterizing them. Both Benedict's and Mead's works may sometimes be bad anthropology, but they nonetheless sometimes constituted effective propaganda for worthwhile causes such as anti-racism and anti-homophobia. Though Rand's works appear to non-Objectivists as neither first-rate literature nor first-rate philosophy, they surely constituted effective propaganda on behalf of capitalism during an era of considerable anti-capitalist rhetoric and policy-making. And they may serve that role again during future waves of statism.

Impact on Investors

Neo-objectivist Walter Donway, editor of the newsletter of the Institute for Objectivist Studies, confided to an interviewer that in

1963, too afraid to ask Rand a question directly at a Ford Hall lecture, he got a friend to ask: "If government intervention in the money supply sets up the economy for a bust and a depression, . . . aren't we going to have one?" Rand replied that she "didn't see how we could go another five years without a major depression. That created a new industry, as you know. . . . I don't know if economic doomsday books were published before that time, but later it became a whole new genre." Donway was referring to books like Douglas Casey's *Crisis Investing*, Robert Ringer's *How to Find Happiness during the Collapse of Western Civilization*, and dozens of similar best-sellers. "I will tell you that years of folly in investing, by me and a lot of other students of Objectivism, began there."

What made the prospect so real to them was the depression in *Atlas Shrugged*, which Rand largely copied from what she had seen in the wake of the Russian Revolution. North America did experience major recessions in 1973–74, 1981–82, 1990–91 but nothing close to a great depression. In fact, these downturns were less traumatic than some depressions of Rand's favorite era, the Gilded Age.

Bidinotto points out that the way Objectivists habitually look at the world lead them to conclude that civilization is near collapse. Objectivist Bob Prechter, who was promoting The Ayn Rand Institute in his investment newsletter just as the stock market began to tank in 1987, and whose track record in his *Elliott Wave Theorist* obliged the Financial News Network to honor him as *the* stock market forecasting guru of the 1980s, predicted the mother of all depressions on the scale of *Atlas Shrugged* between the late 1980s and the mid-1990s. In 1995 he published the 475-page *At the Crest of the Tidal Wave: A Forecast for the Great Bear Market*. As of 1998 he was still insisting that it would happen. Yet while the Dow temporarily crested at 2,700 in August 1987, Prechter was still confidently calling for an ultimate top of 3,800. Following October's market meltdown, he changed from super-bull to super-bear, cancelled his prediction for an additional 2,700 to 3,800 rise and instead forecast a cataclysmic 2,700 to 400 drop, warning investors who had yet to exit the market to do so. Perversely, the

Dow then proceeded to climb 5,500 points higher than the ceiling he had once called for prior to his bull-to-bear transformation. As his British 'Elliott Wave' counterpart Robert C. Beckmann put it in 1992, "I've never been too happy about the Prechter version" of the theory. Many took Prechter for the Elliot Wave messiah, but he has since been relegated to comparative obscurity.

Prechter was taking after Rand, who had forecast in February 1951, the outset of a 20-year golden age of prosperity, that "we are on the brink of economic ruin brought about by policies such as the Marshall Plan." She stuck to that perspective for the rest of her life. The standard view now is that the healthy non-socialist development of Western Europe was in part the result of Marhsall Aid.

Bidinotto, an ardent follower of Rand in the 1960s and 1970s, remembers: "In the worst years of my pessimism, I thought economic collapse was only months or years away." Robert Hunt confirms that "disconnected ideological fragments of *Atlas Shrugged* have dominated non-fiction best-seller lists since the late seventies. Rand has indirectly helped create a genre, and through that genre has shaped the thinking of middle-class America."

The apocalyptic scenario, shared by many other Objectivist or libertarian investment analysts, most notably James Dale Davidson and William Rees-Mogg in *The Great Reckoning: How the World Will Change in the Depression of the 1990s* (1991), dovetails so neatly with *Atlas Shrugged* that in his Ford Hall Forum address in 1992, Peikoff—who knows Prechter—advised the audience to help elect the Democrats, in part so that the coming depression would not be associated with a Republican administration. Instead, the 1993–1996 period featured recessionless sustained economic growth, ensuring Clinton's re-election.

Some libertarian speculators are actually Objectivists or neo-Objectivists, such as Bermuda commodities trader Monroe Trout, who bankrolled Michael Paxton's hagiographic feature documentary *Ayn Rand: A Sense of Life* (1997), or futures trader Victor Niederhoffer, author of *The Education of a Speculator* (1997). A neo-Objectivist newsletter relates that Niederhoffer "considers *Atlas Shrugged* the most important book he has ever read and named three of his children [Kira, Rand, and Galt] after Randian characters." Moreover, all his employees must read *Atlas Shrugged*. Niederhoffer believes: "There are more insights about business in it than in all the" business school "case studies. . . . You can't understand *anything* about the media or the relations between private property and government or the nature of the collective until you've read it." Niederhoffer's book has sold briskly; his futures-trading fund went belly-up.

Rand versus Hayek

Cockett refers to "the Hayekian revolution in economic and political thinking from the 1920s to the 1980s." Skidelsky contends that "Hayek's insistence that a beneficial market system requires a consciously contrived constitutional order is the most important Continental European contribution to the theory of economic liberalism. It underlay the neo-liberal idea of the 'social market economy', and influenced the construction of the European Economic Community."

In one letter Rand wrote, "As an example of our most pernicious enemy, I would name Hayek. That one is real poison." She is lambasting the very man actually leading the movement for economic liberalism, for which in fact she was primarily the fiction propagandist, its Maksim Gorki.

Part of why Rand hated Hayek is explained by Greg Johnson. For Hayek, government intervention in the economy is out. "Redistribution, however, is quite another matter. . . . For instance, social safety-nets, subsidies for the arts, school-vouchers, and taxes on luxuries and 'sins' do not seek to alter or replace the market. Rather, they merely re-direct demand within it." Though Hayek would not necessarily support all such measures, he would argue that they do not inherently menace the survival of capitalism. So Hayek does not completely rule out the government reallocating resources by political means, an absolute no-no for Rand.

Childs thought that Rand "hated Hayek intellectually, because . . . he said reason is limited" and because he did not always favor *laisser faire*. Rand told Barbara Branden that she regarded *The

Road to Serfdom as the most dangerous book ever written. "You'll not find any sentence of hers in print on Hayek," Childs added. "She never promoted a Hayek book or said a kind word about him."

Fabians of Conservatism and Classical Liberalism

Cockett believes that free-market think-tanks "did as much intellectually to convert a generation of 'opinion-formers' and politicians to a new set of ideas as the Fabians had done with a former generation at the turn of the century. Indeed the manifest aim of the Institute of Economic Affairs, in particular, was to reverse the intellectual trend started by the Fabians over a half-century earlier, by employing many of their methods." Deregulation, privatization, tax reduction, and deficit reduction have now become commonplaces of public policy. In the 1980s, as Skidelsky has observed, the state's role was redefined as that of providing public goods—goods which the market cannot adequately supply— rather than supplanting the market in pursuit of state objectives.

Anthony Fisher founded the Institute of Economic Affairs in 1955. Its steady stream of thoughtful, carefully argued, and undogmatic publications gradually exerted a tremendous influence on educated opinion in Britain. Fisher also created or helped to forge the Fraser Institute in Canada (in 1974–75), the Centre for Independent Studies in Australia (in the late 1970s), and the Manhattan Institute (1977) and Pacific Institute (1979) in the U.S. Fisher's Atlas Economic Research Foundation (founded 1981) in 1987 teamed with the Institute of Humane Studies (founded in 1961) to oversee all these think tanks. By 1990, 60 Fisher think tanks were operating worldwide and another 20 think-tanks had been initiated or directly affected by Fisher's activities. All these think-tanks are considerably influenced by Hayek and by Milton Friedman, negligibly if at all by Rand. Almost all the former Soviet-bloc countries availed themselves of the help on offer from the Atlas Foundation Institutes at some time during late 1980s or early 1990s. The Atlas Foundation has been called "the Comintern

of the economic liberals." Cockett writes that "economic liberalism now enjoys an institutional, as well as intellectual, coherence
that would have been unthinkable when the Mont Pèlerin Society
was founded in 1947."

In America, the Goldwater campaign of 1964 was "the first
political expression of a rising conservative movement that was
grounded in moral and intellectual outrage and determined to
repudiate nearly a century of national policy," according to James
Smith. Goldwater advocated a complete victory over international
Communism and an end to federal programs that overstepped the
rights of both states and individuals. After his defeat conservatives
realized that their intellectual infrastructure was still too fragile to
combat pragmatic liberalism. The Liberal Establishment was
deemed to consist of "the nation's major foundations, Ivy League
Universities, New York publishing houses, research institutions,
newspapers, and broadcast media." Far-sighted conservatives set
out to replicate these institutions with a conservative slant.

Irving Kristol argued that the battle had to be engaged on the
plane of ideas and within the intellectual bastions of the New
Class. Universities, think tanks, and foundations were the "idea-
germinating" and "idea-legitimizing" institutions. The new right
had to create its own counterparts, and eventually infiltrate the
political bureaucracy. Those counterparts would come to include
the American Enterprise Institute (AEI), the Hoover Institution,
the Heritage Foundation, and the Cato Institute. At AEI, William
Baroody wanted to forge a conservative Brookings Institute, and
by and large he did so.

All along, economic liberals in the U.S. were guided by Hayek's
Mont Pèlerin Society as in Europe. At the 1980 Mont Pèlerin
Society conference at California's Hoover Institution, 600
attended. Writes James Smith of that year's landmark event:
"Reagan's victory was the culmination of a conservative move-
ment that began in the 1940s and early 1950s. Its intellectual lin-
eage . . . draws on the writings of traditionalists like Richard
Weaver and Russell Kirk, classical liberals like Friedrich Hayek
and Ludwig von Mises, militant anticommunists like Whittaker
Chambers and Frank Meyer, and political philosophers like Leo

Strauss and Eric Voegelin." All of these shared a common belief in the power and primacy of ideas.

Exaggerated Notions of Rand's Influence

In a 1980 interview Rand said: "I had some part in . . . the turn to the right. . . . I gave a moral foundation to a free society, to capitalism." Yet this is exactly what orthodox Objectivists deny, and must deny. If Rand gave the culture this intellectual gift, the very fact that her moral foundation for capitalism has not been *accepted* by the culture has to ensure that the turn to the right cannot be sustained.

Philosopher Antony Flew remarks that the whole way the Objectivist movement developed "provided an example of how *not* to do it if you want to be effective. And I should have thought that her actual effect has . . . really been on *other* people and on people who've been in the organization but left. Many of the people who have free-market ideas such as neo conservatives have at some stage of their life been influenced by something Ayn Rand wrote. Wherever you find ideas of this sort there's some mention of Ayn Rand in the background but the people who mention it are not usually people who have been Objectivists or even subscribe to any of the Objectivist publications. They're just people who've read something and it's influenced them a lot, maybe the novels."

The inbredness and insularity of the Objectivist movement is never so alarmingly evident as when biographer Barbara Branden speaks of Rand's worldwide impact: "Ayn often said that if economic theory and practice would convince men to turn to capitalism it would have happened long ago because the economic theory has been there for a very very long time. . . . what she was convinced of was that if men think something is immoral, say making money, economic theory will not make them embrace it. And that has proven true. Today what is happening is that American and worldwide concepts of morality have been changing in the direction of Ayn Rand's theories." Thirty years ago, "you were considered an idealist insofar as you were a socialist and insofar as human beings are virtuous that is how far we would go in that direction. That has . . . reversed itself and *the sole cause of the reversal is Ayn Rand"* (emphasis added). Elsewhere she reasserts, "That is an unbelievable change in a culture. And *nobody did it but Ayn"* (emphasis added).

Branden must be unaware of the whole institutional countertrend of economic liberalism led by Friedrich Hayek, which certainly had a very strong moral component to it and which started long before Rand made her propaganda-fiction contribution to that contertrend. On the prevalence in today's culture of a 'self'-orientation in general and a concern for self-esteem in particular, Barbara Branden declares, "For one woman to have accomplished that is a bloomin' miracle." Once again this is to ignore a century's worth of historical movement in that direction, movement so culturally overwhelming that Rand's contribution is a drop in the bucket. James Lincoln Collier's *The Rise of Selfishness* (1991) makes no mention of Rand.

Cockett suggests that the Soviet bloc's collapse "owed much to the ideological battle waged by the economic liberals in those countries, some operating from think-tanks supported by Antony Fisher's Atlas Foundation." Leonard Peikoff said in 1991 that "I don't see that the pro-capitalist pro-reason movement [Rand] launched in the U.S. has had any effects in eastern Europe."

Rand would assail the libertarians much as Karl Marx excoriated anarchists like Bakunin, possibly because libertarians/anarchists were so much more knowledgably critical of Rand/Marx than were mainstream parties. Historian Modris Eksteins remarks that even in 1832 one Douglas Goldring writes of himself as a "crusted libertarian." Joan Kennedy Taylor recalls that Rand told her in the late 1950s: "The name for my political philosophy is libertarianism." Her fellow political libertarians had been inspired by a whole pantheon of writers preceding or contemporaneous with Rand, including Murray Rothbard, Lysander Spooner, Albert J. Nock, Frank Chodorov, and Rose Wider Lane. Taylor reminds Objectivists that, "before *Atlas Shrugged,* Ayn worked with and admired libertarians whose general philosophy did not have the same moral base as hers: Isabel Paterson, Mises,

Hazlitt, even Leonard Read of the Foundation for Economic Education." Rand was a part of the libertarian tradition, but withdrew from it before it again became influential.

Philosopher Eric Mack, former Objectivist true believer and still deeply sympathetic to Objectivism, has pointed out sadly: "The striking fact is that Objectivists in good standing have contributed almost nothing within the academic domain to the defense of individualism, moral rights, property rights, free markets, anti-statism, anti-collectivism, or anti-egalitarianism. These doctrines have a considerably greater respectability in philosophical circles today than 25 years ago." Credit for this, in Mack's estimation, is shared about equally between individuals who started out with Rand but then developed independently, and engaged in hard debate, and those who were at most marginally aware of Rand.

ARI has repeatedly flaunted the results of a 1991 Book of the Month Club survey, wherein 778 people replied with the name of a particular book to the question. "Have you read a book that made a difference in your life, and if so, what difference?" A significant but not especially impressive 3 percent cited either *Atlas Shrugged* or *The Fountainhead*. A full 21 percent cited the Bible. Naturally, the part that ARI emphasizes is that *Atlas Shrugged* came in second. It carefully refrains from mentioning how distant a second, or how closely bunched the rest of the top ten were.

Howard Roark is included in a recent volume giving brief descriptions of heroes in American fiction, but such recognition pales compared to that bestowed upon Roark's inspiration. Canadian columnist Robert Fulford noted in 1996 regarding what was only the latest of multiple waves of Frank Lloyd Wright mania, that at least 14 books about him had been published in the preceeding year alone. There are Wright CD-roms, furniture, calendars, postcards, ties, datebooks and so forth. He is the subject of an opera by Daron Aric Hagen, called *Shining Brow*, and the Museum of Modern Art opened the biggest Wright exhibition ever, two whole floors of models, reproductions, and drawings. Howard Roark's aura is dim next to Wright's shining brow.[1]

Objectivism's Future

Americans, maintains sociologist Seymour Martin Lipset, are utopian moralists who press hard to institutionalize virtue, to destroy evil people, and to eliminate wicked institutions and practices. "They tend to view social and political dramas as morality plays, as battles between God and the devil, so that compromise is virtually unthinkable." Americans give to their nation and its creed many of the attributes and functions of a church. The U.S. sees itself as the new Israel, a divinely inspired singularity, and Europe as the Egypt whose clutches it has escaped. The emphasis on the religious chosenness of the U.S. has meant that if the country is perceived as slipping away "from the controlling obligations of the covenant," it is perceived as on the road to hell. "The need to assuage a sense of personal responsibility for such failings has made Americans particularly inclined to support movements for the elimination of evil."

Rand's Objectivism was and is one such movement, currently splintered into at least two warring factions. It brandishes the torch of Reason, but many critics retort: If *this* be reason, make the least of it. Classical scholar Gilbert Highet notes that in what we know of Aeschylus's lost sequel to Prometheus Bound, "the poet showed a final reconciliation between reason and deity, between Prometheus and Zeus." For "when reason fails to harmonize with the other forces that make up reality, there is tragedy." According to historian John Ralston Saul, any one of the qualities, intuition, common sense, imagination, memory, ethics, and reason, isolated from the others and set up as an absolute value in itself, becomes a tool of ideology." Saul adds: "Sensibly integrated along with our other qualities, reason is invaluable. Put on its own as a flagship for society and for all of our actions, it quickly becomes irrational."

It was perhaps inevitable that the two Objectivist excommunicatees with independent followings, Nathaniel Branden and David Kelley, would join forces to provide more tolerant Objectivists with an alternative to the dominant Peikoff-ARI axis.

Does Kelley consider *The Psychology of Self-Esteem* as part of the Objectivist canon? "I certainly do," he replied, calling it "a work that is heavily influenced by and in many ways embodies and develops the basic Objectivist view of human nature." It is "sound Objectivist doctrine," he added. So Nathaniel Branden accepted an invitation to present two lectures on 'Objectivism and the Psychology of Self-Esteem' at the 1996 Summer Seminar organized by Kelley's IOS. In response, Joan and Allan Blumenthal severed their ties with that Institute. Branden recounts with characteristic self-satisfaction that "at the end of my talk, the audience exploded into a standing ovation. . . . There were quite a few tears in the room. Including mine, my wife's, and . . . David Kelley's . . . *I felt like I was coming home*" (my emphasis). Meeting Rand for the first time, too, had been a "coming home."

Peikoff's ARI has the powerful advantage that it receives the mail in cards from all of Rand's books. Kelley's IOS permits more diversity within its ranks, and therefore has a greater capacity to generate interest. While ARI monotonously rounds up the usual suspects to speak at its conferences year after year after year, Kelley apparently has few qualms about presenting at IOS speakers who are borderline Objectivists or avowed non-Objectivists. When I asked the Blumenthals and the Smiths, back in the early 1990s, if they still still considered themselves Objectivists, they gave me a definitive 'No', even if philosophically they remained closer to Objectivism than to any alternative. All four have been featured speakers at IOS events. The question for the IOS approach is: will it turn into a mere Ayn Rand admiration society, sometimes a lukewarm one at that, and perhaps a mere adjunct to the libertarian movement? And how committed will non-fanatics be to financing the organization in the long run? For ARI the question is: will its cult fanatics continue to so take for granted its enormous recruiting advantage as to finally excommunicate one too many high-profile Objectivists, and subsequently see ARI funding evaporate? The predicament of both organizations serves to remind us that the Objectivist movement, once so promising, has been severely damaged by its nature as an Ayn Rand cult.

An Ayn Rand Who Might Have Been

Fiction is of greater philosophical importance than history, because history represents things as they are, while fiction represents them as they might be and ought to be.

Statement quite frequently but quite incorrectly
attributed to Aristotle by Ayn Rand

Ayn Rand arrived in America determined not only to write, but to learn: three years' attendance at a crumbling Soviet university doth not an educated woman make. The more certain she became of her own fundamental ideas, the more ferociously she scoured the literature for ideas that challenged them. Though she was always picking up light detective fiction as a diversion, she got around to reading little of it.

Rand often said that raising a child is a full-time project. So in 1944 her friends were surprised, knowing that a third Rand novel was in the planning stages, to hear that she was pregnant. However she *had* just sold the screen rights to *The Fountainhead* for a cool third-of-a-million (in 1999 dollars). Now she could fully concentrate on her writing *and* accede to her husband's desire to be a father. Frank, who hadn't worked full-time in years anyway, would be happy to provide nearly all the child-rearing. Anticipating arguments of 30 years later that smoking might adversely affect a fetus's health, Rand quit completely and never resumed the habit. Frank Jr. was born in Feb. 1945, just before Rand's 40th birthday. During the most difficult and depressing stretches of work on *Atlas Shrugged*, she could always revitalize herself by playing with her young son.

She would admit decades later that only her attachment to her son and concern for what he might think held her back from an affair with Nathaniel Branden in the 1950s. She later told a friend that Frank might have permitted it but her relationship with Frank Jr. would not.

Rand always thought in the long term; it had taken America a half century to fall into its sorry state in 1957, so it might require another half century for it to recover the liberty it had lost. Frank

Jr. at least would live to see American liberty restored and that was all that mattered to her.

After publishing *Atlas Shrugged* to mixed reviews, Rand threw herself with a vengeance into the film, music, theatre, opera, and literary scenes in New York City. Little was to her liking but she was determined to sample the best of American culture, if only insofar as it challenged her own worldview. She was often seen strolling the streets accompanied by Frank and a bodyguard.

In the early 1960s she managed to coax her young philosopher friend Dr. John Hospers to stick around New York rather than accept a teaching offer in California. Rand was painfully aware of the gaps in her philosophical reading and training, and thought it essential that her essays reflect Hospers's philosophical scrutiny and devil's advocate counter-arguments. (Essays that she wrote prior to knowing Hospers are embarrassingly unsophisticated compared to later efforts.) "Twentieth-century philosophy has not seen fit to come to me; it looks as if I'll have to go and defeat it on its own turf," she announced. "The core of my philosophy is facing reality, and the reality is that the ethos of this era is not that of the late nineteenth century. If it were, my books would not have been needed."

In the mid-1960s, though she couldn't stand the hippies and political radicals, Rand publicly called for America's withdrawal from Vietnam, because, as she put it, "Even a fundamentally moral nation can blunder its way into a fundamentally immoral war. Far better to cut our losses now, and devote our defense budget to defending higher-priority American interests. Should Vietnam go completely Communist, it will eventually go completely broke, and bankrupt nations are not generally a threat."

Rand's favorite forum for debate was William F. Buckley's *Firing Line*, where she and Buckley tangled on a dozen or so occasions. Whereas Buckley was turning from essays to fiction, Rand was turning from fiction to essays, and with Hospers's help was being published now and again in philosophical journals and speaking at meetings of professional philosophers. Her 'withdraw-from-Vietnam' stance helped immeasurably in communicating with professors and students alike. In fact, it hooked thousands of left-wingers onto her philosophy.

The Nathaniel Branden Institute and the *Objectivist* continued to expand throughout the 1970s, during which time Rand and her movement became the butt of savage satire in *The National Lampoon* and on *Saturday Night Live*. Branden's weekly Objectivist radio talk-show *'And I Mean It!'*, while never approaching the kind of ratings Rush Limbaugh would enjoy in the 1990s, was a forerunner of that program. Branden went on to write a handful of conservative and libertarian think-tank books, later running successfully for the senate as a Republican. He headed up the party's very substantial libertarian wing during the Reagan years and was responsible for much of Reagan's resistance to moral majority initiatives. His former wife's cousin Leonard Peikoff took his place as host of *'And I Mean It!'* and spent a good deal of air-time attacking the political compromises Branden at times was obliged to make as senator.

In her late 60s, Rand surmounted her fear of flying and took several trips abroad with her lifelong friends the Blumenthals. Florence and London were two favored destinations.

In 1970 on the Merv Griffin show Rand told admirers that no one treating her as an infallible guru or as an authority on artistic tastes deserves to call himself or herself an Objectivist. She even went so far as to say, "If you believe *everything* I have ever written, then you're not independent enough to call yourself an Objectivist."

In 1974 she became a grandmother with the birth of Hank.

In 1975, Rand published a 175-page memoir of her estrangement from Frank Jr. during the early years of the Vietnam war, and of their eventual reconciliation. Critics who had panned *Atlas Shrugged* 18 years before fell over themselves heaping it with praise. It completed Rand's transition from practically a literary outcast to practically a mainstream icon.

In 1978 Lorne Michaels convinced Ayn Rand to appear as a guest host for a special *Saturday Night Live* show roasting socialism around the world and big government at home. She played a Kafka-esque government inquisitor in one sketch.

In 1979 Rand became a fellow of the Committee for the Scientific Investigation of Claims of the Paranormal (CSICOP) and one of that organization's key promoters of critical thinking— which she considered a prerequisite for and a likely stepping stone toward adopting Objectivism. In the same year she debated Nobel Laureate Friedrich Hayek on the limits of human reason, at Princeton.

Ayn Rand's American Objectivism became what Jean-Paul Sartre's French existentialism aspired to but failed to become—a complete, intelligible, and livable, if still controversial, philosophy adopted consciously and with understanding by millions. Rand never ceased to elaborate upon points raised by her critics, whom she was always goading into public confrontation, preferably on television. In 1980 she published *Refuted: 101 Intelligent but Sadly Misguided Objections to Objectivism.*

Rand acknowledged her intellectual and literary debt to scores of writers, including Nietzsche and Oscar Wilde. And she proudly showed off her novelist 'children'—Kay Nolte Smith, Erika Holzer, Barbara Branden, and Edith Efron.

Liberals in the 1980s developed a sneaking admiration for their two principal opponents: William F. Buckley and Ayn Rand.

In 1984, the ten-hour miniseries of *Atlas Shrugged* appeared on NBC, to reviews as mixed as the book's had been. The novel reappeared in the top ten of *The New York Times* paperback best-seller list for more than three months and inspired 'reappraisal' reviews everywhere, most far more generous than those of 1957.

In 1989, she published *To Joy from Living Death*, co-written with one-time critic of paleo-Objectivism, Dr. Albert Ellis. It recounted Rand's bouts of depression and her experience with non-drug cognitive techniques for coping with them. Rand also acknowledged a number of symptoms of paranoia and how she minimized them.

The *Objectivist*, still edited by Barbara Branden, in 1990 reached a circulation of 45,000.

When she was aged 86, translations of all three of her novels simultaneously became best-sellers in Russia. Rand was flown by her American publisher to St. Petersburg for a triumphant visit, during which a parade was held in her honour and she received 'the keys to the city'. She spent an emotional afternoon with her sister at the apartment their family had once owned and lived in. The following day, a surprisingly warm televised encounter between Rand and Alexander Solzhenitsyn on the latter's interview program replaced his usual tiresome monologue.

In 1993 she and Barbara Branden co-authored a 600-page account of both Rand's life and her Objectivist movement, entitled *Impassioned Reason: An American Renaissance.*

Rand lived to age 93, dying in late 1998, but having played an active role in the resurgence of capitalism in the 1980s, and having witnessed with tremendous satisfaction the collapse of Soviet Communism.

Notes

2 Entrails: The Anatomy of the Cult

1. Galanter 1989; Kramer and Alstad 1993; Singer 1995.
2. When a dictionary gives alternative definitions, only one of them need apply for the word to be used correctly. *Webster's Ninth New Collegiate Dictionary* lists five numbered definitions, including this one (actually two alternatives, both of which indisputably apply to Objectivism): "a. great devotion to a person, idea, or thing, *esp:* such devotion regarded as a literary or intellectual fad. b: a usu. small circle of persons united by devotion or allegiance to an artistic or intellectual movement or figure." I maintain that *all five* definitions in Webster's apply to Objectivism, but some might argue about that, for example by denying that Objectivism is 'religious'. On that question, see later in this chapter.
3. People raised in predominantly Christian cultures often assume that belief in a personal God is the litmus test of any doctrine's claim to be a religion. But a number of recognized religions, such as Confucianism or some branches of Buddhism, either don't believe in a God or pay no attention to the question. *Webster's* gives as one alternative definition of religion: "a cause, principle, or system of beliefs held to with ardor and faith." Among its alternative definitions of faith are: "firm belief in something for which there is no proof" and "complete trust."

3 The Cult After the Guru's Death

1. For more on Hospers's exchanges with Rand, see Chapter 8 below.
2. See Schwartz 1986.
3. 'Libertarian' began to be used to denote free-market or *laisser-faire* ideas in the early nineteenth century.

4 Sex, Art, and Psychotherapy

1. Totalitarianism is the phenomenon of the state knowing no bounds to its actions, interfering at will in any aspect of life. Like all classical liberals, Rand was fiercely anti-totalitarian. 'Totalism', as I am using it here, means any single ideology which tries to explain everything. Totalitarian ideologies have always been totalist, but not all totalist ideologies need be explicitly in favor of totalitarian methods of government.

2. "It means one's total commitment to a state of full awareness, to the maintenance of a full mental focus in all issues, all choices, in all one's waking hours . . . It means a commitment to the principle that all one's convictions, values, goals, desires, and actions must be based on, derived from, chosen and validated by a process of thought—as precise and scrupulous a process of thought directed by as ruthlessly strict an application of logic, as one's fullest capacity permits."

3. A combined reference to Blaise Pascal's famous dictum, "The heart has its reasons, which reason knows not of," and the cliché about letting one's head rule one's heart.

5 Nathaniel Branden: The Godfather of Self-Esteem

1. This is not to deny that there is some scope for improvement by reprogramming cognition, where the reprogramming has demonstrated scientific merit, as in Albert Ellis's Rational Emotive Behavior Therapy.

8 The Mind of the Guru

1. *Webster's Ninth New Collegiate Dictionary* has the following for 'egotism': "1 a : excessive use of the first person singular personal pronoun b : the practice of talking about oneself too much 2 : an exaggerated sense of self-importance." As *Webster's* indicates, 'egoism' can be used for more or less definition 2 of 'egotism', but 'egotism' *cannot* be correctly used for the most usual sense of 'egoism', the sense intended by Rand.

10 The Roots of Objectivism

1. Nietzsche: [In nation states, the Jews'] "energy and higher intelligence, their accumulated capital of spirit and will, gathered from generation to generation through a long schooling in suffering, must become so preponderant as to arouse mass envy and hatred." Kant: "The Jews cannot claim any true genius, any truly great man. All their talents and skills revolve around stratagems and low cunning. . . . They are a nation of swindlers."

11 The Disowned Ancestry of *Atlas Shrugged*

1. Prothro's 1954 book (see my bibliography) brings together excerpts from some of the most memorable of the 1920s business theory

writings, including those of Julius Barnes, Charles Fay, William Feather, Ben Hooper, E.W. Howe, Harper Leech, and Eugene Lombard, which I particularly draw upon here.

2. Saint-Simon is viewed as one of the founders of modern socialism, but at that stage, socialism (the word itself had not come into use) was elitist rather than egalitarian. Saint-Simon's version was pro-technology, pro-rationality, and pro-industry. Saint Simon's associate Comte coined the word 'altruism'.

12 Ayn Rand's Legacy

1. *ID: The International Design Magazine* has complained that *The Fountainhead* recruits disaffected undergraduates into architecture (Fulford 17 January 1996). Andy Pressman's recent book *The Fountainheadache* points to the nervousness prevalent among clients who, having read *The Fountainhead*, worry that their architect may foist upon them a monument to the architect's own ego.

Sources

Some of the usefulness of this book stems from its bringing together hundreds of pieces of information which have already been published separately, often in small or obscure publications, but never before presented in one coherent account.

In *The Ayn Rand Cult*, I frequently offer an observation or judgment and cite one source or a few sources. In such cases, it should cetainly not be assumed that these are my only evidence for the observation or judgment. Often, citations are given for illustration and clarification rather than for proof.

I and my editor at Open Court have spent many hours checking for factual accuracy, and numerous people who read parts of the work in different stages have made valuable suggestions about the factual content. If any errors of fact have slipped through and are drawn to my attention, they will be corrected in future printings.

I give below the sources of all the direct quotations in the book. Those interested in sources should also look closely at the bibliography. To keep the bibliography within reasonable bounds, I excluded from it many illuminating and relevant works upon which I did not draw for any specific passage in this book.

Introduction

Page 1: "If you have . . ." Barbara Branden 1986a, p. 347.

1 The Cult While the Guru Lived

Page 11: "When the disciple . . ." James S. Gordon 1987, p. 47; "She could convince . . ." Holzer and Holzer 1991; "I was fifteen . . ." Ronald E. Merrill 1991a, p. 1; "late" Childs 1991. **Page 12:** "demands the fervent . . ." Robert Hunt 1984; "By the time . . ." Kelley 1991; "Many thought that . . ." Taylor 1991. **Page 13:** "a blinding epiphany . . ." Smith and Smith 1991; "I had always . . ." Nichols 1972. **Page 14:** "people responded less . . ." Kay Nolte Smith 1985, p. 153; "I imagined myself . . ." Gaitskill 1991a, p. 162; "huge blazing hazel . . ." Kobler 1961; "We were young

351

. . ." Smith and Smith 1991; "You could almost . . ." Ronald E. Merrill 1991b. **Page 15:** "I worship you . . ." Nichols 1972; "were *gods*, man . . ." Dennison, personal communication; "commonly held and . . ." Smith and Smith 1991; "discovered true ideas . . ." Peikoff 1989a. **Page 16:** "Hatred is the . . ." Hoffer 1951, p. 85; "they corrupted her . . ." Ronald E. Merrill 1991a, pp. 6–7; "If people didn't . . ." Nathaniel Branden 1996b; "devoid of intellectual . . ." *The Objectivist* (December 1967), p. 380. **Page 17:** "devoted to the . . ." Mack 1997; "cutting yourself off . . ." Ridpath 1991b; "fanatical sects . . ." Rand 1957, p. 354. **Page 18:** "lice" etc. Rand 1957, pp. 82, 851, 1029, 1031, 865; "vermin" Rand 1995, p. 132; "once somebody is . . ." Nathaniel Branden 1996c. **Page 19:** "inherently dishonest ideas . . ." Peikoff 1989a; "the couple pledged . . ." Rothbard 1987a; "When one partner . . ." Singer 1995, p. 322. **Page 20:** "Be rational, and . . ." Scuoteguazza 1991; "The whole Nathaniel . . ." Taylor 1991. **Page 21:** "was generally the . . ." Rothbard 1987a; "They are practically . . ." Hamblin 1967; "The courses were . . ." Sidhu 1989; "the young men . . ." Nichols 1972. **Page 22:** "That was the . . ." Taylor 1991; "we are not . . ." Rand 1995, p. 531; "She wasn't aware . . ." Barbara Branden 1991; "the rather dogmatic . . ." Rand 1995, pp. 531, 532. **Page 23:** "to provoke intelligent . . ." Rand 1995, p. 532; "concern for any . . ." Rand 1995, p. 534; "either accepted everything . . ." Taylor 1991; "never had much . . ." Nathaniel Branden 1996c. **Page 24:** "Our job is . . ." Ronald E. Merrill 1991a, p. 152; "abundantly clear to . . ." Nathaniel Branden 1996b; "everybody around you . . ." etc. Smith and Smith 1991; "a man who . . ." Rand 1983, p. 284; "the kindest thing . . ." Rand 1983, p. 290. **Page 25:** "it is painful . . ." Smith and Smith 1991; "always had an . . ." Kelley 1990a. **Page 26:** "Ayn Rand is . . ." Rothbard 1987a; "Within an order . . ." Volkogonov 1996, pp. 298, 253. **Page 27:** "It was like . . ." Bradford et al. 1995; "I did not . . ." Nathaniel Branden 1989a, p. 134; "barking at her . . ." Childs 1991; "to disparage feelings . . ." Nathaniel Branden 1989a, p. 253. **Page 28:** "posturing, pretentious, humorless . . ." Rothbard 1987a; "you got sucked in . . ." Holzer and Holzer 1991. **Page 29:** "It was like . . ." Rand 1957, p. 1014; "we were ecstasy . . ." Nathaniel Branden 1989a, p. 435; "it could give . . ." Kay Nolte Smith 1985, p. 169; "It's wonderful to . . ." Nathaniel Branden 1989a, p. 195. **Page 30:** "They became shivering-scared . . ." Hospers 1991; "better off with . . ." Bradford 1997; "Anything he said . . ." Barbara Branden 1986a, p. 191; "fear was common . . ." Rothbard 1987a; "there was a . . ." Holzer and Holzer 1991. **Page 31:** "not denounced on . . ." Kelley 1993; "Do not *any* . . ." Hamblin 1967; "We'd see her . . ." Smith and Smith 1991; "vivid *un*pleasant memory . . ." etc. Mack 1997. **Page 32:** "if we said . . ." Holzer and Holzer 1991; "You could say . . ." Smith and Smith 1991; "she would make . . ." Walsh, Reedstrom, and Oyerly 1990; "She taught her . . ." Nathaniel Branden 1971. **Page 33:** "Because of the . . ." Singer 1995, p. 278. **Page 34:** "Remember the young . . ." etc. Childs 1991; "sometimes played the . . ." Nathaniel Branden 1989a, p. 265; "a bitter, febrile . . ." Rothbard 1987a. **Page 35:** "denounced and defiled . . ." Singer 1995, p. 277; "the Heroic Accomplishments . . ." Hamel 1990; "It almost got . . ." Smith and Smith 1991; "along with the . . ." Hospers 1990b. **Page 36:** "But that's the . . ." Smith and Smith 1991. **Page 37:** "kooky" Gaitskill 1991b. **Page 38:** "We sure as . . ." etc. Nathaniel Branden 1996b; "I want to . . ." Binswanger 1994; "Because they had . . ." Barbara Branden 1986a, p. 388; "became so alienated . . ." Childs 1991. **Page 39:** "I'd say there . . ." Smith and Smith 1991; "Rand stood up . . ." Ronald E. Merrill 1991b. **Page 40:** "The sign of . . ." Rand 1995, p. 634; "Oh, that's OK . . ." Rothbard 1987a. **Page 41:** "does not expect . . ." Kelley 1990b, p. 72; Even Peikoff has . . . Peikoff 1991b; "had grandiose ambitions . . ." Childs 1991; "regret their childish . . ." Roxanne Roberts 1997; "made it sound . . ." Donway 1992. **Page 42:**

"if looked into . . ." Ridpath 1991b; "I'll just stick . . ." Holzer and Holzer 1991. **Page 43:** "There was a . . ." Walsh 1991; "with qualifications . . ." Taylor 1991. **Page 44:** "sordid sexual affair" Ronald E. Merrill 1991a, p. 5; "were more upset . . ." Kelley 1990b, p. 75; "religious mania" etc. Nathaniel Branden and Barbara Branden 1968. **Page 45:** "absolutely unintegratable in . . ." Greenberg 1977. **Page 46:** "In the name . . ." Barbara Branden 1986b.

2 Entrails: The Anatomy of the Cult

Page 47: "I am not . . ." Rand 1980. **Page 48:** "A lot of . . ." Taylor 1991; "frying pan to . . ." Holzer and Holzer 1991; "She did not . . ." Hospers 1991; "It was a . . ." Blumenthal and Blumenthal 1991. **Page 49:** "in my not . . ." Barbara Branden 1990; "if I am . . ." Rand 1989, p. 353. **Page 50:** "This is what . . ." Nathaniel Branden 1989a, p. 401. **Page 51:** "Like the carapace . . ." Barash 1994, p. 220; "It's really bizarre . . ." Smith and Smith 1991. **Page 52:** "If you define . . ." Smith and Smith 1991. **Page 53:** "It is the . . ." Hoffer 1951, p. 76. **Page 54:** "by the savagery . . ." Smith and Smith 1991; "You can't do . . ." Smith and Smith 1991. **Page 55:** "exactly true" Ridpath 1991b; "the *only* art . . ." Peikoff 1991b; "she would admit . . ." Smith and Smith 1991; "the in-fighting, warring . . ." Wolf ca. 1994. **Page 57:** "In judging people . . ." Bidinotto 1989; "the illiterate, the . . ." Peikoff 1989a; "treating every intellectual . . ." Kelley 1991; "if we approach . . ." Kelley 1990b. **Page 58:** "a student of . . ." OSG contract, Internet, 1994; "With her, it . . ." Hospers 1990b. **Page 59:** "intentionally induces extreme . . ." Budd 1991; "is reputed to . . ." Galanter 1989, p. 197; "greatest mind on . . ." Nathaniel Branden 1989a, p. 353. **Page 60:** "Gurus and disciples . . ." Kramer and Alstad 1993, pp. 109–110. **Page 61:** "ideological uncaringness" Kramer and Alstad 1993, p. 14. **Page 63:** "No deviation from . . ." Kramer and Alstad 1993, p. 57. **Page 64:** "I am writing . . ." Rand 1957, p. 686; "If we fail . . ." *Objectivist Forum* (April 1982); "Ayn Rand's discoveries . . ." Ridpath 1991b; "who understand the . . ." *Objectivist Forum* (April 1982). **Page 65:** "requires your *total* . . ." *Objectivist Forum* (April 1982); "cultist hallucination, or . . ." Efron 1978. **Page 68:** "Eastern mystics came . . ." W.E. Mann 1987. **Page 69:** "fun house mirror . . ." Gaitskill ca. 1986; "men are so . . ." Cockett 1995, p. 231. **Page 70:** "Especially with certain . . ." Internet posting ca. 1993. **Page 71:** "will follow any . . ." Bidinotto 1985. **Page 72:** "dictatorial, judgmental, structured . . ." Kramer and Alstad 1993, pp. 223–24; "Christianity and Marxism . . ." Kelley 1990b, p. 60. **Page 73:** To neo-Objectivist George . . . George H. Smith 1991, p. 214; "Cults become religions . . ." Kramer and Alstad 1993, p. 32. **Page 74:** "we *can* create . . ." James Gordon 1987, pp. 193, 130.

3 The Cult After the Guru's Death

Page 75: "as the planet's . . ." W.E. Mann 1991, p. 230; "the most wonderful . . ." Gardner 1993, p. 116. **Page 76:** "the greatest mind . . ." Nathaniel Branden 1989a, p. 353; "a once in . . ." Binswanger 1994; "The loneliness for . . ." Rand 1957, p. 339; "the climax of . . ." Nathaniel Branden and Barbara Branden 1962, pp. 114, 104; "the greatest novel . . ." Nathaniel Branden 1991; "I very much . . ." Sures 1992; "The traditional 'Big . . ." Second Renaissance catalog, ca. 1995. **Page 77:** "If Ayn Rand . . ." *Objectivist Forum* (August 1982), p. 9; "If this culture . . ." Berliner 1991; "There just never . . ." Ridpath 1991b; "like a philosophical . . ." *Objectivist*

Forum (June 1992), p. 8; "it would take . . ." Rand 1957, p. 276. **Page 78:** "genius-level intelligence . . ." Locke 1991; "In the centuries . . ." Pearson 1988; "The achievement of . . ." Hoffmann 1988. **Page 79:** "What kind of . . ." Peikoff 1989a; "What about the . . ." Bidinotto 1989; "After Ayn Rand's . . ." Objectivist Forum (April 1982), p. 14. **Page 80:** "simply grotesque . . ." Flew 1991b; "a painfully slow . . ." Barbara Branden 1986a, p. 168; "a super-genius" Peikoff 1992. **Page 81:** "questioners, myself included . . ." Rand 1990, p. 126; Walsh relates elsewhere . . . Walsh 1991. **Page 83:** "requires some very . . ." Berliner 1991. **Page 84:** "every word Schwartz . . ." Bidinotto 1990; "as some guru . . ." Bidinotto 1989. **Page 85:** "listen to a tape . . ." Internet posting, 1993; "If you do . . ." etc. King Weimann, OSG promotion on Internet, 1994; "We don't speak . . ." OSG contract, late 1994. **Page 86:** "What's so sad . . ." Smith and Smith 1991; "she spoke with . . ." Binswanger 1994; "to understand the . . ." Rand 1997, p. 667. **Page 88:** "correspondence among some . . ." Perigo 1997; "an evil intellectual . . ." Brickell 1994. **Page 89:** "the Ayn Rand . . ." etc. Kelley 1990a; "unadmitted anti-Objectivists" Peikoff 1989a. **Page 90:** "deeply saddened" Franck 1992; "I've lost good . . ." Brickell 1994; "started this back-patting . . ." 1994; "Objectivist economist Northrup . . ." Walsh, Reedstrom, and Overly 1990; "religious" etc. Beckmann 1990. **Page 91:** "since it chose . . ." Minsaas 1997; "I think the . . ." Perigo 1997; "expose (for the . . ." etc. Bidinotto 1989. **Page 92:** "struggle to the . . ." Brickell 1994; "the real basis . . ." Bidinotto 1989; "those whose talents . . ." Bidinotto 1989; "Leonard Peikoff and . . ." Edwards 1997; "view Objectivism as . . ." Bidinotto 1989. **Page 93:** "It was very . . ." Kelley 1991; "David Kelley has . . ." *IOS Journal* (1994); "Really amazing. It's . . ." *IOS Journal* (September 1994). **Page 94:** "engaged in various . . ." etc. *IOS Journal* (September 1994); "that mindset, and . . ." Bidinotto 1989; "cause of all . . ." Peikoff 1989a; "most people will . . ." Kelley 1988; "is a crusading . . ." Kelley 1991. **Page 95:** "asking whether he . . ." Machan 1989; "I truly thought . . ." Reisman 1996, p. xlvi; "sheer stupidity" etc. Wolf et al. 1996. **Page 96:** "The leadership of . . ." *Full Context* (October 1996). **Page 97:** "ARI requires Objectivists . . ." etc. Wolf et al. 1996; "intellectual pedigree" etc. Reisman 1996, pp. xlvii, 89, 90. **Page 98:** According to psychiatrist . . . Blumenthal and Blumenthal 1991; "was due to . . ." Walsh 1991. **Page 99:** "idolatry, or worshipping . . ." Kelley 1990b, p. 74; "Do you know . . ." Pressman 1994, p. 65; "likely to lose . . ." W.E. Mann 1991, p. 261; "Randian clones can . . ." George H. Smith 1991. **Page 100:** "closed nature of . . ." Machan 1989; "The most eloquent . . ." Peikoff 1989a; "to give up . . ." Nathaniel Branden 1996b; "liable to judge . . ." Kelley 1990b, p. 16; "demonstrated positive effects . . ." Bidinotto 1985. **Page 101:** "a walking caricature . . ." George H. Smith 1991, p. 222; "relevant facts, motives . . ." Bidinotto 1989. **Page 102:** "I don't know . . ." Nathaniel Branden 1984; "became sarcastic, caustic . . ." Bidinotto 1985; "accused Ayn Rand . . ." etc. Peikoff 1989a. **Page 103:** "the accuser started . . ." Peikoff 1989a; "sees Ayn Rand's . . ." Brickell 1994. **Page 104:** "the seemingly better . . ." Brickell 1994

4 Sex, Art, and Psychotherapy

Page 105: "All questions have . . ." Hoffer 1951, p. 77; "attractive ideologies, attractive . . ." Highet 1954, p. 28. Page 106: "a complete replacement . . ." Cockett 1995, p. 194. **Page 107:** "they must conform . . ." Peikoff 1989a; "If they learned . . ." Greenberg 1977, pp. 50–51; "An unbearable propaganda . . ." Rand 1997, p. 57; "Everything I say . . ." Nathaniel Branden 1984. **Page 108:** "A man falls . . ."

Nathaniel Branden 1969, p. 137; "a meeting of . . ." James S. Gordon 1987, p. 9.
Page 109: "in The Playboy . . ." *IOS Journal* (February 1997). **Page 110:** "if I'll see
. . ." etc. Rand 1957, pp. 714, 600. **Page 111:** "in 1960 Nathaniel . . ." Nathaniel
Branden 1984; "Until his meeting . . ." Rand 1997, p. 96; "My answer is . . ." etc.
Packer 1985b. **Page 112:** "from the impromptu . . ." Chambers 1957; "Citizen
Argounova, what . . ." Rand 1936, p. 172; "Rand was childless . . ." Pierpont 1995.
Page 113: "I think the . . ." Nolte 1995; "if I had . . ." Rift 1997; "against having
children . . ." Nathaniel Branden 1980, p. 206, "never especially wanted . . ."
Nathaniel Branden 1996a, p. 111; "tragedy" Nathaniel Branden 1997a, pp. 78–80.
Page 114: "children would spread . . ." Nathaniel Branden 1996c; "A couple has .
. ." Packer 1988; "Loneliness is all . . ." Scuoteguazza 1991. **Page 115:** "I am a . . ."
Rand ca. 1982; "What she saw . . ." Rand 1983, pp. 398–99. **Page 116:** "merely the
pride . . ." Rand 1997, p. 95; "gave her the . . ." Rand 1957, p. 133; "the boldest
example . . ." Pierpont 1995; "because of the . . ." Gaitskill 1991a; "thousands of fat
. . ." Ephron 1968; "an ideal woman . . ." Rand 1995, p. 623. **Page 117:** "Having a
woman . . ." Rand 1983, p. 195; "unbearable" etc. Rand 1989, pp. 269–270; "I am
a . . ." Rand ca. 1982; "Am not a . . ." Rand 1995, p. 218; "I wouldn't vote . . ." Rand
1994. **Page 118:** "When we behave . . ." Nathaniel Branden 1994, p. 144. **Page 119:**
"Because it involves . . ." Wolf ca. 1994; "From inspection and . . ." Perigo 1997;
"she was absolutely . . ." Nathaniel Branden 1983b. **Page 120:** "homosexuality is
not . . ." Peikoff 1984; "I've said many . . ." Peikoff 1996. **Page 121:** "the essential,
ultimate . . ." Torres and Kamhi 1991–92; "the style and . . ." Rand 1995, p. 408.
"What Ayn held . . ." Joan Mitchell Blumenthal 1993. **Page 123:** "random contor-
tions, arbitrarily . . ." Rand 1971, p. 67; *"You could not* . . ." Blumenthal and
Blumenthal 1991; "All art must . . ." Peikoff 1991b. **Page 124:** "cult of an . . ."
Minsaas 1997; "reveals his naked . . ." Rand 1971, p. 44; "The composite picture .
. ." Rand 1971, p. 130; "I am not . . ." Rand 1971, p. viii. **Page 125:** "she didn't know
. . ." Joan Mitchell Blumenthal 1993; "and if you . . ." Smith and Smith 1991. **Page
126:** *"That* says something . . ." Taylor 1991; "wondering 'What was . . ." Barbara
Branden 1986b; "a dismaying uniformity . . ." Scuoteguazza 1991. **Page 127:** "I
stayed up . . ." Bullock 1997. **Page 128:** "All folk art . . ." Rand 1989, p. 120; "she
was just . . ." Cosman 1997; "An emotion that . . ." Rand 1957, p. 962; "she had
always . . ." etc. Rand 1957, pp. 679, 947. **Page 129:** "The head has . . ." Rand 1995,
p. 526; "I do not . . ." Rand 1957, p. 727; "we are, in . . ." Rand 1957, p. 729; "I don't
think . . ." Rand 1980; *"Either* man's emotions . . ." Rand 1995, p. 521. **Page 130:**
Neo-Objectivist Connie Fawcett . . . Internet, 1994; "a disastrous view . . ." Den Uyl
and Rasmussen 1984, p. 143. **Page 131:** "That's fine, but . . ." Donway 1992. **Page
132:** "a distant pain . . ." Rand 1957, p. 925; "no matter how . . ." Rand 1995, p.
584. **Page 133:** "you can't repress . . ." Barbara Branden 1992; "what a nightmare"
etc. Barbara Branden 1990. **Page 134:** "in discovering the . . ." Rothbard 1989; "a
very strong . . ." Taylor 1991; "I would not . . ." Holzer and Holzer 1991. **Page 135:**
"if Objectivist views . . ." Ellis 1968, pp. 48–49; "Self-evidently yes" Smith and
Smith 1991; "Objectivism drove *everyone* . . ." Blumenthal and Blumenthal 1991;
"And on everything . . ." Plasil 1985, p. 45. **Page 136:** "we know of . . ." Holzer and
Holzer 1991; "patients become like . . ." Singer 1995, p. 173; "a healthy woman
. . ." Plasil 1985, p. 81. **Page 137:** "contradictions cannot exist . . ." Plasil 1985, p.
157; "unwittingly laid the . . ." Plasil 1985, p. 216; "which relates to . . ." etc.
Objectivist newsgroup posting, 1994. **Page 138:** "It could happen" Blumenthal and
Blumenthal 1991; "is an 'arithmetic . . ." etc. Rand 1997, pp. 71, 24, 73; "what is
not . . ." Peikoff 1991b. **Page 139:** "apalled by her . . ." Barbara Branden 1986a, p.
387; "people who were . . ." Smith and Smith 1991.

5 Nathaniel Branden: The Godfather of Self-Esteem

Page 141: "When I was . . ." Nathaniel Branden 1984. **Page 142:** "with the dedication . . ." Nathaniel Branden 1989a, p. 18; "As far as . . ." Nathaniel Branden 1984; "I am in . . ." Nathaniel Branden 1989a, p. 49; "I really mean . . ." Branden and Branden 1968; "I thought that . . ." etc. Rand 1997, pp. 464, 477, 478. **Page 143:** "To my father . . ." Nathaniel Branden 1989a, p. 100. **Page 144:** "Within the movement . . ." Barbara Branden 1990; "I made myself . . ." Nathaniel Branden 1994, p. 126. **Page 145:** "enormous enthusiasm was . . ." Nathaniel Branden 1996b; "this creep" etc. Rothbard 1989; "hideous sessions" etc. Hessen 1991. **Page 146:** "Nathan had the . . ." Barbara Branden 1990; "had an atmosphere . . ." Greenberg 1977, p. 14; "It was certainly . . ." Barbara Branden 1990. **Page 147:** "scribbled half a . . ." Hamblin 1967; "That he was . . ." Barbara Branden 1990; "I can't let . . ." Nathaniel Branden 1989a, p. 326. **Page 148:** "He had a . . ." Smith and Smith 1991; "He created a . . ." Personal communication: name of informant withheld by request; "Everyone was worse . . ." Hessen 1992; "a destroyer of . . ." Efron 1992; "Despite a lot . . ." Blumenthal and Blumenthal 1991. **Page 149:** "that wasn't what . . ." Taylor 1991; "Insofar as Objectivism . . ." Barbara Branden 1990; "repeatedly told me . . ." Branden and Branden 1968; "He was constantly . . ." Barbara Branden 1990; "Nathan was expelling . . ." Barbara Branden 1990. **Page 150:** "I had come . . ." etc. Nathaniel Branden 1989a, pp. 316, 265; "He rewrites his . . ." Barbara Branden 1990; "Can you think . . ." Nathaniel Branden 1989a, p. 200. **Page 151:** "I was betraying . . ." Nathaniel Branden 1989a, p. 328; "Branden turned into . . ." Efron 1992; "Everything he's accomplished . . ." Raico 1992; "I'm not religious . . ." Rand 1995, p. 151; "*His* problem is . . ." Holzer and Holzer 1991; "formation of a . . ." Singer 1995, p. 78; "something most unusual . . ." Efron 1992; "were really desperately . . ." Barbara Branden 1990; "murdered by flattery" Efron 1992; "the Kepler of . . ." Webster 1995, p. 225; "it was really . . ." Nathaniel Branden 1996c; "Miss Rand is . . ." Nathaniel Branden 1971. **Page 152:** "in raising Lenin . . ." Volkogonov 1996; "It is doubtful . . ." Hoffer 1951, p. 82; "brilliantly original and . . ." Branden and Branden, 1968. **Page 153:** "Ayn had originally . . ." Barbara Branden 1990; "He was extremely . . ." Blumenthal and Blumenthal 1991; "was owed me . . ." Nathaniel Branden 1996c; "I thought I . . ." Rand 1995, p. 479. **Page 154:** homeopathic doctor Ebenezer . . . Gardner 1993, p. 28; But the autopsy . . . Hamel 1990, p. 61. **Page 155:** Robert Hessen, who . . . Hessen 1992; Tibor Machan was . . . Machan 1989. **Page 156:** "virtually empty of . . ." Fussell 1991, p. 65; "demand for higher . . ." Nathaniel Branden 1997c. **Page 157:** "and found out . . ." Ellis 1991b; "Would you like . . ." Butler 1992, p. 40. **Page 158:** "Not that this . . ." Nathaniel Branden 1996a, p. 123; "my best means . . ." etc. Nathaniel Branden 1971. **Page 159:** Branden takes to . . . 1989a, p. 128; two unnamed clients . . . Nathaniel Branden 1996a, pp. 72–73. **Page 160:** "In her article . . ." Nathaniel Branden 1996c. **Page 161:** "Dr. Nathanial [sic] . . ." Callahan 1991, p. 75. **Page 162:** "The number of . . ." Callahan Techniques promotional literature; "revolutionary" etc. Nathaniel Branden 1994, pp. 276–77; "I think her . . ." Nathaniel Branden 1996c; "Roger came out . . ." Ellis 1991b. **Page 163:** "It's a sort . . ." Butler 1992, p. 216; "very important research . . ." Alphasonics brochure; "Lucidly written, informative . . ." Shulman 1990, back cover. **Page 164:** "enjoyed the theatricality . . ." Smith and Smith 1991; "uniquely powerful tool . . ." Nathaniel Branden 1997a, p. 113. **Page 165:** "the father of . . ." Learning Annex seminar catalogs. **Page 166:** "the test virtue . . ." Rand 1995, p. 135; "an *unbreached* determination . . ." Nathaniel Branden 1969, p. 114; "dope-addicted dwarf" etc. Nathaniel

Branden 1969, pp. 137–38, 136. **Page 167:** "Without self-acceptance, self-esteem .
. ." Nathaniel Branden 1994, p. 90. **Page 168:** "The first love . . ." Nathaniel
Branden 1996a, p. 149; "speak to me . . ." Nathaniel Branden 1984; "Every aes-
thetic choice . . ." Sciabarra 1995, p. 206. **Page 169:** "a person with . . ." etc.
Kramer 1993, pp. 211, 222; "health or happiness . . ." Nathaniel Branden 1991;
"Old Branden or . . ." Rothbard 1989. **Page 170:** "I am not . . ." Rand 1983, p. 405;
"kindness that is . . ." Nathaniel Branden 1994, p. 141; There is evidence . . .
Nathaniel Branden 1997a, pp. 44–47. **Page 171:** "Their smallest bits . . ." Nathaniel
Branden 1997c; "us giants against . . ." Internet, 8 September 1994; "it breaks my
. . ." Nathaniel Branden 1996c; "is already present . . ." Nathaniel Branden 1984;
"very powerful bias . . ." etc. Nathaniel Branden 1971. **Page 172:** "we were all . . ."
Nathaniel Branden 1996c; "become the masters . . ." Nathaniel Branden 1984; "In
even the . . ." Barbara Branden 1990. **Page 173:** "causing irreparable harm . . ." etc.
Nathaniel Branden 1987b; "The culture of . . ." Nathaniel Branden 1996b; "always
made me . . ." Barbara Branden 1990; "heroic vision of . . ." Nathaniel Branden
1984; "running through Objectivism . . ." Internet, 8 September 1994. **Page 174:**
"Deep thinking is . . ." Coleridge *Collected Letters*, p. 709; "this paragraph or . . ."
Nathaniel Branden 1997b. **Page 175:** "I don't know . . ." Barbara Branden 1990;
"'Ayn wants you . . ." Nathaniel Branden 1989a, p. 398; "would pave the . . ."
Branden and Branden 1968; "Nathan is a . . ." Smith and Smith 1991; "The man
was . . ." Mann 1991, p. 168; "You have betrayed . . ." Gaitskill 1991a, p. 269. **Page
176:** "I wish *desperately* . . ." Nathaniel Branden 1983b; "living in a . . ." Nathaniel
Branden 1994, p. 157; "The hell you . . ." Nathaniel Branden 1984.

6. Leonard Peikoff: From Serf to Pontiff

Page 177: "total awe, as . . ." Peikoff 1995; "he would have . . ." Bradford et al.
1995. **Page 178:** "It's wonderful to . . ." Kay Nolte Smith 1985, p. 208; "more seri-
ous than . . ." Nathaniel Branden 1996b. **Page 179:** "he would not . . ." Machan
1989; "I spoke in . . ." Peikoff 1984a; "It's hard to . . ." Peikoff 1984a; "A Ph.D. today
. . ." Peikoff 1995. **Page 180:** "How would you . . ." Peikoff 1995; "if you took . . ."
Peikoff 1995; "very happily and . . ." Nathaniel Branden 1996b; "know the ins . . ."
Peikoff 1991b. **Page 181:** "Scared to think . . ." Hospers 1991; "This guy can't . . ."
Smith and Smith 1991. **Page 182:** "Wilson in particular . . ." Gaitskill 1991a, pp.
205, 172; "Since he was . . ." Barbara Branden 1991; "We were always . . ." Smith
and Smith 1991; "been under intense . . ." etc. Holzer and Holzer 1991. **Page 183:**
"One day soon . . ." Rand 1995, p. 667; "is now moving . . ." *The Objectivist*
(February 1969); "I urge you . . ." *Objectivist Forum* (April 1982); "I remember once
. . ." Smith and Smith 1991. **Page 184:** "You don't really . . ." Rand 1957, pp. 435,
499; "a troubled relationship . . ." Barbara Branden 1991; Ex-follower Joan
Kennedy Taylor . . . Taylor 1991. **Page 185:** "The empty booze . . ." Nathaniel
Branden 1996c; "from the rapture . . ." Peikoff 1991a, p. 458. **Page 186:** "ripped
out all . . ." Peikoff 1996; "I was in . . ." Peikoff 1984a; "Speaking for myself . . ."
Peikoff 1984a; "I think that . . ." Peikoff 1984a. **Page 187:** "I never read . . ." Peikoff
1991b; "I have one . . ." Peikoff 1989b; "He simply didn't . . ." etc. John Hill 1992.
Page 188: "just yanked the . . ." Snider 1991; "What about Ed . . ." Wolf et al, 1996;
"the excited child . . ." Nathaniel Branden 1996b; "said everything" Nathaniel
Branden 1989a; "times and situations . . ." Peikoff 1984a; "will overturn the . . ."
Objectivist Forum (October 1985). **Page 189:** "I *have* a . . ." Peikoff 1989b. **Page
190:** "best student" Peikoff 1991a, p. xv. **Page 191:** "constant, unending need . . ."

Oyerly 1992a; "He seems to . . ." Steele 1992. **Page 192:** "All these years . . ."
Barbara Branden 1991; "I constantly thought . . ." Blumenthal and Blumenthal
1991; "I certainly do . . ." *Objectivist Forum* (June 1986); "willful falsehoods moti-
vated . . ." Peikoff 1984a. **Page 193:** "brought Peikoff to . . ." etc. (Bidinotto 1989);
"I haven't the . . ." McDonald 1998; "an acquaintance" Nathaniel Branden 1996c.
Page 194: "He hasn't added . . ." Bradford et al. 1995; "he learned from . . ."
Barbara Branden 1991; "Leonard's position is . . ." Blumenthal and Blumenthal
1991; "little Ayn Rand . . ." McDonald 1998; "There are too . . ." Peikoff at an
Objectivist Conference, from a personal communication, name of source withheld.
Page 195: "When I make . . ." Same source as previous quotation; "is a small . . ."
Peikoff 1992. **Page 196:** "irresponsibility" etc. Wolf et al. 1996. **Page 197:** "was
wastebasket stuff . . ." Barbara Branden 1992; "is cashing in . . ." etc. Raimondo
1989; "If anything confesses . . ." Internet posting. **Page 198:** "bizarre . . . in the
. . ." Peikoff 1984a; "hear of somebody . . ." Nathaniel Branden 1996b; "is such a .
. ." Peikoff 1984a. **Page 199:** "I know perfectly . . ." etc. Peikoff 1989b. **Page 200:**
"I've seen Objectivist . . ." Peikoff 1984a; "Peikoff emphasizes . . ." Sciabarra 1995,
p. 219. **Page 201:** Edith Efron, a . . . Efron 1992; "seeks to establish . . ." Internet
posting. **Page 202:** "it is necessary . . ." Internet posting by Chris Wolf, 1998.

7 Alan Greenspan: The Undertaker Takes Over

Page 203: "former Ayn Rand . . ." Foust 1997; "He was very . . ." Holzer and Holzer
1991. **Page 204:** "He was her . . ." Bradford 1997; "It was like . . ." etc. Michael
Lewis 1995; "would compliment Ayn . . ." Nathaniel Branden 1989a, p. 187; "It
became evident . . ." Michael Lewis 1995; "He'd never heard . . ." Bradford et al.
1995; "some great Greenspan . . ." Childs 1991;*"Everybody* went through . . ."
Barbara Branden 1990. **Page 205:** "How's the Undertaker?" Nathaniel Branden
1989a, p. 132; "It was incredible . . ." Bradford 1997; "sometimes you just . . ."
Michael Lewis 1997; "Greenspan was supercilious . . ." Rothbard 1989; "known to
faint . . ." Michael Lewis 1997; "Alan is my . . ." Michael Lewis 1997; "As far as
. . ." Niederhoffer 1997b. **Page 206:** "Greenspan has an . . ." Beckner 1996, p. 14;
"Alan came in . . ." etc. Michael Lewis 1997; "even when he . . ." Hudgins 1993;
"Since I've become . . ." Beckner 1996, p. 18; "Greenspam" *Time* (10 November
1997); "no one seemed . . ." Michael Lewis 1997. **Page 207:** "an ineffectual stunt"
Michael Lewis 1997; "were suffering more . . ." Foust 1997; "kamikaze politics
. . ." Michael Lewis 1997; "put Greenspan in . . ." Beckner 1996, p. 17. **Page 208:**
"at the time . . ." Michael Lewis 1997; "Alan Greenspan is . . ." Sechrest 1994; "If
you have . . ." Beckner 1996, p. 16. **Page 209:** "is a necessary . . ." *IOS Journal*
(November 1993), citing *Investor's Business Daily* (18 October 1993); "it takes the
. . ." Luttwak 1996; "He engineered the . . ." Michael Lewis 1997; "Greenspan gives
Volcker . . ." Beckner 1996, p. 3; "began in earnest . . ." O'Donnell 1990. **Page 210:**
"was to become . . ." etc. Beckner 1996, pp. 28, 34, 35, 36, 62. **Page 211:** "the correct response . . ." Michael Lewis 1997; "a no-brainer" Beckner 1996, p. 55. **Page
212:** "Our nation's monetary . . ." etc. Michael Lewis 1997; "frankly admit conducting . . ." Beckner 1996, pp. 100–01. **Page 213:** "All they're going . . ." etc.
Beckner 1996, pp. 126, 136, 195. **Page 214:** "Greenspan has a . . ." Niederhoffer
1997b; "despite the demonstrable . . ." etc. Beckner 1996, pp. 201, 215, 225, 230;
"Greenspan invariably errs . . ." Luttwak 1996. **Page 215:** "lowered rates in . . ."
etc. Beckner 1996, p. 257, 298; "invariably remain in . . ." Luttwak 1996; "Clinton
was less . . ." Beckner 1996, pp. 293, 318. **Page 216:** "Greenspan admitted that

. . ." Thurow 1996, p. 185; "Just as the . . ." Beckner 1996, p. 391; "He has preserved
. . ." etc. Michael Lewis 1997; "I do know . . ." Bradford et al. 1995; "I have been
. . ." Hitchens 1994; "I haven't changed . . ." Bradford 1997; "when a man . . ."
Niederhoffer 1997b. **Page 217:** "any job in . . ." etc. Bradford 1997; "He is not . . ."
etc. *Intellectual Activist* (July 1997); "Mistakes were clearly . . ." Beckner 1996, p. 8.
Page 218: "perhaps it was . . ." Beckner 1996, p. 127, "If the battle . . ." etc. Thurow
1996, pp. 191, 189, 192.

8 The Mind of the Guru

Page 219: 'You bastard!' Hospers 1990a; "So what if . . ." Hospers 1991. **Page 220:**
"sweetness itself" Hospers 1991; "and that would . . ." Hospers 1991; "I never
engage . . ." Rand 1997, p. 624; "I do not . . ." Kelley 1990b, p. 53. **Page 221:** "born
without the . . ." Rand 1997, p. 94; "everyone makes speeches . . ." Steele 1988;
"went almost immediately . . ." Nathaniel Branden 1996b. **Page 222:** "Today, I am
. . ." Rand 1995, p. 531; "favorite type of . . ." O'Neill 1977, p. 22. **Page 223:** "was-
n't interested" Nathaniel Branden 1991; "Probably someone would . . ." Barbara
Branden 1991. **Page 224:** "I didn't do . . ." Holzer and Holzer 1991; "Why doubt
that . . ." Internet posting, 1993. **Page 225:** "on her side" Mack 1997; "In one sense
. . ." Rasmussen 1997. **Page 226:** "as a preview . . ." Rand 1990, p. 1; "theodicy of
capitalism" O'Neill 1977, p. 16; "offers a definite . . ." etc. Rand 1997, p. 80; "I use
words . . ." *Objectivist Forum* (December 1985), p. 11; "I found her . . ." Hospers
1990b; "absolutely zilch" etc. Flew 1991b. **Page 227:** "egregiously poor scholarship" Gary Merrill 1993; "Do what you . . . Flew 1991; "the exact meaning . . ." Rand
and Branden 1964, p. vii. **Page 228:** "most" Sciabarra 1995, p. 252; While Rand
always . . . *Objectivist Forum* (June 1982); "The absolute egotist" Rand 1995, p. 224.
Page 229: "Genuine conflicts of . . ." Dwyer 1974; "As Madison argued . . ." Franck
1997; "'The virtue of . . ." Steele 1988; "what is good . . ." etc. Rand 1997, pp. 27,
78. **Page 230:** "special favors sought . . ." Ryerson 1986; "vulgar selfishness"
Sciabarra 1995, pp. 234–35. **Page 231:** "In the ideal . . ." Eksteins 1989, p. 177.
Page 232: "To claim that . . ." Franck 1995; "Since he is . . ." Wolf nd. **Page 233:**
"A little bravura . . ." Pierpont 1995; "cult of the . . ." Collier 1991, p. 64; "torches
of freedom" Torrey 1992, p. 32 "fire held in . . ." Rand 1957, p. 65. **Page 234:** "If
value judgments . . ." Peikoff 1989a. **Page 235:** "*not* 'Man must . . ." Rand 1997, p.
276; "a sketch of . . ." Fred Miller Jr 1992; "underdeveloped and very . . ." Nathaniel
Branden 1996b; "her arguments about . . ." Mack 1997; "I understand that . . ."
Kelley 1992. **Page 236:** "Ayn Rand's position . . ." Franck 1992; Objectivist philosopher Allan Gotthelf . . . Gotthelf 1991. **Page 237:** "organic process" Johnson 1993;
"leads . . . to Hitler . . ." Mayhew 1995, p. 40; "evasion of reality . . ." Peikoff 1989a;
"Kant is a hater . . ." Ridpath 1991b. **Page 238:** "read a primary . . ." Walsh 1993.
Page 239: "and the strict . . ." etc. Walsh 1993; "I want to . . ." Flew 1991.

9 The Dark Side of the Guru's Soul

Page 242: "Russia was just . . ." etc. Binswanger 1994. **Page 243:** "Once I could .
. ." Binswanger 1994; "insecurity that led . . ." Blumenthal and Blumenthal 1991;
"when the Soviet . . ." Hospers 1991. **Page 245:** "We can be . . ." Hoffer 1951, p. 76;
"Outside the territory . . ." Nathaniel Branden 1989a, p. 346; "There is no . . ." Rand
1971, p. 78; "She knew, as . . ." Hospers 1991; "I do *not* . . ." Barbara Branden

1986a, p. 295; "I have no . . ." Nathaniel Branden 1989a, p. 226; "She often said
. . ." Barbara Branden 1991. **Page 246:** "The secret of . . ." Rand 1997, p. 48; "individualism . . . the theme . . ." Binswanger 1994; "I have never . . ." Rand 1995, pp.
668–69; "His emotions are . . ." etc. Rand 1997, pp. 95, 93, 95, 479. **Page 247:** "The
difference is . . ." Singer 1995; "Ayn lived very . . ." Smith and Smith 1991; "Ayn had
disappeared . . ." Nathaniel Branden 1989a, p. 225; "I could not . . ." Nathaniel
Branden 1989a, p. 196; Steele 1988; "created an entire . . ." Blumenthal and
Blumenthal 1991; "according to your . . ." Rand 1994; "I don't think . . ." Smith and
Smith 1991. **Page 248:** "the only thing . . ." Smith and Smith 1991; "Remember
that New . . ." Smith and Smith 1991. **Page 249:** "I have always . . ." Rand 1995, p.
188; "deathly afraid of . . ." Barbara Branden 1986a, p. 293; "malevolent adversaries whose . . ." Nathaniel Branden 1989a, p. 65; "would last almost . . ." Barbara
Branden 1986a, p. 301; "To spend more . . ." Barbara Branden 1992; "this world
has . . ." Nathaniel Branden 1989a, p. 246; "destined to rank . . ." Quoted in
Barbara Branden 1986a, p. 298. **Page 250:** "and there was . . ." Smith and Smith
1991; "My attitude always . . ." Barbara Branden 1986a, p. 117; "the man who . . ."
Branden and Branden 1968; "She didn't say . . ." etc. Blumenthal and Blumenthal
1991. **Page 251:** "We knew there . . ." etc. Blumenthal and Blumenthal 1991; "I
want to . . ." Rand 1994; "totally motivated" Rand 1997, p. 706; "I hate bitterness
. . ." Nathaniel Branden 1989a, p. 287; "What pain?" Pierpont 1995; "She would see
. . ." Barbara Branden 1991. **Page 252:** "she opposed Reagan . . ." Hospers 1991;
"she was very . . ." Barbara Branden 1990; "infinitely better people . . ." etc.
Branden and Branden 1968; "there were no . . ." Barbara Branden 1991; "the one
topic . . ." Barbara Branden 1986a, p. 283; "I always found . . ." Childs 1991. **Page
253:** "are the ones . . ." Rand 1995, p. 80; "not only is . . ." Barbara Branden 1991;
"That was for . . ." Smith and Smith 1991; "She wanted someone . . ." etc. Barbara
Branden 1991; "Ayn would have . . ." Barbara Branden 1992. **Page 254:** "She
seemed unable . . ." Barbara Branden Barbara Branden 1986a, p. 283; "*The God of
. . .*" etc. Rand 1995, pp. 102, 367; "discovered" Rand 1997, p. 673; "What is magnificent . . ." Nathaniel Branden 1989a, p. 363; "I cannot consider . . ." Rand 1995,
p. 453; "Lots of well-known . . ." Efron 1992. **Page 255:** "she was such . . ." Holzer
and Holzer 1991; "a girl who . . ." Branden and Branden 1968; "you're going to
. . ." Branden and Branden 1968; "I feel a . . ." Rand 1995, p. 473; "he's a replica
. . ." Rand 1995, p. 185; "It was a . . ." Nathaniel 1996c; "You're going to . . ."
Nathaniel Branden 1989a, p. 117. **Page 256:** "It's a project . . ." Nathaniel Branden
1989a, p. 345; "in every case . . ." Johnson 1988, p. 216; "Never. *Never.* There . . ."
Barbara Branden 1991; "then reality went . . ." Nathaniel Branden 1996c; "You
have no . . ." etc. Nathaniel Branden 1989a, pp. 374, 371; "all my life . . ." Rand
1995, p. 153. **Page 257:** "I am becoming . . ." Rand 1995, p. 179; "What I am . . ."
Rand 1995, p. 203; "Yes, . . . I do . . ." Rand 1983, p. 215; "is the only . . ." Rand
1995, p. 671; "A book like . . ." Rand 1995, p. 359; "Can't you be . . ." *The Objectivist*
(November 1967); "I do like . . ." Rand 1995, p. 153; "Frank says that . . ." Rand
1995, p. 106. **Page 258:** "the looks of . . ." *Objectivist Forum* (June 1981); "She had
no . . ." Nathaniel Branden 1996b; "She turned her . . ." Efron 1992; "She very
much . . ." Barbara Branden 1991. **Page 259:** "It's a failure . . ." Barbara Branden
1991; "did not understand . . ." Barbara Branden 1991; "that sewer" etc. Nathaniel
Branden 1989a, p. 116; "she made it . . ." Nathaniel Branden 1989a, p. 347; "pain
happens but . . ."Barbara Branden 1991; "joy is all-pervading . . ." Rand 1997, p.
512; "She was obsessed . . ." Nathaniel Branden 1989a, p. 287. **Page 260:** "All her
energies . . ." Nathaniel Branden 1989a, p. 377; "were alike in . . ." Barbara
Branden 1986a, p. 274; "I told her . . ." Gotthelf 1991; "She did not . . ." Barbara

Branden 1986a, p. 390; "a terrible human . . ." Kay Nolte Smith 1985, p. 58. **Page 261:** "shows little concern . . ." Kramer and Alstad 1993, p. 83; "disposition to use . . ." Nathaniel Branden 1989a, p. 373; "about whether or . . ." Childs 1991; "In the early . . ." Nathaniel Branden 1996c; "I suggested to . . ." Blumenthal and Blumenthal 1991; "Mr. Rand" Rothbard 1989; "bottomless agony" Barbara Branden 1986a, p. 88; "He was just . . ." Smith and Smith 1991. **Page 262:** "strikers" etc. Rand 1997, p. 398; "No, he was . . ." Barbara Branden 1991; "For the ugly . . ." Smith and Smith 1991; "we think in . . ." Rand 1995, p. 661; "She used to . . ." Smith and Smith 1991; "But he *hated* . . ." Barbara Branden 1986a, p. 384; "Frank has gone . . ." Rand 1995, pp. 165–66, 291. **Page 263:** "Who is Frank . . ." Rand 1997, p. 229; "my best proof . . ." etc. Rand 1995, pp. 670, 418, 615; "She loved him . . ." Ronald E. Merrill 1991b; "Dagny finally crashes . . ." Pierpont 1995. **Page 264:** "I would see . . ." Barbara Branden 1992; "would watch Scotch . . ." Kay Nolte Smith 1985, pp. 161, 158; "the first thing . . ." Barbara Branden 1992; "He would just . . ." Smith and Smith 1991; "torturing him" Barbara Branden 1986a, p. 365. **Page 265:** "massive works of . . ." Paul Johnson 1988, p. 69; "It is thought . . ." Blumenthal and Blumenthal 1991; "back all the . . ." Peikoff 1995; "I do think . . ." Taylor 1991; "There is no . . ." etc. Efron 1992. **Page 266:** "In her grandiosity . . ." Nathaniel Branden 1989a, pp. 347, 349. **Page 267:** "always thinking of . . ." Secrest 1992, p. 554; "I have seldom . . ." Rand 1995, p. 188; "her one chance . . ." Barbara Branden 1991; "there was never . . ." Barbara Branden 1986a, p. 293; "You still tell . . ." Rand 1995, p. 185; "Frank actually enjoyed . . ." Smith and Smith 1991; "a very unpleasant . . ." Wheeler 1996; "I know she . . ." Childs 1991. **Page 268:** "because at times . . ." Nathaniel Branden 1996c; "She did not . . ." Blumenthal and Blumenthal 1991; "kept chain-smoking and . . ." Secrest 1992, p. 497; "a fire at . . ." Quoted in Kluger 1996, p. 16; "When a man . . ." Rand 1957, p. 65. **Page 269:** "She didn't do . . ." Blumenthal and Blumenthal 1991. **Page 270:** "the result of . . ." Barbara Branden 1986a, p. 383.

10 The Roots of Objectivism

Pages 273–74: Count Alfred Korzybski . . . Gardner 1957, pp. 281–291. **Page 276:** "disgust . . . and humiliation . . ." etc. Rand 1997, pp. 26, 37, 38. **Page 277:** Objectivism absorbed Nietzsche . . . Ridpath 1985; "Nothing could have . . ." Barbara Branden 1991. **Page 278:** "I don't like . . ." Barbara Branden 1986a, p. 203. **Page 279:** "is the greatest . . ." Rand 1957, p. 827. **Page 287:** The number three . . . Schwartz 1988; Leonard Peikoff has . . . Peikoff 1996. **Page 288:** "Propaganda is the . . ." Rand 1995, p. 159. **Page 289:** "history shows that . . ." etc. Prothro 1954, pp. 65, 39, 216; "the ultrareality theory . . ." Gaitskill 1991a, p. 259. **Page 290:** "went beyond politics . . ." etc. Gaitskill ca. 1986; "unadorned fact" etc. Prothro 1954, pp. 32, 41, 58. **Page 291:** "the guru and . . ." Barbara Branden 1986a, p. 166; "hair-trigger temper, her . . ." Barbara Branden 1986a, p. 309; "increasingly belligerent toward . . ." Nathaniel Branden 1989a, p. 124; "a vigorous, if . . ." Nash 1976, p. 131.

11 The Disowned Ancestry of *Atlas Shrugged*

Page 295: Quoted in *Liberty* (May 1991). **Page 296:** "use emotional manipulation . . ." Gaitskill ca. 1986; "because her writing . . ." Gaitskill ca. 1986. **Pages 297–98:**

"the cartoon increasingly . . ." etc. Robert Hunt 1984; Nathaniel Branden recollects . . . Nathaniel Branden 1989a, p. 225. **Page 299:** "the idea is . . ." Barbara Branden 1991. **Page 300:** "recognize the peculiar . . ." Prothro 1954, p. 62; "History proves conclusively . . ." etc. Prothro 1954, pp. 20, 52; "Nature builds no . . ." Quoted in Sciabarra 1995, pp. 291–92; "The machine, the . . ." Rand 1957, p. 886, and see p. 988. **Page 301:** "by far the . . ." etc. Henry Nash Smith 1964; "Rand is one . . ." Ronald E. Merrill 1991b; "the entrepreneurial businessman . . ." Ronald E. Merrill 1991a, p. 68; "We have a . . ." Hawley 1955. **Page 302:** "in which the . . ." Hayek 1952, pp. 131–32. **Page 303:** "we certainly must" Rand 1995, p. 238. **Page 305:** "taking over a . . ." etc. Henry Nash Smith 1964. **Page 306:** "I'm the driver" Garrett 1922, p. 155; "After 1896 the . . ." Garrett 1922, p. 167; "solitary serenity" etc. Garrett 1922, pp. 158, 161, 157, 188, 40, 41. **Page 307:** "You put the . . ." Garrett 1922, p. 24; "Who knew what . . ." Garrett 1922, p. 230. **Page 308:** "money is only . . ." Rand 1957, p. 388; "What if all . . ." Barbara Branden 1986a, p. 218. **Pages 310–12:** "who in their . . ." etc. Bramah 1995, pp. 191, 51, 41, 176, 125, 209, 53, 189, 111, 145, 80, 81, 210, 214, 171, 184, 77, 78, 97, 262, 264, 263. **Page 313:** "stopped suddenly, jerked . . ." etc. Bramah 1995, pp. 205, 218, 155, 163; "It wasn't real . . ." Rand 1957, p. 993; "I have found . . ." Bramah 1995, p. 267. **Page 315:** "Except from the . . ." etc. Bossum 1934, pp. 14, 28, 37, 9; "there was nothing . . ." Pierpont 1995. **Page 316:** "this marvel of engineering . . ." *Skyscraper Souls;* "Well Mr. Roark . . ." *The Fountainhead* (movie); "You despise me . . ." *Casablanca;* "A leash is . . ." Nathaniel Branden 1989a, p. 22; "a Carlylean hero . . ." etc. Secrest 1992, pp. 384, 385, 384. **Page 317:** "association with Louis . . ." etc. Secrest 1992, pp. 496, 258, 552; A key plot . . . Reidy 1989; "If I take . . ." etc. Rand 1997, pp. 142, 118, 120. **Page 318:** "We are all . . ." Quoted in Rand 1997, p. 145; "as if the . . ." etc. Reidy 1997; "Why not, then . . ." etc. Rand 1997, pp. 120, 121; "friendly, late-night intimacy . . ." etc. Reidy 1993. **Page 319:** In an article . . . *The Eye* (Toronto, 11 March 1993); "mostly insipid, sometimes . . ." Reidy 1997; "It's a piece . . ." etc. Tafel 1979, pp. 100–01; "an unintended comedy . . ." Pierpont 1995. **Page 320:** "For the first . . ." etc. Rand 1995, pp. 415, 456, 475, 204; "Miss Rand declined . . ." Reisman 1996, p. xiv. **Page 321:** "insistence on morally . . ." Torres and Kamhi 1991–92; "the stronger the . . ." Smith and Smith 1991; "Galt was explicitly . . ." Ronald E. Merrill 1991a, p. 74; "I believe that . . ." Barbara Branden 1990; "Very few authors . . ." Nathaniel Branden 1996b; "had three men . . ." Smith and Smith 1991; "I don't think . . ." Taylor 1991; "she's perfection from . . ." Barbara Branden 1990. **Page 322:** "characters aren't people . . ." Rand 1995, p. 290; "not really . . ." Cox 1993; "It is I . . ." Rand 1957, p. 538; "Man is only . . ." Rand 1957, p. 920; "a monument to . . ." Rand 1995, pp. 109, 111; "He lived from . . ." Pierpont 1995. **Page 323:** "I don't think . . ." Barbara Branden 1990; "a moral label . . ." Smith and Smith 1991; "People don't change . . ." Childs 1991; "I would say . . ." Minsaas 1997; "A reader can . . ." Pierpont 1995; "I think people . . ." Holzer and Holzer 1991. **Page 324:** "She is great . . ." Hospers 1991; "a truncated intellectual . . ." Gaitskill 1991b; "a sprawling triple-decker . . ." Pierpont 1995; "robust but . . . naive . . ." Dipert 1985. **Page 325:** "utterly, utterly humorless . . ." Breslin 1991; "This is a . . ." John Hill 1992.

12 Ayn Rand's Legacy

Page 327: "there has probably . . ." Pierpont 1995; "It's a shame . . ." Smith and Smith 1991. **Page 328:** "I cannot tell . . ." Holzer and Holzer 1991; "They talk about . . ." Smith and Smith 1991; "In the meantime . . ." Gaitskill 1991a, pp. 24, 13. **Page**

329: "Justine was morbidly . . ." Gaitskill 1991a, p. 21; "I don't think . . ." Gaitskill 1991b; "There is something . . ." Breslin 1991; "No, the only . . ." Kress 1993, pp. 30–31. **Page 330:** "Zillions" etc. Childs 1991; "I had never . . ." Hospers 1991; "An awful lot . . ." Smith and Smith 1991. **Page 331:** "is three-quarters based . . ." Taylor 1991; "There would be . . ." Hospers 1991; "the Democrats were . . ." Taylor 1991; "mainly 'libertarian' in . . ." Cockett 1995, p. 189. **Page 332:** "If government intervention . . ." etc. Donway 1992; Objectivist Bob Prechter . . . *Elliott Wave Theorist* (5 October 1987). **Page 333:** "I've never been . . ." Beckman 1995, pp. 186–87; "we are on . . ." Rand 1995, p. 490; "In the worst . . ." Bidinotto 1985; "disconnected ideological fragments . . ." Robert Hunt 1984; "considers *Atlas Shrugged* . . ." Niederhoffer 1997b. **Page 334:** "the Hayekian revolution . . ." Cockett 1995, p. 321; "Hayek's insistence that . . ." Skidelsky 1995, p. 81; "As an example . . ." Rand 1995, p. 308; "Redistribution, however, is . . ." Internet posting; "hated Hayek intellectually . . ." Childs 1991. **Page 335:** "did as much . . ." Cockett 1995, p. 5; "the Comintern of . . ." Cockett 1995, p. 308. **Page 336:** "economic liberalism now . . ." Cockett 1995, p. 308; "the first political . . ." James A. Smith 1991, pp. 167, 169, 181, 22. **Page 337:** "I had some part . . ." *Objectivist Forum* (August 1980); "provided an example . . ." Flew 1991; "Ayn often said . . ." etc. Barbara Branden 1992. **Page 338:** "owed much to . . ." Cockett 1995, p. 329; "I don't see . . ." Peikoff 1991b; "crusted libertarian" Eksteins 1989, p. 295; "The name for . . ." Taylor 1993; "before *Atlas Shrugged* . . ." Taylor 1993. **Page 339:** "The striking fact . . ." Mack 1997. **Page 340:** Lipset 1990, p. 77; "the poet showed . . ." Higher 1954, p. 115; "Sensibly integrated along . . ." Saul 1995, p. 99. **Page 341:** "I certainly do" Kelley 1991; "at the end . . ." Nathaniel Branden 1996c.

Select Bibliography

Abramson, Glenda, ed. *The Blackwell Companion to Jewish Culture*. New York: Blackwell, 1989.

Adrian, Cheri. Inside Branden's Intensive. *Reason* (December 1977): pp. 27–30.

Allen, Jay, ed. The Kelleyite Posts. Internet, 1994.

Allen, Steve. The Jesus Cults: A Personal Analysis by the Parent of a Cult Member. *Skeptic*, vol. 2, no. 2 (1993).

American Psychiatric Association. *DSM IV: The Diagnostic and Statistical Manual of Mental Disorders, Fourth Edition*. Washington, D.C.: American Psychiatric Association, 1994.

Anderson, Martin. *Revolution: The Reagan Legacy*. Stanford: Hoover Institute Press, 1990.

Angeles, Peter A. *The HarperCollins History of Philosophy*. New York: HarperCollins, 1992.

Arbel, Avner, and Albert E. Kaff. *Crash: Ten Days in October . . . Will It Strike Again?* New York: Longman Financial Services, 1989.

Aristotle. *Ethics*. Revised translation by Hugh Treddinick. London: Penguin, 1976.

Ayn Rand Letter. The Volumes 1–4, 1971–1976. New Milford. Second Renaissance, 1990.

Baida, Peter. Poor *Richard's Legacy: American Business Values from Benjamin Franklin to Michael Milken*. New York: Morrow, 1990.

Baker, James T. *Ayn Rand*. Boston: Hall, 1987.

Baker, Marc. Objectivism In Israel. *Full Context* (November 1992): pp. 9–11.

Baker, Robert A. *They Call It Hypnosis*. Buffalo: Prometheus, 1990.

Barash, David P. *Beloved Enemies: Our Need for Opponents*. Amherst: Prometheus, 1994.

Barnes, Hazel. *An Existentialist Ethics*. New York: Random House, 1967.

Barrow, John D. *Theories of Everything: The Quest for Ultimate Explanation*. London: Vintage, 1991.

Barry, Norman P. *On Classical Liberalism and Libertarianism*. London: Macmillan, 1986.

——. *The New Right*. London: Croom Helm, 1987.

Bast, Joseph L., Peter J. Hill, and Richard C. Rue. *Eco-Sanity: A Commonsense Guide to Environmentalism*. Lanham, Maryland: Madison Books, 1996.

Beckman, Robert C. *Elliott Wave Explained*. Chicago: Probus, 1995.

Beckmann, Petr. Interviewed by Karen Reedstrom. *Full Context* (September 1990).

Beckner, Steven K. *Back from the Brink: The Greenspan Years*. New York: Wiley, 1996.

Berger, Peter L. *The Capitalist Revolution: Fifty Propositions about Prosperity, Equality, and Liberty*. New York: Basic Books, 1986.

Bergland, David. *Libertarianism in One Lesson*. Costa Mesa: Orpheus, 1990 [1984].

Berliner, Michael. Personal interview with Jeff Walker, 2 October 1991.

Bidinotto, Robert. *The Oasis*. Audiotape. 1985.

——. *Individualism as if Individuals Mattered*. Robert Bidinotto, 1988.

———. Facts, Values, and Moral Sanctions: An Open Letter to Objectivists. Internet, 21 July 1989.

———. Interviewed by David Oyerly. *Objectivist Club of Eastern Michigan* newsletter (March 1990): pp. 1–9.

———. *The Green Machine.* 32-page pamphlet. Poughkeepsie: Institute for Objectivist Studies, 1993.

———. Survive or Flourish: A Reconciliation. *Full Context* (February 1994): pp. 1–5. Concludes with Part II in April 1994 issue.

Binswanger, Harry. Letter to the Editor on Norah Ephron's article. *The New York Times Book Review* (9 June 1968).

———, ed. *The Ayn Rand Lexicon.* New York: New American Library, 1986.

———. Ayn Rand's Life: Highlights and Sidelights. Two audiotapes. New Milford: Second Renaissance, 1994.

Blake, Peter. Letter to the Editor on Nora Ephron's article. *The New York Times Book Review* (9 June 1968).

Block, Walter. Libertarianism versus Objectivism: A Response to Peter Schwartz. Audiotape. San Francisco: Laissez Faire, ca. 1988.

Bloom, Alexander. *Prodigal Sons: The New York Intellectuals and Their World.* New York: Oxford University Press, 1986.

Blumenthal, Allan, and Joan Mitchell Blumenthal. Personal interview with Jeff Walker, 31 October 1991.

Blumenthal, Joan Mitchell. Interviewed by Karen Reedstrom. *Full Context* (March 1993).

Blumenthal, Sidney. *The Rise of the Counter-Establishment: From Conservative Ideology to Political Power.* New York: Harper and Row, 1986.

Bossum, Alfred C. *Building to the Skies: The Romance of the Skyscraper.* London: The Studio, 1934.

Bourgin, Frank. *The Great Challenge: The Myth of Laissez-Faire in the Early Republic.* New York: Braziller, 1989.

Bradford, R.W. The Real Judge Thomas. *Liberty* (September 1991): pp. 18–21.

———. Freedom's Rose. Review of biography of Rose Wilder Lane. *Liberty* (March 1994): pp. 53–64.

———. Was Ayn Rand a Plagiarist? *Liberty* (May 1994).

———. Deep Cover Radical for Capitalism? *Liberty* (November 1997).

———. Review of the film *Ayn Rand: A Sense of Life. Liberty* (May 1998).

Bradford, R.W., et al. 1995 *Liberty* Editors' Conference. Ayn Rand: The Woman Behind the Myth. Audiotape. Port Townsend: Liberty.

Bramah, Ernest. *The Secret of the League: The Story of a Social War.* Atlanta: Specular Press, 1995 [London: John Murray, 1907. Original title: *What Might Have Been: The Story of a Social War,* changed to present title in 1909 edn.].

Branden, Barbara. *The Passion of Ayn Rand: A Biography.* New York: Doubleday, 1986a.

———. An Evening with Barbara Branden: 24 June 1986. Audiotape. *Liberty* Audio, 1986b.

———. Liberty Interview. *Liberty* (January 1990), pp. 49–76.

———. Personal interview with Jeff Walker, 29 September 1991.

———. Interviewed by Karen Reedstrom. *Full Context* (October 1992).

———. Passion Play. *Liberty* (July 1998): pp. 29–30.

Branden, Barbara, and Nathaniel Branden. *See* Branden, Nathaniel, and Barbara Branden.

Branden, Nathaniel. *The Psychology of Self-Esteem: A New Concept of Man's Psychological Nature.* New York: Bantam, 1969.

———. Break Free! An Interview with Nathaniel Branden. *Reason* (October 1971): 4–19.

———. *The Disowned Self.* Los Angeles: Nash, 1972.

———. On Self-Discovery and Self-Responsibility: An Interview with Nathaniel Branden. Interviewed jointly by Roy Childs Jr., Tibor Machan, and George H. Smith. *Reason* (May 1973).

———. Thank You Ayn Rand, and Goodbye. *Reason* (May 1978): pp. 58–61.

———. *The Psychology of Romantic Love.* New York: Tarcher, 1980.

———. *Honoring the Self: The Psychology of Confidence and Respect.* New York: Tarcher, 1983a.

———. Love and Sex in the Philosophy of Ayn Rand. Audiotape. 1983b.

———. The Benefits and Hazards of the Philosophy of Ayn Rand: A Personal Statement. *Journal of Humanistic Psychology,* vol. 24, no. 4 (Fall 1984): pp. 39–64.

———. *How to Raise Your Self-Esteem.* New York: Bantam, 1987a.

———. Review of Ellen Plasil, *Therapist. Free Inquiry* (Summer 1987b). Reprinted in *Liberty* (May 1988).

———. *Judgment Day: My Years with Ayn Rand.* Boston: Houghton Mifflin, 1989a.

———. Nathaniel Branden: New York City—June 22, 1989b. Audiotape. Liberty Audio and Film Service.

———. Personal interview with Jeff Walker, 29 September 1991.

———. Positive Selfishness. *New Woman* (October 1993): pp. 48–49.

———. *The Six Pillars of Self-Esteem.* New York: Bantam, 1994.

———. *Taking Responsibility: Self-Reliance and the Accountable Life.* New York: Simon and Schuster, 1996a.

———. Objectivism Past and Future. Audiotape. Recorded 23 November 1996b. San Francisco: Laissez Faire Audio.

———. Interviewed by Karen Reedstrom. *Full Context* (September and October 1996c).

———. *The Art of Living Consciously.* New York: Simon and Schuster, 1997a.

———. Objectivism and Self-Acceptance. *IOS Journal* (February 1997b).

———. Self-Esteem in the Information Age. In Frances Hesselbein, Marshall Goldsmith, and Richard Beckhard, eds., *The Organization of the Future.* Drucker Foundation. San Francisco: Jossey-Bass, 1997c.

Branden, Nathaniel, and Barbara Branden. *Who Is Ayn Rand?* New York: Random House, 1962.

Branden, Nathaniel, and Barbara Branden. In Answer to Ayn Rand. 1968.

Branden, Nathaniel, and Devers Branden. *What Love Asks of Us.* New York: Bantam, 1992 [1982].

Brandes, Georg. *Friedrich Nietzsche.* New York: Haskell House, 1914.

Breslin, Mark. Personal interview with Jeff Walker, 19 November 1991.

Brickell, Diana Mertz, compiler. Kelley/Peikoff Split. Internet (February and March 1994).

Briggs, Dorothy Corkville. *Your Child's Self-Esteem.* New York: Doubleday, 1970.

———. *Celebrate Your Self.* New York: Doubleday, 1977.

Brody, Nathan, Martha Murdock, and Leslie Prioleau. An Analysis of Psychotherapy versus Placebo Studies. *Behavioral and Brain Sciences,* vol. 6 (1983): pp. 275–310. With a follow-up rejoinder and author response in vol. 7 (1984): pp. 756–762.

Brownmiller, Susan. *Against Our Will: Men, Women, and Rape.* New York: Simon and Schuster, 1975.

Buckley, William F. *In Search of Anti-Semitism.* New York: Continuum, 1992.

Budd, Eric Merrill. The ABC's of Mind Control. *Free Inquiry* (Fall 1991).

Bullock, Scott. A Rebel and a Drummer (Who Is Neil Peart?). *Liberty* (September 1997).

Burns, James McGregor, and Stewart Burns. *A People's Charter: The Pursuit of Rights in America.* New York: Knopf, 1991.

Butler, Kurt. *A Consumer's Guide to Alternative Medicine.* Buffalo: Prometheus, 1992.

Callahan, Roger J. *The Five Minute Phobia Cure.* Wilmington: Enterprise Publishing, 1985.

———. *Five Minute Phobia Cure: How to Do It.* Videotape. Indian Wells, California: Callahan Techniques, ca. 1988.

———. *Why Do I Eat When I'm Not Hungry?* New York: Doubleday, 1991.

Cantor, Norman. *Inventing the Middle Ages.* New York: Morrow, 1991.

———. *The Civilization of the Middle Ages.* New York: HarperCollins, 1993.

Casey, Douglas R. Crisis *Investing: Opportunities and Profits in the Coming Great Depressions.* New York: Stratford, 1980.

Chambers, Whittaker. Big Sister Is Watching You. Review of Rand 1957. *National Review* (28 December 1957): pp. 594–96.

Champagne, Maurice. Translated by Bill Bucko. *The Mysterious Valley.* Lafayette, Colorado: Atlantean Press, 1994 [Paris: Librairie Delagrave, 1915].

Childs, Roy A., Jr. Ayn Rand: 1905–1982. *Inquiry* (26 April 1982), pp. 33–34.

———. Personal interview with Jeff Walker, 1 November 1991.

———. Ayn Rand, Objectivism, and All That. Interviewed by Jeff Walker. *Liberty* (April 1993): pp. 31–42.

Cockett, Richard. *Thinking the Unthinkable: Think Tanks and the Economic Counter-Revolution, 1931–1983.* London: HarperCollins, 1995.

Cody, John. Ayn Rand's Promethean Heroes. *Reason* (November 1973).

Collier, James Lincoln. *The Rise of Selfishness in America.* New York: Oxford University Press, 1991.

Collier, Peter, and David Horowitz. *Destructive Generation: Second Thoughts about the Sixties.* New York: Summit Books, 1989.

Conquest, Robert. *The Harvest of Sorrow: Soviet Collectivization and the Terror Famine.* New York: Oxford University Press, 1986.

Conway, Flo, and Jim Siegelman. *Snapping.* New York: Delta, 1979.

Cosman, Madeleine Pelner. Interviewed by Karen Reedstrom. *Full Context* (December 1997).

Costantino, Maria. *Frank Lloyd Wright.* London: Bison, 1991.

Cox, Stephen. Review of *The Early Ayn Rand. Reason* (April 1985).

———. Interviewed by Karen Reedstrom. *Full Context* (December 1993).

———. Review of *Journals of Ayn Rand. Liberty* (July 1998).

Craig, Gordon A. *The Germans.* New York: New American Library, 1982.

Crawford, Susan, and Lyn Salsman. Rational Parenting. Audiotape. New Milford: Second Renaissance, 1994.

Crowley, Brian. *Friedrich Hayek: The Vindication of Doubt.* CBC Ideas Transcript, 1990.

Damasio, Antonio R. *Descartes's Error: Emotion, Reason, and the Human Brain.* New York: Grosset/Putnam, 1994.

Davidson, James Dale, and William Rees-Mogg. *The Great Reckoning: How the World Will Change in the Depression of the 1990s.* New York: Summit, 1991.

Davis, L.J. The Encyclopedia of Insanity: A Psychiatric Handbook Lists a Madness for Everyone. *Harper's Monthly* (February 1997).

Den Uyl, Douglas J., and Douglas B. Rasmussen. Nozick on the Randian Argument. *Personalist* 59 (April 1978): 184–205.

Den Uyl, Douglas J., and Douglas B. Rasmussen, eds. *The Philosophic Thought of Ayn Rand*. Urbana: University of Illinois Press, 1984.

Dennison, Shane. *Sidehill Gouger or What's So Deadly about Caterpillars?* New York: Doubleday, 1977.

Dershowitz, Alan M. *Chutzpah*. New York: Simon and Schuster, 1991.

———. *The Vanishing American Jew: In Search of Jewish Identity for the Next Century*. Boston: Little, Brown, 1997.

Dickman, Howard. Interviewed by Karen Reedstrom. *Full Context* (November 1990).

Dibacco, Thomas V. *Made in the U.S.A.: The History of American Business*. Harper and Row, 1987.

Dimont, Max I. *Jews, God, and History*. New York: Simon and Schuster, 1962.

Dipert, Randall. Taking Ayn Rand Seriously. *Reason* (January 1985): pp. 58–62.

Ditko, Steve. *The Avenging World*. A comic book. San Jose: Bruce Hershenson, 1973.

Donway, Walter. Interviewed by Karen Reedstrom. *Full Context* (May 1992).

Dreiser, Theodore. *The Titan*. New York: New American Library, 1965 [1914].

———. *The Financier*. New York: New American Library, 1967 [1912].

Drucker, Peter F. *Post-Capitalist Society*. New York: HarperCollins, 1993.

Dwyer, William. The Argument Against 'An Objective Standard of Value'. *Personalist* 55 (Spring 1974): 165–181.

Dyson, Freeman. Tool-Driven Scientific Revolutions. *Skeptical Inquirer*, vol. 18, no. 2 (Winter 1994): p. 169.

Economist, The. Philosophy Comes Down from the Clouds. *The Economist* (26 April 1986).

Edwards, Keith. Interviewed by Karen Reedstrom. *Full Context* (March 1997).

Efron, Edith. Viewpoint. *Reason* (August 1978).

———. *The Apocalyptics: How Environmental Politics Controls What We Know about Cancer*. New York: Simon and Schuster, 1984.

———. Telephone interview with Jeff Walker, 9 November 1992.

———. Can the President Think? *Reason* (November 1994): pp. 20–44

Eksteins, Modris. *Rites of Spring: The Great War and the Birth of the Modern Age*. Toronto: Lester and Orpen Dennys, 1989.

Elliott Wave Theorist. Monthly newsletter . Gainesville, Georgia: New Classics Library.

Ellis, Albert. *Is Objectivism a Religion?* New York: Institute For Rational Living, 1968.

———. *Why Some Therapies Don't Work: The Dangers of Transpersonal Psychology*. Buffalo: Prometheus, 1989.

———. Personal interview with Jeff Walker, 31 October 1991a.

———. Telephone interviews with Jeff Walker, 28 October 1991b and subsequently.

Ellison, Bryan. Interviewed by Karen Reedstrom. *Full Context* (November 1994).

Ephron, Nora. A Strange Kind of Simplicity. *The New York Times Book Review* (5 May 1968).

Erickson, Peter. *The Stance of Atlas: An Examination of the Philosophy of Ayn Rand*. Portland: Herakles Press, 1997.

Evans, J.St.B.T., D.E. Over, and K.I. Manktelow. Reasoning, Decision-making, and Rationality. *Cognition* 49 (1993): pp. 165–187.

Evans, M. Stanton. The Gospel According to Ayn Rand. *National Review* (3 October 1967): pp. 1059–1063.

Eysenck, Hans. *The Decline and Fall of the Freudian Empire*. New York: Viking, 1985.

Feinberg, Joel, ed. *Reason and Responsibility: Readings in Some Basic Problems of Philosophy*. Belmont: Wadsworth, 1995.

Feldman, David. Rush: Quality Rock. *Full Context* (January 1990): pp. 6–7.

——. Review of *The Ideas of Ayn Rand* by Ronald Merrill. *Full Context* (January 1992): pp. 10–12.

Ferguson, Tim W. Seeing Dollar Signs. *Forbes* (23 March 1998).

Feuer, Lewis. *Imperialism and the Anti-Imperialist Mind*. Buffalo: Prometheus, 1986.

Fletcher, Max E. Harriet Martineau and Ayn Rand: Economics in the Guise of Fiction. *American Journal of Economics and Sociology*, vol. 33, no. 4 (October 1974): pp. 367–379.

——. A Rejoinder. *American Journal of Economics and Sociology*, vol. 35, no. 2 (April 1976): p. 224.

Flew, Antony. *Thinking about Thinking*. Glasgow: Fontana/Collins, 1975.

——. *Thinking about Social Thinking: Escaping Deception, Resisting Self-deception*. London: Fontana, 1991a [1985].

——. Personal interview with Jeff Walker, 15 October 1991b.

Florman, Samuel C. *Blaming Technology: The Irrational Search for Scapegoats*. New York: St. Martin's, 1981.

Foust, Dean. Alan Greenspan's Brave New World. *Business Week* (14 July 1997).

Franck, Murray I. Interviewed by Karen Reedstrom. *Full Context* (June 1992).

——. Taxation Remains Moral. *Full Context* (September 1994).

——. Emergencies and Ethical Consistency. *Full Context* (May 1995).

——. Rationality as a Source of Conflicts of Interest. *Full Context* (October 1997).

Fremantle, Anne. *This Little Band of Prophets: The Story of the Gentle Fabians*. New York: Allen and Unwin, 1960.

Friedman, Milton. Say 'No' To Intolerance. *Liberty* (July 1991): pp. 17–20.

Fulford, Robert. Who Speaks for Capitalism? *Globe and Mail* (4 January 1995).

——. The Appalling Charm of Rand's *Fountainhead*. *Globe and Mail* (17 January 1996).

——. Rand Fans Band Together when Attack at Hand. *Globe and Mail* (24 January 1996).

Fussell, Paul. *Bad, or the Dumbing of America*. New York: Simon and Schuster, 1991.

Gabler, Neal. *An Empire of Their Own: How the Jews Invented Hollywood*. New York: Doubleday, 1989 [1988].

Gaitskill, Mary. Unpublished article on Ayn Rand, ca. 1986.

——. *Two Girls, Fat and Thin*. New York: Simon and Schuster, 1991a.

——. Personal interview with Jeff Walker, 2 December 1991b.

Gotthelf, Allan. Personal interview with Jeff Walker, 4 December 1991.

Galanter, Marc. *Cults: Faith, Healing, and Coercion*. New York: Oxford University Press, 1989.

Gardner, Martin. *Fads and Fallacies in the Name of Science*. New York: Dover, 1957.

——. *The Healing Revelations of Mary Baker Eddy: The Rise and Fall of Christian Science*. Buffalo: Prometheus, 1993.

Garrett, Garet. *The Driver*. New York: Dutton, 1922.

——. *The People's Pottage*. Includes *The Revolution Was* [1944]. Caldwell, Idao: Caxton, 1953.

Gay, Peter. *The Cultivation of Hatred: The Bourgeois Experience from Victoria to Freud.* New York: Norton, 1993.

Gellner, Ernest. *The Psychoanalytic Movement: Or the Coming of Unreason.* London: Granada, 1985.

Gilder, George. *Wealth and Poverty.* New York: Basic Books, 1981.

Gilman, Sander L. *Smart Jews: The Construction of the Image of Jewish Superior Intelligence.* Lincoln: University of Nebraska Press, 1996.

Gilovich, Thomas. *How We Know What Isn't So: The Fallibility of Human Reason in Everyday Life.* New York: Free Press, 1991.

Gladstein, Mimi Reisel. *The Ayn Rand Companion.* Westport, Connecticut: Greenwood Press, 1984.

Goertzel, Ted. *Turncoats and True Believers: The Dynamics of Political Belief and Disillusionment.* Buffalo: Prometheus, 1992.

Goldman, Daniel. *Vital Lies, Simple Truths: The Psychology of Self-Deception.* New York: Simon and Schuster, 1985.

Gordon, David. Review of *Atheism, Ayn Rand, and Other Heresies* by George H. Smith. *Journal of Libertarian Studies* (Fall 1992): pp. 191–99.

Gordon, James S. *The Golden Guru: The Strange Journey of Bhagwan Shree Rajneesh.* Lexington: Stephen Greene, 1987.

Gray, David. *Thomas Hastings, Architect: Collected Writings, together with a Memoir.* Boston: Houghton Mifflin, 1933.

Greenberg, Sid. *Ayn Rand and Alienation: The Platonic Idealism of the Objectivist Ethics.* San Francisco: Sid Greenberg, 1977.

Greenwood, Robert. Ayn Rand and the Literary Critics. *Reason* (November 1974).

Gullison, Leisha. Telephone interview with Jeff Walker, Fall 1992.

Gutheim, Frederick, ed. *Frank Lloyd Wright on Architecture.* See Frank Lloyd Wright.

Hackett, A. P., and J. H. Burke. *Eighty Years of Bestsellers 1895–1975.* New York: Bowker, 1977.

Hamblin, Dora Jane. The Cult of the Angry Ayn Rand. *Life* (7 April 1967): pp. 92–102.

Hamel, Virginia L.L. *In Defense of Ayn Rand.* Brookline, Massachusetts: New Beacon Publications, 1990.

——. Telephone interview with Jeff Walker, Fall 1992.

Hawley, Cameron. *Executive Suite.* Boston: Houghton Mifflin, 1952.

——. *Cash McCall.* Boston: Houghton Mifflin, 1955.

Hayek, F.A. *The Road to Serfdom.* Chicago: University of Chicago Press, 1944.

——. *The Counter-Revolution of Science: Studies on the Abuse of Reason.* Glencoe, Illinois: Free Press, 1952.

Hazlitt, Henry. *Economics in One Lesson.* New York: Arlington House, 1979 [1946].

Heilbroner, Robert. *Twenty-first Century Capitalism.* Concord, Ontario: Anansi, 1992.

Heinlein, Robert. *The Moon Is a Harsh Mistress.* New York: Putnam, 1966.

Hertzberg, Arthur. *The Jews in America: Four Centuries of Uneasy Encounter.* New York: Simon and Schuster, 1989.

Hessen, Robert. A Noble Savages . . . Letter to the Editor. *Liberty* (September 1989): pp. 4–6.

——. Telephone interview with Jeff Walker, Fall 1992.

Highet, Gilbert. *Man's Unconquerable Mind.* New York: Columbia University Press, 1954.

Hill, Jim. Interviewed by Karen Reedstrom. *Full Context* (June 1994).

Hill, John. Interviewed by Karen Reedstrom. *Full Context* (January 1992).

Himmelfarb, Gertrude. *The De-Moralization of Society: From Victorian Virtues to Modern Values.* New York: Knopf, 1995.

Hines, Terence. Antidote to Science-Bashing. *Skeptical Inquirer,* vol. 18, no. 2 (Winter 1994), pp. 179–181.

Hitchcock, Henry-Russell. *In the Nature of the Materials: The Buildings of Frank Lloyd Wright 1887–1941.* New York: Da Capo, 1973 [1942].

Hitchens, Christopher. Minority Report. (On Alan Greenspan) *The Nation* (16 March 1994).

Hobsbawm, Eric. *The Age of Extremes: A History of the World, 1914–1991.* New York: Pantheon, 1994.

Hoffer, Eric. *The True Believer.* New York: Harper and Row, 1951.

Hoffman, Wallace. Letter to the Editor. *Liberty* (July 1988).

Holzer, Erika. *Eye for an Eye.* New York: Forge, 1993.

———. Interviewed by Karen Reedstrom. *Full Context* (February 1996).

Holzer, Erika, and Hank Holzer. Personal interview with Jeff Walker, 3 December 1991.

Hook, Sidney. Each Man for Himself. *The New York Times Book Review* (9 April 1961): pp. 3, 28.

———. *Out of Step: An Unquiet Life in the Twentieth Century.* New York: Harper and Row, 1987.

Horkheimer, Max. *The Eclipse of Reason.* New York: Seabury, 1947.

Hospers, John. Conversations with Ayn Rand. *Liberty* (July 1990a): pp. 23–36.

———. Conversations with Ayn Rand. Part Two. *Liberty* (September 1990b): pp. 42–52.

———. Personal interviews with Jeff Walker, 26 September and 1 October 1991.

———. Leaving a Margin for Error. *Liberty* (September 1997): pp. 67–69.

Hubbard, L. Ron. *Dianetics: The Modern Science of Mental Health.* Los Angeles: Bridge, 1985 [1950].

Hubner, John, and Lindsey Gruson. *Monkey on a Stick: Murder, Madness, and the Hare Krishnas.* New York: Penguin, 1988.

Hudgins, Edward. Interviewed by Karen Reedstrom. *Full Context* (September 1993).

Hughes, William. *Critical Thinking: An Introduction to the Basic Skills.* Lewiston, N.Y.: Broadview, 1992.

Hugo, Victor. *Les Misérables.* New York: Penguin, 1980 [1862].

———. *Ninety-Three.* Introduction by Ayn Rand. New Milford: Second Renaissance, 1994 [1872].

Hull, Gary. The Black Hole of Contemporary Philosophy. Audiotape. New Milford: Second Renaissance, ca. 1990.

Hunt, Lester. Review of *Ayn Rand: The Russian Radical* by Chris Matthew Sciabarra. *Liberty* (March 1996).

Hunt, Robert. Science Fiction for the Age of Inflation: Reading *Atlas Shrugged* in the 1980s. In George E. Slusser, Eric S. Rabkin, and Robert Scholes, eds., *Co-ordinates: Placing Science Fiction and Fantasy. Alternative Series.* Carbondale and Edwardsville: Southern Illinois University Press, 1984, pp. 80–98.

Jacobs, Jane. *Systems of Survival: A Dialogue on the Moral Foundations of Commerce and Politics.* New York: Random House, 1992.

Jacoby, Russell. *The Last Intellectuals: American Culture in the Age of Academe.* New York: Farrar, Straus, and Giroux, 1987.

Jefferson School. Doctors' Panel Q and A. Audiotape. Jefferson School, 1989.

Johnson, Gregory R. Did Rand Stack the Ethical Deck? *Liberty* (November 1992): pp. 62–63.

Johnson, Paul. *A History of Christianity.* New York: Penguin, 1976.

———. *A History of the Modern World.* London: Weidenfeld and Nicolson, 1983.

———. *A History of the Jews.* New York: Harper and Row, 1987.

———, *Intellectuals* New York: Harper and Row, 1988.

———. *The Birth of the Modern: World Society 1815–1830.* London: Weidenfield and Nicholson, 1991.

———. Blessing Capitalism. *Commentary* (May 1993).

Kalmar, Ivan. *The Trotskys, Freuds, and Woody Allens: Portrait of a Culture.* New York: Viking, 1993.

Kamhi, Michelle Marder. Ayn Rand's *We The Living:* New Life in a Restored Film Version. *Aristos: The Journal of Aesthetics,* vol. 4, no. 4 (December 1988).

Kamiya, Gary. Iron Maiden. Review of *Journals of Ayn Rand. Los Angeles Times* (4 January 1998).

Kelley, David. *The Evidence of the Senses: A Realist Theory of Perception.* Baton Rouge: Louisiana State University Press, 1986.

———. Objectivism and the Struggle For Liberty. Audiotape. Laissez Faire Supper Club, 10 November 1988. San Francisco: Laissez Faire.

———. Objectivism: The Philosophy and the Movement. Audiotape. San Francisco: Laissez Faire, 1990a.

———. *Truth and Toleration.* New York: Institute for Objectivist Studies, 1990b.

———. Interviewed by David Oyerly. *Full Context* (May 1990c).

———. Personal interview with Jeff Walker, 30 October 1991.

———. How Principles Work. *Liberty* (November 1992): pp. 63–76.

———. Interviewed by Raymie Stata. *Full Context* (June 1993).

———. Better Things to Do. *IOS Journal* (March 1994).

Kelley, David, et al. Reader's Forum: More on Ayn Rand. Letters from David Kelley, John Ridpath, Ayn Rand Institute, and Tibor Machan, with rejoinders from Jeff Walker. *Free Inquiry,* vol. 15, no. 1 (Winter 1994–95): pp. 51–52.

King, Florence. Hillarique Shrugged (After Ayn Rand). *National Review* (26 September 1994): p. 61.

Kirkpatrick, J. Pragmatism and the Harvard Case Method. Audiotape. August 1989.

Kluger, Richard. *Ashes to Ashes: America's Hundred-Year Cigarette War, the Public Health, and the Unabashed Triumph of Philip Morris.* New York: Knopf, 1996.

Kobler, John. The Curious Cult of Ayn Rand. *Saturday Evening Post* (11 November 1961): pp. 98–101.

Kosko, Bart. *Fuzzy Thinking: The New Science of Fuzzy Logic.* New York: Hyperion, 1993.

Kotkin, Joel. *Tribes: How Race, Religion, and Identity Determine Success in the New Global Economy.* New York: Random House, 1992.

Kramer, Joel, and Diana Alstad. *The Guru Papers: Masks of Authoritarian Power.* Berkeley: North Atlantic, 1993.

Kramer, Peter D. *Listening to Prozac: A Psychiatrist Explores Antidepressant Drugs and the Remaking of the Self.* New York: Viking, 1993.

Krefetz, Gerald. *Jews and Money: The Myths and the Reality.* New Haven: Ticknor and Fields, 1982.

Kress, Nancy. *Beggars in Spain.* New York: Morrow, 1993.

Kristol, Irving. *Two Cheers for Capitalism*. New York: New American Library, 1978.

Krogh, David. *Smoking: The Artificial Passion*. New York: Freeman, 1991.

Kurtz, Paul. Personal interview with Jeff Walker, 28 September 1991.

Lamont, Stewart. *Religion Inc.: The Church of Scientology*. London: Harrap, 1986.

Lane, Rose Wilder. *The Discovery of Freedom: Man's Struggle against Authority*. Laissez Faire Books, 1984 [1943].

Lapham, Lewis H. *Money and Class in America: Notes and Observations on the Civil Religion*. New York: Ballantine, 1988.

Lennox, James G. Fletcher's Oblique Attack on Ayn Rand's Economics and Ethics. *American Journal of Economics and Sociology*, vol. 35, no. 2 (April 1976): 217–224.

———. Interviewed by Karen Reedstrom. *Full Context* (March 1991).

Paul Lepanto. *Return to Reason: An Introduction to Objectivism*. New York: Exposition, 1971.

Lewin, Tamar. The Quiet Allure of Alan Greenspan. *Sunday New York Times* (5 June 1983).

Lewis, Martin W. *Green Delusions: An Environmentalist Critique of Radical Environmentalism*. Durham: Duke University Press, 1992.

Lewis, Michael. Beyond Economics, Beyond Politics, Beyond Accountability. (On Alan Greenspan.) *Worth* (May 1995).

Lewis, Sinclair. *It Can't Happen Here*. New York: New American Library, 1935.

Lipset, Seymour Martin. *Continental Divide: The Values and Institutions of the United States and Canada*. New York: Routledge, 1990.

Livingston, Kenneth. To Awaken the Hero Within. Review of *The Six Pillars of Self-Esteem* by Nathaniel Branden. *IOS Journal* (March 1994).

Locke, Edwin. The Nature of Human Intelligence. Audiotape. New Milford: Second Renaissance, 1991.

———. Psycho-epistemology of the Arab World. Audiotape. New Milford: Second Renaissance, 1994.

———. Traits of Business Heroes. Audiotape. New Milford: Second Renaissance, 1995.

Locke, Edwin, and S. Sapontzis. Do Animals Have Rights? A debate. Audiotape. College of Marin, March 1990.

Long, James de. The Way it Was. *Journal of Taliesin Fellows* 21 (Spring 1997).

Lugenbehl, Dale. The Argument for an Objective Standard of Value. *Personalist* (Spring 1974).

Lukacs, Georg. *The Destruction of Reason*. Atlantic Highlands: Humanities Press, 1981 [1954].

Luttwak, Edward. Central Bankism. *London Review of Books* (14 November 1996).

Machan, Tibor R. Nozick and Rand on Property Rights. *Personalist* 58 (April 1977): 192–95.

———. Ayn Rand and I. *Liberty* (November 1989): pp. 49–54.

———. Interviewed by Jack Criss. *Full Context* (May 1994).

Mack, Eric. Interviewed by Karen Reedstrom and Rick Minto. *Full Context* (May 1997).

McDonald, Marci. Fighting over Ayn Rand: A Radical Individualist's Followers Can't Get Along. *U.S. News and World Report* (9 March 1998).

McIlhany, William H. Interviewed by Karen Reedstrom. *Full Context* (December 1995).

Mann, Arlene. The Rationality of the Common Law. Audiotape. New Milford: Second Renaissance, 1992.

Mann, W.E. Guruship, in America. *Energy and Character* (April 1987).
———. *The Quest for Total Bliss: A Psycho Sociological Perspective on the Rajneesh Movement*. Toronto: Canadian Scholars Press, 1991.
Marcus, G. Plato, Kant, and Aristotle in Mathematics. Audiotape. Thomas Jefferson School. New Milford: Second Renaissance, 1991.
Masson, Jeffrey Moussaieff. *Against Therapy: Emotional Tyranny and the Myth of Psychological Healing*. New York: Atheneum, 1988.
——— *Final Analysis: The Making and Unmaking of a Psychoanalyst*. Reading, Massachusetts: Addison-Wesley, 1990.
Maxmen, Jerrold S. *Essential Psychopathology*. New York: Norton, 1986.
Mayhew, Robert, ed. *Ayn Rand's Marginalia*. New Milford: Second Renaissance, 1995.
Merrill, Gary. Rand's Work: Style and Quality. Internet, 1993.
Merrill, Ronald E. *The Ideas of Ayn Rand*. La Salle, Illinois: Open Court, 1991a.
———. Personal interview with Jeff Walker, 1 October 1991b.
Merwin-Webster (Merwin, Samuel, and Henry K. Webster). *Comrade John*. New York: Macmillan, 1907.
———. *Calumet 'K'*. Introduction by Ayn Rand. New York: NBI Press, 1967 [1901].
Metz, Robert. Interviewed by Karen Reedstrom. *Full Context* (February 1995).
Miller, Fred, Jr. Interviewed by Karen Reedstrom. *Full Context* (March 1992).
Miller, Russell. *Bare-Faced Messiah: The True Story of L. Ron Hubbard*. New York: Holt, 1987.
Mills, David. Overcoming 'Self-Esteem': Why Our Compulsive Drive for 'Self-Esteem' is Anxiety-Provoking, Socially Inhibiting, and Self-Sabotaging. REBT essay of the month, obtained from Internet in early 1998.
Minsaas, Kirsti. Interviewed by Karen Reedstrom and Thomas Gramstad. *Full Context* (February 1997).
Mises, Ludwig von. *Economic Policy: Thoughts for Today and Tomorrow*. Washington, D.C.: Regnery Gateway, 1979.
Morris, Tom. *If Aristotle Ran General Motors: The New Soul of Business*. New York: Holt, 1997.
Moulton, William P. Mrs. O'Connor, Call Your Literary Agent. *Liberty* (May 1991): p. 9.
Mozes, Eyal. Review of *Objectivism: The Philosophy of Ayn Rand* by Leonard Peikoff. *Full Context* (February 1992): pp. 10–12.
Munz, Peter. Sense Perception and the Reality of the World. Review of Kelley 1986. *Critical Review*, vol. 2, no. 1 (Winter 1987).
Nash, George H. *The Conservative Intellectual Movement in America Since 1945*. New York: Basic Books, 1976.
Nichols, Rosalie. *Confessions of a Randian Cultist: An Open Letter to Ayn Rand regarding the Branden Interview*. Brian Eenigenburg, 1972.
Niederhoffer, Victor. *The Education of a Speculator*. New York: Wiley, 1997a.
———. Interviewed by Karen Reedstrom. *Full Context* (April 1997b).
Nietzsche, Friedrich. *The Will to Power*. Walter Kaufmann, editor. Walter Kaufmann and R.J. Hollingdale, translators. New York: Random House, 1967.
———. *The Portable Nietzsche*. Walter Kaufmann, editor and translator. New York: Viking, 1968.
———. *Basic Writings of Nietzsche*. Walter Kaufmann, editor and translator. New York: Modern Library, 1992 [1968].
Noll, Richard. *The Jung Cult: Origins of a Charismatic Movement*. Princeton: Princeton University Press, 1994.

————. *The Aryan Christ: The Secret Life of Carl Jung.* New York: Random House, 1997.

Nolte, Eric. Interviewed by Karen Reedstrom. *Full Context* (March 1995).

Norton, Rob. In Greenspan We Trust. *Fortune* (18 March 1996).

Nozick, Robert. On the Randian Argument. *Personalist*, vol. 52, no. 2 (Spring 1971): p. 282.

Objectivist, The. Volumes 5–10, 1966–1971. Palo Alto Book Service. Palo Alto, 1982.

Objectivist Forum, The. Volumes 1–8, 1980–1987. New York: TOF Publications, 1993.

Objectivist Newsletter, The. Volumes 1–4, 1962–1965. Palo Alto: Palo Alto Book Service, 1982 [1967].

Odendahl, Teresa. *Charity Begins at Home: Generosity and Self-Interest Among the Philanthropic Elite.* New York: Basic Books, 1990.

O'Donnell, Jim. Interviewed by Karen Reedstrom. *Full Context* (November 1990): pp. 8–10.

O'Neill, William F. *With Charity toward None: An Analysis of Ayn Rand's Philosophy.* Totowa: Littlefield, Adams, 1977 [1972].

————. Personal interview with Jeff Walker, 4 October 1991.

Ortega y Gasset, Jose. *The Revolt of the Masses.* New York: Norton, 1932.

————. *On Love: Aspects of a Single Theme.* New York: Meridian, 1957.

Overbeek, Ross. Rand-Bashing: Enough is Enough. *Liberty* (July 1988): pp. 56–58.

Oyerly, David. Review of *Objectivism: The Philosophy of Ayn Rand* by Leonard Peikoff. *Full Context* (January 1992a): pp. 8–10.

————. Comments On Chapter 10 of Leonard Peikoff's *Objectivism: The Philosophy of Ayn Rand. Full Context* (May 1992b): pp. 7–11.

Packer, Edith. The Art of Introspection. 16-page. pamphlet reprinted from the *Objectivist Forum*, 1985a.

————. Q and A. Audiotape. New Milford: Second Renaissance, 1985b.

————. The Role of Philosophy in Psychotherapy. Audiotape. The Jefferson School, October 1986.

————. Toward a Lasting Romantic Relationship. Audiotape. New Milford: Second Renaissance, 1988.

Paterson, Isabel. *The God of the Machine.* New York: Putnam's, 1943.

Paterson, R.W.K. *The Nihilistic Egoist: Max Stirner.* London: Oxford University Press, 1971.

Pearson, Scott. Letter to the Editor. *Liberty* (July 1988).

Peikoff, Leonard. The Philosophic Base of Capitalism—Q and A, Chicago, 1981. Audiotape.

————. *The Ominous Parallels: The End of Freedom in America.* New York: New American Library, 1982.

————. Understanding Objectivism. Audiotape: A Twelve-lecture Course. Los Angeles: Second Renaissance, 1984a.

————. Why Johnny Can't Think. Ford Hall Forum talk, 1984b. Audiotape.

————. Objectivism Q and A. Audiotape. Los Angeles: Second Renaissance, 1985.

————. A Rational Curriculum. Audiotape. The Jefferson School, October 1986.

————. Fact and Value. *The Intellectual Activist* (18 May 1989a).

————. Moral Virtue. Several lectures, Q and A, 1989b. Audiotape.

————. *Objectivism: The Philosophy of Ayn Rand.* New York: Dutton, 1991a.

————. Personal interview with Jeff Walker, 3 October 1991b.

————. Some Notes about Tomorrow. Ford Hall Forum talk, 1992. Audiotape.

———. Modernism and Madness. Ford Hall Forum Lecture, 1993. Audiotape. New Milford: Second Renaissance, 1994.

———. Interviewed by James Valliant on 5 August 1995. *WJM Productions*.

———. The Leonard Peikoff Show: Editions 1–5 Excerpt Tape. Audiotape. New Milford: New Milford: Second Renaissance, 1996.

Perigo, Lindsay. Interviewed by William Minto and Karen Reedstrom. *Full Context* (September 1997).

Pierpont, Claudia Roth. Twilight of the Goddess. *New Yorker* (24 July 1995).

Plasil, Ellen. *Therapist*. New York: St. Martin's, 1985.

Potok, Chaim. *Wanderings: Chaim Potok's History of the Jews*. New York: Fawcett Crest, 1978.

Powers, William. Ayn Rand Was Wrong. *Washington Post* (25 August 1996).

Pratkanis, Anthony, and Eliot Aaronson. *Age of Propaganda: The Everyday Use and Abuse of Persuasion*. New York: Freeman, 1992.

Prechter, Robert R. Jr. *At the Crest of the Tidal Wave: A Forecast for the Great Bear Market*. Gainesville, Georgia: New Classics Library, 1995.

Prothro, James Warren. *The Dollar Decade: Business Ideas in the 1920s*. Baton Rouge: Louisiana State University Press, 1954.

Pressman, Steven. *Outrageous Betrayal: The Dark Journey of Werner Erhard from est to Exile*. New York: St. Martin's, 1994.

Quoile, Martin. Review of Bramah 1995. *Liberty* (May 1998).

Raico, Ralph. Telephone interview with Jeff Walker, 11 November 1992.

Raimondo, Justin. The Voice of Bitterness. *Liberty* (May 1989): pp. 49-54.

———. *Reclaiming the American Right: The Lost Legacy of the American Right*. Burlingame: Center For Libertarian Studies, 1993.

Rand, Ayn. *We the Living*. New York: Macmillan, 1936.

———. *The Fountainhead*. Indianapolis: Bobbs-Merrill, 1943 [25th anniversary edition. New York: Signet, 1968].

———. *Atlas Shrugged*. New York: Random House, 1957.

———. *Anthem*. New York: Signet, 1961 [Caldwell, Idaho: Caxton, 1946].

———. *For the New Intellectual*. New York: Random House, 1961.

———. *The New Left: The Anti-Industrial Revolution*. Revised 2nd edn. New York: Signet, 1963.

———. Interviewed by Alvin Toffler. *Playboy* (March 1964).

———. *The Romantic Manifesto*. Revised 2nd edn. New York: Signet, 1971 [Cleveland: World Publishing, 1969].

———. The Foreign Policy of a Mixed Economy. 1965 talk. Audiotape. New Milford: Second Renaissance.

———. Speaking Freely: Ayn Rand Interviewed. Edwin Newman, interviewer. Audiotape. New Milford. Second Renaissance.

———. An Interview with Ayn Rand. Raymond Newman, interviewer. Audiotape. Los Angeles: Second Renaissance.

———. Appearance on *Donahue* show, 29 April 1980. Transcript.

———. *Philosophy: Who Needs It?* Indianapolis: Bobbs-Merrill, 1982.

———. 'The Money-Making Personality' and 'The Brain Drain'. Audiotape. Los Angeles: Second Renaissance.

———. Intellectual Bankruptcy of Our Age—Q and A. Audiotape. New Milford: Second Renaissance.

———. The Age of Mediocrity. Ford Hall Forum, 1981. Audiotape, ca. 1982.

———. *The Early Ayn Rand: A Selection from Her Unpublished Fiction*. New York: NAL Books, 1983.

————. Conservatism: An Obituary—Q and A. Audiotape. New Milford: Second Renaissance, 1993.

————. Let Us Alone/The Structure of Government. Audiotape. New Milford: Second Renaissance, 1993.

————. *The Night of January 16th.* New York: Plume, 1987 [Cleveland: World Publishing, 1968].

————. *The Voice of Reason: Essays in Objectivist Thought.* New York, New American Library, 1989.

————. *Introduction to Objectivist Epistemology.* Expanded 2nd edn. New York: NAL Books, 1990.

————. Rand's 1979 appearance on *Donahue*. With Milton Friedman appearance on a different *Donahue* show. Videotape. No Free Lunch Distributors, 1994.

————. *Letters of Ayn Rand.* Edited by Michael S. Berliner. New York: Dutton, 1995.

————. *Journals of Ayn Rand.* Edited by David Harriman. New York: Dutton, 1997.

————. Ayn Rand Speaks. Videotape. Interviewed by James Day. San Francisco: Laissez Faire.

Rand, Ayn, and Nathaniel Branden. *The Virtue of Selfishness.* New York: New American Library, 1964.

Rand, Ayn, et al. *Capitalism the Unknown Ideal.* New York: New American Library, 1966.

Ayn Rand's Marginalia. See Mayhew 1995.

Randall, John Herman, Jr. *Aristotle.* New York: Columbia University Press, 1960.

Rasmussen, Douglas B. Interviewed by Karen Reedstrom. *Full Context* (April 1997).

Reisman, George. *The Toxicity of Environmentalism.* Laguna Hills: The Jefferson School, 1990.

————. *Capitalism: A Treatise on Economics.* Ottawa, Illinois: Jameson, 1996.

Reidy, Peter. Rand the Second-Hander. Letter to the Editor. *Liberty* (November 1989): p. 4.

————. Review of Rand 1995. *Journal of the Taliesin Fellows* 21 (Spring 1997).

Riasanovsky, Nicholas V. *A History of Russia.* Fourth edn. New York: Oxford University Press, 1984.

Ridpath, John B. Fletcher's Views of the Novelist's Aesthetic Purpose in Writing. *American Journal of Economics and Sociology,* vol. 35, no 2 (April 1976): 211–17.

————. Nietzsche and Individualism. Audiotape. New Milford: Second Renaissance, 1985.

————. Adam Smith and the Founding of Capitalism. Audiotape. Conceptual Conferences, 1988.

————. Interpreting Kant's Political Philosophy. Audiotape. New Milford: Second Renaissance, 1991a.

————. Personal interview with Jeff Walker, 9 November 1991b.

————. Figures in Intellectual History. Audiotape. New Milford: Second Renaissance, 1992.

————. Ayn Rand and the History of Individual Rights. Audiotape. New Milford: Second Renaissance, 1993.

————. Virginia, the Virginians, and the Founding of America. Audiotape. New Milford: Second Renaissance, 1993.

————. Letter to the Editor. *Globe and Mail* (5 January 1994).

Ridpath, John B., and Bob Rae. Is Capitalism or Socialism the Moral System? A debate. Audiotape. New Milford: Second Renaissance, 1992.

Rift, Laura. The Generation of Life. *Full Context* (September 1997).

Riggenbach, Jeff. The Disowned Children of Ayn Rand. *Reason* (December 1982).

Robbins, John W. *Answer to Ayn Rand: A Critique of the Philosophy of Objectivism.* Washington, D.C.: Mount Vernon, 1974.

———. *Without a Prayer: Ayn Rand and the Close of Her System.* Trinity Foundation, 1997.

Roberts, Roxanne. The Me Celebration: Gala Marks Anniversary of Rand's *Atlas Shrugged. Washington Post* (6 October, 1997).

Rosen, Gerald M. Self-Help Treatment Books and the Commercialization of Psychotherapy. *American Psychologist* (January 1987): pp. 46–51.

Rosenstand, Nina, ed. *The Moral of the Story: An Introduction to Questions of Ethics and Human Nature.* Mountain View: Mayfield, 1994.

Ross, David. Interviewed by Karen Reedstrom. *Full Context* (April 1995).

Ross, David Justin. Le Morte d'Alger. *Liberty* (April 1993): pp. 57–63.

Rothbard, Murray N. *The Sociology of the Ayn Rand Cult.* Port Townsend: Liberty, 1987a.

———. Review of Barbara Branden 1986. *American Libertarian* (1987b)

———. My Break with Branden and the Rand Cult. *Liberty* (September 1989): pp. 27–32.

———. Telephone interview with Jeff Walker, 10 November 1992.

Ryerson, André. Capitalism and Selfishness. *Commentary* (December 1986).

Ryerson, André, et al. Letters to the editor by Michael Berliner, Roger Donway, and Cynthia Peikoff, and a rejoinder by André Ryerson. *Commentary* (March 1987).

Sanger, Larry. Twenty-eight Objections to Objectivism. Internet, 1994.

Sachar, Howard Morley. *The Course of Modern Jewish History.* New York: Delta, 1977 [1958].

Salsman, Richard M. Wall Street Under Siege. Audiotape. New Milford: Second Renaissance, 1990.

———. Article on Alan Greenspan as Fed Chairman. *Intellectual Activist* (July 1997).

Salzman, Jack, and Pamela Wilkinson. *Major Characters in American Fiction.* New York: Holt, 1994.

Sass, Louis A. *Madness and Modernism: Insanity in the Light of Modern Art, Literature, and Thought.* New York: Basic Books, 1992.

Saul, John Ralston. *Voltaire's Bastards: The Dictatorship of Reason in the West.* London: Viking, 1992.

———. *The Unconscious Civilization.* Toronto: Anansi, 1995.

Schneider, Norbert. *Vermeer.* Köln: Benedikt Taschen, 1994.

Schwartz, Peter, ed. *The Battle for Laissez-Faire Capitalism: Essays Reprinted from the Intellectual Activist.* New York, 1983.

———. Libertarianism: The Perversion of Liberty. Audiotape. New Milford: Second Renaissance, 1985

———. Libertarianism—Q & A. Audiotape. The Jefferson School, 1985.

———. *Libertarianism: The Perversion of Liberty.* New York. Intellectual Activist, 1986.

———. Objectivity in Journalism. Audiotape. Conceptual Conferences, 1988.

———. Analyzing Libertarianism. Audiotape. New Milford: Second Renaissance, 1992.

———. Objectivism, Religion, and Libertarianism: An Interview. Audiotape. New Milford: Second Renaissance, 1993.

————. Contextual Knowledge. Audiotape. New Milford: Second Renaissance, 1995.

Sciabarra, Chris Matthew. Letter to the Editor. Full Context (May 1993): pp. 9–10.

————. *Ayn Rand: The Russian Radical.* Pennsylvania State University Press, 1995.

————. Bowdlerizing Ayn Rand. *Liberty* (September 1998).

Scuoteguazza, Henry. Is Self-Interest Enough? Audiotape. San Francisco: Laissez Faire, 1991.

————. Man's Life versus the Fulfilled Life. *Full Context* (April 1993): pp. 7–10.

Secrest, Meryle. *Frank Lloyd Wright: A Biography.* New York: Knopf, 1992.

Sechrest, Larry. Interviewed by Karen Reedstrom. *Full Context* (December 1994).

Sheaffer, Robert. *Resentment against Achievement.: Understanding the Assault on Ability.* Buffalo: Prometheus, 1988.

————. *The Making of the Messiah: Christianity and Resentment.* Buffalo: Prometheus, 1991a.

————. Personal interview with Jeff Walker, 30 September 1991b.

Shermer, Michael. The Unlikeliest Cult in History. *Skeptic,* vol. 2, no. 2 (1993).

————. *Why People Believe Weird Things: Pseudoscience, Superstition, and Other Confusions of Our Time.* New York: Freeman, 1997.

Shulman, Lee M., Joyce Shulman, and Gerald Rafferty. *Subliminal: The New Channel to Personal Power.* Santa Monica: InfoBooks, 1990.

Shulman, Lee, and Joan Kennedy Taylor. *When to See a Psychologist.* Los Angeles: Nash, 1970.

Sidhu, Gurdip S. Chain Reaction. Letter to the Editor. *Liberty* (May 1989).

Simonton, Dean Keith. *Greatness: Who Makes History and Why.* New York: Guilford, 1994.

Singer, Margaret Thaler. *Cults in Our Midst.* San Francisco: Jossey-Bass, 1995.

Skeptic. Banned by Rand. In the Skeptic News section. *Skeptic,* vol. 5, no. 3 (1997), p. 27.

Skidelsky, Robert. *The World after Communism: A Polemic for Our Times.* London: Macmillan, 1995.

Skinner, B.F. *Walden Two.* New York: Macmillan, 1948.

Smith, George H. *Atheism, Ayn Rand, and Other Heresies.* Buffalo: Prometheus, 1991.

Smith, Henry Nash. The Search For a Capitalist Hero: Businessmen in American Fiction. In Earl Cheit, ed., *The Business Establishment* (New York: Wiley, 1964).

Smith, James A. *The Idea Brokers: Think Tanks and the Rise of the New Policy Elite.* New York: Free Press, 1991.

Smith, Kay Nolte. *The Watcher.* New York: Coward, McCann, and Geoghegan, 1980.

————. *Elegy for a Soprano.* New York: Villard, 1985.

————. Romanticism, Rand, and Reservations. 15 June 1990. Audiotape. Laissez Faire Books, 1990.

Smith, Kay Nolte, and Philip Smith. Personal interview with Jeff Walker, 2 November 1991.

Sniechowski, James. A Call to Consciousness. Review of *Six Pillars of Self-Esteem.* by Nathaniel Branden. *Reason* (November 1994): pp. 66–69.

Snider, Ed. Interviewed by Karen Reedstrom. *Full Context* (April 1991).

Sobran, Joseph. Ayn Rand, American. *National Review* (1 August 1986): pp. 39–40.

————. Mussolini Shrugged. *National Review* (27 January 1989): pp. 52–53.

Spencer, Herbert. *The Man versus the State*. Caldwell, Idaho: Caxton Printers, 1940 [1892].

Starker, Steven. *Oracle at the Supermarket: The American Preoccupation with Self Help Books*. New Brunswick: Transaction, 1989.

Steele, David Ramsay. Alice in Wonderland. *Liberty* (May 1988): pp. 35–43.

———. Peikoff's Objectivism: An Autopsy. *Liberty* (January 1992): pp. 60–66.

Steinem, Gloria. *Revolution from Within: A Book of Self-Esteem*. Boston: Little, Brown, 1992.

Storm, Rachel. *In Search of Heaven on Earth*. London: Bloomsbury, 1991.

Sures, Mary Ann. Ayn Rand and the *Atlas Shrugged* Years: Reminiscences and Recollections. Audiotape. Additional material by Harry Binswanger. New Milford: Second Renaissance, 1992.

Sutherland, Charles W. *Disciples of Destruction: The Religious Origins of War and Terrorism*. Buffalo: Prometheus, 1987.

Sutherland, Stuart. *Irrationality: The Enemy Within*. London: Penguin, 1992.

Tafel, Edgar. *Apprentice to Genius: Years with Frank Lloyd Wright*. New York: McGraw-Hill, 1979.

———. *About Wright: An Album of Recollections by Those Who Knew Frank Lloyd Wright*. New York: Wiley, 1993.

Taylor, Joan Kennedy. Personal interview with Jeff Walker, 2 December 1991.

———. *Reclaiming the Mainstream: Individualist Feminism Rediscovered*. Buffalo: Prometheus, 1992.

———. Interviewed by Karen Reedstrom. *Full Context* (October 1993).

Teachout, Terry. The Goddess that Failed. *Commentary* (July 1986): pp. 68–72.

Thomas, William, and J. Donal Wales. Is the Truth the Whole? *Full Context* (January 1993): pp. 7–8.

Thomas Jefferson School. *See* Jefferson School.

Thurow, Lester C. *The Future of Capitalism*. New York: Penguin, 1996.

Todd, Trish. Looking Back Objectively. *Trade News* (1988).

Torres, Louis, and Michelle Marder Kamhi. Ayn Rand's Philosophy of Art. *Aristos: The Journal of Aesthetics*, vol. 5, nos. 2–5 (January 1991, September 1991, January 1992, September 1992).

Torrey, E. Fuller. *Freudian Fraud: The Malignant Effects of Freud's Theory on American Thought and Culture*. New York: HarperCollins, 1992.

Tracinski, Robert W. Notes on 'A Question of Sanction'. Internet, 22 January 1990.

Tracy, Honor. Here We Go Gathering Nuts. Review of *Capitalism: the Unknown Ideal*. *New Republic*, 1964.

Tuccille, Jerome. *It Usually Begins with Ayn Rand*. New York: Stein and Day, 1971.

Twain, Mark. *A Connecticut Yankee in King Arthur's Court*. Harper, 1889.

Unamuno, Miguel de. *The Tragic Sense of Life*. New York: Dover, 1954 [1921].

Volkogonov, Dimitri. *Trotsky: The Eternal Revolutionary*. New York: Free Press, 1996.

Veatch, Henry B. Might Objectivism Ever Become Academically Respectable? *Liberty* (January 1992): pp. 61–65.

Virkkala, Timothy. Review of *Unrugged Individualism: The Selfish Basis for Benevolence* by David Kelley. Liberty (September 1998).

Volkov, Solomon. *St. Petersburg: A Cultural History*. New York: Simon and Schuster, 1995.

Walker, Jeff. *Ayn Rand*. Transcript of CBC *Ideas* radio program. 1992.

———. Understanding Ayn Rand. Eleven hours of interviews. Audiotapes. Port Townsend: Liberty, 1993.

Walsh, George. Interviewed by Karen Reedstrom. *Full Context* (February 1991).

———. Interviewed by Karen Reedstrom. *Full Context* (November 1993).

Walsh, George, Karen Reedstrom, and David Oyerly. Compare and Judge for Yourself. *Full Context* (September 1990): pp. 11–12.

Waters, Ethan O. (pseudonym for R.W. Bradford) The Two Libertarianisms. *Liberty* (May 1988): pp. 7–11.

———. Passport to Galt's Gulch. *Liberty* (September 1989): p. 8.

Webster, Richard. *Why Freud Was Wrong: Sin, Science, and Psychoanalysis*. New York: Basic Books, 1995.

Wells, H.G. *Things To Come*. Boston: G.K. Hall, 1935.

Wheeler, Jack. Interviewed by Karen Reedstrom. *Full Context* (May 1996).

Wills, Garry. *Under God: Religion and American Politics*. New York: Simon and Schuster, 1990.

Wistrich, Robert S. *Anti-Semitism: The Longest Hatred*. London: Thames Mandarin, 1992 [1991].

Williams, Walter. Interviewed by Karen Reedstrom. *Full Context* (November 1992).

Wolf, Chris. Transcript of Columbia University WKCR student radio interview of Ayn Rand in the early 1960s, nd.

———. What's Wrong with Objectivism? FAQ on Internet, ca. 1994.

———. Leonard Peikoff Unjustly Smears Alan Greenspan. An extended internet posting in an Objectivist newsgroup, 22 February 1998.

Wolf, Chris, et al. An internet <www.all-media.com/ari/docs.htm> compilation of documents by Linda Reardan, Jerry Kirkpatrick, Genevieve Sanford, and others, relating to the excommunication of the Reismans and their supporters from ARI, 1996.

Wolpert, Lewis. *The Unnatural Nature of Science*. London: Faber and Faber, 1993.

Wortham, Anne. Interviewed by Karen Reedstrom. *Full Context* (March 1994).

Wright, Frank Lloyd. *An Autobiography*. Expanded version, 1943. Horizon Press, 1977 [1932].

———. *Frank Lloyd Wright on Architecture: Selected Writings 1894–1940*. New York: Grossett and Dunlap, 1941.

Yeager, Leland B. Review of *Liberty and Nature: An Aristotelian Defense of Liberal Order* by Douglas Rasmussen and Douglas Den Uyl. *Liberty* (July 1992).

Zagorin, Adam. Greenspan and His Friends. *Time* (10 November 1997).

Zamiatin, Evgeny. *We*. New York: Penguin, 1993 [1924].

Index

A

Adler, Alfred, 165
Aeschylus, 340
Agliaro, John, 188
Allport, Gordon, 165
Alphasonics, 163
Alstad, Diana: on authoritarianism,
245; on cults, 19, 35, 61, 63, 73;
on gurus, 15, 50, 60, 261; on
hierarchy, 25; on moral certainty,
function of, 66
American Enterprise Institute, 293
American Renaissance High School,
137
Anderson, Martin: *The Reagan
Revolution*, 207
Angell, Wayne, 214
Arendt, Hannah, 79
Aristotle, 99, 298, 323; and
Objectivism, 235; *Organon*,
273; and Rand, 1, 3, 26, 75, 76,
78, 145, 223, 225, 266
Ashby, Thaddeus, 255
Atlas Foundation, 335, 338
Atlas Shrugged: as alternate reality,
37–39, 247; as apocalyptic, 64;
appeal of, 286; attempt to
embody, 27; and business theory,
299–300; contempt in, 328; as con-
verting world, 60; critical reaction
to, 6, 112, 144, 222, 249, 323–24;
as derivative, 4; on emotion, 128–
29; emotional power of, 298; as
entry to Objectivism, 13; "evil" in,
102; gold in, 278, 299; as the
greatest novel, 76; implausibility
of, 321–22; influence of, 333; message of, 6; pain in, 132, 174, 260,
298; as ranked by *Chicago Tribune*,
295; precursors of, 299–314; as
pro-capitalist, 288; as Promethean,
17; as pulp fiction, 297; Rand on,
253; on reason, 221; as sacred
text, 37; as screenplay, attempts
for, 87–88, 253, 260, 320; setting
of, 297–98; sexuality in, 109–110,
116; smoking in, 268–69; as sterile
world, 112; story of, 295–96;
themes of, 66, 279; use of insults
in, 18; as utopian, 110; word
counts in, 298–99; word repetition
in, 80; youthful readers of, 201
Austin, John, 225
Ayn Rand: A Sense of Life (documentary movie), 2, 193, 333
Ayn Rand Institute (ARI), vii, 8, 73,
82–87; activities of, 83–87; and
college campus clubs, 83; launch-
ing of, 82; and Peikoff, 8, 73, 196,
341; recruits to, 201; thought control in, 54
Ayn Rand Lexicon, 36

B

Bacon, Francis: *Novum Organum*,
273
Bakunin, Mikhail, 338
Barash, David, 51
Baroody, William, 336
Beard, Charles, 272
Beauvoir, Simone de, 79
Beckmann, Petr, 90–91, 238
Beckmann, Robert C., 333
Beckner, Steven, 211, 213, 214, 216,
217; on Greenspan, 207, 209, 210,
212, 215, 216
Beethoven, Ludwig van, 42, 75, 121
Bellamy, Edward, 4, 272–73; *Looking
Backward*, 272–73
Belloc, Hilaire: *The Servile State*, 308
Benedict, Ruth, 331
Berlin, Isaiah, 106
Berliner, Michael, 77, 83, 95–96,
196
Bernstein, Andrew (Andy), 77, 137

THE IDEAS OF AYN RAND
— Ronald E. Merrill —

The Ideas of Ayn Rand is a comprehensive survey of Rand's wide-ranging contributions: her literary techniques; her espousal and then rejection of a Nietzschean philosophy; her contradictory attitude to feminism; her forays into ethics, epistemology, and metaphysics; the development of her political creed; her influence on—and hostility to—both conservatism and libertarianism.

Dr. Merrill's standpoint is friendly yet critical. He presents an original and sympathetic interpretation of Rand's ideas, exposing unexpected facets of the Objectivist vision and arguing that Rand's thought is more complex, more subtle, and more profound than her enemies, or even her friends, have suspected. 203 pages. 1991.

ISBN 0 8126 9158 X (Paper) ISBN 0 8126 9157 1 (Cloth)

WHAT ART IS
The Esthetic Theory of Ayn Rand
— Louis Torres and Michelle Marder Kamhi —

According to today's arts establishment, anything can be art if a reputed artist or expert says it is.

An alternative to this view is provided by philosopher-novelist Ayn Rand, whose analysis of art's cognitive and emotional function validates the instinctive reaction of the lay public that much of today's purported 'art' is not in fact art at all.

Torres and Kamhi provide a restatement and critical evaluation of Rand's esthetic philosophy, bringing out its similarities and dissimilarities with rival theories of fine art. They conclude that, despite some shortcomings, Rand's account of the nature of art is compelling, fruitful, and supported by evidence from anthropology, neurology, cognitive science, and psychology. ca. 460 pages.

To order, call toll-free 800-815-2280 or fax 419-281-6883.